MEMORIALS OF
ANGUS AND THE MEARNS

AN ACCOUNT HISTORICAL, ANTIQUARIAN, AND TRADITIONARY, OF THE
CASTLES AND TOWNS VISITED BY EDWARD I., AND OF THE BARONS,
CLERGY, AND OTHERS WHO SWORE FEALTY TO ENGLAND IN 1291-6;
ALSO OF THE ABBEY OF CUPAR AND THE PRIORY OF RESTENNETH,

BY THE LATE ANDREW JERVISE, F.S.A. SCOT.

DISTRICT EXAMINER OF REGISTERS; AUTHOR OF THE "LAND OF THE LINDSAYS,"
"EPITAPHS AND INSCRIPTIONS," ETC.

REWRITTEN AND CORRECTED BY

REV. JAMES GAMMACK, M.A. ABERDEEN

CORRESPONDING MEMBER OF THE SOCIETY OF ANTIQUARIES, SCOTLAND; AND MEMBER OF THE
CAMBRIAN ARCHÆOLOGICAL ASSOCIATION.

MEMORIALS

OF

ANGUS AND MEARNS

AN ACCOUNT

HISTORICAL, ANTIQUARIAN, & TRADITIONARY.

VOL. I.

EDINBURGH: DAVID DOUGLAS

M DCCC LXXXV

EDINBURGH: David Douglas, 1885.

A Facsimile Reprint
Published 2000 by

HERITAGE BOOKS, INC.
1540E Pointer Ridge Place
Bowie, Maryland 20716
1-800-398-7709
http://www.heritagebooks.com

ISBN: 0-7884-1438-0

A Complete Catalog Listing Hundreds of Titles
On History, Genealogy, and Americana
Available Free Upon Request

EDITOR'S PREFACE TO THE SECOND EDITION.

As the First Edition of this work was evidently an object of much satisfaction to the Author, and as its authority has been recognised by its being used so freely by later writers, I have felt in preparing this Second Edition that I was acting under a weighty responsibility both to the public and to Mr. Jervise's memory.

Many fields have presented themselves for independent research, but as the plan of the work and its limits belonged to the author and not to the editor, I did not feel justified in materially altering either of them. The lines I have followed are generally those that I pursued in my edition of *The Land of the Lindsays*. By the fuller treatment of some of the family histories in that book I have been enabled to give them here in a shorter form than Mr. Jervise considered necessary, and I have also in several instances condensed the accounts of other matters that are dealt with in that work and are likewise treated in this. I have thereby been enabled to present a considerable amount of new matter without unduly increasing the size or scope of the Book.

The lapse of nearly a quarter of a century since the publication of the First Edition has called for many alterations upon the account of the later condition of Angus and the Mearns ;

yet, without departing from the original scope of the work or converting it into anything approaching the character of the mere guide-book, I have sought to present an accurate statement of the more recent condition of the two counties.

The list of Authors consulted and used, apart from the personal applications for information, and the personal visits to the places that I have required to make, will show that the labour bestowed in bringing out this edition has not been slight. But from the outset I have had the assurance of its appreciation, and the constant feeling of sympathy on the part of all to whom I had occasion to speak or write. All have been willing to afford abundant aid, and have also continued to evince a growing interest in the progress of the work.

It is impossible for me to mention the names of all those who have thus assisted; but I should fail in my duty if I omitted to express the debt of gratitude I owe to Mr. Jervise's Trustees for the confidence they have reposed in me, and for the readiness with which they have acquiesced in and carried out my wishes; as also to Mr. James Davidson, Solicitor, Kirriemuir, for his co-operation and ready assistance throughout the whole of my undertaking.

JAMES GAMMACK, M.A.

ABERDEEN, *October*, 1885.

PREFACE TO THE FIRST EDITION.

IN compiling this volume, the Author may state that the chief objects he had in view were—first, to give an account, historical and traditionary, of the different Towns and Castles in Angus and the Mearns at which King Edward I. resided when on his subjugating tour through Scotland in 1296 ; and, secondly, notices of the families and possessions of such of the Barons, Churchmen, and others, as recognised the supremacy of England as well during that year, as in 1291, and afterwards in 1303.[1]

During the period of the disputed monarchy, when Scotland was prostrated under the sway of King Edward, and

---

[1] Among the authorities regarding these times, the following are the chief :—

(1.) *A Diary of Edward the First [his] Journey into Scotland, in the time of John Kinge of Scottis. Aᵒ Regni* 24, 1296. The best edition is in the *Ragman Rolls*, Edinburgh, 1834 : see also one with Introduction and Notes, by P. F. Tytler, Esq., in the *Bannatyne Club Miscellany*, vol. i. In the *Archæologia*, vol. xxi., an English version is printed, with Introduction and Notes by Sir N. Harris Nicolas.

(2.) *The History of King John, King Henry III., and the most Illustrious King Edward the I.*, by William Prynne, Keeper of the Records in the Tower of London, 1308, pp. fol., 1670. This is volume iii. of his *Exact Chronological and Historical Demonstration*, etc.

(3.) *Fœdera Conventiones, Literæ, et cujuscunque generis Acta publica inter Reges Anglice et alios quosvis Imperatores Reges, etc., ab anno* 1101 *ad nostra usque tempora habita aut tractata.* By Thomas Rymer and Robert Sanderson. London, 1704-35.

(4.) *Instrumenta Publica sive processus super Fidelitatibus et Homagiis Scotorum Domino Regi Angliæ factis,* A.D. MCCXCI.—MCCXCVI., or *Ragman Rolls.* Printed by the Bannatyne Club, 4to, 1834.

(5.) *Documents and Records illustrating the History of Scotland, and the Transactions between the Crowns of Scotland and England, preserved in the Treasury of Her Majesty's Exchequer*, with Introduction by Sir Francis Palgrave, K.H., Keeper of the Records. Printed by Royal Command, royal 8vo, 1837.

when every person of note had sworn allegiance to England —SIR WILLIAM WALLACE alone excepted—nearly a hundred of the chief men of Angus and the Mearns are recorded among the rest ; the history, and even the names of the greater part of whom have been hitherto unknown to ordinary readers. Still, as they had all more or less a share in the achievement of our National Independence, the Author trusts that the notices of them and their estates, which occupy so much of the present volume, may not only be read with interest, but be looked upon as a humble attempt to supply a deficiency in our local annals during one of the most important periods of the national history.

The volume was at first intended merely to embrace comparatively short accounts of persons and places, and a history of the period of the Interregnum ; but, on second thoughts, the Author, considering that so much had already been written regarding the Wars of the Independence, believed that the work would be of much more value and interest were it exclusively devoted to a collection of particulars regarding personal and territorial history, rather than that any part of it should be a repetition of facts which could neither be improved upon, nor added to with safety. This change of plan, it need scarcely be said, incurred a vast amount of labour and research beyond what was at first contemplated—so much so, that, with other unavoidable causes of delay, it has not only been the means of retarding the publication of the volume, but has nearly doubled its size.

To show how far these remarks are applicable, it need only be stated, that instead of a few pages being allotted to the history of each of the towns and castles, as was at first proposed, this portion of the work alone extends to about 230 pages, embracing an account of all that is most interesting, trustworthy, and rare regarding each place (in most cases to the exclusion of matter generally known), extending from the most remote down to the latest times.

From the length of time which has unavoidably elapsed between the printing and the publication of certain portions of the volume, as well as from a desire to take advantage of information which sometimes came under the Author's notice after the MS. was prepared for press, a sameness in style and expression will not infrequently be noticed. For these, and other shortcomings (of many of which the Author is but too sensible), he craves the indulgence of the reader, trusting that they may be outweighed, to some extent at least, by the mass of facts which has been collected, and which he has done his best, by the occasional introduction of traditions, to make as *readable* and as attractive as possible.

The Author must not forget to mention that, during the progress of the work, he has been indebted to literary friends and others for some important communications, which will be found acknowledged in their proper places. In an especial manner, he begs to acknowledge the deep obligations under which he lies to Joseph Robertson, Esq., Superintendent of Searches in the Literary and Antiquarian Department of the General Register-House, Edinburgh, not only for the trouble which Mr. Robertson has so kindly taken in revising the sheets before going to press, but for many valuable suggestions and additions, for which his extensive acquaintance with the literary and antiquarian history of Scotland renders him so well qualified.

The Author has also to express his gratitude to the Right Honourable the Earl of Dalhousie, for the kind and courteous manner in which his Lordship granted the use of many valuable family and other MSS., in which, as is well known, the Panmure Library is peculiarly rich. To John Inglis Chalmers,

Esq. of Aldbar, the Author is likewise greatly indebted for the use of his large and excellent library, as well as of many of the valuable MSS. of his late lamented brother, by whose death the science of Scottish Archæology lost one of its best patrons, and its students one of the warmest friends.

To the Society of Antiquaries of Scotland, the Author is obliged for the use of some valuable wood-cuts, among which are those of the beautiful seal of the Chapter of the Cathedral of Brechin.

In conclusion, the Author conceives that some apology may be necessary for the numerous attempts which have been made throughout the volume to interpret the Gaelic names of places. Probably no branch of Archæological study is more interesting than that of etymology, while, on the other hand, none is more unsatisfactory in its results ; for it very frequently happens that accomplished Gaelic scholars give very different interpretations of the meaning of the same word. The Author, therefore, begs that the reader will attach no undue weight to such attempts as appear here, although the greater part of them have met the approval of some eminent teachers of the language, and natives of the land of Ossian.

ANDREW JERVISE.

BRECHIN, *January*, 1861.

CONTENTS.

VOLUME FIRST.

Part First.

INTRODUCTION.

OUTLINE OF THE EARLY HISTORY, AND ANTIQUITIES OF ANGUS AND THE MEARNS.

SECTION I.

SECTION II.

SECTION III.

Part Second.

CASTLES AND TOWNS VISITED BY EDWARD I.,
A.D. 1296.

CHAPTER I.

THE CASTLES AND TOWN OF FORFAR.

Section I.

Section II.

Section III.

SECTION IV.

SECTION V.

CHAPTER II.

FARNELL CASTLE, AND KINNAIRD.

SECTION I.

SECTION II.

CHAPTER III.

CASTLE, CONVENT, AND TOWN OF MONTROSE.

SECTION I.

SECTION II.

SECTION III.

SECTION IV.

SECTION V.

CHAPTER IV.

CASTLES OF KINCARDINE, GLENBERVIE, AND DURRIS.

SECTION I.—KINCARDINE AND FORDOUN.

SECTION II.—CASTLE AND KIRK OF GLENBERVIE.

SECTION III.—CASTLE OF DORES OR DURRIS.

CHAPTER V.

THE ROUND TOWER, CATHEDRAL, CASTLE, AND CITY OF BRECHIN.

Section I.

Section II.

Section III.

Section IV.

SECTION V.

SECTION VI.

CHAPTER VI.

THE ABBEY, AND TOWN OF ABERBROTHOC.

SECTION I.

SECTION II.

CHAPTER VII.

THE CHURCH, CONVENTS, CASTLE, AND TOWN OF DUNDEE.

VOLUME SECOND.

Part Third.

THE BARONS WHO SWORE FEALTY TO EDWARD I.,
A.D. 1291-6.

CHAPTER I.

THE MAULES OF PANMURE.

Section I.

Section II.

CHAPTER II.

THE UMPHRAVILLES ; LEIGHTONS ; FENTONS ; BEATONS ; AND GRAHAMS.

Section I.

THE UMPHRAVILLES, EARLS OF ANGUS.

Section II.

THE LEIGHTONS OF USAN.

Part Fourth.

THE BARONS OF ANGUS WHO SWORE FEALTY TO KING EDWARD I., A.D. 1296.

Part Fifth.

THE BARONS OF THE MEARNS WHO SWORE FEALTY TO KING EDWARD I., A.D. 1296.

Section I.

THE ALLARDICES OF ALLARDICE.

Section II.

THE FALCONERS AND THE FYNDONS.

The Falconers of Halkerton.

Fyndon of Fyndon.

Section III.

THE MIDDLETONS AND THE MONTFORTS.

The Middletons of Middleton.

The Montforts of Kinneff.

———

Part Sixth.

THE ABBEY OF CUPAR AND THE PRIORY OF RESTENNETH.

CHAPTER I.

THE ABBEY OF CUPAR.

SECTION I.

CHAPTER II.

THE PRIORY OF RESTENNETH.

SECTION I.

SECTION II.

SECTION III.

Part Seventh.

CHAPTER I.

THE CHURCHES OF DUNLAPPY, IDVIES, KINNETTLES, AND LOGIE, IN ANGUS.

CHAPTER II.

THE CHURCHES OF GARVOCK, KINNEFF, AND

DUNNOTTAR, IN THE MEARNS.

Section I.

THE CHURCH OF GARVOCK.

Section II.

THE CHURCH OF KINNEFF.

Section III.

THE CHURCH OF DUNNOTTAR.

CHAPTER III.

KNIGHTS TEMPLARS AND HOSPITALLERS OF ST. JOHN, THE HOLY TRINITY, AND ST. GERMAINS.

CHAPTER IV.

THE LADIES OF DECEASED BARONS, A.D. 1296–1306.

CHAPTER V.

HOMAGES OF BARONS, A.D. 1306.

LIST OF AUTHORS.

ABERCROMBY (Pat.), Martial Achievements of the Scots Nations. 2 vols.
Edinb. 1711.
Aberdeen—Collections for a History of the Shires of Aberdeen and Banff.
Robertson. Aberd. 1843.
„ Antiquities of the Shires of Aberdeen and Banff. 4 vols.
Aberd. 1847-69.
Acta Dominorum Concilii (1478-95, and 1466-95). 2 vols. Rec. Comm.
1839.
Acts of Parliament of Scotland. 11 vols. 1814.
Aikman (James), History of Scotland. 4 vols. Glasgow, 1827.
Allan (David), Historical Sketches of Kirriemuir and its Neighbourhood.
Dund. 1864.
Anderson (James), Black Book of Kincardine. Aberd. 1879.
„ (James), Selectus Diplomatum et Numismatum Scotiæ. Ruddi-
man. Edinb. 1739.
„ (Jos.), Scotland in Early Christian Times. Rhind Lectures. Series
Nos. i., ii., iii., iv. Edinb. 1881-4.
„ (William), Scottish Nation. 3 vols. Edinb. 1863.
Anglo-Saxon Chronicle. Bohn Ed. 1849.
Annals of Ulster. O'Connor. Dublin, 1786.
Antiquaries of Scotland, Proceedings of. Old and new series. Edinb.
1855-84.
„ Transactions (Archæologia Scotica). 2 vols. Edinb. 1792-
1818.
Arbuthnott Missal. Forbes. Burntisland, 1864.
Arnot (H.), Celebrated Criminal Trials in Scotland, 1536-1784. Edinb. 1785.
Ayloffe (Sir Jos.), Calendars of the Ancient Charters. Lond. 1774.

BALMERINACH, Liber S. Marie de. Turnbull. Edinb. 1841.
Balfour (Alex.), Contemplation and other Poems. Edinb. 1841.
„ (Sir James), Historical Works. 4 vols. Edinb. 1824-5.
Bannatyne Miscellany. 3 vols. Edinb. 1827-55.
Barbour (John), Life and Acts of King Robert Bruce. Ed. Pinkerton.
3 vols. Lond. 1790.
Beatson (Rob.), Political Index. 3 vols. Lond. 1806.
Beattie (George), John o' Arnha'. Montrose, 1882.
Bede, Ecclesiastical History. Bohn Ed. Lond. 1849.
Betham (Sir W.), Etruria Celtica. 2 vols. 1842.
Billings (R. W.), Baronial and Ecclesiastical Antiquities of Scotland. 4 vols.
Edinb. 1845-52.
Blind Harry, Sir William Wallace. Jamieson. Edinb. 1820.
Book of the Official of St. Andrews. Abbotsford Club. Edinb. 1845.
Book of the Universal Kirk of Scotland. Bannatyne Club. 3 vols. Edinb.
1839-45.

Borthwick (Wm.), Remarks on British Antiquities. Edinb. 1776.
Boutel (Chas.), Christian Monuments of England and Wales. Lond. 1854.
Bowick, Character and Sketches. Montr. 1827.
„   Life of Erskine.
Brechin, Bailie Court Minutes. MS.
„   Diocesan Synod Minutes. MS.
Brown (Wm.), History of the Royal Palaces of Scotland. Jamieson.
    Edinb. 1840.
Browne (Jas.), History of the Highlands. 4 vols. Glasg. 1837-8.
Brunton and Haig, Historical Account of the Senators of the College of
    Justice. Edinb. 1832.
Buchanan (George), History of Scotland. 2 vols. Edinb. 1766.
„   (Wm.), Ancient Scottish Surnames and Clans. Glasg. 1818.
Burke (Sir Bern.), Peerage, Baronage, and Knightage. 42 ed. Lond. 1880.
„   Visitation of the Seats and Arms.
Burnet (Bp. Gilb.), History of his own Time. 2 vols. Oxf. 1823.
Burns, Life and Works. Chambers. 4 vols. Edinb. 1853.
„   „   Scott-Douglas. 4 vols. Edinb. 1877.
„   Chronicle of the Hundredth Birthday. Ballantine. Edinb. 1859.
Burton (J. H.), History of Scotland. 7 vols. Edinb. 1876.
„   Criminal Trials. 2 vols. Lond. 1852.
Butler (Alb.), Lives of the Saints. 2 vols. Lond. 1863.

CALDERWOOD (David), History of the Kirk of Scotland. Thomson. 8 vols.
    Edinb. 1842-9.
Calendar of Documents relating to Scotland. Pub. Rec. Off., London. Bain,
    vol. i. Edinb. 1881.
Camden (Wm.), Britannia. Gough. Lond. 1789.
Campbell (Rev. Jas.), History of Balmerino and its Abbey. Edinb. 1867.
Cardonnel (Adam de), Numismata Scotiæ. Edinb. 1786.
„   „   Picturesque Antiquities of Scotland. Lond. 1788-93.
Catalogue of the Museum of the Archæological Institute of Great Britain
    and Ireland, held in Edinburgh 1856. Edinb. 1859.
Chalmers (Geo.), Caledonia. 3 vols. Lond. 1807-24.
„   (Pat.), Ancient Sculptured Monuments of the County of Angus.
    Bann. Club. Edinb. 1849.
Chamberlain Rolls of Scotland. Bann. Club. 3 vols. Edinb. 1817-45.
Chambers (R.), History of the Rebellion of 1745-6. Edinb. 1847.
„   Popular Rhymes of Scotland and Poems. Edinb. 1847.
Chronica de Mailros. 735-1270. Gale. Oxf. 1684.
Colman (Geo.), Random Records. 2 vols. Lond. 1830.
Crawford Peerage Case. 1845.
Crawford (George), Peerage of Scotland. Edinb. 1716.
„   „   Lives of the Officers of the Crown and of the State in
    Scotland, vol. i. Edinb. 1726.

DALRYMPLE (Sir D.) [Lord Hailes], Annals of Scotland, 1057-1370. 3 vols.
    Edinb. 1797.
Dalzell (Sir John), Darker Superstitions of Scotland. Edinb. 1835.
Davidson (Rev. Dr. John), Inverurie and the Earldom of the Garioch. 2 vols.
    Edinb. 1878.
Defoe (Dan.), Journey through Great Britain. 3 vols. Lond. 1724-27.
Diurnal of Occurrents in Scotland. 1513-75. Edinb. 1833.
Douglas (Francis), General Description of the East Coast of Scotland in 1780.
    Aberd. 1826.
Douglas (Sir Robert), The Baronage of Scotland. Edinb. 1798.

Douglas (Sir Robert), The Peerage of Scotland. Wood. 2 Ed. 2 vols. Edinb. 1813.
Dugdale (Sir Wm.), Monasticon Anglicanum. 6 vols. Lond. 1846.
„ „ Baronage of England. 3 vols. Lond. 1675-6.
Dundee Year-Books. 1882-1885-6.

EDINBURGH ENCYCLOPÆDIA. Brewster. 18 vols. Edinb. 1830.
Edmondson (Jos.), Complete Body of Heraldry. 2 vols. Lond. 1780.
Edward (Rev. Rob.), Description of Angus in 1678. Trans. by Trail. Dund. 1793. (Reprinted in Warden's *Angus*, ii. p. 234 sq.)
Exchequer Rolls. 5 vols. Lond. 1835-6.
Extracta e variis Cronicis Scocie. Abb. Club. Edinb. 1842.

FORBES (Bp. A. P.), Kalendars of the Scottish Saints. Edinb. 1872.
Fordun (John de), Scotichronicon. Skene. 2 vols. Edinb. 1872.
Forfarshire Illustrated. Dund. 1843.
Fosbroke (Thos. D.), Encyclopædia of Antiquities. 2 vols. Lond. 1843.
Franck (Rich.), Northern Memoirs. Edinb. 1821.
Fraser (Wm.), History of the Carnegies, Earls of Southesk, and of their Kindred. 2 vols. Edinb. 1867.
Fraser (Rev. W. R.), History of the Parish and Burgh of Laurencekirk. Edinb. 1880.
Fuller (Thos.), Holy Warre. Nichols. Lond. 1841.

GILLIES (R. P.), Memoirs of a Literary Veteran. 3 vols. Lond. 1851.
Gordon (Alex.), Itinerarium Septentrionale. Lond. 1727.
„ (Dr. Jas. F. S.) Monasticon and Scotichronicon. Glasg. 1867-68.
„ (Jas.) Hist. Scot. Affairs. 1637-41. Robertson and Grub. 3 vols. Aberd. 1841.
„ (Sir Rob.), Genealogical History of the Earldom of Sutherland to 1630. Continuation by G. Gordon to 1651. Edinb. 1825.
„ (Wm.), History of the Family of Gordon. 2 vols. Edinb. 1726.
Grose (Fras.), Antiquities of Scotland. 2 vols. Lond. 1797.
Grub (Dr. George), Ecclesiastical History of Scotland. 4 vols. Edinb. 1861.
Gamble (Dr. Th.), Life of General Monck. Lond. 1671.
Guthrie (Hen.), Memoirs of Scottish Affairs, Civil and Ecclesiastical. Glasg. 1747.
Guthrie (Wm.), History of Scotland. 10 vols. Lond. 1767-8.

HARDYNG (John), Chronicle in Metre. Ellis. Lond. 1812.
Hart (Rich.), Ecclesiastical Records. Camb. 1846.
Hay (George), History of Arbroath. Arb. 1876.
„ „ Charters, etc., of Dundee. Dund. 1880.
Headrick (James), General View of the Agriculture of Angus. Edinb. 1813.
Hewlett (James), Scotch Dignities.
Holinshed (R.), Scottish Chronicle. 2 vols. Arbroath. 1805.

IMPERIAL DICTIONARY. Annandale. 4 vols. Glasg. 1884.
Inquisitionum retornatarum abbreviatio. Inquis. Spec. Inquis. Gen. Inquis. de Tutela. 3 vols. Lond. 1811.
Innes (Cosmo), Scotland in the Middle Ages. Edinb. 1860.
„ „ Sketches of Early Scotch History. Edinb. 1861.
„ „ Lectures on Scotch Legal Antiquities. Edinb. 1872.
Innes (Th.), Critical Essay on the Ancient Inhabitants of Scotland. 2 vols. Lond. 1729.

Innes (Th.), Civil and Ecclesiastical History of Scotland, 80-818. Grub.
    Aberdeen, 1853.
Irving (David), Lives of Scottish Writers. 2 vols. Edinb. 1851.

JAMIESON (John), Scottish Dictionary. Johnstone. 4 vols. Edinb. 1840-1.
Jervise (And.), Epitaphs and Inscriptions. 2 vols. Edinb. 1875-9.
    „   Land of the Lindsays. Gammack. Edinb. 1882.
Johnson (Dr. Sam.), Journey to the Western Isles. Lond. 1775.
Johnston (Arthur), Musæ Aulicæ, etc. 2 vols. Aberd. 1637.
Johnstone (Jas.), Extracts from the Annals of Ulster, etc. Copenh. 1786.

KEITH (Rob.), Historical Catalogue of the Scottish Bishops. Russell. Edinb.
    1824.
Kincardineshire, Black Book of. (See Anderson, Jas.)

LAING (Alex.), Wayside Flowers. Edinb. 1878.
    „   (Henry), Ancient Scottish Seals. 2 vols. Edinb. 1850-66.
Lamont (John), Diary, 1649-72. Edinb. 1810.
Lawson (C. S.), Guide to the Abbey of Arbroath and St. Vigeans.   Arb.
    1872.
Leech (John), Epigrammata and Poems. Lond. 1620.
Legendary Ballads (Chand. Class.). Lond. N.D.
Lellan, Roll of Battle Abbey.
Leslie (Col. Charles), Historical Records of the Family of Leslie. 3 vols.
    Edinb. 1869.
Liber Sanctæ Mariæ de Lindores. Turnbull. Edinb. 1841.
    „   Ecclesiæ de Scon. Edinb. 1843.
Lindsay (Lord), Lives of the Lindsays. 3 vols. Lond. 1849.
    „   (R. of Pitscottie), Chronicles of Scotland. Dalzell. 2 vols. Edinb.
    1814.
Lockhart (John G.), Life of Burns. Lond. 1847.
Longmuir (John), Dunnottar Castle. Aberd. 1876.
Lowson (Alexander), The Forfar Pulpit. Dund. 1884.
Lyell (Sir Chas.), Elements of Geology. Lond. 1852.

MAITLAND (Wm.), History and Antiquities of Scotland to 1603. 2 vols.
    Lond. 1757.
M'Crie (Th.), Life of John Knox. 2 vols. Edinb. 1831.
    „   „   Life of Andrew Melville. Edinb. 1856.
    „   (Th., jun.), Sketches of Scottish Church History, 1528-1688. Edinb.
    1841.
M'Pherson (Dr. J. G.), Strathmore : Past and Present. Perth, 1885.
Matthew of Westminster's Flowers of History, to 1307. Bohn. Ant. Lib.
    Lond. 1853.
Maxwell (Alex.), Old Dundee. Edinb. 1884.
Melville (Jas.), Autobiography and Diary, with Continuation. Pitcairn.
    Edinb. 1842.
Miller (D.), Arbroath and its Abbey. Edinb. 1860.
Miscellanea Aldbarensis, MS., at Aldbar Castle.
Mitchell (Dr. Arthur), The Past in the Present. Rhind Lectures. Edinb. 1880.
Monipennie (John), Abridgment of the Scotch Chronicle. Glasg. 1818.
Monteith (Rob.), Theatre of Mortality. Edinb. 1704.
Montrose, Original Dukedom of, Case. Lond. 1855.
Morer (Thos.), Short Account of Scotland. Lond. 1702.

Morton (Jas.), Monastic Annals of Teviotdale. Edinb. 1832.
Myles (Jas.), Rambles in Forfarshire. Dund. 1850.

NAPIER (Mark), Life and Times of the Marquis of Montrose. Edinb. 1840.
Nisbet (Alex.), System of Heraldry. 2 vols. Edinb. 1804.
„ Historical and Critical Notes on the Ragman Roll. Edinb. 1804.

OCHTERLONY (John), Account of the Shire of Forfar, 1684-5. (Reprinted in *Spottiswoode Miscellany*, pp. 317 sq., and Warden's *Angus*, ii. pp. 252 sq.)
Oliver and Boyd, New Edinburgh Almanac. Edinb. 1883-5.
Original Letters of the Reign of James VI.

PALGRAVE (Sir Francis), Parliamentary Writs. 2 vols. Lond. 1827-34.
Pennant (Th.), Towns in Wales in 1770. Lond. 1778.
Peter (D. M'G.), Baronage of Angus and Mearns, Edinb. 1856.
Petrie (Alex.), History of the Catholic Church, 600-1600. The Hague, 1662.
„ (Geo.), Round Towers of Ireland. Dubl. 1845.
Pinkerton (John), History of Scotland, 1371-1542. 2 vols. Lond. 1797.
„ Literary Correspondence. Lond. 1858.
Pitcairn (Rob.), Criminal Trials in Scotland, 1488-1624. 3 vols. Edinb. 1833.
Pratt (Rev. J. B.), Buchan. Aberd. 1870.
Presbytery of Brechin from 1639 to 1660, Extracts from the Records of Dundee, 1876.
Presbytery of Arbroath, Brechin, Dundee, Fordoun, Forfar, and Meigle, Current Registers. MS.
Prynne (Wm.), History of Edward I. Lond. 1670.
Pulleyn (Wm.), Churchyard Gleanings and Epigrammatic Scraps. Lond. N.D.

RAGMAN Rolls, 1291-6. Bann. Club. Edinb. 1834.
Ramsay (Wm.) Astrologia Restaurata. Lond. 1653.
Reeves (Dean), The Culdees of the British Islands. Dubl. 1864.
Register of Ministers, Exhorters, and Readers, and of their Stipends, 1567. Maitl. Club. Edinb. 1830.
„ of Ministers and Readers in the Kirk of Scotland, 1574. Wodrow Soc. Edinb. 1844.
„ Parochial, of the Parishes in Angus and the Mearns. MS.
„ Privy Council of Scotland, 1545. Vol. i. Edinb. 1877.
„ of Probative Writs. Brechin. MS.
„ of Services in Chancery Office.
Registrum Episcopatus Aberdonensis. Spald. Club. 2 vols. Edinb. 1845.
„ Episcopatus Brechinensis. Bann. Club. 2 vols. Aberd. 1856.
„ de Panmure. 2 vols. Edinb. 1874.
„ Magni Sigilli Regum Scotorum, 1306-1424. Lond. 1814.
„ Nigrum Aberbrothoc. Bann. Club. Edinb. 1856.
„ Vetus de Aberbrothoc. Bann. Club. Edinb. 1848.
„ Prioratus de St. Andree. Bann. Club. Edinb. 1841.
Reliquiæ Antiquæ Scoticæ. Edinb. 1848.
Report of Grievances.
Rickman (Thos.), Gothic Architecture. Lond. 1825.
Riddell (John), Remarks on Scotch Peerage Law. Edinb. 1833.
„ Tracts, Legal and Historical, chiefly relating to Scotland. Edinb. 1835.
Robertson (E. Wm.), Scotland under her Early Kings, 843-1285. 2 vols. Edinb. 1862.

Robertson (Jos.), Statuta Ecclesiæ Scoticanæ, 1225-1559. 2 vols. Edinb. 1866.
Robertson (Wm.), Proceedings relating to the Peerage of Scotland, 1707-88. Edinb. 1790.
„ „ Index of Missing Scottish Charters. Edinb. 1798.
„ (D. H.), History of Leith and its Sculptured Stones. Edinb. 1851.
Rogers (Dr. Ch.), Monuments and Monumental Inscriptions in Scotland. 2 vols. Lond. 1871.
„ „ Rental-Book of the Cistercian Abbey of Cupar. 2 vols. Lond. 1879-80.
„ „ Memoirs of R. Burns. Lond. 1877.
Rotuli Scotiæ in Turri Londinensi, etc., 1291-1516 : Hardy. 2 vols. Lond. 1814-19.
Roy (Wm.), Military Antiquities of the Romans in Britain. Lond. 1793.
Ruddiman (Thos.), Introduction to Anderson's Diplomata Scotiæ. Edinb. 1773.
Ryley, Placita.
Rymer (Thos.), Fœdera, etc. : 1101-1625. 19 vols. Lond. 1704-32.

Scots Magazine. Edinb. 1739-1745.
Scott (H.), Fasti Ecclesiæ Scoticanæ. 3 vols. Edinb. 1866-71.
„ (Sir W.), Border Antiquities of England and Scotland. 2 vols. Lond. 1814.
„ „ Letters on Demonology and Witchcraft. Lond. 1830.
Scottish Journal of Topography, Antiquities, Traditions, etc. 2 vols. Edinb. 1848.
Setts of Royal Burghs. 1785-89.
Sharpe (C. K.), Historical Account of Belief in Witches in Scotland. Lond. 1884.
Simpson (Sir J. Y.), Archaic Sculptures of Cups, etc., on Stones and Rocks. Edinb. 1867.
„ „ Archæological Essays. 2 vols. Edinb. 1872.
Sinclair (Geo.), Satan's Invisible World discovered. Edinb. 1685.
Six Old English Chronicles. Bohn, Ant. Libr. Lond. 1875.
Skene (Dr. W. F.), Chronicles of the Picts and Scots. Edinb. 1867.
Slezer (John), Theatrum Scotiæ. Edinb. 1814.
Smart (Alexander), Rambling Rhymes. Edin. 1845.
Smith (Aw.), Roman Antiquities recently discovered in Fife. Edinb. 1823.
Smith (Dr. Wm.), and Prof. Cheetham, Dict. Christian Antiquities. 2 vols. Lond. 1876-80.
Smith (Dr. Wm.), and Professor Wace, Dict. Christian Biography. Vols. i., ii., iii. Lond. 1877-82.
Spalding Club Miscellany. 5 vols. Aberd. 1841-52.
„ (John), History of the Trubles in Scotland, etc. Stuart. 2 vols. Edinb. 1850-51.
Spottiswood (John), Religious Houses in Scotland. Edinb. 1734. (Reprinted in Keith's Catalogue of Scottish Bishops. Edinb. 1824.)
Statistical (New) Account of Scotland. 15 vols. Edinb. 1845.
„ (Old) Account of Scotland. 21 vols. Edinb. 1791-99.
Stodart (R. R.), Scottish Arms, being a Collection of Armorial Bearings, A.D. 1370-1678. 2 vols. Edinb. 1881.
Stuart (Dr. John), Notices of the Spalding Club, etc. Edinb. 1871.
„ „ Sculptured Stones of Scotland : Spald. Club. 2 vols. Aberd. 1856-7.
Stuart (Prof. John), Essays on Scottish Antiquities. Aberd. 1846.
„ (And.), Genealogical History of the Stewarts. Lond. 1798.

THOMSON (Jas.), History of Dundee.   Dund. 1847.
Theiner (Aug.), Vetera Monumenta.   Rom. 1864.
Toland (John), History of the Druids : Huddleston.   Montr. 1814.
Tytler (Pat. Fraser), History of Scotland.   9 vols.   Edinb. 1841-3.

WALCOTT (Mackenzie E. C.), Ancient Church of Scotland.   Lond. 1874.
Walford (E.), County Families of the United Kingdom.   Lond. 1881-85.
Warden (A. J.), Angus or Forfarshire.   5 vols. Dundee, 1880-84.
Willis's Current Notes.
Wilson (Prof. Daniel), Prehistoric Annals of Scotland.   2 vols.   Lond. 1863.
Wodrow (Rob.), History of the Sufferings of the Church of Scotland : Burns.
          Glasgow, 1829-30.
     „   „   Analecta : Leishman.   Glasg. 1842-3.
     „   „   Collections upon the Lives of Reformers, etc.   Glasg. 1834.
Wood (J. P.), Account of the Parish of Cramond.   1794.
Wyntoun (Andrew of), Orygynale Cronykil of Scotland : Laing.   3 vols.
          Edinb. 1872-9.

YORK BUILDINGS COMPANY Memorandum-Book.   MS.

ILLUSTRATIONS.

ETCHINGS BY W. B. HOLE, A.R.S.A.

VOL. I.

VOL. II.

MEMORIALS OF ANGUS AND THE MEARNS.

PART FIRST.

INTRODUCTION, AND OUTLINE OF

The Early History and Antiquities

OF

ANGUS AND THE MEARNS.

MEMORIALS OF

ANGUS AND THE MEARNS.

PART FIRST.

INTRODUCTION—OUTLINE OF THE EARLY HISTORY, AND ANTIQUITIES OF ANGUS AND THE MEARNS.

SECTION I.

A welcome guest in hall and bower,
He knows each castle, town, and tower.

SCOTT, *Marmion.*

Principal rivers—Lakes—Ancient and modern towns—Origin of towns—Chiefs, or Maormors—Origin of Sheriffdoms and Sheriffs—Hereditary Sheriffs—Lists of Sheriffs-Principal—Royal hunting forests—Origin of Thanedoms and Thanes —Local Thanedoms.

ANGUS and MEARNS, or the counties of Forfar and Kincardine, are situated in the north-east of Scotland, between the rivers Tay and Dee.

The principal rivers in these two counties are the North Esk and the South Esk—the *Tina* and *Esica* of old geographers.[1] Both rivers rise in Forfarshire. The first named forms the boundary between that county and Kincardineshire for a distance of several miles, commencing near Dooly in Glenesk, and terminating at Kinnaber, near Montrose; while the latter is wholly in Angus, rising in Loch Esk and the mountains at the head of Glen Clova, passing the castles of Cortachy and Inverquharity, the latter now in ruins, the city

---

[1] We owe these names to Richard of Cirencester. It is to be regretted that so much of our early Scotch history and geography is based upon the more than doubtful authority of Gildas, Nennius, and "our Richard," as even Chalmers calls him. But acknowledged ignorance is better than accepted error.

and castle of Brechin, and joining the sea at Montrose. The chief tributaries of the North Esk are the Mark and the Tarf, the Dye or West Water, the Cruick, and the Luther, of which the last named rises in the Mearns ; while those of the South Esk are the White Water, the Prosen, the Carity, the Lemno, the Noran, and the Pow. The district of the South Esk being chiefly pastoral, the scenery is not, after the river leaves its mountain birthplace, so bold and striking as that on the North Esk. There are, however, several stretches of more than ordinary beauty. At Cortachy and Shielhill, where the river flows over a rocky bed through rock-bound banks, its late untroubled course is rudely broken, and the picturesque grandeur of the scenery is much to be admired. On the tributaries also many rich and varied scenes are to be met with : the Prosen rushes proudly down from rock to rock, while the Noran, clear and pellucid, throws itself time after time over the precipices in its course, and forms several waterfalls of considerable height and unusual interest. The North Esk, on the other hand, is almost throughout its entire length remarkable for its beautiful mountain scenery and its richness in geological and botanical treasures, particularly between the Mooran burn on the west, and Arnhall on the east.

Next in importance to the Esks is the river Isla, which rises in the Highland district of Glenisla, and joins the Tay near Kinclaven in Perthshire. The waterfalls of Reeky Linn and Slugs of Auchrannie are upon the Isla, and it receives in its course the waters of the Lunan, Ericht, and Alyth burn on the right bank, and those of the Melgam and Dean on the left. The chief of these tributaries are the Ericht, whose parent springs are in the Grampian range in the north of Perthshire, and which is formed by the junction of the Ardle and Shee ; the Melgam, that comes down from the hills of Lintrathen ; and the Dean, that flows from the loch of Forfar, and is joined in its course by the Kerbet.

The lesser rivers are the Dichty, another Lunan, and the

Elliot. The first issues from the lochs of Lundie, the second, rising at Lunanhead, within a short distance of Forfar, flows through the lochs of Rescobie and Balgavies, and the third has its source in Dilty Moss, Carmyllie. The Elliot joins the sea to the west of Arbroath, the Lunan at Redcastle, and the Dichty falls into the Tay near Monifieth.

Besides the Luther, which has its source among the hills in Fordoun, and traverses the Mearns for a distance of twelve or fifteen miles, the waters of Bervie, Carron, and Cowie are all considerable streams, which rise in the more northern parts of the county, and join the sea—the first at Bervie, the others at Stonehaven. The Cowie passes in its course the mansion-houses of Rickarton and Urie, and the Carron the old church of Fetteresso—one of the most romantic spots in the district. This church was dedicated to St. Caran, bishop, whose feast-day is variously stated as the 21st and 23d December.[1]

Through Strachan run the Dye, the Aan, and the Feugh. The first two are tributaries of the third, which falls into the Dee at the village of Banchory-Ternan, where the channel, wild and rocky, shaded by mountain pine, birch, and copse-wood, presents a singularly romantic appearance.

Although the more important of the Forfarshire rivers have their origin in lakes or lochs, many of the smaller and some of the larger of the lochs have been almost completely drained within the last hundred years; among these we may name the lochs of Kinnordy, Logie, Hyndcastle, Baikie, and Restenneth in Angus, and Leys in the Mearns. Leys seems to have been the most considerable of the lakes in that county; and, from the fact that it contained one of those singular works called *crannogs*, or artificial islands, of which there are still some interesting specimens in Ireland, it had doubtless been a place of note in old times. The greater portion of the island still remains, and some curious bronze pots, in good preservation,

---

[1] *Collect. on Aberd. and Banff*, p. 550; *Reg. Ep. Aberd.* i. pref. p. 86; *Proc. Soc. Ant. of Scot.* ii. p. 272.

have, with other relics of antiquity, been found in its neighbourhood.[1]

The principal lochs in Angus are those of Forfar (of which some account will be found in the next chapter), Lintrathen—now enlarged and used by the Dundee Water Commissioners as a water supply for Dundee,—Loch Lee, Lundie, Rescobie, and Balgavies. Tradition says that the celebrated Alan Durward had castles near the lochs of Lintrathen and Lundie; and those of Rescobie and Balgavies are supposed to have been within the boundary of the old hunting forest of Drimmie.

The loch of Feithie, near Forfar, and that of Kinnordy, near Kirriemuir, present some points of considerable interest. The geological features of the former, according to Sir Charles Lyell, are unique, for although it contains neither springs nor shell-marl, it is surrounded by calcareous deposits, and is otherwise favourably situated for the presence of the one and the production of the other. The latter abounded in peat and shell-marl, and about sixty years ago an ancient canoe, still preserved at Kinnordy House, was found imbedded among the peat-moss.[2] It had previously been drained to a considerable extent, and is now little more than a marsh.

But regarded as to extent, grandeur of natural scenery, or historical interest, Loch Lee—the chief source of the North Esk—is probably the most remarkable. It is nearly two miles long by about half a mile broad, and is surrounded by almost perpendicular rocks and steep mountain declivities. At the west or upper end it receives the conjoined waters of the Unich and the Lee, also those of the interesting little lake of Carlochy, which lies in the bosom of the rugged rock of Craig Maskeldie, and somewhat resembles that of Lochnagar. At the east or lower end there are the old parish church and churchyard, and the picturesque tower of Invermark, so often resorted to by "the lichtsome Lindsays," ancient lords of the district, and made the scene of their more important

---

[1] New Stat. Acct. Kincardineshire, p. 327.   [2] Allan, Kirriemuir, p. 2.

actions; while, in pleasing contrast to this hoary ruin, and perched upon the side of a grassy mountain on the north, stands the modern shooting-lodge of the Earl of Dalhousie, commanding a varied and extensive view of the valley of the Esk. It was by the side of this romantic loch, when Christianity was in its infancy in Scotland, that St. Drostan is said to have planted a church. Near the same spot, in times not so remote, the author of *The Fortunate Shepherdess* taught the youth of the parish, and preserved, by his writings, much of that old Doric language of his native country, which otherwise would have been lost.[1]

Little is recorded of the ancient towns of the district. Brechin appears to have been a considerable place towards the close of the reign of Kenneth III.; and a few years later, when the country was invaded by the Danes, we are told that they burned the towns of Brechin and Montrose.[2] It is much more certain, however, that Montrose, Forfar, and Dundee were places of some trade in the time of Malcolm the Maiden, since that prince made grants from the revenues of these towns towards the support of the Priory of Restenneth.

It was around the seats of kings, bishops, and abbots that towns and villages were originally planted. The first were accounted royal burghs, the others burghs of bishops and abbots respectively. Of the first class were Forfar and Montrose, and in all probability Kincardine, of the next Brechin, and of the third Coupar-Angus and Arbroath. Brechin, from having been the seat of a cathedral and bishop, has the style of *city*.

Besides numerous populous villages in Forfarshire, the chief seats of commerce now-a-days are much the same as they were

---

[1] For a detailed account of the district and its antiquities, see Mr. Jervise, *Land of the Lindsays*, ch. ii.

[2] Holinshed, *Scot. Chron.* pp. 305, 329. Our Scotch authors, like Boetius, Dempster, Holinshed, etc., write too much in the spirit of romancers to be quoted as historical authorities regarding the events in ancient Scotland, yet they may at times embody in their works the traces of an older tradition, and may have taken as a groundwork the meagre notices in the Scotch and Irish Monastic Chronicles that, extant then, may now be lost.

in ancient times. From earliest record Dundee appears to
have been the largest town, then Montrose, Brechin, Forfar, and
Arbroath. But the position of the last-named four burghs is
now altered : Arbroath, according to the number of its inhabitants, ranks next to Dundee, and then Montrose, Forfar, and
Brechin. But to these ought to be added the rather ancient
and now thriving town of Kirriemuir, of which the old Earls of
Angus were superiors. Kirriemuir (anciently *Kil-marie*) is a
burgh of barony, as are Glamis, Edzell, and some other villages.

Forfar is the chief seat of the sheriff-courts in the one
county, and Stonehaven of those in the other. Inverbervie is
the only royal burgh in Kincardineshire, while Stonehaven,
Laurencekirk, Fettercairn, and Auchinblae, are the larger
places, that, with some lesser hamlets, were erected into burghs
of barony at different times, and are held of different superiors.

Like other districts in Scotland, Angus and Mearns are said
to have been governed in old times by hereditary Maormors,
or Earls. Dubican, the son of Indrechtaig, together with his
son, Maolbride, and Cunech or Cunechat, the father of Lady
Finella, are said to have been Maormors of Angus during the
greater part of the tenth century. Finella, who is believed to
have been the cause of the death of Kenneth III., is described
as the wife of the Maormor of the Mearns, and Malpender, or
Maolpeder, the Maormor of the period, is said to have assas-
sinated King Duncan in 1094.[1]

It is supposed that Sheriffs were first appointed by David I.,
but it was not until the time of David II. that the office
became hereditary in Scotland.[2] The heritable sheriffship of
Angus appears to have been first conferred upon Ramsay of
Auchterhouse, from whom, through a female, it was carried to
the Ogilvys. On the resignation of the office by a female
descendant of that family, it was acquired by David, Earl of
Crawford, afterwards Duke of Montrose; but from the part

[1] Stuart, *Ant. Essays*, p. 99.
[2] Chalmers, *Caled.* i. pp. 452, 714 sq. ; Ryley, *Placita*, p. 504 ; Innes, *Sketches*,
pp. 399, 465 ; Robertson, *Scotland under her Early Kings*, i. pp. 253-7, 438-9.

which he took in favour of James III. against the rising of his son at Blackness, he was deprived of the office on the succession of James IV. It was then given to the family of Gray, with whom it continued down to the early part of the reign of Charles I., when it appears to have been abolished as a hereditary right. The Keith-Marischals were probably hereditary Sheriffs of the Mearns—at least they appear to have held the office from much about the same time as the Ramsays did that of Forfarshire.

Though very incomplete, it is believed that the following lists of the Sheriffs-Principal of Angus and Mearns, extending over a period of more than five hundred years, may be perused with interest, if not by the general reader yet by the representatives of the older families of these counties.[1]

Sheriffs of Angus.

William Cumyn, justiciary of Scotland, was sheriff of Forfar in 1209-18.—Douglas, *Peer.* i. p. 161 ; *Reg. Vet. Aberbr.* pp. 5, 73.

David de Haya, 1211-14.—*Reg. Vet. Aberbr.* p. 43.

Hugo Cambrun, sheriff, 1214-25.—*Reg. Ep. Br.* ii. p. 3 ; *Reg. Vet. Aberbr.* p. 162.

Thomas of Malherbe (of Rossy), sheriff, 1226.—*Reg. Vet. Aberbr.* pp. 163, 262, 335 ; *Acta Parl.* i. p. 81.

Henricus Cambro (but perhaps Hugo, as above), 1226-39.—*Reg. Vet. Aberbr.* p. 335, cf. p. 262.

William of Hwuctyruus (Auchterhouse), sheriff, 1245.—*Reg. Vet. Aberbr.* p. 200.

E. and W. Montealt (of Fern), sheriffs, 1264.—*Chamb. Rolls,* i. pp. 11*, 41*.

R. of Montealt, quondam sheriff, 1266.—*Ibid.* p. 54*.

John of Fenton (of Baikie), sheriff, 1266.—*Chamb. Rolls,* i. p. 34*.

Matthew de le Chene, " tunc vicecomes de Forfar," 1272.—Fraser, *Hist. Carnegies of Southesk,* ii. p. 480.

Sir William Maule of Panmure was sheriff in 1286, and at the death of Alexander III.—Douglas, *Peer.* ii. p. 350.

David of Betun (of Ethiebeaton), knight, 1290.—*Chamb. Rolls,* i. p. 79*.

[1] *Reg. Episc. Br.* i. p. xxi *n.*

William of Herth (? Airth), appointed by King Edward I., 1305.—
Acta Parl. i. p. 15.

John of Trequer was sheriff, 9th June 1328.—*Chamb. Rolls,* i. p. 12.

Hugh of Ross, and William, Earl of Ross, sheriffs and bailies of
Forfar, 1347.—*Miscell. Aldbar,* MS., p. 208.

Robert of Ramsay (of Auchterhouse), sheriff, 9th April 1359.—
Chamb. Rolls, i. p. 342.

John of Ramsay, collector of one of the Quarters of Angus,
1359.—*Ibid.* p. 355.

Robert of Ramsay, sheriff, 1359-62.—*Ibid.* pp. 352-98.

Malcolm of Ramsay, 1365.—*Reg. Mag. Sig.* pp. 42, 116. He was
alive in 1407.—*Reg. Ep. Br.* i. p. xxi.

Sir Walter of Ogilvy, temporary sheriff, 31st Oct. 1380.—*Antiq. of
the Shires of Aberdeen and Banff,* ii. p. 43.

Alexander of Ogilvy, 1388-90.—*Reg. Ep. Br.* p. xxi; Robertson,
Index, p. 149.

Walter of Ogilvy, lord of Auchterhouse, 1390.—*Reg. Mag. Sig.*
p. 193, No. 2.   Slain at Glasklune, 1392.—Wyntoun, *Chron.* ii.
p. 369.

Alexander of Ogilvy, 1405-7.—*Chamb. Rolls,* ii. p. 634 ; *Reg. Mag.
Sig.* pp. 243-2.

Alexander de Ogilvy, dominus de Ouchtirhouss, vicecomes de
Anguss, 2d July 1410.—*Reg. Ep. Br.* i. p. 27.

John of Ogilvy, "under schref," 10 Jan. 1410-11.—*Ibid.* i. p. 32.
1432, "Subvicecomes de Angus."—*Balcarres Ch. Chest.*

Sir Alexander of Ogilvy, vicecomes de Angus, 1417.—Macfarlane,
Coll. Adv. Lib.

Alexander of Ogilvy, 1420.—*Chamb. Rolls,* iii. p. 103 ; Robertson,
Index, pp. 149, 165.

Sir Patrick of Ogilvy, knight, 2d May 1425, *Reg. de Pan.,* i. p. 212 ;
and 2d Aug. 1428, *Reg. Mag. Sig.* No. 110, p. 21.

Alexander of Ogilvy, son and heir of "nobilis viri Johannis de
Ogilvy ; this Alexander "was sub-vicecomes de Angus," Nov.
26, 1426.—*Reg. de Pan.* i. p. 247.

Sir Alexander Ogilvie, of Auchterhouse, knight, sheriff of Forfar
1446.—H. Laing, *Scot. Seals,* i. p. 109.

Walter of Ogilvy, sheriff of Angus, May 20th, 1455 (*Misc. Spald.
Club,* iv. p. 128); and Sept. 2d, 1458 (*Reg. Mag. Sig.* No. 615,
p. 137 ; but he had been also on 1st Feb. 1453 (*ibid.* No. 1038,
p. 215).

Margaret Ogilvy of Auchterhouse, afterwards Countess of Buchan,
resigned the sheriffship of Angus about 1464.—*Misc. Spalding
Club,* v. p. 286.

David, Earl of Crawford, afterwards Duke of Montrose, appointed
hereditary sheriff of Angus by James III., 19th Oct. 1466,
was compelled to resign the office by James IV., 29th Oct. 1488
—*Reg. Mag. Sig.* No. 886, p. 164 ; Lord Lindsay's *Report on
the Montrose Claim*, pp. 519, 524. Probably Lord Innermeath, and Alexander Guthrie of that Ilk, were deputes to the
Earl of Crawford. The first appears in 1478, the latter in
1481.—*Acta Aud.* pp. 64, 95.

Andrew, Lord Gray, was appointed hereditary sheriff on the resignation of the Duke of Montrose, 6th Nov. 1488-95.—*Reg. Mag.
Sig.* No. 1806, p. 383 ; *Montrose Claim*, p. 524. The office was
held by the Lords Gray until Charles the First's time, when
the eighth Lord Gray resigned it, on the promise of receiving
50,000 merks.—Douglas, *Peer.* i. p. 672.

While the hereditary sheriffship was held by the Grays,
their deputes[1] were probably, in 1494, William Monor-
gond of that Ilk, and Alexander Boyis (*Acta Aud.*
p. 206); in 1514, Henry Lovell of Ballumby, knight, and
William Ouchterlowny of Kelly (*Miscell. Aldbar*, MS.,
p. 47); in 1516, Gilbert Middleton of that Ilk (Douglas,
Peer. ii. p. 230) ; in 1541, John Stewart, Lord Innermeath (*Account of Senators of the College of Justice*, p. 82);
in 1560 and 1578, Ninian Guthrye of Kingenny (*Reg.
de Pan.* ii. p. 309 ; *Crawford Case*, p. 178).

William Ouchterlowny of Kelle, sheriff of Forfar, 1514.—Fraser,
Hist. Carnegies of Southesk, ii. p. 544.

" Alexandro Erskine de Dun novissimo Vicecomiti dicti Vice-
comitatus."—*Charter of grant of Sheriffship to Sir P. Maule*,
5th Sept. 1632.

Sir Patrick Maule, afterwards Earl of Panmure, was created
" sheriff principal of the shire of Forfar," by charter under the
Great Seal, dated at Holyrood, 5th Sept. 1632.—*Reg. de
Pan.* ii. p. 319. He died in Dec. 1661.

Henry Maule of Dunbarrow, sheriff-depute, 19th March
1635.—*Reg. de Pan.* ii. p. 77.

David Nevoy of Reidie, sheriff-depute, 1651.—*Deed at Panmure.*

David, first Earl of Southesk, " for many years sheriff of Forfar "
before 1658.—Fraser, *Hist. Carnegies of Southesk*, i. p. 108.

Archibald sone of Chapelton, sheriff-depute, 7th January
1642.—*Crawford Case*, p. 131.

---

[1] For the Sheriffs-depute generally see *Reg. Mag. Sig.*, pass. ; Warden, *Angus*,
ii. pp. 229 sq.

James Keith of Caldhame, sheriff-depute of Forfar, 1662.—
Reg. de Pan. ii. p. 136.

Sir James Keith of Powburne, knight-baronet, sheriff-depute
of Forfar, November 1663.—*Paper at Panmure* (Discharge).

James, second Earl of Southesk, had re-grant of the sheriffship in
1643, with Robert, Lord Carnegie, for their joint lives—Fraser,
Hist. Carnegies of Southesk, i. p. 142 ; sheriff, 1669—Douglas,
Peer. ii. p. 515.

Robert, third Earl of Southesk, had a new grant for himself and
son in 1682.—Fraser, *Hist. Carnegies of Southesk,* i. p. 147.

John Lindsay of Edzell, sheriff, died 1671.—*Lives of the Lindsays,* ii.
p. 58.

Patrick, third Earl of Kinghorn, who died 15th May 1695, was
appointed sheriff, 1694.—*Family papers at Glamis.*

David, fourth Earl of Northesk, sheriff, 1702.—Douglas, *Peer.* ii.
p. 323.   Fraser, *Hist. Carnegies of Southesk,* ii. p. 376.

David, fifth Earl of Northesk by patent 1702 to succeed his father
(1729).—Fraser, *Hist. Carnegies of Southesk,* ii. p. 376.

Sheriffs of the Mearns.

"Osbert Olifard, sheriff of the Merns under Malcolm IV."—
Chalmers, *Caled.* i. p. 516 ; Douglas, *Peer.* i. p. 78.

John of Hastinkes (lord of Dun in Angus) was sheriff and forester
of the Mearns, 1163-78.—*Spalding Club Miscell.* v. p. 210.

Robert Senescald, sheriff of the Mearns, 1214-25.—*Reg. Ep. Br.* ii. p. 3.

Philip of Maleville (of Mondynes), 1222-40.—*Reg. Vet. Aberbr.*
pp. 88-9.[1]

Robert le Chein, 1263-6.—*Chamb. Rolls,* i. p. 20*.

Reginald le Chein, 1266.—*Ibid.* p. 32*.

Richard of Dummor, appointed by King Edward I., 1305.—*Acta
Parl.* i. p. 15.

Alexander of Stratoun (of Lauriston), sheriff, 9th June 1328.—
Chamb. Rolls, i. p. 12.

Robert of Keith, Marischal of Scotland, 11th August 1348-58.[2]—
Ibid. pp. 289, 300.

---

[1] Although the story of a Melville having been sheriff of the Mearns, and boiled in
a caldron at Garvock, is common, and given below (p. 150), the above is the only
authentic notice that the author has seen of the Melvilles as sheriffs of the district.
One of the Melvilles may have been a sub-sheriff under James I.

[2] Douglas, *Peer.* ii. p. 178, says that Robert Keith, Marischal of Scotland, fell at
Durham, 17th Oct. 1346 ; but this is probably a mistake, since there was no other
Robert in the family until long after 1358.

William of Keith, 1359, and on 15th March 1391.—*Chamb. Rolls,*
   i. p. 338 ; ii. p. 175.
Robert Keith, knight, lord of Troup, 12th March 1406-7.—*Reg.*
   Mag. Sig. p. 223.
Sir William Keith, sheriff, 20th May 1442, died 1476.—Douglas,
   Peer. ii. p. 189.
     Alex. Ogilvy of Inverquharity, sheriff-depute of Kincardine,
     1443.—*Coll. for Shires of Aberdeen and Banff,* iii. p. 268.
Patrick Barclay, sheriff-depute, 1st April 1448.—*Reg. Ep.*
   Br. i. p. 113.
William, second Earl Marischal, about 1483.—Nisbet, *Heraldry,*
   ii. App. p. 238.
William, third Earl Marischal, 7th July 1492.—*Acta Dom. Concil.*
   p. 243.
William, fourth Earl Marischal, 22d April 1525, died 1581.—Douglas,
   Peer. ii. p. 191.
William, Lord Keith, 1621, died 1635.—*Acta Parl.* iv. p. 630.

It would appear from the list of sheriffs of the Mearns that
the offices of sheriff and forester were often united. The
royal forester had jurisdiction in offences against the forest
laws, and had certain payments or privileges allowed for
keeping or superintending these sporting fields, of which
Cowie, Durris, and the Month were the more important in
the Mearns, as those of Monrommon, Kingenny, Drimmie,
Plater, and Kilgery were in Angus.

Apart from sheriffdoms, there were districts called thane-
doms, and their possessors assumed the title of Thane.[1]
There was also another division, as when King William the
Lion granted to the Abbey of Arbroath " the church of St.
Mary of Old Munros, with the lands of that church, which in
Scotch is called Abthen."[2] Thanes, originally stewards over
king's lands, became ultimately hereditary tenants of the
king, and the title and lands descended accordingly. The

---

[1] On the question of Thanes and Thanedoms, see Chalmers, *Caled.* i. pp. 456,
716-719 ; Robertson, *Scotland under her Early Kings,* i. pp. 185, 234, 237, ii. pp.
444-471.
[2] *Reg. Vet. Aberbr.* p. 67, 1292-3 ; Abthenage of Ketenes (Kettins), Rogers,
Coupar Abbey.

fine paid by a thane was a hundred cows, being the same number as that payable by an Earl's son.

Probably these divisions were more numerous in this district than in most other parts of Scotland, as there were at least nine of them in Angus, and seven in the Mearns :—

Thanedoms in Angus.

A bounding charter of the thanedom of ABBERLENNOCHE, or ABERLEMNO, was granted by Robert the Bruce to William Blunt, a cadet of an old Dumfriesshire family.[1]

Sir Alexander Lindsay, knight, had the thanage of DOUNEY, or DOWNIE, from Robert II. in 1331.[2]

John de Logy (probably the father of Margaret Logy, Queen of David II.) had the reversion of the thanedoms of GLAMIS and TANNADICE from King David in 1363. The reddendo of the first was a red falcon, to be delivered yearly at the feast of Pentecost, and that of the second a sparrow-hawk. Both thanedoms were afterwards given to Sir John Lyon, ancestor of the Earls of Strathmore, in dowry with his wife, Jane, daughter of Robert II.[3]

Robert II., with consent of his eldest son, John, Earl of Carrick, gave to Walter Ogilvy an annual rent out of the "thanedom of KINGALTY." This probably refers to Kinalty in the parish of Tannadice, near the castle of Cortachy, since the lands of Kinalty, in the parish of Airlie, are described, in a nearly contemporary charter, as being in the barony of Rethy, or Reidie.[4]

In the year 1220, Malcolm, Earl of Angus, grandson of Gilchrist, gave Nicholas, the priest of Kirriemuir, and his heirs, the ABTHEIN LANDS OF MONIFIETH. "Patricius capitalus medico," had a charter of the lands of Ballegillachie, or Balgillo, in the thanedom of MONIFIETH, from Robert I.[5]

---

[1] Robertson, *Index*, p. 18 ; *Reg. Mag. Sig.* No. 3583, p. 771 (A.D. 1511), classes together the Thanages of Vetus Montrose, Duny, Glammys, Kingalteny, and Aberleminock.

[2] Robertson, *Index*, p. 96.

[3] Willis, *Current Notes* for July 1854 ; *Reg. Mag. Sig.* pp. 32, 90 ; Laing, *Scot. Seals*, i. p. 130.

[4] Robertson, *Index*, pp. 132, 137 ; *Reg. Mag. Sig.* p. 171.

[5] *Reg. Vet. Aberbr.* p. 330 ; Robertson, *Index*, p. 18.

Gyles, thane of EDEVYN, EDEVY, or IDVIES, flourished about the year 1219.[1]

Donald, eighth Earl of Mar, had from Robert I. a charter of his thanage of Colvith (probably Clova) in Angus.[2]

In 1360 Andrew Dempster of Auchterless and Careston, and William and John Collace of Balnamoon, granted confirmation of an annual payment to the Priory of Restenneth out of the thanedom of MENMUIR.[3]

In 1365 David II. gave Sir Alexander Lindsay of Crawford, father of the first Lindsay of Glenesk, "all the king's lands in the thanedom of NEWDOSK."[4] These lands lie in the Kincardineshire portion of the parish of Edzell.

Thanedoms in the Mearns.

The thanedom of ABERBOTHNET, or ARBUTHNOTT, was granted by Robert I. to John Fraser, a cadet of the Saltoun family.[5]

Charters of the reversion of the thanedoms of ABERLUTHNOT [Marykirk], KINCARDINE, and FETTERCAIRN, were granted from William, Earl of Sutherland, in the time of David II. to Walter Lesley.[6]

William Fraser, and his spouse, Margaret Murray, had the thanedoms of COLLY, or COWIE, and DURRIS, from David II., in succession to his father, Alexander Fraser.[7] The former had previously belonged to Fraser's father. Robert, son of William Keith Marischal, had a charter from Robert II. of the forests of Cowy and the Month, the lands of Ferachy, Glastolach, Cragy, and Clochnahill, "which of old was in the thanedome of Cowie." Long before this, however, in 1281, Thomas, son of the Thane of Kolly, is witness to a deed regarding the division of the lands of Nigg.[8]

David II. granted John Gray five chalders of victual, and David Fleming an annual, out of the thanage of MEIKLE MORPHIE.[9] Conveth was also a thanage.[10]

---

[1] *Reg. Vet. de Aberbr.*, p. 163.   [2] Douglas, *Peer.* ii. p. 200.
[3] *Reg. Mag. Sig.* p. 43.   [4] Robertson, *Index*, p. 79 ; *Reg. Mag. Sig.* p. 45.
[5] Robertson, *Index*, p. 18.
[6] *Ibid.* pp. 65, 89 ; *infra*, p. 139 ; *Reg. Mag. Sig.* p. 71.
[7] Robertson, *Index*, pp. 60, 65, 117 ; *Reg. Mag. Sig.* p. 68 ; *infra*, p. 160.
[8] *Reg. Vet. Aberbr.* p. 164.
[9] Robertson, *Index*, p. 32.
[10] Innes, *Scot. Leg. Ant.* pp. 79, 80.

SECTION II.

Stern tide of human Time : that know'st not rest,
But sweeping from the cradle to the tomb,
Bear'st ever downward on thy dusky breast
Successive generations to their doom.

SCOTT, *Waterloo.*

Castles : Redcastle, and its siege by Gray of Dunninald—Black Jack—Origin of the
present Castle of Glamis, and of the paintings in the chapel—Guthrie Castle
—Affleck—Inverquharity—Broughty—Dunnottar—Fortar—Braikie—Newtyle—
Balfour—Colliston—Bannatyne—Crathes—Balbegno—Careston—Inglismaldie—
Muchalls, etc.

WITH the exception of the ruins of the ancient castle at Kincardine in the Mearns, there is probably no certain trace of
any stronghold existing in either county before the fifteenth
century, about which date it is supposed that the square
tower of three or four stories, with the lower one always, and
the second one generally, vaulted, was introduced into Scotland.

Although a few of the castles present interesting architectural features, and have been the scene of important historical
events, yet our limits will not allow us now to enlarge upon
these particulars.   This, however, is the less to be regretted,
since notices of the more important of them, with the exception of Redcastle and Glamis, will be found in different parts
of the work.   As little has been hitherto written regarding
the former, while much fable has been circulated as to the age
and origin of the latter, a few facts may add somewhat to the
interest of the one, and place the history of the other in its
true, and not less agreeable light.

The ruins of Redcastle, which are among the oldest in
Forfarshire, occupy a rising ground on the west side of Lunan
Bay, fully a mile north-east of the parish kirk of Inverkeilor.
They consist of little more than a roofless square tower, greatly
dilapidated.   The lands of Inverkeilor and the manor of
Redcastle were given by King William the Lion in 1165 to his
chamberlain, Walter de Berkeley, and through his daughter's
marriage they were carried to Ingleram of Baliol, ancestor of

King John.[1] A descendant of Baliol married an Englishman of the name of Fishburn, whose son possessed Redcastle in 1306. Subsequently it was given by Robert the Bruce to Donald Campbell, on the forfeiture of Henry Percy and Ingleram of Umphraville.[2] On the resignation of Sir Andrew Campbell, in 1366-7, the barony was acquired by Sir Robert Stewart of Innermeath, father of the first Lord Lorn. The tower of the castle was probably built by one of the Lords Innermeath— at least the family were in possession of the lands from the last-named date, and occupied the house down to about the close of the sixteenth century.[3]

It was in the spring of 1579, during the widowhood and old age of Lady Innermeath, that Andrew Gray, son of Patrick, Lord Gray, proprietor of the neighbouring estate of Dunninald, along with a number of his followers, attacked the house of Redcastle, for the purpose of plundering and burning it, and killing the inmates. It was then occupied by Lady Innermeath, in company with a son and daughter, the latter being wife of Lindsay of Vayne.[4] She is recorded to have been pregnant at the time; and Gray, having succeeded in gaining

---

[1] Walter de Berkeley, made Chamberlain of Scotland in 1165, received from King William a grant of the extensive manor of Inverkeilor in Forfarshire, and built Redcastle, hence he is sometimes called the lord of Redcastle. He granted the church of Inverkeilor to the monks of Arbroath, and was a hostage for King William, but the date of his death, in the beginning of the thirteenth century, is unknown : he left an heiress, who married Ingleram de Baliol. Humphry de Berkeley was probably a brother of this Walter, and granted Balfeich, etc., to Arbroath.—Chalmers, *Caled.* i. p. 529. Humphry received from King William the manor of Conveth, Monbodach, Balfeich, Culback, Kinkell, Glenferchar, and other lands in Fordoun parish.—*Ibid.* i. p. 529 *n.* Another branch in the twelfth century were progenitors of the Mathers Barclays.—*Ibid.* i. p. 529 *n.*

[2] Crawford, *Off. of State*, p. 253 ; Robertson, *Index*, p. 18.

[3] *Reg. Priv. Counc. Scot.* iv. p. 449.

[4] Our author received from the late P. Arkley, Esq. of Dunninald, the following interesting notices of the occupiers of Redcastle at the time of Gray's attack :— "The Lady of Innermeath was Elizabeth, daughter of Sir John Betoun of Creich, and widow of John Stewart, Lord Innermeath, to whom she was married about 1530. Before then she had borne a daughter to James v. This daughter was the well-known Jean, Countess of Argyle, who was sitting with Queen Mary when the murderers of Rizzio rushed in upon their victim ; and, in Dec. 1567, the General Assembly subjected her to stringent discipline because she had acted as proxy for Queen Elizabeth at the baptism of James vi., as that ceremony was performed accord-

possession of the whole buildings, except the tower of the castle, in which the occupants took refuge, burned down the rest, and, so it is stated, caused Lady Vayne, almost suffocated with smoke, to miscarry.

Although royal mandates were specially addressed to Gray, ordering him to desist from his heartless, and, so far as known, unprovoked attack, yet he paid no heed to them, but continued his " cruel invasion of said castle and persons " from 27th February till 12th March following, when matters assumed so serious an aspect that the provost and bailies of Dundee were ordered by the King to join Erskine of Dun, in an attempt to relieve the inmates. This seems to have had, for a time at least, the desired effect, for on seeing the approach of Erskine and his followers, Gray and his accomplices are said to have abandoned the siege, and betaken themselves to Gray's "locum de Dunenald, *alias* Blak Jack," carrying great spoil along with them.

This cessation of hostilities, however, appears to have been only temporary, for Gray, watching an opportunity for further outrage, made a second attack, on 3d February 1581, during the absence of the family. He was then accompanied by seventy followers, and the house being in charge of only two men and one woman (and these he confined in the stocks or prison for twenty days), he had no difficulty in making himself master of the place, including the tower. At that time he burned and destroyed a great part of the building both within

ing to the Roman Catholic manner.—(*Book of the Universal Kirk*, p. 90.) It is stated by many writers that the mother of the Countess of Argyle was Elizabeth, daughter of Sir John Carmichael (afterwards wife of Sir John Somerville of Cambusnethan), who was mother, by James V., of John Stewart, Prior of Coldingham. But this is an error, as it is expressly stated in the Countess's legitimation, under the Great Seal, 18th October 1580, which I have examined in the Register House, that she was the daughter of Elizabeth Betoun. Douglas (*Peerage*, i. pp. 92, 139), with his not unusual inaccuracy, in one place calls the Countess the daughter of Elizabeth Carmichael, and in another of Elizabeth Betoun. John Stewart, who was in Redcastle along with his mother, was the second son of Lord Innermeath. A charter of the lands of Laithers, in Aberdeenshire, was given to his father and himself in 1561. Marjory Stewart, the daughter of Lady Innermeath, must have been the wife of one of the Lindsays of Vayne."

and beyond the fortifications, and after keeping possession for some weeks, returned home with the plunder.

A messenger was forthwith sent to serve an indictment upon Gray at his house of Dunninald; but the messenger quaintly declares that although Gray spoke to him " our the wall of Dunenald and out of the windois thairof, he causit hade the zett and durris fast and wald not latt me in, [so] I deliuerit ane coppie of this sumondis to the said Androis spous, and that eftir I hade knokit nyne knokis at the zett of the said place."[1] When Gray failed to answer to the charge preferred against him, his lands and goods were confiscated to the Crown, and he himself was outlawed.[2] Still, he seems by some means to have got the sentence of outlawry removed, as in 1586, he was one of the assize on the trial of Archibald Douglas, parson of Glasgow, who was accused of being concerned in the murder of Darnley.[3]

Little else of interest is recorded of Redcastle. The barony became the property of Ruthven of Gardyne before the middle of the seventeenth century, and the house is said to have been roofed and in pretty good repair down to about 1770. It was subsequently in the hands of the Earls of Northesk ; but was purchased by the Countess, Lady Margaret Hamilton, for the Panmure estate in 1724. This apparently was the purchase of the castle and lands as well as the barony, but several additions were made within the barony to these purchases from 1756 to 1760.[4]

The castle of *Black Jack* was in olden times the residence of the lairds of Dunninald. It occupied the top of a perpendicular rock which rises from 100 to 200 feet above the level of the sea, near a place called Boddin Point. Foundations are still visible upon the rock, which is connected with the mainland by a narrow neck of land, where there are also

---

[1] In *Miscell. Spalding Club*, iv. pp. 60-68-9, Gray's name is given as *James*, not Andrew.   [2] *Acta Parl.* iii. pp. 206-10.   [3] Pitcairn, *Crim. Trials*, i. p. 148.
[4] *Reg. de Panmure*, i. p. lxvii., ii. p. 360. On Redcastle and Lunan, see APPENDIX No. I.

traces of a foss or ditch. The Grays were in possession of
Dunninald down to at least the year 1608.   It was afterwards
in the hands of the Erskines of Dun, from whom it passed to
James Allardyce, in part payment of his wife's portion.[1] Subsequently it was owned by the descendants of an old burgess
family of Montrose, of the name of Scott, and now belongs to
the representatives of the late Mr. Patrick Arkley, formerly
one of the sheriffs of Edinburgh, whose father built the present
mansion-house, which was designed by the late Mr. Gillespie
Graham in the English baronial style.

Although there was a royal residence at Glamis from a
remote date, and record shows that the noble family of Lyon
were settled there about the middle of the fourteenth century,
it does not appear that the building of the present castle was
begun until the time of the first Earl of Kinghorn, who succeeded his father in 1578.   This Earl, who also built certain
parts of Castle Lyon, now Castle Huntly, in the Carse of
Gowrie (originally constructed by the second Lord Gray,
about 1452)[2] unfortunately did not live to finish the work ;
and the justly admired ceiling of the great hall was not completed until 1620—such at least is the date it bears ; and the
initials, in monogram, of John, second Earl of Kinghorn, and
his Countess, Margaret Erskine, third daughter of the Earl of
Mar, correspond with that period.   The fine iron railing round
the top of the centre tower was put up in 1682, and the
paintings on the walls and ceiling of the chapel were executed
in 1688 by Jacob De Witt, a Dutchman, who, in 1684-6,
painted the portraits of the Kings of Scotland in the Picture
Gallery of Holyrood.   It was agreed between the Earl of
Kinghorn and the artist, that each of the fifteen large panels
in the roof of the chapel should contain " a full and distinct
story of Our Blessed Saviour, conforme to the cutts in a bible
here in the house, or the service-book."   The lesser panels

---

[1] *Inq. Spec. Forfar.* No. 60 ; *Miscell. Spalding Club*, iv. pref. p. lxxix.

[2] Douglas, *Peer.* i. p. 667.   See *Forf. Illust.* pp. 141 sq., for an account of the
family and castle.

were to be filled " with the angels as in the skie, and such other things as he (De Witt) shall invent, and be esteemed proper for the work." The crucifixion was to form the altar piece, and " the doore piece the ascenscione." In the panels around the chapel our Saviour was to be painted, and his twelve apostles, " in als full stature as the panels will permitt," also " King Charles the Martyr," and St. Paul and St. Stephen, all conform to the cuts in the books referred to. Each picture was to have the same name painted above, and " at the foot a scroll containing the same words as are exprest in the cutt."

The agreement between De Witt and the Earl came to be disputed ; and instead of the claim of 200 merks which the artist made, the Earl writes, " I would give now, after full deliberation, for the roofe of the chapel, £15 sterling : For Our Saviour, the 12 Apostles, the King's father, the 2 Martyrs, St. Paul, and Stephen, the altar and door pieces, £20 sterling."[1] Such are some of the details relating to the building and decoration of this castle, which the Chevalier de St. George, who spent a night there in January 1715, is said to have declared to be the finest he had anywhere seen.

It need only be added that, since the seventeenth century, many alterations and additions have from time to time been made upon the building, the latest being the work of the present Earl of Strathmore, who, as thirteenth Earl, succeeded in 1865. In 1866 his lordship had the chapel re-arranged internally to suit a purer ecclesiastical taste. The pictures were cleaned, and the heavy black enclosing mouldings gilded, so that at the re-opening service (by the late Bishop Forbes of Brechin) the prevailing feature was one of lightness and beauty without the air of antiquity being in the least interfered with. Apart from the paintings in the chapel, other objects of interest, such as historical portraits, and pieces of fine tapestry, adorn the interior of the castle ; and among the

---

[1] *Family Papers at Glamis.*—The scrolls and letters were executed by William Rennie, a painter in Dundee.

curiosities is an excellent specimen of the dress of the domestic fool or jester, to the cap and other parts of which the bells are still attached.

To much the same age as Redcastle, probably belongs the tower or older portion of Guthrie Castle. Sir David Guthrie, who was son of the laird of Kincaldrum, and Treasurer to James III., bought the barony of Guthrie from the Earl of Crawford, about the year 1465, and became founder of the family of that Ilk.[1]

The castles of Affleck, or Auchenleck, in the parish of Monikie,[2] and of Inverquharity, near Kirriemuir, are among the best and most entire in Forfarshire. They are of fine ashlar work, and at both there stood the old iron gates or *yetts*, that were so needful for the protection of life and property in feudal times, and for the erection of which special licences were granted by the king;[3] but, while the yett at Inverquharity remains, that of Affleck has disappeared.

Possibly also the older portions of the castles of Airlie, Brechin, and some others, belong to much the same period as those previously noticed, as well as the interesting keep of Broughty (built in 1496, and now restored), the tower of Dunnottar in the Mearns (probably erected by Sir William Keith), and that of Lauriston, by the Straitons. The same may also be said of the castle of Mathers, now reduced to a fragment, in the parish of St. Cyrus, and of the tower of Benholm, with its thick walls and broad massive battlements and turrets.

Of a subsequent date to the castles just named, varying probably from about the middle of the sixteenth to the beginning of the seventeenth century, are the Lindsay castles of Edzell, Finhaven, and Farnell (the last being a residence of the Bishops of Brechin), and Aldbar, which was built by Sir Thomas Lyon. Powrie Castle,[4] near Dundee, was built by the Fotheringhams,

---

[1] Jervise, *Land of the Lindsays*, p. 372.   [2] *Ibid.* p. 386.

[3] For a copy of the licence given to Ogilvy of Inverquharity, see Jervise, *Land of the Lindsays*, p. 346.

[4] "T.F.," upon a shield over chimney of dining-room or hall.

and Fortar, in Glenisla, by the Ogilvys. Fortar and Airlie were both burned by the Earl of Argyle in 1640,[1] and it was from the former that Lady Ogilvy, in the absence of her lord, was expelled by Argyle, an incident which gave rise to the fine old ballad regarding the burning of "the Bonny House o' Airlie." Melgund Castle is believed to have been erected by Cardinal Beaton, and Mains by the Grahams of Fintry. Hatton of Newtyle was erected by the Oliphants, and Pitcur by the Hallyburtons. Braikie, built by Fraser, a cadet of the house of Lovat, bears the date of 1581, and Claypotts, built by a descendant of Strachan of Carmyllie, has two dates, the one 1569, the other 1588.[2] The older portion of the castle of Gardyne was built by the family of that name; and the castle of Kelly near Arbroath—one of the best specimens of its kind in Angus—was probably erected by an Ochterlony. Balgavies, destroyed by order of James VI. in 1593 so that some arches and foundations only remain, together with Vayne and Invermark, were built by the Lindsays. Possibly the old gateway of Dun—the only remaining portion of the castle where Knox, Richard Melville, and others, so often met with Erskine to consult respecting the best means of promoting the Reformation—belongs to the early part of the sixteenth century. Balfour castle, in Kingoldrum, now in ruins, is said to have been built by Cardinal Beaton;[3] this, however, appears to be a popular error. Balfour, which was held of the Abbots of Arbroath, was possessed by Ogilvys from at least 1478, and the castle may have been the work of Beaton's contemporary, Walter Ogilvy, third son of Lord Airlie, and brother of Marion Ogilvy, mother of Cardinal Beaton's children. The castle of Colliston, near Arbroath (apparently one of the latest examples

---

[1] *New Stat. Acct.*, Forfarshire, p. 676 sq.

[2] *Forf. Illust.* p. 65, suggests that Claypotts Castle was built by John, son of Gilbert Strachan, or that the latter date belongs to John.

[3] Jervise, *Epitaphs*, i. p. 385, gives a copy (to some extent condensed) of a charter in Balfour in Kingoldrum, by Card. Beaton to James Ogilvy of Cookstone, 20th February 1539 (1540), but (*ibid.* i. p. xxv) he thinks that Melgund was the only castle really built by the Cardinal.

of the period referred to), is also said to have been erected by
the Cardinal. This impression seems to have originated in
much the same way as that regarding Balfour Castle, for the
lands of Colliston were also held under the superiority of the
Abbey of Arbroath ; and, during the abbotship of the future
Cardinal, they belonged to his relative Beaton of Creich.

The castle of Ballantyne or Bannatyne at Newtyle, was
erected, or at least enlarged, by Lord Ballantyne, or Bannatyne,
there being a contract extant " for building a house at Newtyle, betwixt Lord Ballantyne and John Mylne, and George
Thomson," dated 28th February 1589.[1]   Lord Ballantyne was
the elder brother of George Bannatyne, the famous collector of
the early poetry of Scotland, whose name was adopted by a
well-known Scottish literary club.   Local story says that it
was in the turret on the north-east corner of the house that
Bannatyne compiled his MSS., and that he came here to escape
the plague which raged in Edinburgh in the autumn of 1568.
But had the contract in question been executed (a supposition
which the style of the building rather tends to favour), the
most interesting part of this story must necessarily disappear.
Lord Ballantyne's father was a writer in Edinburgh, and
proprietor of the lands of Kirkton of Newtyle, in which he
was succeeded by his eldest son.   This interesting little castle
is still inhabited, and known as Bannatyne House.

But the finest examples of this period are Glamis Castle before mentioned and Crathes Castle.   The latter, situated in the
Mearns, was erected by one of the Burnetts, the first of whom
had charters of Crathes from Robert I.   In the same county,
the older portions of Thornton bear date in the earlier part
of the sixteenth century ; those of Hallgreen, Arbuthnott, Til-

---

[1] *Note from the late Mr. D. Hill.*—In an obituary notice of Mr. Mylne,
C.E., F.R. S., in 1858, *The Morning Post* says : " So early as 1587, his ancestor, John
Mylne, was engaged on Dundee Harbour and Town Works, and in building Lord
Bannatyne's house at Newtyle; and in 1600 in building a stone bridge of eleven
arches over the Tay at Perth.   Still later, in 1671, Robert Mylne, King's Master
Mason in Scotland, constructed the present Holyrood Palace, and executed a vast
number of public works."

whilly, and Balbegno, in the latter.   Tilwhilly was built by a
Douglas ; Balbegno, with arched hall, and medallion portraits
round the bartisan, was erected by a cadet of the knightly
house of Bonnington, in Angus—the date, " ANO 1569," and
the names of the erector, " I. WOD," and his wife, " E. IRVEIN,"
being carved near one of the upper windows.   This latter
property, situated in the regality of Kirriemuir, belonged
anciently to the Earls of Angus.

Of the castles of the seventeenth century so many exist,
either in whole or in part, both in Angus and Mearns, that
it would be superfluous to enumerate the whole of them, and
only a few of the more important need be named.   In Forfarshire there are Careston, built by one of the Lindsays ; Ethie,
by an ancestor of the Earls of Northesk ; Craig, by a cadet
of the noble house of Southesk ; and Dudhope, perhaps by
Scrymgeour, Earl of Dundee.   In Kincardineshire are Inglismaldie, built by Carnegie of Northesk, but much added to,
especially by the present Earl of Kintore ; Fiddes, by one of
the Arbuthnotts ; Monboddo, by an Irvine ; Allardice, by a
member of that family ; and Muchalls, by one of the Burnetts
of Leys.   The first and last named of these are probably the
most interesting.   Careston contains some curious ornamental
carvings in armorial bearings, and other insignia ;[1] while the
hall at Muchalls has a fine stucco ceiling, containing portraits
of Old Testament personages and heroes famous in Roman
history, with the royal arms of Scotland over the chimney.[2]

---

[1] For an account of Careston Castle, see Jervise, *Land of the Lindsays*, p. 290 sq.
[2] A stone on Muchalls Castle bears the inscription, " This work begun on the east
and north be Ar. Burnet of Leyis 1619, ended be Sr Thomas Burnet of Leyis his
sonne 1627." See Billings, *Bar. Arch.* iv. plate 18, and letterpress.

SECTION III.

Even the wild outlaw, in his forest walk,
Keeps yet some touch of civil discipline.
For not since Adam wore his verdant apron,
Hath man with man in social union dwelt,
But laws were made to draw the union closer.

OLD PLAY.

Battles of Dunnichen, A.D. 685—Pitalpin, A.D. 836—Aberlemno—Montrose—Lunan Bay—Barry—Restenneth, A.D. 833-6—Murder of Malcolm I.—Kenneth III. —Duncan II.—Death of Donald Bane, and King Edgar—Alexander I. surprised at Invergowrie—Battle of Stracathro, A.D. 1130—Sepulchral remains found in these Districts—Notes regarding the Wars of the Independence, and those of subsequent periods.

APART from the invasion of the Romans, which occurred about the year 84 of our era, when, as conjectured by some writers, the celebrated battle of the Grampians was fought in Angus, and by others in the Mearns (although for neither of them is there any conclusive evidence), it is recorded that on 2d May, 685, Egfrid, king of Northumbria, and Bridei, king of the Picts, fought in the neighbourhood of Dunnichen, and the former was slain.[1] This conflict is called *Cath-Duin-Nechtan*, or the battle of Nechtan's fort, because Nechtan, who reigned king of the Picts from 710 to 725, is said to have afterwards occupied a fort on the adjoining hill.[2] A swamp, or lake, in the neighbourhood, called Nechtan's Mere, was only finally drained by the late Mr. George Dempster. Traces of ancient sepulture have been got in the neighbourhood, and in a field called the *Cashel*, or Castle Park, a well-known sculptured stone monument was found, and below this a stone cist containing bones.[3]

---

[1] See Chalmers, *Caled.* i. pp. 210, 255 ; *Annals of Ulster*, A.D. 685 ; *Anglo-Saxon Chron.* A.D. 685.

[2] Skene, *Chron.* pp. cxix, 72, 351, 402 ; Bede, *Hist.* iv. c. 26 ; Chalmers, *Caled.* i. p. 210.

[3] On the antiquities of Dunnichen, see Stuart, *Sculp. Stones*, i. p. 28 and plate xcii. ; *Proc. Soc. Ant. Scot.* ii. p. 187.

It was in the year 836, that Aengus defeated Elpin, king of Scots, in the parish of Liff, near Dundee.[1] According to Boece, the latter was beheaded upon the stone on which he raised his standard. The stone is still called the "King's cross;" and "Pit Alpin," the name of the mound upon which it stands, is supposed to imply that the king was buried there; but he lies in Galloway.[2] About thirty years ago, the remains of a human skeleton were found about 18 inches below the surface. Towards the close of last century, eight or ten graves, constructed of rude flag-stones, were discovered in the same locality; and a fine "snake bracelet," now in the National Museum of the Society of Antiquaries of Scotland, was found there in 1732.[3]

According to the account given of the defeat of the Danes by Malcolm II., at Aberlemno[4] and other places in Forfarshire, one portion of the Northmen landed in the South Esk, at Montrose, another at Lunan Bay, and a third at Barry[5] where Camus, the reputed leader of the Northmen, was killed.[6]

Be the cause what it may, it is certain that in no part of Angus have there been found so many traces of ancient sepul-

[1] Another date given for this defeat is 730, but the whole question is doubtful, and 836 is Chalmers's date for Alpin son of Eocha's death. Chalmers, *Caled.* i. pp. 302-4; Holinshed, *Scot. Chron.* pp. 245 sq.; *New Stat. Acct.*, Forfarshire, p. 580.

[2] Skene, *Chron. Picts*, p. clxxxiv.

[3] Chalmers, *Caled.* i. pp. 211, 302-4 *n.*; *Proc. Soc. Ant. Scot.* ii. pp. 442 sq.; *Old Stat. Acct.* xiii. pp. 115 sq.

[4] Chalmers, *Caled.* i. pp. 400, 465; Gordon, *Septent.* p. 151, giving an account of the Aberlemno sculptured stones.

[5] Johnstone, *Extracts*, p. 59. It may probably be found that the district was the scene of the battles of Moncarno and Drumberg-Blathmig, both of which are said to have been fought in the year 728 (*Annals of Ulster*, in O'Conor, *Rex. Hib. Scrip.* iv. p. 81). In the former fell Bisceot M'Moneit and his son, and in the latter, Drust, or Drostan, king of the Picts. The first happened at a place described as "Monit-carno, near Loch Loegdea, or "Month-curno, near the lake of Leogdye," and the latter at "Droma-dearg-blatmig," or "Druim-derg Blathmig." A place called Moncur, or Monquhirr, is in the parish of Carmyllie, and near it Lochlair, and a farm called Dustydrum, (?Drustydrum). In Glenisla there is a place called Drumdarg. Near Arbroath is the ridge, or rising ground, of Kinblethmont, the soil of which is of a peculiarly red colour. In *Caledonia* (vol. i. p. 211), it is conjectured that the battle of Moncur was fought near Inchture, and that of Drumberg-Blathmig on the west side of the Isla. Others have suggested that Cairn-o'-Mount and Glendye, in the Mearns, may be the places meant by the Irish annalist.

[6] Jervise, *Land of the Lindsays*, p. 387.

ture and tumuli, as in the districts of Carnoustie and
Aberlemno; and below the cruciform sculptured stone at
Camuston, where the leader of the Danes is said to have been
buried, Commissary Maule is reported to have found a large
skeleton, with a part of the skull cut away, and also a rude
clay urn, and a thin bracelet of gold, still preserved at Brechin
Castle, and here represented.

It ought to be noticed that local tradition uniformly avers
(although there is no ground for such a belief) that the sculptured stone monuments had their origin in the defeat of the
Danes by King Malcolm.[1] The peasantry also believe that
the curious symbols engraved upon the stones are a species of
hieroglyphic, and that those at Aberlemno were once read by
a Danish soldier! This tale has long been common, and the
interpretation of the figures is preserved in these rude
couplets :—

> " Here lies the King o' Denmark's son,
>   Wi' twenty thousand o' his horse and men ; "

And—

> " Here lies the King o' Denmark sleepin' ;
>   Naebody can pass by this without weepin'."

About a mile south-east of the church of Aberlemno, in a
hillock upon the estate of Pitkennedy, there was found a rudely

---

[1] For further accounts of the sculptured stones of Angus, see Mr. Chalmers's work
on the subject, and Mr. Stuart's *Sculptured Stones of Scotland*. In the latter will
be found notices of sepulchral remains which have been discovered at some of
them as well as at single unembellished boulders and circles of stones. Notices of
similar discoveries in the two counties will also be found in the *Proceedings of the
Society of Antiquaries of Scotland*, pass., but for Aberlemno, *ib.* ii. 190 sq.

constructed stone coffin, containing a clay urn. Near the urn were scattered a number of beads, composed of jet or cannel coal, of which upwards of a hundred were recovered. With the exception of four pieces of a square shape, and two of a triangular, the rest were oblong, and pierced laterally, the square pieces being each pierced with four holes, and in the same direction, while the triangular bits were pierced obliquely. The square and triangular pieces have on one side a dotted ornament resembling a lace pattern, very similar to that figured on beads found in a barrow near Assynt, in Sutherlandshire, with this difference, that the spots of those, unlike the marks on the ones found at Pitkennedy, are said to have been studded with gold. The Pitkennedy necklace is in the possession of Patrick Chalmers, Esquire of Aldbar, proprietor of the lands upon which it was discovered, and it is probably the most complete hitherto found in Scotland.[1]

It is not, however, with the defeats of the Danes alone that the district of Aberlemno had to do, for Hector Boece tells us that, between 833 and 836, the Picts and Scots had a great battle near Restenneth, three or four miles to the westward. In this encounter, in which both armies are reported to have "fought right fiercely so long as any day light was on the skie," Ferideth, king of the Picts, is said to have been slain and his army defeated.[2] With this affair the two large unembellished obelisks at the Blackgate of Pitscandly are locally associated; and on one of them being overturned some years ago, a clay urn was found containing burnt ashes.

It is related by old writers that Malcolm I. fell at Fetteresso, in the Mearns, in the year 953, in a contest with a band of Morayshire men whom he met on their way south to revenge the death of their Maormor, or chief, whom King Malcolm is said to have killed,[3]

---

[1] *Proc. Soc. Ant. Scot.* iii. pp. 78, sq.
[2] Holinshed, *Scot. Chron.* pp. 244-5.
[3] Chalmers, *Caled.* i. p. 390, etc. Prof. Stuart, *Essays*, pp. 103 sq. Some lay the scene of the murder in Moray.

"quhill at the last
He was at *Colly* slayne in fycht."
WYNTOUN, *Chron.* ii. p. 92.

Traces of ancient burial are common in the district of Fetteresso ; and Professor Stuart says that in a gravel hillock lying
a little to the westward of Stonehaven Station fragments of a
human skeleton were found imbedded in a vegetable substance.
Over the skeleton was a covering of beautifully executed network, and around it a number of small black balls of the form
of acorns.   Remains of hair, of an auburn colour, were also
got, and pieces of an oval-shaped box, elegantly carved, lay
upon the breast.[1]   These are preserved in Fetteresso Castle.

Historians generally agree, that it was near Fettercairn that
Kenneth III. came by his death ; but some incline to the view
that it was near Stracathro ; all are at one, however, in
attributing the cause of it to Finella, wife of the Maormor of
the Mearns.[2]

Duncan II. is said to have been slain at Mondynes in that
county by Maolpeder, the Maormor of the Mearns.   A rude
unembellished boulder, near Mondynes, called the *Coort Stane,*
about 7½ feet high, is supposed by Professor Stuart to have
been the place of his burial.[3]   The name at least seems to
imply that the stone had been used as the site of the courts of
the barony of Mondynes, which was gifted by William the
Lion to one of his Anglo-Norman followers.

Donald Bane, who had assumed the sovereignty on the
death of his brother, Malcolm III., was dispossessed by Duncan,
Malcolm's son, and returned again to the throne at Duncan's
death.   In 1097 he was a second time overthrown, and imprisoned by King Edgar in the castle of Rescobie, in Angus,
where he died, having previously, according to the barbarous
custom of the times, had his eyes put out with red-hot irons.[4]

[1] *Essays*, p. 103.
[2] *Infra*, pp. 137 sq.
[3] Chalmers, *Caled.* i. p. 423 ; Prof. Stuart, *Essays*, p. 115.
[4] Chalmers, *Caled.* i. p. 424.

Towards the south-west end of the Loch of Rescobie, there is a long ridge or hillock, which, it is affirmed, was surrounded by water in old times and joined to the land by a causeway. Here, without however any apparent foundation, some have fixed the site of the castle of Rescobie. On the summit of the adjoining hill of Turin, there are traces of a building called "the castle," but neither history nor tradition preserves any record of the house or its occupiers.

Some say that King Edgar, the nephew and torturer of Donald Bane, died at Dundee;[1] and it is recorded that his successor, Alexander I., was surprised in his castle of Invergowrie in 1107, by a band of rebels from Morayshire and the Mearns.[2] This castle is said to have occupied a tongue of land, formed by the junction of two burns at a place called Hurley Hawkin, near the church of Liff.[3] The foundations of an old circular building were discovered here, and among them were found some pieces of human and animal bones, and rings of iron and bronze.

In the year 1130, King David I. defeated Angus, Earl of Moray, in a battle at Stracathro, in which, it is said, the Earl and nearly all his followers were killed.[4] Quantities of stone cists have been found in this neighbourhood; and when the *Re* or *Rye* Hillock, near the church of Stracathro, was being reduced some years ago, a carefully constructed grave, in which were human remains, was found about two feet below the surface. According to local story, the grave contained the figure of a fish, made of gold, from 4 to 5 inches in length.

The only warlike transactions of note that occurred in the district during subsequent centuries, were the defeat of Lord Montfort, near Panmure, by the Earls of Fife and March, in 1336-7; and the battles of Arbroath and Brechin about a

---

[1] Wyntoun, *Chron.* ii. p. 173; but Chalmers, *Caled.* i. p. 618, places his death at Dun-Edin.

[2] Wyntoun, *Chron.* ii. p. 174; but Chalmers, *Caled.* i. p. 620, at Stirling.

[3] *New Stat. Acct.*, Forfarshire, p. 580.

[4] Hailes, *Annals*, i. p. 76; Balfour, *Hist.* i. p. 11; Chalmers, *Caled.* i. p. 621.

hundred years later.[1]   The siege of the castle of Glenbervie by
Adam Gordon of Auchendown in 1571, and the "bourd of
Brechin," in 1570, when it is said Regent Lennox had "32
suddarts hangit," were perhaps the most serious local affrays
of the time of Queen Mary;[2] while the burning and besieging
of the town of Dundee—the former by the Marquis of Montrose
and the latter by General Monck—were the more remarkable
incidents which occurred in the district during the Civil Wars.[3]

SECTION IV.

Didst mark in thy journey, at dew-dropping eve,
Some ruin peer high o'er thy way,
With rooks wheeling round it, and ivy to weave
A mantle for turret so gray?

BISHOP COXE, *Christian Ballads.*

Introduction of Christianity—SS. Palladius, Drostan, and Boniface—The Culdees
—Religious Houses Founded—Origin of Parishes—Ancient and Modern Ec-
clesiastical Divisions—Examples of Ancient Church Architecture at Brechin,
Restenneth, Arbroath, Dundee, Cowie, and Arbuthnott—Tomb of Hugh le Blond
—Arbuthnott Family Mausoleum—Sepulchral Slabs at Dundee, Finhaven, &c.

ALTHOUGH it is said that Christianity was introduced into the
Mearns by St. Palladius, who settled at Fordoun during the
fifth century, and that St. Drostan and St. Boniface planted
churches in different parts of Angus during the two succeeding
centuries,[4] yet little reliance can be placed upon the ecclesiastical history of the country till we receive the accounts of a much
later date.   It was just about the dawn of our genuine Scotch
history that the Keledei or Culdees were introduced into
Scotland, and among their houses appear to have been those at
Abernethy in Perthshire, and Brechin in Forfarshire.[5]

Brechin had doubtless been a place of ecclesiastical note in

---

[1] Abercromby, *Wars,* ii. p. 70; Guthrie, *Scot.* ii. p. 395; *infra,* pp. 188 sq.
[2] Lamont's *Diary,* p. 227; Tytler, *Hist. Scot.* vii. p. 280.
[3] *Infra,* pp. 283 sq.
[4] Butler, *Lives of the Saints;* Dr. Wm. Smith and Prof. Wace, *Dict. Chr. Biog.*
i. pp. 330, 907.   [5] *Infra,* p. 164.

the year 990, when King Kenneth is said to have given the town to the Lord; but apart from this, and the facts before adverted to, little is known of the true state of the church here, or in any part of Scotland until the time of David I. The liberality of the latter in building and endowing religious houses is well authenticated, and among these were the Cathedral of Brechin—probably also the Priory of Restenneth. His grandson and successor, Malcolm the Maiden, founded the Abbey of Coupar-Angus, and King William the Lion that of Arbroath.

It seems also to have been in King David's time that Scotland was divided into parochial districts; and, from about that period down to the Reformation, there were eighty-one churches and chapels in our two counties. Of these, fifty-two belonged to the diocese of St. Andrews, twenty-three to that of Brechin, four to that of Dunkeld, and two to that of Aberdeen.[1] The bishops of the different dioceses of the Scottish Episcopal Church still adhere in the main to this arrangement; while, under presbyterial rule, there are, besides those merely *quoad sacra*, fifty-five separate *quoad omnia* parishes in Forfarshire. These in effect form five presbyteries, Arbroath, Brechin, Dundee, Forfar, and Meigle, as only three of the thirteen that constitute the presbytery of Meigle, and four of the like number in the presbytery of Dundee, are situated in the county of Perth. In Kincardineshire there are twenty parishes and one presbytery, but seven of the parishes, being those situated in the north-east portion of the county and at Deeside, belong to the presbyteries of Aberdeen and Kincardine O'Neil, while the others constitute the presbytery of Fordoun.[2]

It was while the religious houses of the twelfth and thirteenth centuries were being reared that the Anglo-Saxon and Anglo-Norman families came to Scotland. Of the lineage and possessions of the most of such as were in Angus and

---

[1] *Registers of Arbroath and Brechin; Archæologia*, xvii.
[2] A small portion of Edzell also is in Kincardineshire.

Mearns, some account will be found in this work, and their liberality, combined with that of the different sovereigns, tended greatly to increase the wealth and influence of the church.

It was also during the same period that the First Pointed (or Early English) style of architecture prevailed, and some good specimens of this are to be seen about the Cathedral and the Hospital or *Maisondieu* of Brechin, the Priory of Restenneth, and the Abbey of Arbroath. A portion of the west front of that Abbey shows traces of the Romanesque or Norman, or that style of architecture which is supposed to have preceded the First Pointed, but no other example of the kind is known in the district; while the Round Tower of Brechin, which belongs to a period anterior to the Norman style of building— probably to the end of the tenth century—is still in fine preservation, and a good example of the high state of the art of masonry in early times.

Kincardineshire is singularly devoid of the remains of ancient architecture; indeed, with the exception of the mere mention of a Priory, which is recorded to have stood at Ecclesgreig, or St. Cyrus, and to have been ancient in the days of King William the Lion,[1] there is but the slightest trace, even in history, of any convent in that county, and that obscure foundation is the Priory of the Carmelite Friars at Inverbervie, regarding the time of the endowment of which, and the style of its architecture, nothing is known.[2]

In specimens of the architecture of a later period, both Angus and Mearns are comparatively meagre. The bell-towers of Dundee and Brechin, however, and more particularly the first-named, present some interesting examples of the Decorated, or Second Pointed style. The old churches of Auchterhouse in Angus, and Arbuthnott in the Mearns, both of which have been unfortunately long since demolished, had, so far as can be gleaned from stray window-mullions and other pieces of

---

[1] *Reg. Prior. S. Andree*, p. 27.
[2] Walcott, *Scot. Ch.* pp. 337, 408. See APPENDIX No. II.

hewn work, possessed more than ordinary interest for the student of ancient church architecture. To these ought to be added the picturesquely situated ruins of the chapel of St. Mary at Cowie, near Stonehaven, that was consecrated on May 22, 1276, and the Burial Howff at Urie, built in 1741.

The belfry of the church of Arbuthnott (though by an ill-executed drawing of it a late eminent English antiquary was so far misled as to suggest a resemblance betwixt it and the old round towers)[1] is still a curious, if not unique object, while the adjoining burial-aisle of the family is the only structure in the district entitled to the name of a mausoleum. It is in the Gothic style of architecture, about fifty feet in height, and was built in 1505 by Sir Robert Arbuthnott of that Ilk. The upper story was set apart as a library, which Alexander Arbuthnott, son of the laird of Pitcarles, afterwards Principal of King's College, Aberdeen, bequeathed at his death to the clergy of the county, but the books have long since disappeared. The room is still more specially interesting in the fact of its having probably been the place where Mr. James Sybbalde, chaplain of St. Ternan, penned the psalter and office used in the chapel of St. Mary, and the missal used in the parish church. These are beautiful specimens of penman-ship, though even more important as pre-Reformation documents, and they have been carefully preserved in Arbuthnott House.[2] In the lower part of the aisle, formerly the chapel of St. Mary, there is the burial-place of the family of Arbuthnott, and a recumbent effigy, shown as that of Sir Hugh le Blond, the reputed founder of that family. Fable says that he received large additions to his estates in consequence of having killed some wild animal that frequented the Den of Pitcarles and was considered dangerous to the neighbourhood ; and a *cannon ball,*

---

[1] Pinkerton, *Literary Correspondence,* ii. p. 420.

[2] They were printed in 1864, at the Pitsligo Press, Burntisland, by the editors, Bp. Forbes and the Rev. G. H. Forbes. See *New. Stat. Acct.,* Kincardineshire, pp. 156 sq. ; *Old Stat. Acct.* xvii. p. 391.

preserved in the awmrie of the aisle, is shown as the *stone* with which Sir Hugh killed the animal ! [1]

The reputed tomb of Sir Hugh is ornamented with armorial bearings, which some heraldic writers have strangely interpreted, for it is certain that, if the shield which is said to have been charged with *three chevrons* (upon which has been founded the idea that Sir Hugh's wife was of the old family of De Moreville, Constable of Scotland) ever existed, it is not now to be seen. Four shields, however, still remain: two of them bear the Arbuthnott coats, and a third has two mullets-in-chief (and this possibly had at one time borne also the Arbuthnott arms, since the lower portion seems to have been chiselled off). A fourth shield is charged with the *fesse chequé* of the Stewarts of Atholl, to a daughter of which house James Arbuthnott, who died in 1521, was married. Possibly to this baron the tomb belongs; he was uncle of the builder of the aisle. It is much more probable that the coffin-slab which lies beside that effigy, and is embellished with a cross, two shields, and a sword, had been the tombstone of Le Blond, if he had had one. Its style, at least, corresponds more with that of the funeral monuments of the thirteenth century, during which he flourished.

This class of monuments is by no means common, yet there are several good examples in Scotland, and probably the best are at Dundee. Their chief feature is a cross, sometimes of exquisite design, and generally occupying the whole length of the stone. Along with the cross are the more ordinary representations of swords and hunting horns, compasses and squares—doubtless indicating the favourite pursuits and occupations of the persons over whom they were reared. One of the slabs at Dundee bears the figures of a ship, a ship-carpenter's hatchet, and other interesting objects. Two of them are thus inscribed; one contains a

---

[1] Another legend is given in the ballad of "Sir Hugh le Blond," *Legendary Ballads*, p. 206.

shield, charged with the Hay arms, and these words are carved
perpendicularly on the stone :—

✠ 𝔥𝔦𝔠 . 𝔦𝔞𝔠𝔢𝔱 . 𝔍𝔬𝔞𝔫𝔫𝔢𝔰 . 𝔣𝔦𝔩𝔦𝔲𝔰 . 𝔓𝔥𝔦𝔩𝔦𝔭𝔭𝔦 . 𝔠𝔦𝔰𝔰𝔬𝔯𝔦𝔰.

The other, adorned with a pair of scissors and a bodkin, contains
this pious legend :—

✠ 𝔒𝔯𝔞𝔱𝔢 : 𝔭𝔯𝔬 : 𝔞𝔫𝔦𝔪 : 𝔐𝔞𝔱𝔦𝔩𝔡 : 𝔣𝔦𝔩𝔦𝔞[𝔢] : 𝔗𝔥𝔬𝔪𝔞[𝔢] :

Similar ancient monuments were found in the old churchyard of Finhaven, situated near the confluence of the Lemno
and South Esk.[1]

Before closing these brief introductory remarks, it may be
added that, differing in style both from the ancient sculptured

stones of the Aberlem-
no and Meigle type,
and from those just
noticed, a peculiarly
interesting example of
an early Christian mo-
nument is preserved
at the Manse of Ar-
birlot, near Arbroath.[2]
This stone, which is
here represented, was
discovered in the foun-
dations of the old
parish kirk of Arbirlot
some fifty years ago.
It is about 5½ feet
high, by about 2¾ feet
broad, bears the repre-
sentation of two crosses near the top and bottom of the stone,
of two open books, and a small circle. One of the volumes has
a clasp, and the line which connects the upper book with the

---

[1] For these see Jervise, *Land of the Lindsays*, pp. 162-4.
[2] *Proc. Soc. Ant. Scot.* ii. p. 449.

cross below is probably intended to represent a rope or chain, and thus shows that the custom of preserving in this way the sacred writings and the works of the Fathers had been in use at the time when this stone was erected, but that time is, of course, unknown.

This is probably the monument of some former ecclesiastic of Arbirlot (or Abereloth, as the name was anciently written), the first recorded of whom is William of Eglisham, who flourished in the time of King Robert the Bruce. The church was in the diocese of St. Andrews, was granted to the Abbey of Arbroath, and dedicated to St. Ninian.

Very early in the thirteenth century, a person called "Maurice Abbe de Abireloth" witnessed grants to the monastery of Arbroath, by both King William the Lion and the Earl of Angus;[1] and, in consequence of the surname *Abbe* being assumed by ancient owners of properties in this and other parts of the country, some antiquarians are of opinion that those who bore this name were either hereditary lay abbots, or descended from the principal ruler of some Culdee establishment, such as were the Abbes of Edale or Edzell, and Brechin.

[1] *Reg. Vet. Aberbr.* pp. 29-32.

MEMORIALS OF ANGUS AND THE MEARNS.

PART SECOND.

THE HISTORY AND TRADITIONS OF THE

Castles and Towns

VISITED BY KING EDWARD THE FIRST,

A.D. 1296.

PART SECOND.

CASTLES AND TOWNS VISITED BY EDWARD I., A.D. 1296.

CHAPTER I.

The Castles and Town of Forfar.

SECTION I.

I grudge not Wellington his fame:
I grudge not Beresford a name,
Or ' glory to the gallant Graeme'!
But should not every honour due
Be paid the dead, and living too ?

BEATTIE, *John o' Arnha.*

Record of Two Castles—Queen Margaret's Inch—Supposed Origin of the Inch—
Religious House upon it—Parliaments at Forfar—William I.—Alexander II.
and III.—Gardeners of Forfar and Menmuir—Expenses of Royal Household—
Castle Surrendered to Edward I.—Edward's Visit—Castle Captured and
Destroyed by Bruce—Ancient Armour, Bronze Celts, etc.—The Constable's
House—Tenures of Old Farms—King's Falconer, etc.

THE history of both the Castle and Town of Forfar is lost in
the mists of antiquity. Hector Boece makes the apocryphal
assertion that Forfar had a castle at the time of the Roman
invasion under Agricola. Tradition, which in this case seems
borne out by the names of certain adjacent places,[1] has it that a
castle existed there during the reign of Malcolm Canmore. This
latter point may now be considered pretty well established,
since record shows that, within a hundred and fifty years from
the death of that king, Robert de Quincy made over to Roger
de Argenten what he terms "my place of the *old castle* of
Forfar, which our lord King William gave to me in lieu of a

---

[1] *e.g.* King's Muir, Palace Dykes, Queen's Well, Queen's Manor, Court Road,
King's Burn, King's Seat, Wolf Law, etc.

toft, to be held of me and my heirs by him and his heirs, well
and peacefully, freely and quietly." [1]

This, the only charter evidence of *an old* castle at Forfar in
the time of William the Lion, is of much value, not only as
proving that *two* castles were there at one and the same time,
but also as showing that, although the authority of Boece is
often questionable, he is sometimes more accurate than is
supposed, for in regard to this point he says, Forfar was
" strengthened with *two* roiall castles, as (he continues) the
ruins doo yet declare." [2]

Probably the *old castle* given over by De Quincy was that of
King Malcolm, which, according to tradition, stood upon an
island called *Queen Margaret's Inch*, on the north side of the
Loch.   Foundations of an extensive building are still visible
there, among which, till of late, there was " an oven almost
quite entire." [3]   This island was partly artificial, composed, as is
yet apparent, of large piles of oak and loose stones, with layers
of earth above.   Although now accessible from the land, the
belief is that it was formerly reached by a drawbridge; and
it may be inferred, since it is understood that insular fortifications were not introduced into Scotland till after the Norman
Conquest, that it owed its origin to King Malcolm, who
flourished subsequently to that time, and whose Queen was
born and educated in England.   But whether the island in the
Loch of Forfar was wholly or only partly artificial, or the site
of King Malcolm's castle, it is certain that a religious house
was established upon it by Alexander II. in 1234, and that,
besides money and other privileges, he gave to the two officiating monks pasture for six cows and a horse on his lands of
Tyrbeg.[4]   The chaplaincy of St Margaret's Inch was granted
by the Abbot and Convent of Coupar-Angus in 1508 to Sir
Alexander Turnbull, the chaplain, who was bound to give

---

[1] *Reg. Prior. S. Andree*, p. 354.
[2] Holinshed, *Scot. Chron.* i. p. 11, following Boece.
[3] Brown, *Royal Palaces of Scot.* p. 266; *Old Stat. Acct.* vi. p. 528 *n.; Proc.
Soc. Ant. Scot.* ii. p. 64.   [4] Rogers, *Coupar Abbey*, i. pp. xiii. 329.

personal residence upon the Inch, see to the building and
repair of the chapel and houses, and generally to preserve
the Abbot's interests there.[1] Probably the more recent castle
or fort at Forfar occupied the Castlehill, a conical mound near
the centre of the town, upon which also were the remains
of a building. The mound is about fifty feet in height, had
at one time been moated, and upon it was placed, some years
ago, a picturesque tower of modern masonry, from which a
pleasing view of the surrounding country is obtained.

Assuming, then, that the old castle of Forfar stood upon
Queen Margaret's Inch, it had been there, according to Boece
and others, that King Malcolm held his first Parliament, instituted titles of distinction, restored the children of those that
Macbeth had forfeited, and abolished the *marcheta mulierum*
law of the fabulous Evenus III., which apparently was nothing
else than a mere money payment on the marriage of a vassal.[2]
There too, probably, were performed by Queen Margaret many
of those holy deeds for which her life was so pre-eminent, and
whose history tradition has linked so closely with the town
and neighbourhood of Forfar.[3]

It is not, however, until late in the reign of King William
the Lion, that there is any record of a Court having been held
at Forfar—indeed, not until between 1202 and 1207, when King
William was present, and held an Assembly there. Forfar was
certainly a favourite residence of the last two Alexanders,[4] and
in 1225, the former of these monarchs held a Parliament there
in person. Another Assembly took place on the 14th of
January 1227, but from that the King was absent.[5] Several
charters of the same prince are dated from Forfar towards the
close of his reign.[6]

But it was during the time of the last Alexander, while the

---

[1] Rogers, *Coupar Abbey*, i. p. 273.

[2] Holinshed, *Scot. Chron.* i. p. 351. But the Parliament is probably fabulous;
see Innes, *Sketches*, p. 328 *n*.

[3] Hailes, *Annals*, Appendix No. I., and A.D. 1093. Butler, *Saints*, June 10.

[4] Fordun, *Chron.* ii. pp. 278, 285.   [5] *Acta Parl.* i. pp. 58, 59.

[6] *Illust. of Aberd. and Banff*, ii. p. 109.

commerce of the kingdom, its agriculture, and even its horticulture, were in a state of considerable advancement, that Forfar was most patronised by royalty ; and it is curious that, but for a passing notice relative to the King's gardeners at Forfar, Menmuir, and two or three other places, the interesting fact of the art of horticulture having been known and cultivated in Scotland in those days would have been little else than matter of conjecture.   The gardeners of Forfar and Menmuir are the only gardeners mentioned in this part of Scotland at that period ; and it is probable that both places were frequently resorted to by royalty.   The yearly wages of the gardener of Forfar was five marks, while the gardener of Menmuir had only one mark [1]—a fact which perhaps indicates the smallness of the labours of the gardener at Menmuir as compared with those of his brother at Forfar.

It is in 1263-4 that those interesting notices occur, when Alexander III. was but fourteen years on the throne ; [2] and the accounts of the two Montealts, ancient lords of Fern, and sheriffs of the county, furnish some interesting particulars regarding the items of rent received from the royal manors or demesnes of Forfar and Glamis.   During the year 1264, the return is 24 cows from Forfar, and 13½ from Glamis, exclusive of an arrear of 21, making a total of 58½ cows.   Of these 48 were expended in the King's service, and Montealt acknowledged himself debtor for 10½ cows.   Out of 75 hogs received from the two manors, 25 were spent in the King's service.

These accounts also abound with entries as to cheese, butter, hens, and malt, which were in the same year received from Forfar and Glamis.   It appears that 4 chalders and 10 bolls of barley-meal were used in feeding seven whelps and their dam for purposes of the chase.   William of Hamyll, hunting at Forfar with the king's hawks, had, for the space of 29 weeks and two days, in the year 1263, 8½ chalders, with three parts

[1] *Chamb. Rolls*, i. p. *13 ; Jervise, *Land of the Lindsays*, p. 307.
[2] *Chamb. Rolls*, i. pp. *12, *13.

of a boll of grain, together with £8, 12s. 6d. in money. During the same time, the king's horses hunting at Forfar had 14 chalders and 6 bolls of grain, and the grooms, besides being found in forage, had £4, 7s. in wages. Still further, the carriage of 16 pipes of wine from Dundee to the castle of Forfar, a distance of about fifteen miles, cost £4, 8s., and at Easter, 30 sheep, valued at 25s., were brought from Barry, and 40, computed at 33s. 4d.,[1] from the Grange of Strathylif, now Glenisla.

Such are a few of the glimpses, which the industry and research of learned antiquaries have given of the value of certain commodities in bygone days, and the economy and mode of living adopted by our ancient sovereigns. Unfortunately, from the above date until the year 1291, when King Edward demanded but was refused seisin of the castle of Forfar, nothing is recorded of its history. It was then held for the Estates of the kingdom by Umphraville, Earl of Angus, and, along with the castle of Dundee, was surrrendered by him into the hands of the English—only, however, on Umphraville receiving a formal letter of indemnity, guaranteeing him from all blame.

Soon after this, on Tuesday, the 3d of July 1296, King Edward and his suite visited Forfar, and took up their abode in the castle, where they resided until Friday the 6th. At that time Forfar was, as now, the chief or county town, and, the King of England, accompanied by Anthony Beck, the celebrated Bishop of Durham, and others, came thither from the secluded stronghold of Inverqueich, in Perthshire, a distance of about twelve miles. During King Edward's stay at Forfar, two churchmen and four barons, from different and distant parts of the kingdom, appeared and owned his superiority over Scotland.[2]

The castle had probably been then entire; but in the following year, while it was held by Brian Fitzadam, a retainer of King Edward, it is said (upon what authority is not apparent), that it was captured by Sir William Wallace. If so, it had

[1] *Chamb. Rolls*, i. pp. *11-15.
[2] *Ragman Rolls*, pp. 77-80; Prynne, *Hist.* p. 650; Palgrave, *Writs*, pp. 162-5. See APPENDIX No. III. for a detailed Itinerary of King Edward's visit to Scotland in 1296.

soon again fallen into the hands of the English, who long afterwards kept possession of it; for, towards the close of the year
1308, King Edward granted a mandate to John of Weston,
"constable of *our* castle of Forfare," to supply it with the
necessary provisions and fortifications.[1] Soon after this date,
if not even before, it yielded to the conquering arms of Bruce,
and the merit of its capture on that occasion is said to rest
with Philip, forester of the forest of Platane or Plater, near
Finhaven. The manner in which he accomplished the deed
is thus quaintly described by Barbour :—

> " The castell of Forfar was then
> Stuffit all with Inglismen,
> Bot Philip the forestar of Platane
> Has of his frendis with him tane,
> And with ledderis all prevely
> Till the castell he can him hy,
> And clam out our the wall of stane,
> And sagat has the castell tane
> Throu falt of wach with litill pane,
> And syn all that he fand has slane :
> Syn yhald the castell to the king
> That mad him richt gud rewarding,
> And syn gert brek doun the wall,
> And fordid the castell all."[2]

The castle thus destroyed,—

> " And all the touris tumlit war
> Doun till the erd "—

was never rebuilt, and when the Court visited the neighbourhood afterwards, it seems to have resided either at Glamis
Castle, or at the Priory of Restenneth, as from both of these
places charters were granted in presence of royalty.[3]

Fable affirms that Malcolm II. was murdered in "his lodging"
at Glamis, and that the murderers were drowned in the Loch of
Forfar.[4] Pieces of chain and plate armour, more or less entire,
together with several other warlike remains, including swords,

---

[1] *Rotul. Scot.* i. p. 61.
[2] Barbour, *Brus*, p. 203 ; Jervise, *Land of the Lindsays*, p. 171.
[3] *Reg. Mag. Sig.* p. 116 ; *Reg. Ep. Brechin.* i. p. 29.
[4] Holinshed, *Scot. Chron.* i. p. 334. But Malcolm II. died peaceably in 1033.

battle-axes, and bronze celts, as also a bronze cabinet ornament, have at various times been found, while excavations were made in and about the drained parts of the Loch and near the Castle-hill. The celts and cabinet ornament are preserved in the National Museum of the Society of Antiquaries of Scotland ;[1] and the armour, some of which is at Glamis Castle, and said to be that of the regicides, had most probably belonged to soldiers who fell at the capture of the castle of Forfar in 1308.

Of the size or appearance either of the older castle mentioned in De Quincy's charter, or of the more modern one which King Robert the Bruce destroyed, it were idle to conjecture. It is true that the armorial bear-ings of the town, and also the ornament which formed the top of the cross of the burgh,[2] erected in 1684, are said to be represen-tations of one or other of these strongholds.

It is probable that the ruins of the two castles to which Boece alludes had not long survived his time; for, within half a century after the publication of his History, an anonymous writer is altogether silent on the matter of the castle, and only condescends upon the Constable's house :—" In Foirfar," he says, " I saw tua durs chekis, with ane myd trie betuene the durris maid verray clenely and verray substantious, quhairin the constabill of Forfair Castell duelt in the tyme of King Malcolme Kanmore : thay ar of blak aik, and appeirandlie as thai war not maid v. zeir of eild."[3]

There is reason to conclude that, by the time the last-quoted writer visited Forfar, both castles were heaps of ruins, as otherwise he would, in all probability, have noticed them. It is certain that in 1674, which is the next mention that is

[1] *Proc. Soc. Ant. Scot.* ii. p. 64.

[2] The ornament lies on the Castlehill, but is broken into two pieces.

[3] (1569) *Extracta e Cron. Scocie*, p. 250.

made of *the castle,* it is declared to have been "now long time ruinous." About ten years later, Mr. Ochterlony says, the ruins of Canmore's castle "are yet to be seen;" while another writer, who visited the town about five years afterwards, observes that "Forfar had once the King's Palace, though now we scarce see the ruins of it."[1]

With the exception of traces of the building upon the Island before referred to, nothing remains there or on the Castlehill to show that either of these places had been occupied by strongholds; the site of the Constable's residence is unknown. The Hereditary Constableship of the King's house itself, long held by the noble family of Gray, and more recently by that of Strathmore, and ultimately merged into that of the burgh, was abrogated in 1748, on the abolition of heritable jurisdictions.[2]

Still, it is interesting to find that record has preserved some of the curious tenures by which certain of the royal farms were held in old times, the same, doubtless, as obtained when the palace was occupied by King William the Lion and the two Alexanders. In the year 1372 it appears that the middle lands of Kerringtonfields, now Ferridan or Ferryton fields, were held "pro seruiciis debitis et consuetis manerio nostro de Forfar;"[3] while Tyrbeg, or Torbeg (the place of the "little tower"), and Balmashannar ("the town of the high hill"), were held upon the *reddendo* of furnishing the royal household with three hundred cartloads of peats from the muirs of these lands, when the Court should have residence at Forfar—a holding which was subsequently changed (whether owing to a scarcity of peats, or from other causes, it is not stated) to the furnishing

[1] *Paper in Archives of Burgh; Spot. Miscell.* i. p. 321 ; Morer, *Acct. of Scot.* p. 104 ; Monipenie (1612) gives this random description :—" The towne of Forfarre with an old castle, with a loch and an isle therein, with a tower."—*Miscel. Scot.* i. p. 163.

[2] It may be noticed that Walter, Lord Aston, was created Baron Forfar by Charles I. in 1627 ; and Archibald Douglas, second Earl of Ormond, was created Earl of Forfar by Charles II. in 1661. The first of the titles became extinct in 1845 ; the latter in 1761, with the last Duke of Douglas.

[3] *Reg. Mag. Sig.* p. 89 ; again in 1391, *Ib.* p. 123.

of a sufficient quantity of fuel in general.[1]   It is also averred that the neighbouring lands of Heatherstacks (a name of which there is found no earlier trace than towards the close of the fifteenth century),[2] were held under a similar tenure in regard to the furnishing and winnowing of *heather* for the use of the royal kitchen, and this idea the name itself, even in the absence of charter evidence, may be held to corroborate.

As an instance of the manner in which fact and fiction are sometimes commingled, it may be mentioned that, among the officers belonging to the household of King Malcolm at Forfar, tradition speaks of a *falconer* who was buried at Kirriemuir, and upon his tombstone, it is said, were the figure of a *plover*, and an inscription to the effect that the stone marked the grave of a fowler to that king, who dwelt at Pluckerston. It is further stated that Pluckerston, which is in the neighbourhood of Kirriemuir, had its name because the feathers were there *plucked* off the birds which were killed by the royal sportsmen.   But it appears that in old writings the name is written Locarstoun, or Lockartstoun;[3] and, although the gravestone referred to is said to have disappeared, yet it is probably the curiously carved figures upon the old sculptured stones, now in the new cemetery of Kirriemuir, that had given rise to the idea of the plover, as one of these stones bears allegorical or other representations of figures with birds' heads.[4]

It is quite certain that falconers, apart from the menials that kept the hawks, were attached to the households of the kings who resided at Forfar.   In the year 1327, King Robert I. granted and confirmed to Geoffrey of Foullertoune and Agnes his wife, the lands of Fullartoun in Forfarshire, with the office of King's falconer within the shire of Forfar, and entertainment in the King's house at Forfar, when the King sojourned there, for the Falconer himself, a servant, a boy, and two horses.[5]

---

[1] *Chamb. Rolls*, i. p. 343; *Reg. Mag. Sig.* p. 116.
[2] *Acta Dom. Con.* p. 332.
[3] *Acta Parl.* ii. p. 379-82.   [4] *Sculp. Stones of Scot.* plate xliii.
[5] Hadington's *Collection of Charters, MS.*, Adv. Lib. Edin.

SECTION II.

O! I fling my spirit backward,
And I pass o'er years of pain :
All I loved is rising round me,
All the lost returns again.

AYTOUN, *Misc. Poems.*

Ecclesiastical Notices of Restenneth-Forfar—Change of Glebe Lands—Inscriptions
on the Church Bells—Funeral Monuments—Episcopacy—Declaration against
the Solemn League and Covenant—Dr John Jamieson.

ALTHOUGH Forfar had a royal palace, and was of considerable
antiquity as a town, it was of late erection as a separate
parochial district, being at first a portion of the old parish of
Restenneth, and as such called *Rostinoth-Forfar.*[1] In the
ancient *taxatio* the church of Restenneth and the chapel of
Forfar are rated together at the small sum of 24 merks. Restenneth was given to the Abbey of St. Mary of Jedburgh by King
Malcolm ; and subsequently, during the reign of Alexander II.,
David, bishop of St. Andrews, not only confirmed the gift
of the church of Restenneth to Jedburgh, but added the chapel
of Forfar, which was dedicated to St. James the Great, to the
same convent.[2] Both houses were in the diocese of St.
Andrews ; and, so far as ascertained, the names of John and
Dionysius, who were deacons, and Simon who was cleric, are
the only traces that remain of the old ecclesiastics.[3]

In 1567, the churches of Forfar, Restenneth, and Aberlemno
were served by one and the same minister, David Lindsay of
Pitairlie, who had a salary of £200 Scots, and in 1570 the
reader of Forfar had the sum of £20. From that time, down
to 1643, when an alteration took place in the situation of the
glebe, there is no record of the clergy of the town, with the
exception of Mr. James Elliot, who entered upon the office of

---

[1] The etymology of the name is doubtful—*Feur-fuar*, means "cold meadow-
land ;" *barr-fuar*, "a cold point, a height."

[2] See notice of RESTENNETH below, Part VI.

[3] *Reg. Vet. Aberbr.* pp. 31, 93, 115, 263 ; *Reg. Prior. S. Andree*, p. 346 ;
Reg. Ep. Brechin. i. p. 7.

the ministry in 1593 and no doubt as minister of Forfar, sat in the General Assembly at Glasgow in 1610.[1]

Until the year 1643, the glebe of Rostinoth-Forfar was situated within what may have been the parish of Restenneth ; and as it was fully a mile distant from the kirk of Forfar— the original parish or district church of Restenneth having been previously suppressed—Mr. Thomas Pierson, the clergyman, succeeded in getting it removed nearer to the town, while, in lieu of the "gleib allottit to him furth of the lands of Restennett, belonging to James Fletcher," he had " All and heall that croft of arrabill land callit the Bread croft lyand within the territorie of the said burgh of Forfar, betuix the lands of William Scott at ye wast, The lands of Jhon Morgoun on the east, The Ferritoun fields on the south, and the Kings gait ledand to Dundie at the north pairts, Extending to four ackers of arrabill land or thairby, To be holden in frie burgage and heretage for ye yeirlie payment of the Kings meall and wther common anuells and debbit furth yrof of befoir, by the said Mr. Thomas Pierson, and his successors, ministers [of Forfar], serueing the kirk and cuire y^{r}of, as a constant gleib to him and them in all time coming."[2]

The kirk of Restenneth had been suppressed, and Forfar made the place of worship sometime between 1586 and 1643, as at the former date we find Forfar and Restenneth spoken of as separate parishes. The lands within the burgh of Forfar, " great and small," have belonged to the town from time immemorial, and were confirmed to it by the charter of Charles ii., together with those of the greater part of the parish of Forfar-Restenneth, as also the patronage of the kirk of Forfar, which had been previously disponed to the town by Sir George Fletcher, to whom, and his brother James, the patronage belonged.[3]

The parish of Forfar proper is a single ecclesiastical charge,

[1] *Booke of the Kirk*, pp. 804, 1086.
[2] *Paper* (1643) *in Archives of Burgh.*
[3] *Acta Parl.* vii. 615 ; *Old Stat. Acct.* vi. p. 513 *n. ; New Stat. Acct.*, Forfarshire, p. 695.

but in 1835-6 a chapel-of-ease was built, and, a district having
been assigned to it, it was erected into a parish *quoad sacra*,
called St. James's. Both churches are plain, comfortable
buildings ; and the old kirk, erected in 1791, but considerably
altered in 1836 so as now to accommodate upwards of 1600
worshippers, is conspicuously situated upon a rising ground
near the centre of the town. The interior, which was reseated
and thoroughly renovated in 1882, is fitted up with galleries
on all sides excepting the south ; and prior to the building of
the present steeple in 1814, a short old tower with battlements
and spire occupied its place, adding little to the beauty of
either the kirk or the town.[1]

The date of the erection of that tower is unknown ; but in
1657, through the liberality of Robert and William Strang,
merchants in Stockholm, natives of the burgh of Forfar, of
which their father was sometime Provost, it received the
addition of three bells, which are still in use. The largest
of these is singularly handsome and profusely ornamented,
bearing upon the west side the armorial bearings of the family
of Strang, and these words :—

> "THIS BELL IS PERFECTED AND AUGMENTED BY
> WILLIAM STRANG AND HIS WYFE MARGRET PATTILLO IN STOCKHOLM.
> ANNO 1656."

Upon the east side is inscribed :—

> "FOR THE GLORY OF GOD
> AND LOWE HE DID BEARE TO HIS NATIWE TOUNE
> HATHE VMQ' ROBERT STRANG FRIELY GIFFTED THIS BELL
> TO THE CHURCHE OF THE BURGHE OF FORFAR,
> WHO DECEASED IN THE LORD IN STOCKHOLM THE 21 DAY OF APRILL.
> ANNO 1651."

Surrounding the rim of the bell, at top and bottom respectively,
are these quotations from the Evangelist and the Psalmist :—[2]

> " GLORIA IN EXCELSIS DEO
> ET IN TERRA PAX HOMINIBUS BONA VOLUNTAS. ANNO 1656."

> " LAETATUS SUM IN HIS QUÆ DICTA SUNT MIHI IN DOMUM DOMINI.
> IBIMUS STANTES ERANT PEDES NOSTRI IN ATRIIS TUIS JERUSALEM."
> "ME FECIT GEROT MEYER. 1656."

---

[1] *Old Stat. Acct.* vi. pp. 510, sq. 523 ; *New Stat. Acct.*, Forfarshire, pp. 691 sq.
[2] Luke ii. 14 ; Psalm cxxii. 1, 2. See also APPENDIX No. IV.

Until within little more than a quarter of a century ago, the piece of ground which surrounds the old church was the only public place of burial in the parish. A cemetery, elegantly laid out, and ornamented by a handsome monument to the memory of Sir Robert Peel—the first, it is believed, that was erected in Scotland to that eminent and patriotic statesman—was then provided by the Town Council, in the Newmont Hill, on the south side of the town, and now forms the burial-place for the district; this cemetery has been added to lately, and now covers an area of 16 acres. There has also been for many years a burying-ground within the enclosure of St. John's Episcopal Church, but interments, if indeed they are ever made in that ground at the present day, are confined to those of the members of that communion. Although the tombstones in the old churchyard are numerous, the inscriptions possess little general interest. The oldest is in memory of a "cordiner and burgess" called Wood, with a carving of the arms of that family, and date 1607. There are, however, four neat marble tablets within the church—one to the Carnegies of Lour, cadets of the noble family of Northesk, a second to the late Provost Kerr, a third to Quartermaster John Allan of the 46th Regiment, who died in his native town while there in quest of health. This monument is one of those fine specimens of "a soldier's gratitude"—so characteristic of the benevolence of the British warrior—having been "erected by Colonel Garret and the officers of the regiment in testimony of their esteem and regard for their deceased brother officer, and in commemoration of his services in the army for nearly thirty-five years, twenty-three of which he served abroad with his regiment in the East and West Indies, Gibraltar, and North America." The fourth tablet was erected in 1882 by his widow, to the memory of the late Rev. Robert Stevenson, who was the first minister after the Disruption, and died in 1876.

Besides the Established Church, there are churches representative of the Free, United Presbyterian, Episcopal, Congrega-

tional, and Baptist communions in Forfar. Some of the more
recently erected churches, particularly those of the First Free,
and Episcopal congregations, both erected in 1881, are exceedingly tasteful specimens of architecture. St. James's Episcopal
Church, built at a cost, including organ, of about £10,000, has
still its tower incomplete, but is otherwise a very handsome
building, and occupies the site of the one that was built in 1822.[1]
Transferred from the old church, and given a rather less conspicuous place in the new, being placed in the organ chamber, is
the fine stained glass window, put up at the expense of the late
laird of Guthrie, and thus inscribed to the memory of his father
and mother:—" ✠ In Honorem Dei, et Memoriam Joannis
Gvthrie, de Gvthrie, Arm : Qui Obiit, 12. Nov. 1845. Ætatis
svæ 82. Atqve in Memoriam Annæ Dovglas, Conjvgis ejvs,
Qvæ Obiit 2 Dec. 1845, Ætatis svæ 75." Forfar has long been a
stronghold of Episcopacy, and during the time of Charles II. the
magistrates and Council were staunch adherents of that Church.
At that time they declared openly against the legality of
both the National and the Solemn League and Covenant, and
in the following firm and remarkable terms treated the oaths
and obligations, which had been taken to maintain these
Leagues, as frivolous and unimportant :—

" WEE Prowest, Baillies, and counsellers of the burghe of
Forfar under subscryvand, and evry ane of ws Doe sincerly
affirme and declaire That we judge it wnlawfull To subjects
vpon pretence of reformatione or other pretence whatsoever,
To enter into Leagues and Covenants, or to take vp armes
aganest the King or theise commissionated by him : And
that all theise gatherings, conwocationes, petitiones, protesta-
tiones, and erecting and keiping of counsell tables, that were
used in the beginning, and for careing on of the late troubles,
Wer wnlawfull and seditious, And particularlie that these
oathes wherof the one wes comonlie called *The Nationall*

<hr>

[1] See APPENDIX No. V.

Covenant (as it wes sworne and explained in the year jᵐvjᶜ
and thirtie eight, and therefter), and the vther entituled *A
solemne League and Covenant,* Wer and are in themselfes un-
lawfull oathes, and wer taken by, and imposed vpone, the
svbjects of this Kingdome aganest the fundamentale Lawes
and Liberties of the same : And that ther lyeth no obligations vpone ws or any of the subjects from the saids oathes,
or aither of them, to endeavoure any change or alteratione of
the government, aither in churche or state, as it is now
established by the Lawes of this Kingdom : In witnes wher-
off wee put owr handis heirto att Forfar this Tuentie one day
of December jᵐvjᶜ thriescore thrie yeares.

CHARLES DICKESON, prouest

T. GUTHRIE, bailie	JAMES BENNY, counsellor
CHARLES THORNTOUNE, balzie	JHONE MORGAN
A. SCOTT, counseller	TH. BENNY, Consvler
DA. DICKSON, counseller	Mr WILLIAM SUTTIE, cownceller
JAMES BENNEY, counseller	H. CUTHBERT, coonceller
RO. HOOD, Counsellar	JOHNE AIRTH JS. BROUNE, jr
	JOHN COOK JHON BRANDORE."[1]

Dr. John Jamieson, the well-known antiquary, and compiler
of the *Scottish Dictionary,* was pastor of the Anti-Burgher
congregation of this place from 1780 to 1797, when he left
for Edinburgh. He laboured at Forfar for the small sum of
£50 a year, and before leaving for the metropolis he had
made himself popular by the publication of *Sermons on the
Heart, Vindication of the Doctrines of Scripture, in reply to
Dr. Priestley,* and other works of a like character.

While at Forfar he had the good fortune to become
acquainted with George Dempster of Dunnichen, at whose
table he was a frequent guest, and it was there that the idea
of the *Scottish Dictionary* was first suggested to him. This
originated with Grim Thorkelin, the learned Professor of

---

[1] *Original Document in Archives of Burgh.*

Antiquities at Copenhagen, as, before meeting with him, Jamieson had looked upon the Scottish language as merely a species of jargon, or at most a corrupt dialect of the English and Anglo-Saxon.

The Professor, having spent a few months in Scotland before meeting with Mr. Jamieson, had noted some hundreds of purely Gothic words which were then in common use in the counties of Forfar and Sutherland. These, he believed, were unknown to the Anglo-Saxon, though familiar to the Icelandic tongue ; and it was this hint which induced Jamieson to collect the more peculiar words and expressions of the inhabitants of Angus, and gave rise to his *Scottish Dictionary* —one of the most remarkable monuments of industry and learning, and works of utility, of which any country or age can boast.[1]

SECTION III.

We spake of many a vanished scene,
Of what we once had thought and said,
Of what had been, and might have been,
And who was changed and who was dead.

LONGFELLOW, *Poems.*

Forfar, a Royal Burgh—Early Burgesses—Its place among Royal Burghs—Roger Cementarius de Forfar—*Brogue*- or Shoe-makers—Johnston's Panegyric— Drummond's Satire—Provost Strang's Defence of Charles I.—Refusal of Nobles to subscribe the Covenant and stent the Lieges.

THAT the town of Forfar had an origin later than the castle, and arose under its protection, can hardly be doubted, but the time of either its foundation or its erection into a royal burgh is unknown. Like most Scotch burghs in the same position, it is believed to have been so created by David I. It was

---

[1] See the Memoir of Dr. Jamieson in the edition of his *Dictionary Scott. Language* published in 1840. Dr. Jamieson's son Robert, an eminent lawyer, to whose memory the Faculty of Advocates erected a fine monument in St. Cuthbert's church-yard, Edinburgh, was born at Forfar. David Don, originally bred a gardener at Kinnoull, and sometime Professor of Botany, King's College, London, was also a native of that town, having been born there on the 21st December, 1799. His father, George Don, was a " watchmaker and botanist."—*Forfar Parish Register.*

certainly a recognised burgh in 1261,[1] and as one of the
"steddis of warranty in Scotlande," it dates as far back as the
days of King William the Lion.[2]   Before 1244 it was a place
of considerable size, and in that year was almost totally
destroyed by accidental fire;[3] but by the time of the visit of
King Edward I., it had so far recovered from the accident as
to receive the appellation of "bone ville" in the Diary of the
journey of that King, which was far from flattering in its
expressions towards either the towns or people of Scotland.

Among the earliest notices of the burgesses and magistrates
of Forfar, which occur in 1372, are the names of Patrick of
Rynd (perhaps one of the Carse family), who was alderman,
and he, along with five other burgesses, named respectively
William Adamson, John Williamson, William Rede, Simon
Armurer, and Hugh Flesher, are parties to an indenture or
agreement with the inhabitants of Montrose regarding the
freedom of both burghs.[4]   Subsequently, betwixt 1395 and
1434, the bailies were Philip Freck, William Young, John
Wricht, and Alexander of Guthrie.   The last three surnames
are common in the town and neighbourhood at this day.[5]

The king had the disposal of the burgh duties and maills,
and from these, it is said, "be vertew of ane antient gift, dated
the 20th of February 1299," the minister of Finhaven had a
small annuity;[6] and in 1376, Robert II. granted 10 merks out
of the same to Alexander of Lindsay.   Among the missing
charters of Robert III. there is one to the town of Forfar for
£8, 13s. 4d. Scots of feu-duty;[7] while, at a much earlier period
William the Lion and Alexander II. gifted both lands and
money out of the town towards the support of the Abbey of
Arbroath.[8]

The population of the burgh at the early period under

---

[1] *Chamb. Rolls*, i. p. *14.   [2] *Acta Parl.* i. p. 51.
[3] Fordun, *Scotichr.* b. ix. 61.   [4] *Miscell. Aldbar*, MS., p. 90.
[5] *Chamb. Rolls*, ii. and iii. *passim.*   [6] *Paper in Archives of Burgh.*
[7] *Reg. Mag. Sig.* p. 110 ; Robertson, *Index*, p. 144.
[8] *Reg. Vet. Aberbr.* pp. 7, 53, 201 ; *Reg. Nig. Aberbr.* p. 85.

review is unknown; but, by contrasting the payments made
to the king's chamberlain by the bailies of Forfar, with those
of the other burghs of the county, it appears that the payments of Forfar were the least. Nor does the town seem to
have advanced much during the half century which followed,
for, by the modified burgh tax of 1483, it is charged little
more than a fourth part of the amount allotted to Montrose
and Brechin.[1]

The only glimpse which we get of the trades carried on at
Forfar in early times is perhaps in the names of the burgesses
already noticed. In Simon Armurer, for example, the name
may be traced to the occupation of a manufacturer of defensive
weapons, and Hugh Flesher, to that of a dealer in animal
food; but, long prior to the date at which these parties
flourished—contemporary even with King William the Lion—
are found in connection with the town the still more interesting personages Roger Cementarius de Forfar and his son
William. In these, perhaps, we may be able to recognise the
chief builders or superintendents of King William's palace at
Forfar, and of Ingleram of Baliol's stronghold of Redcastle
in Lunan Bay, for both occur as witnesses to charters by that
baron, confirming the grant of the kirk of Inverkeilor to the
monastery of Arbroath.[2] But whether these were the builders
of the earlier castles of Forfar and Redcastle or not—and it
is not improbable that they were—it is more certain that in
Roger and his son we have, in a Latinised form, the now
common surname of *Mason*, which had originated in that
important business.

But from the fourteenth to the seventeenth century no trace
is found of the occupation of the inhabitants of the old county
town. Doubtless the trades carried on were as varied in
character as the necessities of the community required, while
the exports also must have been limited. The first incorporation of trades[3] took place in 1653, and these were four in

---

[1] *Misc. Spald. Club*, v. p. 27.   [2] *Reg. Vet. Aberbr.* p. 39.   [3] APP. No. VI.

number—shoemakers, tailors, glovers, and wabsters—the first being the most ancient and wealthy.[1] By the time the Incorporated Trades in Forfar were dissolved in 1846, the Hammermen had been added, but their deacon did not have a seat, while those of all the other crafts were *ex-officio* councillors of the burgh.[1]

Forfar is chiefly famous in the old annals of commerce for the manufacture of shoes, and these were of a peculiar kind, called "brogues," from the Gaelic word *brog*, literally "a shoe." Light and coarse, made of horse leather instead of nolt, they were admirably adapted for travelling among the hills, and were a type of the shoes worn by the old inhabitants of Scotland, which, in more modern times, were denominated *rough rullions,* the brogues differing from these only in the hair being taken off.

It is uncertain when the manufacture of brogues was introduced into Forfar; and, it will be seen by the following translation of a fanciful epigram by the learned Arthur Johnston (in which a fabulous antiquity is assigned to the trade), that we are not made by him any wiser upon the point. But as the town was proverbially associated with the trade in Johnston's time, it could not have been introduced later than the sixteenth century :—

> " The ruines of a Palace thee decore,
> A fruitfull Lake, and fruitfull Land much more,
> Thy Precincts (it's confest) much straitened be,
> Yet Ancient SCOTLAND did give power to thee :
> Angus and other places of the Land,
> Yield to thy Jurisdiction and Command.
> Nobles unto the People Laws do give,
> By Handy-Crafts the Vulgar-sort do live.
> They pull off Bullocks-hydes and make them meet
> When tann'd, to cover handsome Virgins feet ;
> From thee are Sandals to light Umbrians sent,
> And solls with latchets to Rope-Climbers lent :

---

[1] By the old Sett of the burgh of Forfar, the town was governed by a provost, two bailies, a treasurer, and fifteen councillors. There are now a provost, three bailies, a treasurer, and ten councillors.

And Rullions wherewith the Bowrs do go
To keep their feet unhurt with Yce and Snow.
The ancient Greeks their Boots from this Town brought
As also hence their Ladies slippers sought.
This the Tragedians did with Buskings fit,
And the Commedian-shooes invented it.
Let not Rome henceforth of its Puissance boast
Nor Spartans vaunt much of their warlick-host :
   They laid their Yoak on necks of other Lands,
   Farfar doth tye their feet and leggs with bands."[1]

There is a tradition that, during the summer of 1645, while Drummond of Hawthornden, the historian and poet, was journeying through Scotland, he visited Forfar, and was refused shelter for the night. This want of hospitality is only to be accounted for, we hope, by a fear on the part of the inhabitants that he might communicate the plague, which was then raging in many parts of the kingdom. But be the reason what it may, Drummond found a hearty welcome in the adjoining town of Kirriemuir, and, learning that a feud pended between the inhabitants of those two places regarding the commonty of Muir Moss, he determined to play off a joke upon the magistrates of Forfar, by addressing a letter to the Provost on the day following. The Estates of Parliament were then sitting at St. Andrews, and, believing the communication to be from that body, the chief magistrate had the council and clergymen of the burgh convened, to hear and deliberate upon the contents of the letter. But, much to their astonishment and chagrin, this was found to consist only of the following reproachful rhyme upon themselves, in which there is a pointed allusion to the brogue-makers :—

   "The Kirriemarians an' the Forfarians met at Muir Moss,
   The Kirriemarians beat the Forfarians back to the Cross ;
   Sutors ye are, an' Sutors ye 'll be—
   Fye upo' Forfar, Kirriemuir bears the gree !"

The town of Forfar, thus famous in old times for the number of its *souters* or shoemakers, had among these craftsmen persons of the highest integrity and independence of character, one in

---

[1] See APPENDIX, No. VII. (A).

particular, who, in the face of the assembled Parliament of the kingdom, stood almost alone and single-handed, and boldly denounced the sale of Charles I. to his English enemies—a fact thus quaintly noticed by Sir Henry Spottiswoode in his poem of *The Rebel States*:—

> "Neither did all that Parliament agree
> To this abhorred act of treacherie.
> Witness that still to be renowned *sutor*,
> Forfar's commissioner, and the State's tutor
> In loyaltie ; who being asked his vote,
> Did with a tongue most resolutely denote
> In loyal heart, in pithie words, tho' few—
> 'I disagree, as honest men should doo.'"

—This noble-minded "sutor" was Alexander Strang, Provost and commissioner of the burgh to the Parliament of 1647, " in respect of whose faithfull testimony and dissent against the passing of the Act concerning his Majestie's persone, and for diverse other good causes and considerations," Charles II. ratified the ancient, and granted some new privileges, to the burgh.[1]

Before this, however, in the memorable year 1639, the inhabitants of Forfar had a good example of loyalty set them by a number of the nobles who there convened in Committee for the purpose of having the Covenant for stenting the lieges and numbering and arming the men subscribed—projects which completely failed, owing chiefly to the firmness displayed by the Earl of Southesk,[2] in confronting his son-in-law, the future Marquis of Montrose, who was then on the side of the Covenant.

Subsequently, in 1644, committees of the loyalists were held daily at Forfar ; and in the following year, while General Baillie was in pursuit of the Marquis of Montrose (by this time an Anti-Covenanter), he encamped here with his army,[3]

---

[1] *Acta Parl.* vii. p. 615. In *Spot. Miscel.* i. Pref. pp. iv. and 184, the name of the commissioner is erroneously given as *Hunter.* The only other burgh commissioners that voted against the sale of King Charles were those of Brechin, Tain, and Ross. There were also six peers and four commoners, making in all fourteen.— Bp. Guthrie, *Memoirs,* p. 237.

[2] Spalding, *Trubles,* i. p. 135.   [3] *Ibid.* ii. p. 347.

on the night before his ineffectual pursuit after Montrose, who upon that occasion accomplished his celebrated retreat, and took refuge among the Grampians.[1]

SECTION IV.

Speak of me as I am : nothing extenuate,
Nor set down aught in malice.
SHAKESPEARE, Othello.

Imprisonment of an English Spy—his Release—Destruction of the Burgh Records—
Glamis Castle garrisoned—Conduct of Mackay's Troops—Introduction of Linen
Trade—General Improvement of the Town—County Hall and its Paintings—
Markets—Disputes concerning the Customs of St. James's Fair—Notices of the
Town during the 17th Century—Date of Ochterlony's *Account of the Shyre
of Forfar* ascertained.

IT was during the wars of the Commonwealth that the town suffered most at the hands of the soldiery, and this arose from a wish on the part of the inhabitants to support the deposed monarch.   Ever ready in the cause of their unfortunate king, and in the punishment of his enemies, the magistrates, in the year 1651, discovered Captain Buchan "an intelligencer, and [one who] did keep correspondence with the English his Majestie's enemies," and had him secured in their tolbooth. But before they had time to come to a decision respecting his conduct, the English had captured the neighbouring town of Dundee.   Colonel Ocky, hearing of Buchan's imprisonment, marched from thence to Forfar, "with a considerable body of horse and dragoons," and not only liberated Buchan, but pillaged and harassed the town ; then, breaking open the charter room, he " took forth all their rights and records, and cancelled and destroyed the same."[2]   To this we must trace the want of early records relative to the burgh of Forfar—the oldest extant bearing the late date of 1665.

Within four years from the time the burgh was pillaged by Ocky and its old records destroyed, a part of the army of the

---

[1] Jervis, *Land of the Lindsays*, pp. 294 sq. ·
[2] *Paper in Archives of Burgh*—(1674).

Commonwealth was quartered at Glamis Castle, and during that time the bakers of Forfar were bound to supply them with "fower dussen of wheate breade for each day in the weeke," and the fleshers "beefe, mutton, or lambe, each Munday and Wedensday," under pain of the same being forcibly exacted.[1]

The stay of the garrison at Glamis, however, was short; and, so far as can be gleaned from the few remaining documents of the period, little occurred for many years beyond what has been already noticed. There was nothing of note until after the battle of Killiecrankie, when a detachment of the forces of William and Mary were stationed at Forfar to watch the movements of the rebels that were constantly passing along the front of the Grampians, between Brechin and Dunkeld, plundering as they went. But it would seem that, so far as regarded honesty and decorum, the conduct of the royalists was much on a par with that of the rebels; for, during the short time the former were stationed at Forfar, they had "eattin and destroyed" all kinds of victual to the value of £8000, forced horses and carts and free lodgings from the inhabitants to the extent of an additional £2000, left the tolbooth and schoolhouse in a state of ruin, and were otherwise guilty of such oppressive conduct that many of the people altogether deserted the town.[2]

Forfar does not appear to have borne a more conspicuous part in the rebellions of 1715 or 1745 than other burghs in the county, though it is true that the accidental murder of the Earl of Strathmore during day and on the open street (elsewhere noticed),[3] had its rise in the first of these. It is also certain that the number of rebels in Forfar at the latter rising was great, and, as in the curious case of Councillor Binny, they sometimes resorted to strange plans for carrying out their purpose;[4] still, oddly enough, the town was selected as the place for confining the rebel lairds of Pitrichie and Echt.[5] This was in January 1746, and within a month thereafter, when the Duke of

---

[1] (1654)—APPENDIX No. VIII.
[2] *Burgh Records*, 1689-90.
[3] Jervise, *Land of the Lindsays*, p. 200.
[4] APPENDIX No. IX.
[5] *Misc. Spalding Club*, i. p. 369.

Cumberland's army rested at Glamis, the Forfarians displayed their favour for the exiled family by stealthily going there under night and cutting the girths of the horses, so that the Duke's progress northward might, as much as possible, be retarded.

The town may be said to have been then without rulers, and it was only after the return of peace that the Council and magistrates found themselves in a position to take the oaths of allegiance, as they had been prevented from doing so at the time of their election by " the influence of a military force, and also by the numbers of rebels." But it is curious to observe that previous to that date, even so late as the beginning of last century, the number of business men was so few that it was feared " a penury of fitt persons for representing the magistracy may happen;" and in consequence the Council resolved to continue the same persons as magistrates for two or three consecutive years, instead of one year as the law provided.[1] After the middle of last century, however, the population of the town and parish rapidly increased, and, where there were 2450 in 1755, and 4756 in 1792, there were 13,579 in 1881.[2]

This increase has arisen chiefly from the introduction, subsequent to the Rebellion of 1745, of linen manufactures. The linen at first made here was of a coarse sort, called *Osnaburg,* for the superiority of which Forfar acquired considerable repute. Of late years the manufactures have mostly consisted of *brown linens* and the prosperity of the trade is amply shown in the opulence of the employers and the comfortable condition of the workers.[3] It is also apparent in the recently much improved state of the town, in regard to both its public and private buildings. Many of the shops are spacious and elegant, and most of the modern buildings are in tasteful and varied styles of architecture.

---

[1] *Sets of Royal Burghs of Scot.* p. 41.

[2] On Forfar in the beginning of this century, see Headrick, *Agriculture of Angus,* pp. 189, 190.

[3] On the manufactories of Forfarshire up to the beginning of this century, see *ibid.* pp. 539 sq. ; and its population, *ibid.* pp. 554 sq.

The Sheriff Court and Prison Buildings, built on the high ground beside the railway, on the west, have a very imposing appearance. The Infirmary has been found most useful in the town, since its erection about twenty years ago; and the Reid Hall, built by Provost Peter Reid in 1871, as a memorial to his parents and family, and since added to at a total cost of about £9000, is a very handsome addition to the grace and convenience of the town. The Council Buildings, situated near the middle of the High Street, were formerly used as the Sheriff Court Buildings; but, having been latterly found insufficient and inconvenient for that purpose, the new Sheriff Court Buildings were erected, and those vacated acquired by the town. The old Court-room forms the present Council Chamber, and accommodation is provided in the building for the Town Clerk and other officials. Adjoining these buildings is the old Town House, in which is the County Hall, which is embellished with excellent portraits of the noble hero of Camperdown, Dempster of Dunnichen, Scott of Dunninald, and the famous Henry Dundas, Lord Melville. The first of these was painted by Opie, the last by Sir H. Raeburn. Soon after Melville's picture was placed in the hall, a county dinner took place, at which the late Lord Panmure, then the Honourable Mr. William Maule, was present, and Dundas being as staunch a supporter of the Tory party as Maule was of the Whig, the latter, in an after-dinner humour, put a lighted taper to Melville's portrait. The picture was but little injured; and the Honourable Miss Wortley, a daughter of a house of the same politics as Dundas, having heard of the circumstance, wrote the following verse upon the subject:—

> "To vent his spleen on MELVILLE'S patriot name,
> MAULE gave his picture to the ruthless flame;
> Nor knew that this was MELVILLE'S fame to raise—
> Censure from MAULE is MELVILLE'S greatest praise."[1]

---

[1] Copied by the late P. Chalmers, Esq. of Aldbar, from a paper at Dunnichen, in the handwriting of G. Dempster, Esq.

The weekly and certain statutory fairs or markets held at Forfar are of a highly important character, and have long contributed to the interests of the community. The first of these, as in other ancient towns, and coeval with the rise of the town itself, was held on Sunday, a custom which originated at a very remote period ; and, from the long time the practice continued, it had doubtless been found convenient both for exposer and purchaser. The same course was carried on even after the Reformation ; and it was not until the year 1593 that Parliament thought of legislating upon the point, when an Act was passed "to discharge, remove, and put away all fairis and marcattis haldin an Sondayis ;"[1] but the people were so much prejudiced in favour of the custom that nearly a century elapsed before the terms of the Act were generally complied with.

During the same year the burgh of Forfar had a special grant from Parliament, changing its weekly market from " Sondaie to Fridaie, with the like priviledges and freedomes " as before ; and subsequently, notwithstanding that an Act had been previously passed prohibiting the holding of fairs on Saturdays and Sundays, upon the plea of their interfering with the sanctity of the Sabbath, and " under the paine of ane hundredth merks,"[2] the market-day of Forfar was again altered to Saturday, and upon that day the principal weekly market was long held.

The other statutory fairs were those of St. Valentine ; All Saints ; St. Peter, probably held at one time near the Priory of Restenneth, to which saint that church was dedicated ; St. James, so named in honour of the patron of the old chapel of Forfar ; and *St. Trodline*, properly St. Triduana, a fair which is said to have been held originally at the kirk-stile of Roscobie, and removed to Forfar soon after the Earl of King-horn, superior of the regality and patron of the kirk of Roscobie,

---

[1] *Acta Parl.* iv. p. 16.
[2] *Ibid.* iv. p. 39 ; vii. p. 481 ; *Forf. Illust.* p. 136.

succeeded to the office of Constable of Forfar. There was also the Fair of St. Margaret, in honour of the Queen of Malcolm Canmore; and St. Ethernan, to whom some chapel in the neighbourhood had probably been inscribed.[1]

St. James's, however, had long been the chief market of the district, but is now limited to only one day. In old times it lasted from the 20th to the 30th of July, and the magistrates were empowered " to arme with halberts twenty foure men duering the time of the faire, for keeping the peace, and collecting the customes thereof."[2] Although the Act of Charles II., already alluded to, seems to exclude the probability of the right to the customs belonging to any private individual, and implies that they belonged to the burgh itself, they were sometimes claimed by the Constable,—a proceeding which produced much bad feeling in the community.

Shortly before the year 1672, a serious dispute took place between the town and the Constable in consequence of the market being proclaimed by William Gray of Invereighty, Hereditary Constable, " in his Majestie's name and his owen," without mentioning the town of Forfar. It would appear from the magistrates' account, that Gray conducted the affair in a singularly bold and arbitrary manner, since, not satisfied with going through the form of proclaiming and " ryding " the market (a custom which, having its origin in the same principle as that by which the King rode on horseback in procession to Parliament, was long kept up in Scotland), he called together about eighty persons, who invaded and assaulted the magistrates and burgesses, and committed several deeds of outrage, " by fyreing of pistolls, beating of them with drawen swords, and tradeing their bailies under foot." The matter was brought under review of the Privy Council, and they, favouring the pretensions of Gray, took as evidence against the burgh

---

[1] The markets now held in Forfar are the weekly markets on Monday and Saturday; and the monthly, called the April, May, June, St. Peter's, St. James's, St. Triduan's, October, and St. Ethernan's markets.

[2] *Orig. Warrant by Ralph Cobbett*, 1652, in *Archives of Burgh.*

the testimony of several of his own tenants, though some of them accompanied him upon the occasion complained of, and " fyred the first pistolls, and drew the first swords."[1] How the difference was settled, we are left to conjecture : it is certain, however, although the issue here is also doubtful, that in the course of another year or two the Earl of Kinghorn, who had been recently appointed Constable,—following up the object which Gray had in view,—also laid claim to the customs ; but his lordship's claim was denied upon the narrative set forth in the charter of 1665, and upon the ground that the " Constabulary of Forfar imported no more but the keeping of the King's house in Forfar while the same stood."[2]

Such is a brief notice of the past and present state of Forfar. The notices in the *Old* and the *New Statistical Accounts of Scotland*, written the former in the year 1793 and the latter in 1843, are both of them extremely meagre in regard to the ancient memorials of the place ; and yet no other history of it exists, as these for the most part have merely been abridged for the numerous gazetteers that have since been published. It is true that Boece speaks of it as having been "in time past a notable citie, though now [1526] it is brought to little more than a countrie village, replenished with simple cottages ;" while a local writer towards the close of the century which followed, passes over all notice of the town, merely remarking in reference to the lakes of the county, that "the principal are those of Dodd and Forfar, where there is a chain of them adorned with fishing boats and wears."[3] But Mr. Ochterlony of Guynd, who wrote a few years later, shows more discrimination ; and in his brief account says, "Forfar is a considerable little toune, and hath some little trade of cremerie ware [small goods sold to pedlars], and linen cloath, and such lyke. It is pretty well built, many good stane houses sklaited therein, and are presently building a very stately Cross ; hath a large church and steeple

---

[1] *Paper*, 1672, *in Archives of Burgh.*
[2] *Paper*, 1674, *ibid.*   [3] Edward, *Descrip. of Angus*, p. 19.

well plenished with bells ; they have some public revenue, and a good deal of mortifications to their poor, doled by the bountie of some of their toun's men, who going abroad became rich ; they have a good tolbuith, with a bell in it ; they have four great faires yearly, and a weekly mercat. The Shieref keeps his courts there ; and all publick and private meetings of the shyre, both in tyme of peace and war, are kept there."[1] Soon after the period to which these remarks refer, the town of Forfar was visited by a Scotch regiment of the line, and the English chaplain, in his published notes of the towns he visited, describes it as " a place of no great noise, saving that it is a county-town, a royal borough, and anciently the seat of several Parliaments."[2]

Upon these, the only printed notices of Forfar in early times (excepting a worthless and very grotesque story by Captain Franck), little remark need be made. Its fast-growing importance as a town and burgh has already been adverted to, and there is no doubt that the old writers just quoted have for the time given faithful accounts of the place. With regard to the " very stately Cross," which was being erected in Ochterlony's time, it ought to be remarked that from the way in which he mentions the subject, compared with the reference in the Burgh Records, he seems to settle the exact date of his valuable *Account of the Shyre of Forfar*, which has hitherto been very uncertain. It is ordinarily given as being written *about* 1682 ; but as the treasurer's accounts of the burgh, towards the close of 1684, contain several entries regarding the construction of the Cross, such as the hewing of the stones, and the carriage of the chief or top stone, which was got from Glamis Quarry, it is much more probable that Mr. Ochterlony's pamphlet was not written before the end of 1684—perhaps not till early in 1685.[3]

---

[1] *Spottiswoode Miscellany*, i. p. 321.
[2] Morer, *Acct. of Scotland*, p. 104.   [3] APPENDIX No. x.

SECTION V.

And O! the strange sichts and the uncos that fell,
Nae livin' could think o', nae language could tell.

LAING, *Wayside Flowers.*

Notices of Witches—Their Treatment and Trials—Kinked, Witch-pricker, made an
Honorary Burgess of Forfar—Feuds between the Farquharsons and M'Comies
of Glenisla.

THE trial and execution of Witches is a dark subject, with
which not only the town of Forfar, but the whole British
Islands, and many other countries, had unfortunately too
much to do, and by which a vast number of human lives were
sacrificed to the credulity and ignorance of the times. That
deplorable state of matters evidently arose from a narrow and
misconceived construction of the words in Exodus, " Thou shalt
not suffer a witch to live ;" and the literal manner in which
that passage was interpreted, and its injunction enforced, leaves
a stigma upon the old legislature of Great Britain, both civil
and sacred, which can never be effaced from her history.[1]

The evils attendant upon the passing of the celebrated
statute of James VI. for the punishment of witches, and his
work on Demonology and Sorcery, are well known, and have
been often alluded to. Suffice it to say that while the last
execution for witchcraft in Scotland took place in 1722 at
Dornoch in Sutherland, in virtue of the no less heartless than
illegal decision of Captain David Ross of Littledean, then
Sheriff-substitute, the penal statutes against it were only
repealed in 1736.[2] The victim upon the occasion referred to
was a poor insane woman, who was so crazed that she

---

[1] On this phase of thought in Scotland, see Sir John Dalyell, *Darker Superstitions of Scotland ;* Sir W. Scott, *Demonology and Witchcraft ;* Pitcairn, *Criminal
Trials ;* Sinclair, *Satan's Invisible World Discovered ;* J. H. Burton, *Trials in Scotland,* i. pp. 236 sq. ; C. K. Sharpe's *Hist. Acct. of Belief in Witches in Scotland,*
contains also, in the Appendix, a list of *Scottish Books on Witchcraft.*

[2] Scott, *Demonology and Witchcraft,* p. 382.

gloried in beholding the fire that was kindled to consume
her person.

It is not known that any executions for witchcraft took
place at Forfar later than the year 1662 ; but during the preceding half-century they were numerous in this and in every
other town of the county. Indeed, there is scarcely a presbytery or session book of contemporary date that does not bear
record of these deplorable proceedings, either in the form
of precognitions and examinations, or in the significant intimation of the ministers of rural parishes being present
in the chief towns of their neighbourhood "at the tryal of
witches and charmers," instead of attending to their parochial
duties.[1]

Records of the declarations, and the details of the trials of
some of those unfortunate creatures, are extant in the archives
of the burgh ; and, however absurd these would appear now-
a-days, were they collected and printed they would form a
curious chapter in the history of the district during that
really dark age. But we shall content ourselves with only a
slight notice of some of the minutes on the subject, which,
while lacking the sad disclosures of human depravity contained in the more formal records of the trials, are sufficiently
curious to be referred to with some degree of interest by all.

It appears that, in the year 1661, the town of Forfar was
divided into eight districts, with a councillor in each district,
"for setting and changing the gairds for the witches." It was
also decreed that "persones jmprisoned for witchcraft shall
have no watch with them jn ther prisones, nor fyre nor candle,
but that sex men nightly and dayly attend and watch them jn
the vper tolbooth, and that the quarter-master shall order the
watchmen to wisit them at evry three houres end night and
day." It appears that, for the sin of looking out of the window
of the prison, two of these unfortunate women were ordered to

---

[1] For some account of the confessions and trials of the witches of Forfar, 1661,
see *Reliq. Ant. Scot.* pp. 113 sq.

be " put jn the stockes," or to have the window of their chamber nailed up. In such an arbitrary state of matters it will not appear very wonderful to find the Council, with all due solemnity, approving of the " care and diligence " of Alexander Heigh, a dealer in " aquavitie " (from whom, as appears in evidence, much of the liquor was got that " the devill " gave to the unfortunate dupes whom he met periodically in the churchyard), " for his bringing over Johne Kinked, for trying of the prisoners suspect of witchcraft." Nay, so well pleased were the Council with the manner in which Kinked performed his business, that within ten days after Keith of Caldhame, Sheriff-depute of the county of Forfar and a cadet of the noble family of Keith-Marischal, had been admitted a burgess and freeman of the burgh, the same honour was conferred by the same magistrates upon " Johne Kinked, pricker of the witches in Trennent "!

About that time, the Council appears to have had some difficulty in procuring an executioner, and the magistrates of Perth sent their hangman to carry out the extreme penalty of the law upon two unfortunate prisoners. Having in view some more criminals who were to undergo the like awful punishment, a deputation of the Council was appointed to " speak with David Soutar to be their executioner," and to this was to be added the extraordinary and heartless office of " scourger of the poore "! By a free interpretation of this singular entry, it would appear that, in those days, the sin of being *poor* was sufficient ground for being scourged and whipped. But it is clear also that, if Soutar found himself honoured by the distinction which the Council proposed to confer upon him, he did not long retain the office ; for, in the course of a few months one of the burgesses had to whip or scourge his own maid-servant " throw the towne," upon pain of being himself banished the same ![1]

---

[1] *Burgh Records of Forfar, passim.* The office of "scourger of the poore " was perhaps synonymous with that of "rung the beggars "—a petty policeman.

Numerous other instances of the strange doings of the period could be added from the same impartial record. Suffice it to say, that the men and women of Forfar who were so unfortunate as to incur the petty spleen and envy of persons more opulent in circumstances than themselves—and that the great majority of those who were convicted of witchcraft, and suffered accordingly, owed their misery to one or other of these heartless passions, there is too much reason to suspect—were executed and buried near the present public washing-green. The site of the gallows, where the remains of human bones are often found, is now occupied by a sawmill and other works of industry, which add their mite to the growing importance of the town. The branks, or bridle—a well-known instrument of punishment for scolds, and those suspected of witchcraft —is still preserved, among other curiosities, in the Town Buildings. It is made of various pieces of iron united by hinges, with an arrow-headed projection on the inner side. It surrounds the head of the delinquent, while the arrow-head enters the mouth, to prevent the wearer from speaking.

In little more than ten years after the last witch-burning at Forfar, the immediate neighbourhood of the town was the scene of a characteristic quarrel between two Highland clans, and, as was the case in most of these skirmishes, it had a fatal termination. The conflicting parties were the Farquharsons and the M'Comies. The former, owners of Brochdarg in Glenshee, and of Westmill and Downie in Glenisla, were ancestors of the lairds of Baldovie in Kingoldrum; and the latter possessed the barony of Fortar in Glenisla, and the lands of Finziegand in Glenshee. Of these M'Comies an ancestor had a charter as "John M'Comy-Moir" (the big or great M'Comie), 9th September 1571.[1] M'Comy-More's family are said at that date to have been "*ab antiquo* tenants and possessors" of Finziegand, and, under the name of Clan M'Thomas, they are

---

[1] *Orig. Charter in Charter Chest at Dalrulzion.*

specially mentioned in the Roll of the clans and broken men, both in 1587 and 1594.[1]

M'Comie, having acquired a wadset of the barony of Fortar from the Earl of Airlie, built a mansion-house at Crandart, about a mile to the north of the fine old castle of Fortar. He also appears to have received a right of forestry in the adjoining forest of Glascorie, and the Earl afterwards granted the same in tack to Farquharson of Brochdarg, upon some real or supposed right. This was most probably done with the view of curtailing M'Comie's influence in the district, for he is described as " haveing great power with the late Vsurpers as their intelligencer and favorite."[2]   But M'Comie naturally denied the plea of reservation on which Lord Airlie appears to have made the grant to Farquharson, and this, perhaps, was the more immediate cause of quarrel, for it seems that Farquharson had seized some of M'Comie's property in that forest.

M'Comie, opposing Airlie's proceedings, raised an action of spulzie against Farquharson before the Sheriff of Forfar, and succeeded in obtaining letters of caption. But this was a much easier matter than the seizure of Brochdarg himself, which was often attempted in vain, as he had sworn that " no messenger should take him alive."   After some little time, however, the M'Comies learned that he and several retainers were in the neighbourhood of Forfar. Mustering their followers and going there, they had Alexander Strachan, " the messenger of the burgh," put upon the alert, and thus met with Farquharson and his friends near the Muir of Forfar. This was on the 28th of January 1673 ; and, as was to be expected, Brochdarg refused " to lay aside his arms and become prisoner."   Upon this Strachan craved the assistance of the

---

[1] *Acta Parl.* iii. p. 467 ; iv. p. 71.   The names of M'Thomas and M'Intosh are the same as M'Comie, and mean "the son of Thomas."   In the *Justiciary Records or Books of Adjournal*, in H. M. Gen. Reg. House, Edinburgh, vol. xiii. (1673), from which the following account of the fray at Forfar is taken, those engaged in it are called sometimes M'Intosh, sometimes M'Comie ; the father is " John M'Intosh of Forther alias M'Comie."

[2] *Acta Parl.* vii. pp. 193-4.

M'Comies, and John, the elder brother, seized Robert Farquharson, and held him so firmly "that he was not able to do any present hurt." Upon this the Farquharsons fired and wounded John M'Comie, who fell disabled to the ground ; the same shot killed his brother Robert, and soon afterwards the Farquharsons returned to vent their bitter feelings upon John, whom, as he lay wounded, they butchered "with their durks and swords." Brochdarg, who had fled across the moss, was soon overtaken by the M'Comies ; and the prevaricating messenger, who was ultimately deprived of his office and imprisoned, quaintly depones that after this "he broke his wand of peace against them all."[1]

Both parties had their retainers along with them. Robert of Brochdarg and his brother John were both killed, and two of the four M'Comies shared the same fate, but their father was not engaged in the affair.

Counter prosecutions were afterwards raised by the surviving relatives, but this ended in the diet being deserted against both parties ; and the sons of the Farquharsons and of the M'Comies, as well as the adherents of each party present at the fight, were all outlawed. The subsequent fate of the Farquharsons is not exactly known ; but one of the M'Comies went to the south, and another, Donald, settling in the Highlands of Aberdeenshire, became ancestor of the M'Combies of Easter Skene, Lynturk, and Tillyfour, and died (as mentioned on his gravestone) at Mains of Tonley, in the parish of Tough, July 9, 1714.

The feuds between the Farquharsons and the M'Comies had been of long standing. The first referred to in the law-process occurred on the 1st of January 1669, when the Farquharsons, with fifty or sixty accomplices, went to Crandart, "under cloud and silence of night, bodin in fear of war." They there lay in ambush "until near the break of day," when old M'Comie

---

[1] Alexander Strachan, the messenger, was threatened afterwards by both families, and thus gave contradictory reports of service.

went abroad, and, having seized and carried him off to Brochdarg, they kept him there until night. They then took him " to
a certain place in a wildernesse and desert called Tombeg in
Glenshie," and kept him several days and nights in that place,
along with five of his sons who had gone to interpose for his
liberty. But this boon was granted only on obtaining a bond
for 1700 merks. Before long, however, we find the M'Comies
resented this insult in much the same way. Lying in wait for
Brochdarg, they found him in the forest of Glascorie, and " per-
vaded and pursued him ;" but, as the writ states, "by God's
providence, he escaped at that time." They afterwards searched
for him in the house of Tombeg, stabbing " the beds and other
places with their durks and swords ;" and they continued to
hunt him down until they traced him to the neighbourhood
of Forfar on the day of the fatal occurrence above narrated.

Some striking instances of the insatiable revenge of old
M'Comie are brought out in the course of the evidence in
this affair. On one occasion his servants had met with
Brochdarg in the forest of Glengarnie, and, on talking over the
matter at Crandart, old M'Comie got into a great passion—
upbraided them for not bringing to him " ane legg, ane arme,
or the lyff " of Farquharson, and declared that " he should have
bein their warrand " had they done so ; and, to obtain him
" dead or alive," he swore that he would " ware tuo of his best
sones in the quarrell "—adding in the strain of a bold undaunted
Highlander, and bidding defiance to all law, " Who would or
durst speir after it ?"   The evidence also goes on to show that,
when friends were endeavouring to mediate, M'Comie declared
that all was of no purpose, and that " the sword behooved to
decyd it !"—that, since the murder, " he wished he were but
twenty years of age againe," and that, if he were, " he should
make the Farquharsons besouth the Cairne of Month thinner, and
should have a lyff for ilka finger and toe of his tua dead sones !"
Angus M'Comie, who is charged as the person that hounded
out his kinsmen against the Farquharsons, appears to have had

much the same revengeful and savage feeling as his father; for, "when his sister wes regretting the lose of hir tuo brothers that had fallen in the scuffle," he coolly replied, "that she had no reason to lament for them, since they hade gott the liff they wer seekin!"—meaning that of Brochdarg.[1]

Stories of "the scuffle" at Forfar, and of the personal strength and gallantry of the M'Comies, are even now nearly as common in Glenisla and Glenshee, as they undoubtedly were a century ago. There are also remains of M'Comie's house at Crandart, where upon one of the chimney lintels is the date 1660, and the initials of the founder and of his wife Elizabeth Campbell, a daughter of Donald Campbell,[2] the laird of Denhead, near Coupar-Angus, with these words—" THE · LORD · DEFEND · THIS · FAMILIE · "[3] · Upon another stone, which is said to have been taken from Crandart, and built into a house near by, but which is now removed to Balharry, near Meigle, is the same date, and the words—" I · SHALL · OVERCOM · INVY · VITH · GODS · HELP : TO · GOD · BE · AL · PRAIS · HONOVR · AND · GLORIE." To Balharry the stone was taken from the ruins of the cottage at Dalnasnaught into which it had been 'built, and if it had originally been carried from Crandart the first part of the inscription may relate to the differences between the families.

The elder M'Comie, who died about the year 1676, was of great stature and strength. As was the case with most Highlanders of that period, he was naturally superstitious, and, like the more celebrated Rob Roy Macgregor, considered that the chief part of the education of his sons ought to lie in wielding the claymore, or in feats of strength and daring; and, in regard both to his credulity and to the novel manner he took to develop the latter in his family, some interesting stories still live in the Highlands.

By the time alluded to, "the big M'Comie" had attained a

---

[1] *Books of Adjournal* (*Justiciary Rec.*), vol. xiii.

[2] Son of Donald Campbell, the last Abbot of Coupar-Angus.

[3] The lintel is now permanently built into a prominent part of Crandart farmsteading.

good old age. He is said to have had seven sons. The eldest
of these possessed, as he supposed, least of the courageous spirit
of his ancestors, and, for the purpose of testing his prowess, the
hardy chief waylaid him one dark night, at a large stone in the
solitude of Glenbaynie, known at this day as *M'Comie's Chair*,
and, as he pounced upon him unawares, a dreadful struggle took
place between the old man and his son. The father, finding his
son's strength and courage fully a match for his own, at length
disclosed himself, and his astonished son is said to have
allowed the sword to drop unnerved from his hand.

Caenlochan, a romantic and secluded part of M'Comie's
property in Glenisla, was a favourite place of resort for this
old Highlander. There he often joined his tenants and servants
in the well-known test of strength called " the putting stone;"
and two round stones, each of great weight, which he is said to
have thrown far beyond any of his companions, still lie there,
and are known by his name. There also he is said to have
had frequent interviews with a Mermaid, who revealed some
wonderful stories to him; and it is told that on one occasion
she leaped up behind him, and took advantage of his horse to
enjoy a trip down Glenisla! Among other prophecies, she
warned him that he would die with his head upon a certain
stone which projected from the craig above his house of
Crandart, and, believing in the weird tale and afraid he might
come by an untimely end, he had the stone removed, and laid
under the bed where he slept and in which he died![1]

---

[1] The death of " big M'Comie " was looked upon by the cateran, whom he always
kept in check, as a great and fortunate event; and it is recorded that one of their
number, returning from the Lowlands at the time, joyously exclaimed, in answer to
the question—" Ciod an sgeul?"   " Sgeul! agus deagh sgeul! Beannaichte gu robh
an Oighe Muire! Cha bheo MacOmie mor am braigh na macharach,—ge'd bu mhor
agus bu laidir e!" *i.e.* " What news?"   " News! and good news! Blessed be the
Virgin Mary! The great M'Comie in the head of the Lowlands is dead, for as big
and strong as he was!"

CHAPTER II.

ſarnell Castle, and Kinnaird.

SECTION I.

The arm is strong where heart is true,
And loyal hearts are a' that.

JACOBITE BALLAD.

King Edward at Farnell Castle—Duncan of Fernevel—Castle of Farnell a "Palace,"
and the lands a Grange of the Bishops of Brechin—Dispute regarding the Muir
—Mode of declaring Sentence by a Doomster—Farnell alienated by Bishop
Alexander Campbell to the Earl of Argyll—Acquired by the first Earl of Southesk—State of the Lands, and character of Tenants in 1729—The present and
improved state of both.

So far as known, the fact of King Edward I. having visited
the Castle of Farnell, when on his victorious march throughout Scotland, is the only old historical incident of importance
relating to the district. It was on the 6th of July 1296 that
the king rode from Forfar to Farnell, a distance of about ten
miles. Next day he went to Montrose Castle, but during his
stay at Farnell he received the homage of William Fraser, who
is designed son of the late Alexander Fraser.[1] Who these
individuals were, it cannot now be said.

From earliest record the lands of Farnell belonged to the
see of Brechin, and the castle was a grange or residence of the
Bishop. Whether the Episcopal chair was occupied or vacant
at the time of King Edward's visit, is not certain; but the
late Mr. D. D. Black has it that the Bishop was probably one
named Nicholas.[2] Although long prior to that period the
Bishop had vassals that assumed their surname from these
lands, it is uncertain whether they existed at that date. The

---

[1] *Rag. Rolls*, pp. 82, 178; Palgrave, *Writs*, p. 165; Prynne, *Hist.* p. 650.
[2] Black, *Hist. Brechin*, p. 303.

only individual mentioned as bearing the name was a Duncan of Fernevel, who witnessed charters of the old Earl of Angus as early as 1214 and 1227.[1]

The Castle of Farnell, as it now stands, is a plain building, of two stories, with a circular staircase on the south side or front. Though only a fragment of what it was when erected, probably about the end of the 16th century, it is kept in good repair, and has long been appropriated by the noble family of Southesk as an asylum for poor and aged female pensioners. It is pleasantly situated upon the north bank of the pretty den of Farnell, and surrounded by fine old trees ; the park or lawn, which has been kept under grass for many years, is pastured by sheep and cattle of the most approved breeds. The south-west, or oldest part of the castle, seems to have been built during the sixteenth century, and two skew-put stones, on the north or back part of the house, bearing carvings of shields,

 are charged respectively with the figures here represented. The first of these, being less wasted than the other, is perhaps the more modern of the two, and bears the sacred monogram Iħs, ornamented by a cross. The second presents a crown in chief, with the letter M in base, which the late Dr. Joseph Robertson supposed to be illustrative of the crowning of the Blessed Virgin as Queen of Heaven, by her Son Jesus Christ—one of the many beautiful legends of the mediæval church.[2]

Although the lands of Farnell belonged in property to the Bishopric of Brechin, it appears that in 1410 the joint lairds of Kinnaird—a domain which had been carried by the marriage of three co-heiresses to the persons undernamed—laid claim to the " moir lyand to the Manyss of Fernwell," but this

---

[1] *Reg. Vet. Aberbr.* pp. 34, sq. ; Black, *Hist. Brechin*, p. 303 ; Fraser, *Hist. Carnegies of Southesk*, i. pp. xlvi. sq.

[2] *Reg. Ep. Brechin.* ii. p. 169. To the Earl of Southesk our author owed the favour of the *casts* of those curious stones, and from these the engravings are made.

proceeding Bishop Walter successfully resisted in the courts
of law. The case was tried at the county town of Forfar
before the Duke of Albany, "vpon ye law day eftir Zuill;"
and, in the passing of judgment in the case, which was done
through the dempster or doomster, we have one of the
clearest notices of the mode of declaring sentence through
that ancient functionary. "Rowine of Deere," for such was
the doomster's name, is described as giving "dome in yis forme
sayand," that the "Bischop of Brechineis borrowis foirsaid is
of wertu and force, and Dauid Panter Dutho of Carnegy and
William of Crawmond in sic amerciament as yai aw to tyn in
to yis court for ye wranguss reconteryng of the said borch
[surety] fundyne throu the bischop."[1]

This sentence put an end to encroachments on the privileges
of the Bishop of Brechin in this quarter, or at least there is no
further notice of any, and until 1566 the lands of Farnell
were held by the Church. It was then that the titular Bishop,
Alexander Campbell, brother of the laird of Arkinglass, Comptroller of Scotland, acquired unfortunately the power to dispose
of all the benefices within the diocese, a privilege of which he
took every advantage; for it appears that he not only disposed
of all the Church property of Farnell, and resigned the lands,
towers, fortalice, manor and mains, with four acres of land
adjoining the church—now occupied as the glebe—as well as
the Croftheads of Farnell, and the lands of Maryton, with the
salmon fishings, and the land of Esauxtoun, but also made
over the office of bailie of the whole lands belonging to, or
under the jurisdiction of the Bishop, to his relative, the Earl of
Argyll. The rental of the property thus alienated amounted
to £357, 10s. 8d. Scots.[2] It was through the interest of Argyll
that Campbell received the bishopric; and, seeing the pre-
carious state of ecclesiastical matters, while desirous at the

---

[1] *Reg. Ep. Brechin.* i. pp. 29 sq. This David Paneter of Montrose got a charter
on Cragoch and Ardoch in the barony of Logy, 20th March, 1407-8, on the resignation of "David de logy de Cragoch."—*Reg. Mag. Sig.* p. 231.

[2] *Reg. Ep. Brechin.* ii. pp. 205 sq.; *infra*, p. 175.

same time of augmenting their own private resources, the Bishop and his patron united their energies to reduce the rental of the Church, until barely so much was left of the revenues of the see of Brechin as would maintain an ordinary minister.[1]

It was in this way that the castle and lands of Farnell became the property of the Earl of Argyll, who, sometime before 1568, granted them—upon what ground is not apparent —to his own relative, Catherine, Countess of Crawford. In that year she gave "the demesne lands of Fernwel" to her younger sons.[2] They passed for a very short time to the Ogilvys of Airlie, and then became part of the lands held by the Carnegies.[3] The first Earl of Southesk, whose wife was grand-daughter of Catherine, Countess of Crawford, was the first Carnegie of Farnell. In the hands of that family these lands have ever since continued, with the exception of the time when they were under forfeiture in consequence of the fifth Earl having espoused the cause of the Chevalier de St. George.

From the forfeiture until 1764 these estates were possessed by the York Buildings Company, by whom a lease or tack of them was given in 1729 to Grant of Monymusk and Garden of Troup. The lessees, aware that most of the tenantry were in arrear of rent, investigated narrowly into their individual circumstances, and unhesitatingly reported upon each, in regard to both his financial and his more private matters. In consequence of this a sad picture is presented of the state of the farmers of the period, in respect of both their poverty and their lack of a sense of honourable and straightforward dealing. Some of these memoranda are extremely quaint and curious :— Mains and Mill of Farnell were then tenanted by a widow who declared herself unable to pay up any arrears. But further inquiry brought out the bad features of her character, and it is accordingly recorded :—" 'Tis uncertain what she may be able to pay, but she should by no means be spared, for she is

---

[1] *Panmure Catalogue of Bishops*, MS., p. 110.
[2] *Crawford Peerage Case*, p. 219.   [3] Jervise, *Land of the Lindsays*, p. 244 n.

a very cheeping [complaining or murmuring] woman, and can do better than she lets on [admits], her being of a very strange temper, and conveys her effects to her children, in order to defraud the heritor." The tenant of Tillysoil adjoining was ground officer or bailiff over the property. With a view of getting quit of his arrears he disponed his effects to a neighbour, and he is described as " not only poor, but also houseless and graceless, and [one] who certainly should be removed from being officer, and made of what can be." The farm of Egypt was then occupied by a father and son ; the first is called " ane old sickly man, who may pay up anything that is resting," and the latter, " a poor silly fellow, good for nothing."

But it must not be inferred from this roll of delinquents that the old Southesk tenantry were altogether bad, for there were a few well spoken of. The farmer of Greenlaw, for example, is described as " a very honest-like man, and has undertaken to pay all : however," adds the writer (who, to his honour be it told, never fails to speak favourably of the deserving), " 'tis alleged he is fully as frank [desirous] as able at the bottom." The tenant of Gateside is called " very mean [poor] and cannot pay much, and his wife is melancholy ;" while John Lyall, ancestor of the late factor on the estate of Southesk, then farming a part of Meikle Carcary, is recorded as " a good tenant, and may pay anything that is resting."[1]

These curious entries might be multiplied, for there are similar notices regarding the Panmure and Marischal tenantry, but enough has been given to show the miserable condition of the country during those unsettled days. It is curious to contrast these with the present times. Tile-draining and the reclaiming of marshes and other waste land, though as well known to the Romans more than 2000 years ago as in Scotland at the present time, had fallen into disuse, and only a dry gravel hillock, or a patch on the margin of a burn or river, was now and then brought under the plough. The *bauk an' rig* or

---

[1] *York Building Co.'s Mem. Book*, the property of the Earl of Dalhousie.

runrig and rennel system was in full force, by which one-half
of the ground—good or bad, it did not signify—was rendered
useful only for depositing stones and the larger weeds. Fences
were considered needless or troublesome, and the time of able-
bodied men and women, which was loitered away in keeping a
few half-starved oxen from trespassing among a sorry crop of
grain, was deemed well spent. The cultivation of green crop
was but little practised, and foreign and artificial manures
not at all heard of, while half-a-dozen of what were then considered large farms would scarcely satisfy a modern farmer of
even humble ambition.

Between the housing of the husbandman and his cattle there
was but little difference. In the case of the former the light was
admitted into the house by the same aperture in the roof as that
by which the smoke ascended; but now-a-days, thanks to the
philanthropy of the late minister of Oathlaw and others, and
the kindness of many landlords, farm labourers are lodged
much more comfortably than the majority of masters were
within the past hundred years, while the employer in his turn
enjoys a better residence and more of personal comfort than
did the mass of Scottish proprietors down till after " the
Forty-five."

It is only fair to add that in the improvement of agricultural
dwellings, as well as in that of the too long neglected school-
house and parish church, the noble proprietor of Farnell has
shown an example which cannot be too closely followed
throughout the country, in respect to both the personal
comfort of the labourers and the chaste style of the architecture of their cottages—things that always have a salutary
influence on the morals and habits of the people.

SECTION II.

The small birds rejoice in the green leaves returning,
* The murmuring streamlet runs clear through the vale ;*
The hawthorn trees blow in the dews of the morning,
* And wild scatter'd cowslips bedeck the green dale.*

BURNS, *The Chevalier's Lament.*

Origin of the name of Farnell—the Kirk—Ancient Sculptured Monument—Kirk of
  Cuikstone—its removal to Kinnaird—Old Portioners of Cuikstone—Pottery
  Work—Story of Young Reiden—Easter Fithie—Account of the Carnegies of
  Kinnaird—Creation, Forfeiture, and Restoration of the Earldom of Southesk—
  The New Castle, and Deer Park, etc.

THE Kirk of Farnell is picturesquely situated upon a rising
ground nearly opposite the castle. Upon the north side is the
Red Den Burn, here traversing a finely wooded valley, and
upon the south runs the stream of the Pow. Like so many
local names, the derivation of the word Farnell must remain
uncertain. Some have supposed it to signify the " stream of
alders," as the Gaelic *Fearn* and *Allt* respectively denote
stream and alder, but there we must leave it. The earliest
known form of the name is Ferneval, which occurs in charters
of 1219 and 1225.

William Herwart, in 1435, is the earliest known vicar of
the parish ;[1] but the saint to whom the kirk was inscribed is
unrecorded. The sculptured stone monument found there some
years ago and afterwards placed in the Montrose Museum, is
decorated on one side with a beautifully interlaced cross, and
on the other displays the figures of Adam and Eve at the tree
of the forbidden fruit, and standing between two serpents of
great comparative size. This may perhaps have marked the
grave of some former ecclesiastic.[2]

In Episcopal times the vicar of Farnell held the office of
Dean of the church of Brechin, and in the old *taxatio* the
kirk is rated at 20 merks. As now constituted, Farnell comprises two old ecclesiastical districts, for anciently there was a

[1] *Reg. Ep. Brechin.* i. p. 67.   [2] Stuart, *Sculp. Stones of Scot.* plate lxxxvi.

chapel at Cuikstone, or Quygstone. The names of two of the
rectors of it have been preserved,[1] and the supposed site is about
a mile north of the present parish church, near a mound called
Rume's Cross, a name which, although now of doubtful origin,
perhaps refers to the patron saint of the kirk.[2]

The kirk of Cuikstone was supported by the teinds of the
lands of Kinnaird, Balnamoon on the Southesk, Pantaskal
near Balbirnie mill, and Over Dalgetty; and also by the
vicarage and small teinds of Middledrums, Greenden, and
others. But having, towards the close of the sixteenth
century, become "altogidder ruynous and decayit,"[3] it was
rebuilt by Carnegie of Kinnaird about half a mile to the
eastward, in front of his own castle. From that time the
name of the church and parish was changed to *Kinnaird*, and
they were served by a separate clergyman until 1787, when
the kirk was suppressed. The north-west portion of the parish
was then added to Brechin, and the rest to Farnell.

The site of the manse of Kinnaird is yet traceable about
three hundred yards north of the church, and the road betwixt
the two places is known as the *Manse Ride*. There was no
schoolmaster's house there in 1729—perhaps no teacher was
required—and the kirk and kirkyard dikes appear to have
then stood much in need of repair.[4] The foundations of the
church are yet to be seen, surrounded by several well-sculp-
tured gravestones; and an adjoining spring, called *Pader* or
Pater Well, is noticed in an old rhyme regarding the love-story
of a young lady of Kinnaird.

The lands of Cuikstone or Quygstone, like those of Farnell,
were held of the Bishop of Brechin. Being divided into

---

[1] *Reg. Ep. Brechin.* i. pp. 72, 90, 156.—Robert Wyschart (1435); Andrew
Walter (1443, 1451).

[2] It is open to question whether there may not be a connection between Rume's
Cross and the adjacent Monrommon Moor, *moine* being a moss or moor—Moine-
Rumon, the moor of [St.] Rumon.

[3] *Acta Parl.* iv. p. 358. On the church and parish of Kinnaird, see Fraser, *Hist.
Carnegies of Southesk.* i. pp. xlii sq.

[4] *York Building Co.'s Inventory Book, MS.*

several portions, they were occupied in 1410 by persons
called William Johnson, Robert Adyson, John Alexanderson
(Saunderson), and Nicholas Speid.[1] The last named was
ancestor of George Speid, who had the lands of Auchdovie,
or Ardovie, from Sir Robert Carnegie of Kinnaird in exchange
for his part of Cuikstone in 1549.[2] From that date the Speids
have continued to possess Ardovie. Cuikstone was a pretty
extensive hamlet in old times. It had a brick or pottery
work from at least the middle of the seventeenth century,[3]
down to within the recollection of some old residenters; and
a number of the cinerary urns found in ancient stone coffins
in this quarter seem to be composed of the same sort of clay
as that which was got in the neighbourhood of Cuikstone.

Although Farnell is a place of considerable antiquity, it is
meagre in traditionary lore. At Red Den, on the west side of
the parish, where traces of early sepulture have been found,
the spring, called *Reiden's Well*, is locally described as the scene
of the tragedy of "Young Reiden," celebrated in the ballad of
that name. This idea, except in the third line of the opening
stanza of the ballad as rehearsed by the old people of Farnell,
is not borne out by the context, and it appears to have originated
in the peculiarity of the name, and in the freak of some local
rhymster, who (although he preserves "Clyde water" and
other associations of the older ballad) makes his version open
prosily thus :—

> "Young Reiden was a gentleman,
> A gentleman of fame ;
> An' he 's awa' to *East Fithie*,
> To see his comely dame."

The lands of Fithie gave surname to a family that held a
respectable position in the county from about the middle of
the thirteenth century until within these two hundred years.[4]
These lands also paid feu-duties to the Bishop of Brechin, and
probably the De Fithies were vassals of the Bishops down to

[1] *Reg. Ep. Brechin.* i. p. 84.   [2] *Orig. Charter in Ardovie Charter Chest.*
[3] (1646)—*Presbytery Records of Brechin.*   [4] *Reg. Vet. Aberbr.* p. 322.

the year 1457, as at that time George Leslie, the first Earl of Rothes, had a grant of Easter Fithies, and this was confirmed by charter, under the Great Seal, to the third Earl in 1511.[1] In little more than a century afterwards the property came into the hands of Sir Robert Carnegie of Kinnaird.[2] At one time Fithie had a castle, the remains of which form the back wall of a cottar house ; and upon an adjoining knoll to the east, popular story avers that the "lady fair" was burnt for the murder of young Reiden !

Of all these proprietors the Carnegies have been longest settled in Farnell, and they are still represented there by their chief, the Earl of Southesk. Their original surname was *De Balinhard*, assumed from the small property of Balanhard, or Balanard, locally called *Bonhard*, in the parish of Arbirlot.[3] Martin of Clermont says the first of the "*Carnegies* was Constable to the King's house at Fettercairn in William the Lion's time, and for that service he got the lands of Fesdow, and those also of Pitnemoone."[4] As *Balinhard* they may have held that office, but certainly not as *Carnegie*, that surname to all appearance being then unknown.

The earliest notice of the De Balinhards occurs about the year 1230, when Gocelynus witnesses several charters to contemporary monasteries both in Angus and Fife, but his connection with the Arbirlot De Balinhards cannot be established, though various circumstances are in favour of its existence. John de Balinhard, possibly Gocelyn's son, the first recorded ancestor of the Southesk family, died about the year 1270, and his property, which lay within the lordship of Panmure, was, it is supposed, exchanged by his great-grandson for the lands of Carnegie in the parish of Carmyllie, which the latter acquired from Sir Walter de Maule about 1340. From these

[1] *Reg. Mag. Sig.* No. lxii. p. 35.
[2] Douglas, *Peerage*, ii. pp. 425-512.
[3] *Bal-an-ard*, in Gaelic, means " the town on a height ;" *Kin-ard*, " a high point, or head." The names are quite descriptive of the position of both places.
[4] Macfarlane's *Collec.*, Adv. Lib. Edin.

lands, as appears by the charter,[1] the surname of De Carnegie, in place of De Balinhard, was then assumed by the progenitor of the Carnegies " of that ilk " and of Kinnaird.

Having elsewhere given an account of this ancient and noble family,[2] it is superfluous to recount their lineage here, especially as it was lately so satisfactorily established before the House of Lords.

Suffice it to say that Duthac de Carnegie, presumed to have been the second son of John de Carnegie, first " of that ilk," purchased from Richard Ayre part of the lands of Kinnaird in 1401, and subsequently acquired the remainder from Mariota de Kinnaird by charter dated 21st February 1409. According to tradition, Mariota was an heiress, and brought her lands to Duthac in marriage, but, owing to the loss of documents when the house of Kinnaird was burnt by Crawford after the battle of Brechin in 1452, much obscurity rests on the earlier history of the Carnegies. Duthac fell at Harlaw in 1411, and Sir David Carnegie, sixth in lineal succession from Duthac, and an eminent lawyer and statesman, was elevated to the peerage, first in 1616 as Lord Carnegie of Kinnaird, and next in 1633 as Earl of Southesk. He had four successors in the Earldom, all noblemen of tried and approved loyalty ; but, in consequence of the part taken by the last of these against the Government in 1715, their titles as well as their estates, which were scattered over seven counties, were forfeited, and the Earl died an exile in France in 1730.

In 1764 the York Buildings Company, which had purchased so many of the forfeited estates, became insolvent, and those of Southesk were bought back by Sir James Carnegie of Pitarrow, great-grandfather of the present Earl of Southesk. The present, who is sixth Earl, succeeded his father as sixth baronet of Pitarrow in 1849, and prosecuted the claim to the Earldom of Southesk, that had previously been raised by his

[1] Jervise, *Land of the Lindsays*, pp. 104, 238-9 ; Fraser, *Hist. Carnegies of Southesk*, i. pp. 1 sq.

[2] Jervise, *Land of the Lindsays*, pp. 238 sq.

father. The Committee of Privileges of the House of Lords, on Tuesday the 24th July 1855, finding "the claim proved in a very satisfactory manner," were pleased to restore to him, with the original precedence, the dignities and titles of Earl of Southesk and Lord Carnegie of Kinnaird and Leuchars, which were forfeited by James, fifth Earl, in 1716.[1] In 1869 the present Earl was created a peer of the United Kingdom, with the title of Baron Balinhard of Farnell, and in the same year a Knight of the Order of the Thistle.

The present Castle of Kinnaird, which, from its elevated position, overlooks a great part of the surrounding country—including the eastern portion of the fertile valley of Southesk, with the town and basin of Montrose—is supposed to occupy almost the same place as the castle which the Earl of Crawford burned down in 1452. Nearly two hundred years ago, Kinnaird and Farnell were quaintly described as "without competition the fynest place, taking all together, in the shyre;" and, as regards the castle and park of Kinnaird at least, the description is not inapplicable at the present day.

Since the accession of the present noble owner, the castle and neighbourhood have undergone a complete transformation. The park-wall has been rebuilt and greatly extended. It now encloses between 1300 and 1400 acres within its bounds, and in this wide extent the deer-park (containing many fallow-deer of the old Kinnaird breed), occupies more than a thousand acres imperial.

The castle has been remodelled, after the design of Mr. Bryce of Edinburgh, in the style of architecture which prevailed throughout France towards the beginning of the sixteenth century, and which differs from the usual Scottish development of the same type, in its larger openings, its higher and heavier roofs, its freer use of Italian and classical forms, and its generally more ornate character. The present building is nearly square. The west and principal front looks

---

[1] Fraser, *Hist. Carnegies of Southesk,* i. pp. 238-40.

towards the deer-park, from which it is separated by a balus-traded terrace wall, and a stone balcony of similar character, with a double flight of steps at the centre, traverses the greater part of its length, which altogether is 208 feet. The carriage entrance is on the north side ; on the south is the conservatory and flower garden.

From the ground to the vane on the highest turret the height is 115 feet; but the platform upon the central tower, which nearly ranges with the tops of the corner towers, is 30 feet lower. The interior is furnished with a well-selected library, and a still more valuable collection of paintings adorns the walls. Among these pictures are some choice originals by Filippo Lippi, Bellini, Bronzino, Albano, Velasquez, Domeni-chino, Cuyp, Vandyck, Teniers, Lely, Jamesone of Aberdeen, and others ; also various interesting historical portraits, and numerous engravings by well-known ancient masters.[1]

[1] For a more extended account of Kinnaird Castle, see Fraser, *Hist. Carnegies of Southesk*, i. pp. xxxiii sq. ; Jervise, *Land of the Lindsays*, p. 245 n.

CHAPTER III.

Castle, Convent, and Town of Montrose.

SECTION I.

O sweet is the calm dewy gloaming,
When saftly by Rossie-wood brae,
The merle and mavis are hymning
The e'en o' the lang summer's day !

LAING, *Wayside Flowers.*

Castle of Montrose—Gatekeeper appointed by William I.—Visited by Edward I.—
Destroyed by Wallace—Tenures of the lands of Inyaney, Bonnyton, Kinnaird,
etc.—Bailie and Burgesses did homage to Edward I. at Berwick—Convent of
Dominican Friars founded by Alan Durward—Removed nearer the town by
Panter of Newmanswalls—Discontent of the Friars—Their lands of Carsgownie
plundered by the Earl of Crawford.

THE Castle of Montrose had a commanding position upon
or near to the Forthill, about a mile above the point where
the South Esk falls into the sea. The time of its erection
is unknown ; but in the year 980, the Danes are said to
have obtained anchorage in that river, and to have begun
those predatory incursions which were ultimately checked
by Kenneth III. at Luncarty. They destroyed both the town
and castle of Montrose, and put the citizens to the sword.[1]

But the real history of the castle dates from the time of
King William the Lion. He made it an occasional residence,
dated charters from it between the years 1178 and 1198,[2] and
appointed a person named Crane to be its gatekeeper. For
that office Crane had the heritable fee of the lands of Inyaney,

---

[1] This is based upon Holinshed and Boece, and its general probability is confirmed by the *Irish Annals* ; see Chalmers, *Caled.* i. pp. 393 sq.

[2] *Reg. Vet. Aberbr.* ii. p. 86.

on the south side of the river, and was succeeded by his son Swayne, and grandson Simon. The latter, dying without male issue, left five daughters, who on the death of their father made a joint claim to Inyaney. Their right being questioned, the matter came before the courts of law, and an inquest was instituted in 1261-2. It is gratifying to know that the assize, which consisted of eighteen of the chief barons of the county, gave decision in favour of the five co-heiresses, who thereupon possessed the property.[1]

From that time, until the Wars of the Independence, no trace of the castle is found. It was captured and the garrison put to the sword by Wallace in 1297. In the previous year King Edward and his retinue went there from Farnell, on the 7th of July, and remained until the 12th of the same month. During that time the English king received the homage of a great number of barons and clergy from all parts of the kingdom, near and remote.[2] He also received, though not personally in Montrose, the submission of King John Baliol, who, as quaintly remarked by the writer of the Diary of Edward's expedition, "did render quietly the realme of Scotland, as he that had done amiss."[3]

The facts regarding this event seem to be these : The submission of Baliol took place, first in the churchyard of Stracathro before Anthony Beck, Bishop of Durham, on the evening of Saturday, July 7th, and had the form of a personal repentance and amendment, by withdrawing from the French League ; and on Tuesday, July 10th following, he again appeared before the English prelate, in the Castle of Brechin, and at this time handed over his kingdom and all his rights in it to King Edward, in the presence of several of the Scotch nobles as witnesses. But Edward was not personally present at either act of Baliol's humiliation.[4]

---

[1] *Acta Parl.* i. p. 90. See APPENDIX No. XI.
[2] *Ragman Rolls*, pp. 89-92 ; Prynne, *Hist.* p. 651 ; Palgrave, *Writs*, pp. 167-173.
[3] *Bannatyne Miscell.* i. p. 277 ; *Ragman Rolls*, p. 83.
[4] *Ragman Rolls*, pp. 82, 84 ; Prynne, *Hist.* pp. 647, 650.

Although King David II. was frequently at Montrose towards the close of his reign,[1] no further mention occurs of the castle after the visit of Sir William Wallace, save the casual notice of it in the patent of the original Dukedom of Montrose. That patent was granted by King James the Third to David Lindsay, Earl of Crawford, in 1488, for his loyal services at the battle of Blackness, and it is therein stated that, along with "the greater and loftier title" of Duke of Montrose, Crawford had hereditarily the capital messuage and castlested of Montrose, the burgh and town, with the great and small customs of its ports, harbours, fisheries, etc.[2]

As a grant with the Dukedom, the castle, if destroyed to any extent by Wallace, had probably, by the close of the fifteenth century, been made worthy of being presented to the royal favourite, and suitable for his residence. The mention of the "capital messuage and place of the castle," and the further definition of the place of the castle, "as what is commonly called the Castlested," would naturally lead us to infer that both the castle, as "capital messuage" or chief residence, and the site on which the castle stood, were given with the ducal patent. In the middle of the sixteenth century, the Fort was held by Erskine of Dun, as hereditary keeper, on behalf of the Queen-mother, but this may have been held as a military post without reference to the castle near it. Both occupied a fine situation, and, as already shown, the castle was a place of much importance during and for long after the reign of William I. ; some estates also in the vicinity were held under tenures of certain services to the King's court at Montrose.

---

[1] *Reg. Mag. Sig.* pp. 43-70.

[2] *Report on the Montrose Claim*, p. 375. The question involved in the interpretation of the term *castlested* is at least a very curious one. The word seems to have been a favourite legal term in the charters of the fifteenth and sixteenth centuries (*Reg. Mag. Sig.*), and the evidence appears to lean in favour of "the site" of the castle, as in the similar grant of Roxburgh Castle, to Walter Ker of Cessford ; yet the second grant of the same castle to Ker leaves the matter open. In 1512 we read of the reddendo " apud le Auld-Castel steid de Kincardine."—*Ibid.* No. 3750, p. 815. See Chalmers, *Caled.* ii. p. 98, for the " castle " interpretation.

Besides Inyaney or Aneny, now called *Ananias*,[1] which Crane and his descendants held as heritable gatekeepers, the adjoining lands of Bonnyton were held for supplying fresh fish, and probably the adjoining farm of Fullerton for wild fowl, to the royal table;[2] Kinnaird, Carcary, and some others, for keeping the King's ale cellar;[3] and Muirmills, a little to the westward, went with the keepership of the royal hunting forest of Montreathmont, the forester having in addition fourpence for each spade casting peats in that muir.[4] All these properties, together with a portion of Montreathmont (or Monrommon) Muir, now form part of the Southesk estates.

Soon after King Edward returned to Berwick in August 1296, no fewer than twelve of the burgesses of Montrose went thither, and took the oaths of allegiance to England, for themselves and the community of the town.[5] This, it ought to be observed, is the only instance of *burgesses* of any burgh in Angus owning the superiority of Edward, though those of the principal burghs of almost every other county did so at the place where the king held court—a fact which goes far to show that perhaps no other town in the county had king's burgesses at the same early date, or, in other words, was a *royal* burgh.

The names of those burgesses show a mixed lineage of Anglo-French, Saxon, and Scotch. Persons bearing similar surnames are still to be found in Montrose.

The first is—

𝔄𝔡𝔞𝔪 𝔊𝔬𝔩𝔡, bailie of the burgh. As a surname Gold is

---

[1] The spelling of this name is various—Ananise, Annand, Annane, Annanie, Inyaney, Inieney, Inieneny, Inyoney, Inyanee, Inneane, and Iniancy. *Ean-an-i*, in Gaelic, means "the island of birds."

[2] Inf. from the late P. Chalmers, Esq. of Aldbar.

[3] *Charter by James VI. to Sir John Carnegy of Kinnaird, Oct. 14, 1592.*

[4] *Inq. Special*, Forfarshire, No. 374.

[5] Prynne, *Hist.* p. 653, gives Patrick, Abbot of *Menros*, etc. ; *Ragman Rolls* (p. 117), *Meuros ;* but as the name appears in the same deed with those of the Abbots of Jedburgh, Dryburgh, and Kelso, it doubtless refers to the Abbot of *Melrose*, which is still locally called *Meurose*. The list of burgesses is in *Ragman Rolls*, p. 124 ; Prynne, *Hist.* p. 654.

still common in Forfarshire, and is, doubtless, synonymous with Goold and Guild.

𝕳𝖊𝖓𝖗𝖞 𝖉𝖊 𝕳𝖆𝖐𝖊𝖑𝖞, probably bears a local or territorial name.

𝕵𝖔𝖍𝖆𝖓 𝖋𝖎𝖟 𝕬𝖉𝖆𝖒, 𝕳𝖚𝖜𝖊 𝖑𝖊 𝖋𝖎𝖟 𝕸𝖆𝖚𝖐𝖊𝖑𝖔𝖒, and 𝕵𝖔𝖍𝖆𝖓 𝖋𝖎𝖟 𝕬𝖑𝖊𝖞𝖓, or John Adamson, Hugh Malcolmson or MacMalcolm, and John Alanson, or MacAlan, are all personal or paternal names.

𝕻𝖍𝖊𝖑𝖎𝖕𝖕 𝖉𝖊 𝕷𝖔𝖌𝖞𝖓, a well-known territorial name, famous in ancient history and modern literature, and assumed, doubtless, from the neighbouring territory of Logy-Montrose.

𝕵𝖔𝖍𝖆𝖓 𝖉𝖊 𝕿𝖍𝖔𝖗𝖓𝖊𝖙𝖔𝖓, also a local or territorial name, and belonging in all likelihood to a cadet of the family of that Ilk in the Mearns.

𝖂𝖆𝖚𝖙𝖎𝖊𝖗 𝖑𝖊 𝕸𝖊𝖗𝖈𝖊𝖗, of which name there was also a Stephen, a burgess of Berwick, that did homage to King Edward in 1291, and Austin, and Bernard, respectively burgesses of Roxburgh and Perth, who did the same service about the same time as Walter of Montrose,[1] and from the burgess of Perth the old family of Mercer of Aldie claim descent.

𝖂𝖆𝖚𝖙𝖎𝖊𝖗 𝖉𝖊 𝕽𝖔𝖘𝖘𝖞, doubtless a scion of the family of that Ilk, near Montrose. The family had an early settlement there as vassals of the old Norman family De Malherb, and in consequence derived their surname from the lands.[2] The remaining burgesses were

𝖂𝖎𝖑𝖑𝖎𝖆𝖒 𝕾𝖙𝖗𝖔𝖓𝖌, 𝕿𝖍𝖔𝖒𝖆𝖘 𝕮𝖚𝖋𝖋𝖔𝖈𝖐, and 𝕵𝖔𝖍𝖓 𝕿𝖗𝖔𝖙. Such names are now seldom met with in the district. To these ought to be added,

𝕿𝖍𝖔𝖒𝖆𝖘 𝖑𝖊 𝕻𝖔𝖗𝖙𝖊𝖗 𝖉𝖊 𝕸𝖚𝖓𝖗𝖔𝖘.[3] This individual, recorded by Palgrave alone, had perhaps been connected in some way with the castle; but of his history nothing further is known, although the surname even now is not uncommon in the district.

Such are the few traces of the old castle and burgesses of Montrose, and it is to be regretted that those of its Convent are even still more obscure. The very site of the original foundation is matter of conjecture. It was "biggit and foundit," and likewise dedicated to the Virgin Mary, in 1230, by Alan the Durward or *Hostiarius*, the most daring and

---

[1] *Rag. Rolls*, pp. 12, 121, 122.
[2] *Reg. Vet. Aberbr.* p. 42.　　　　　[3] Palgrave, *Writs*, p. 197.

powerful Scotch magnate of his time, and the last male representative of a family surnamed De Lundin, who had footing in Scotland under David I., from whom, or Malcolm IV., an ancestor obtained the lands of Lundie in Angus.[1] It belonged to the monks of the order of St. Dominic, who, in consequence of the colour of their habit, were commonly called Black Friars, and also *Fratres Prædicatores*, because they were allowed to go about and preach, and beg their living. Alexander II. introduced them into Scotland, where they had fifteen convents; and Spottiswoode quaintly remarks that, though "they professed great poverty, yet when their nests were pulled down they were found too rich for mendicants."[2]

But although the site of Durward's foundation is not known with certainty, it may reasonably be conjectured that it stood on that portion of the common links of Montrose, which is situated a little to the eastward of Victoria Bridge,[3] and still bears the name of *St. Mary*, patroness of the convent. There is no actual warrant for this, however, beyond incidental notices, in 1245 and 1370, of certain annuities which the convent received out of the lands of Rossie, and others;[4] no further record of it exists until 1516, when the celebrated Patrick Panter,[5] of the Newmanswalls family, Abbot of Cambuskenneth, had liberty from Parliament to remove the house to the immediate vicinity of the town. For the better maintenance of "the new place," as it is called, Panter made a grant to it of the teinds of Spitleschelis and Denside in Garvock, and a payment from Balandro in Benholm, also the teinds of Newmanis Wallis, and croft at Balkilly (Balkeelie, in Craig); and those of Claysched and Saundhauch, and the fishings of the nett of the Virgin in the North Esk, called "Marynett." To these he

---

[1] Chalmers, *Caled*. i. p. 533.

[2] *Hist. of Religious Houses*, p. 487.

[3] This bridge on the Lower North Water Bridge Road, which crosses the branch railway from Dubton to Montrose, had its name in consequence of Queen Victoria having landed there *en route* from Balmoral to London, Sept. 28, 1848.

[4] *Reg. Vet. Aberbr*. p. 337; *Chamb. Rolls*, i. pp. 541-5.

[5] Riddell, *Peer. Cases*, pp. 192, 204.

further added twenty merks Scots from the lands of Dun-
hasny (Dalhesney), Dabley (Dooly), Skannach (Shanno), and
Corniscorun (Corneskcorn), in the lordship of Glenesk, which
were alienated by John, Earl of Crawford; fifty merks out of
the barony of Fern; six merks out of the lands of Cukestoun,
in the barony of Rescobie, and parish of Farnell; and six
merks from the lands of Ballindoch and pertinents, at Inverkeilor—reserving to himself and his heirs the patronage of the
hospital, and a burial-place in the northern part of the choir.[1]

Notwithstanding those additional revenues, it appears that
from the moment the convent was removed discontent reigned
within its walls, and in the course of a few years the friars,
dissatisfied with the locality, craved Parliament to allow them
to return to their old abode. Their chief ground of complaint
was the nearness of the convent to the public thoroughfare,
by which they were continually disturbed in their devotions
by the noise and traffic of horses and currocks to and from
the town.[2] Whether the prayer of this memorial was granted
or not is uncertain, for, except in the statement of Spottiswoode,
who says they " were brought back to their former dwelling by
an allowance of Parliament in the year 1524," no notice of the
matter is found.

Remains of the hospital founded by Panter were visible at no
distant date. These stood in the Sandhauch above mentioned,
about a mile nearer the town than the field of St. Mary, before
alluded to, and within the garden ground upon the east side
of Murray Street; but of the character of the architecture of
the fabric nothing is preserved.[3] If it had any special architectural features, there can be little doubt but they disappeared
soon after the Reformation. And even before that time

---

[1] *Acta Parl.* ii. pp. 389-92.   Sir John Erskine of Dun in 1509 resigned the lands
of Spittalschiells in favour of the Hospital of Montrose, because the Master wished
to build a new church from the foundation, the lands being rather a loss to
Erskine than otherwise.—*Miscel. Spalding Club*, iv. p. x. n.

[2] *Acta Parl.* ii. p. 395.

[3] For a notice of a carved door and some panels supposed to have belonged to
the old Hospital at Montrose, see *Proc. Soc. Ant. Scot.* xvi. pp. 61 sq.

certain lands belonging to the convent had been exposed to the ravages of the notorious David Lindsay, eighth Earl of Crawford, who, in his acts of oppression over all classes of society in the district, persecuted among others the poor friars of Montrose in every manner of way, and by "masterful ejection" deprived them of their crops and "thair thre aught pairts of the lands of Carsegowny;" and for this a decree was passed against Crawford at the instance of Friar Patrick Pillane and the rest of the convent.[1]

When the lands of Carsegownie, which are situated in the parish of Aberlemno and barony of Finhaven, were sold, the right of a day's shooting, and the use of the kitchen of the house, as well as a small annual payment, were reserved in favour of the trustees of the hospital. In virtue of that reservation the civic authorities of Montrose, as trustees of that fund, occasionally take advantage of their old right, but without being restricted, we presume, either to the "thre aught pairts of the lands," or to the kitchen of the house of Carsegownie.

<hr>

SECTION II.

How sweitlie shonne the morning sunne
Upon the bonnie Ha'-house o' Dun :
Siccan a bein and lovelie abode
Micht wyle the pilgrime aff his roode.
G. BEATTIE, The Murderit Mynstrell.

Old Church and Altarages—Notices of the Reformation—Erskine of Dun establishes a Teacher of Greek—Wishart and Methven—Rev. John Duray—Inhabitants of Tayock petition the Presbytery—a second Minister appointed—Old Steeple— Herse gifted to the Kirk by Admiral Clark—Episcopal and other Churches— Grammar School—Grant to it by Robert I.—Medals, etc.—Eminent Natives.

THE parish church of Montrose, dedicated to St. John the Evangelist, was in the diocese of Brechin, and rated in the ancient *taxatio* at £20 Scots.[2] From the year 1214, when a

[1] *Crawford Peerage Case*, p. 10.   [2] *Reg. Vet. Aberbr.* p. 241.

person bearing the Christian name of Henry, subscribes a deed
of that period, as "Chaplain of Munros," no further mention
is found of any of the old churchmen until the beginning of
the fifteenth century, when Thomas Bel, canon of the churches
of Aberdeen and Brechin, and perpetual vicar of the parish
church of Montrose, endowed a chaplaincy in the Chapel of the
Holy Rood for certain objects of prayer.[1] There were several
chaplaincies attached to the church, but all are lost from
memory except that in the chapel above named, and another
at the altar of the Holy Trinity, founded by Heliscus and
Thomas Falconer, and supported by the rents of certain lands
in the vicinity.[2]   Another chapel, dedicated to St. John the
Baptist, was near Montrose, and had at last to be united with
Canon Bel's foundation, when the incorporated chaplaincy
was vested in the vicar of the parish church in all future
time.[3]

But, although the ecclesiastical history of Montrose in the
time of Romanism is thus meagre, it becomes more interesting
during the period of the Reformation, the inhabitants being
among the first in Scotland to embrace the Reformed religion
and propagate its principles. This may be attributed to two
causes—first, the influence that was brought to bear upon
them by Erskine of Dun; and, next, the direct intercourse
which their merchants had with the Continent, from which
copies of the Holy Scriptures, which were then strictly prohibited from being read or circulated in this country, were
brought.

Down almost to the very year when the future Superintendent returned from abroad, where he imbibed the spirit of
religious liberty, a series of bitter feuds existed between
the family of Dun and the inhabitants. But old differences
were then forgotten, and Erskine showed his favour for
Montrose by establishing, and maintaining at his own expense,
a teacher of the Greek language, which until that time was

---

[1] *Reg. Ep. Brechin.* ii. p. 261.   [2] *Ibid.* ii. p. 39.   [3] *Ibid.* ii. p. 37.

little known, and even its elements perhaps not publicly taught, in Scotland.[1]

Upon the death or retirement of M. Marsiliers, the first teacher of Greek at Montrose, he is said to have been succeeded by his pupil, the celebrated George Wishart, who taught and circulated the Greek New Testament among his scholars so openly, that Bishop Hepburn of Brechin found it necessary to summon him upon a charge of heresy. But deeming it more advisable to leave the country than to appear before Hepburn, Wishart fled to England, where he remained nearly six years. He returned to Scotland in July 1543, and immediately thereafter commenced to preach publicly " in Montrois within a private house next unto the church except one." After this he went to Dundee for a short season, but returned again to Montrose, and on that occasion administered the communion at Dun.[2] From these parts he was soon expelled a second time, and the people, in consequence of the increased oppression and tyranny which were being constantly manifested towards them, became doubly eager in the cause of the Reformation. A preacher of the name of Paul Methven, originally a baker in Dundee (who, although by no means of unexceptionable character, appears to have been pretty well suited for the times), was invited to Montrose, and, having administered the sacrament " to several of the lieges in a manner far different from the divine and laudable use of the faithful Catholic Church, he was denounced rebel and put to the horn as fugitive,"[3] while the community themselves were commanded to attend mass, and participate in the rites of the Roman Church at Easter.[4]

It is needless to say that these injunctions were but tardily complied with, and within ten years from the date of the

[1] On the study of the Greek language in Scotland, see M'Crie, *Life of John Knox*, pp. 382-4.; and in England see *Ch. Quart. Review*, No. xxxvi. Art. I.

[2] Wodrow, *Biog. Coll.* i. p. 431; Petrie, *Hist. Cath. Church*, Pt. ii. pp. 182-3; Tytler, *Hist. Scot.* v. p. 341 ; J. Melville, *Autobiog.* p. 39; Grub, *Eccl. Hist. Scot.* ii. p. 23.

[3] Pitcairn, *Crim. Trials*, i. p. 406.   [4] Tytler, *Hist. of Scot.* vi. p. 96.

last-mentioned occurrence, the pulpits of many churches were filled by the reformed clergy. The first reformed minister at Montrose was Mr. Thomas Anderson, who was assisted by Mr. John Beattie, a reader, the former having a salary of eight score merks, and the latter £60 Scots.[1] Both these gentlemen are worthy of notice, in consequence of the kind attention they bestowed upon the more celebrated James Melville during his school-boy days. Melville describes the former as "a man of mean gifts, bot of singular guid lyff;" and the latter, as "a godly honest man, wha read the Scripture distinctlie, and with a religious and devot feilling, wherof," continues the truly excellent Melville, "I fand my selff movit to giff guid eare, and lern the Stories of Scripture, also to tak plesure in the Psalmes, quhilk he haid almost all by hart, in prose." It was also at Montrose and under Mr. Anderson, that Melville, at the early age of thirteen, became a communicant of that church, of which at a future period he was so great an ornament.[2]

Perhaps Anderson was succeeded by Mr. John Dury, father-in-law of James Melville. Like most of his reforming brethren, Dury was educated in the Romish faith, and his own brother, the Abbot of Dunfermline, was his preceptor. Expelled that convent for heresy, he was for some time imprisoned at Edinburgh, and then sent "to ward" in Montrose in 1583. This was at a time when ecclesiastical matters were gaining a more liberal footing, and when in the course of ten years the King —with what degree of sincerity is questionable—gave the country to believe, that he was so sensible of the value of the preaching of the true gospel and the sacrifices that had been made by reforming ministers, that he granted £140 a year to this same Mr. Dury, who had long suffered persecution. Dury died in 1600, and perhaps no greater honour could be paid to the memory of any man than that set forth in the simple narrative of the grant of his pension, which tells its own graphic story. According to it the grant was made by the King in con-

---

[1] *Reg. of Ministers*, p. 14.   [2] Melville, *Diary*, p. 22, et pass.

sideration of " the greit lang and ernest travellis and labouris
sustenit be his louit orator Johnne Dury, minister of Goddis
word at Montrois in the trew preaching of Goddis word, besydes
the greit chargis and expenses maid be him thir mony zeirs
bygane in avancing the publict effayres of the kirk—thair-
withall remembring the greit househald and famelie of barnis
quhairwith he is burdynit;" this pension was granted in
favour of Dury, his wife and son, and " the langest levair of
thame thre."[1]

It does not appear that any of Mr. Dury's successors in the
ministry at Montrose made themselves conspicuous in the
subsequent struggles of the Church. They seem indeed to
have been lax even in their parochial duties, and, down to the
close of the year 1642, the ecclesiastical boundaries of the
parish were so ill defined, and the spiritual welfare of the
inhabitants so little cared for, that the people resident upon
the lands of Tayock, Newbigging, and Pugiston, were not
aware whether they belonged to the kirk of Brechin or to that
of Montrose, as they were never visited by any minister or
called upon to attend any church. Nor did even the Presbytery seem to know to which of these churches the people
belonged ; for, when required to decide in the matter, they,
without settling the question of right, merely declared that the
petitioners " may be mor commodiouslie served at the kirk off
Montrose nor at the kirk off Brecheine."[2] But it was in the
latter of these parishes that the lands and town of Tayock
in reality were situated.[3]

The Presbytery's deliverance, however, proved unsatisfactory, and about thirty years afterwards the same people, if they
were not in much the same dilemma as to the parish in which
they resided, were in an equally deplorable position with regard
to spiritual superintendence. For they again complained that
they " wer not looked after nor owned as parishioners by any

[1] *Acta Parl.* iii. p. 551.
[2] *Brechin Presb. Rec. MS.*
[3] *Reg. Ep. Brechin.* ii. p. 239.

minister;" and thereupon "the Presbiterie determined that
the inhabitants of Tayock should be parishioners of Montrose,
there to hear the Word and to be catechised, and to receive
the benefit of baptisme and marriage, and there to communicat
when the occasion served."[1]

Thus far the doubts regarding the parochial district of
Tayock were settled, but these lands and some others to the
west of Tayock Burn were afterwards disjoined from Montrose
and added to the parish of Dun, as had previously been the
kirk and emoluments of Egglisjohn (now Langley Park), which
was " of auld ane chappell erectit for pilgrimage."[2]

Hitherto we have been speaking of Montrose as a single
ecclesiastical charge.   It was not until about the close of the
seventeenth century, during the time of the last Episcopal
minister, that it became collegiate.   It was so incorporated
by special grant of Parliament, and that upon petition of the
inhabitants, who craved Government to allow them to tax
themselves for the support of a second minister.[3]   But this
proceeding led afterwards to much disagreeable feeling in both
Montrose and Edinburgh, where also the tax existed.   These,
in fact, were the only towns in Scotland where the inhabitants
paid what was called the Annuity-tax, and it proved so odious
that it was deemed advisable at last, by arrangement with the
civic authorities in both places, to have it commuted.

A Mr. David Lyell was then parochial minister, and a Mr.
Neill was the first who received the designation of second or
burgh minister.   Of the latter nothing is known; but the
former, originally a Presbyterian, was ordained at Aberdeen
while Mr. Andrew Cant was moderator of that Presbytery.
When Lyell afterwards became an Episcopalian, it was he who
pronounced the sentence of deposition upon his old friend Cant.
The latter, being in the church at the time, stood up and gave

---

[1] (1674)—*Brech. Presb. Rec. MS.*
[2] *Reg. Ep. Brechin.* ii. p. 343. This is probably the Church of S. John Bapt.
(Ecclesia Johannis) that was attached to the church of Montrose.
[3] *Acta Parl.* ix. p. 188.

utterance to the characteristic exclamation—" Davie ! Davie ! I
kent ay you wad doe this sin the day I lyed my hands on your
head !" Lyell, continues the same writer, " was a thundering
preacher," and " some days before his death, as he was walking
in the Links about the twilight, at a pretty distance from the
town, he espyed as it wer a woman, all in white, standing not
far from him, who immediately disappeared, and he coming up
presently to the place, saw nae person there, though the Links
be very plain. Only casting his eye on the place where shee
stood, he saw tuo words drawn or written as it had been with
a staff upon the sand—' SENTENCED AND CONDEMNED !'—upon
which he came home pensive and melancholy, and in a little
sickens and dyes."[1]

Prior to the erection of the present parish church (which
is large and plain, with two sets of galleries), the building was
in the Gothic style of architecture, " originally venerable and
well proportioned," but afterwards " rendered very gloomy and
irregular, by large additions to the galleries, and to the building itself."[2]   The present kirk was built in 1791, and the old
square tower,[3] with octagonal spire, which stood at the west
gable, gave place in 1833-34 to the handsome Gothic steeple,
that is now so great an ornament to the town.   It ought to
be remarked that the old steeple was not only an object of
unknown antiquity, but also of some historical note.   It was
from that " stiple head " that " the fyre of joy " blazed in
June 1566, when the news of the birth of King James was
announced ;[4] and, upon a previous occasion, it was the scene
of the murder of a young priest, an incident which will afterwards be referred to.

The Chandelier, suspended from the roof of the church, is
the oldest existing relic of the kirk of Montrose.   The candle-

[1] Wodrow, *Analecta*, i. p. 107, had this story from Mr. J. Guild, Minr. of Perth.
[2] *Old Stat. Acct.* v. p. 32 ; Douglas, *East Coast of Scotland*, p. 55, speaks in a
style even less flattering regarding the former church.
[3] *Proc. Soc. Ant. Scot.* ii. p. 460, for the remains found in its foundation, in 1832.
[4] Melville, *Diary*, p. 18.

frame, harrow, or *herse* is an article of great antiquity in churches, and originated in tapers being lighted for necessary purposes and ecclesiastical rites. According to the form of the object, it received the name of *arbor* or *herse*, the latter name coming at last to be appropriated to the catafalque or wheeled bier. In early times the candle-supports were made of wood, and when metal came to be used they were variously and elegantly designed.[1] The chandelier, or hanging herse, at Montrose, is made of brass, about four feet in height, and consists of a large globe and shaft, surmounted by an elegant female figure with outstretched wings, and brandishing in her right hand a sword, while, by a chain held in her left hand, she seems to restrain a dragon on which she treads. It has sixteen branches, divided into two rows of eight each, the lower row projecting beyond the upper. The figures of Justice and of St. Michael and the Dragon, amid the armorial insignia of the gallant donor and his wife, Christina Lamb, are engraved upon the globe, round which are also inscribed these words :—

> " RICHARDVS CLARK MONTROSÆ NATVS
> NVNC AVTEM VICE-ADMIRALIS REGIS SVEDIÆ
> CHRISTIANÆ FIDEI TESTIMONIO HVIVS TEMPLI ORNAMENTO
> COGNATIS SVIS CÆTERISQVE
> HVIVS VRBIS INCOLIS PRISTINI ET INTEGRI AMORIS PIGNORI
> ÆNÆVM HOC CANDELABRVM HIC ERIGI
> FECIT ANNO MDCXXIII."

This Candelabrum, as mentioned in the inscription, was presented to the kirk by Admiral Clark, of the Swedish fleet, a native of Montrose ; but so little was it respected by the congregation of the time that, upon the introduction of gas into the church, it was thrown aside as useless, and altogether lost sight of. When it was subsequently discovered in a black-

---

[1] It may be noted how the use of words change. Hearse, from the French *Herse*, was the frame of wood or iron for bearing candles beside a corpse in church, tomb, or funeral procession, and was formed of cross bars like a harrow, or constructed at a later date in a more ornamental style, either for standing or being hung : it finally came to designate the carriage used for conveying the corpse to the tomb. See *Imperial Dictionary*, Ed. Annandale, ii. p. 497 ; Hart, *Eccl. Records*, p. 247, and Plates ii. iii.

smith's shop, it was found to be denuded of its branches. A worthy citizen had it repaired and replaced in its old position, and it was fitted up at last for gas, in the autumn of 1854. The gift is celebrated in verse by a local poet, who thus speaks of it in the opening stanza of his poem :—

> " The bless of Heivin be on thie hedde,
> Thou pious, gude, and nobille Swede,
> For gift so fair and kind !
> I trow, before we got thy licht,
> We sate in darkness black as nicht
> And wanderit like the blind."[1]

There is now a neat church at Hillside, which was built in 1870 ; and the surrounding district, taken entirely from the parish of Montrose, was erected into a parish *quoad sacra* in 1879, with a permanent endowment yielding £123, 7s. 2d. annually. The school at Hillside is the Board School of the landward part of the parish.

The old burial-ground of Montrose, in which lie the remains of William Maitland the historian, and of many notable citizens of the place, surrounds the kirk. It is overcrowded by monuments, some of which are very handsome. The inscriptions on some of the older stones are rather quaint, and the more ancient were published in Monteith's *Theater of Mortality*, early in the last century. The Houff of Kinnaber, near the North Water Bridge, has long been closed, and the Old Churchyard above mentioned is practically so, there being only one or two families, to whom the right of interment in it was reserved, now alive. Rosehill Cemetery, which has twice been extended, and the burial-ground of St. Peter's Episcopal Chapel, are the only other places of interment in the parish.

St. Peter's, founded in 1722, is an English Episcopal Chapel, and, until the time when it fell a prey to accidental fire, was the same house which Dr. Johnson describes in his *Journey to the Western Islands*, as " clean to a degree unknown in any

---

[1] Bowick, *Characters and Sketches*, p. 67.

other part of Scotland, with commodious galleries, and what was less expected, with an organ." This interesting edifice had been greatly extended and repaired in 1856, at a cost of nearly £3000, and was re-opened for Divine service on the 21st of December of that year. But upon the evening of the 7th of February following, by the overheating of the flues of the stove, as is supposed, the building unfortunately caught fire, and the flames spreading rapidly, the internal furnishings, including the fine organ, and the altar-piece, representing Moses and Aaron, were consumed, and within a few hours little remained save the smouldering ruins. St. Mary's of the Scottish Episcopal Church, Melville *quoad sacra* Church, and St. John's of the Free Church are tasteful buildings.

Closely allied to the churches are the Public Schools, and those in Montrose have long been famous. This is sufficiently attested by the number and superior character of the scholars that have been educated there; and it is a remarkable fact that at one and the same time no fewer than four of them were Fellows of the Royal Society of London.[1] Montrose is said to have been the cradle of the Greek language in Scotland, and, even so early as the days of The Bruce, the seminaries had acquired so much celebrity that he granted the sum of 20s. out of the public revenue towards their support[2]—a fact which proves that even in those days the legislature of Scotland took an interest in the great and now engrossing cause of education.

In more recent times the Grammar School has received

---

[1] These were Joseph Hume; Sir William Burnett, M.D.; Sir James and Sir Alexander Burnes. Besides these, Montrose has given birth to many other eminent men, among whom are John Leech, an old Latin poet (Jervise, *Land of the Lindsays*, p. 314); Dr. George Keith, author of the *Farmer's Ha'*, born 1749; Dr. Wm. Hunter, Sec. to the Asiatic Society; David Buchanan, an eminent classical scholar and printer; Wm. and Thos. Christie, the one compiler of a Latin Grammar, and the other author of several philosophical and other works. To these ought to be added, Alexander Smart, one of the most meritorious of the Scottish poets, author of *Rambling Rhymes* and *Songs of Labour*, in which are preserved many reminiscences of his native town.

[2] Tytler, *Hist. of Scot.* ii. p. 296.

many important benefactions, and is known more generally as The Academy. It has a competent staff of teachers, is capable of accommodating at least 700 pupils, and is one of the fifteen Higher Class Schools in Scotland. A valuable library of the classics was long since presented to it, and, besides the medals and book prizes of the Angus Club, which are distributed among all the more important schools in the county, special medals were instituted by the late Sir James Duke, M.P., and by a Masonic Lodge in Bombay. The latter was in honour of Sir James Burnes, who was a native of Montrose, and long Grand Master of the Scotch Lodge in India. Besides these the interest of £100 was also left by the late Sir Alexander Burnes, to be distributed in prizes to the most proficient of the classical scholars.

The names of the early masters of The Academy are unknown ; but, apart from Monsieur Marsiliers, the first Greek master, and George Wishart, his successor, the Grammar School had the honour of being taught by David Lindsay, laird of Dunkenny, and a relative of the laird of Edzell. Lindsay was afterwards Bishop, first of Brechin, and then of Edinburgh, and it was in his presence that Jenny Geddes is said to have flung the stool at the Dean's head, when he began to read the Book of Common Prayer in the High Church of Edinburgh, in July 1637.[1]

---

[1] There was also a teacher of vocal music appointed at Montrose, early in the eighteenth century, the art of singing not being then taught nearer Montrose than Edinburgh.—*Burgh Records, MS.*

SECTION III.

What is grandeur, what is power ?
Heavier toil, superior pain.
What the bright reward we gain ?
The grateful memory of the good.

GRAY, *Ode on Music.*

Salork, and its Kirk—Harbour of Stronnay—Inch Braoch—Basin—Drainer's Dyke
—Origin of names of Montrose, and Ald Montrose—Town burned—a King's
Burgh—Trading Privileges—the Alderman Hostage for David II.—Landing
of Sir William Wallace from France—Royal Grants to Burgh—Earl of Crawford
created Duke of Montrose—Burgh Customs—Fairs.

BOECE says that Montrose was first known by the name of
Celurca,[1] and, without inquiring into the accuracy of the assertion, future writers have followed the same theory. The truth
is, Montrose and Salork seem to have been two totally different, though contiguous places, and the earliest charter evidence
of both shows that Malcolm IV. gave at one and the same time
certain tithes out of both districts to the Priory of Restenneth ;
as also that Salork had a church of its own, and that Montrose
was even then a considerable place, and had some trade.

The next and apparently the only other notice of Salork
occurs in the time of King William I. It is given in the very
same order as in the charter of Malcolm IV., and in enumerating
the grants to Restenneth, both of these charters say that the
abbot and canons shall have " 10s. out of Kinnaber, the whole
teinds of the king's rent of Salork, and 20s. for the light of the
church of Salork itself, as also the teinds of the king's rents of
Montrose and Rossy." [2] No such place as *Salork* is now known
in the neighbourhood of Montrose, but, from the position which
the name has in both of these charters—between Kinnaber

---

[1] Holinshed, *Scot. Chron.* p. 304.

[2] . . . . "x solidos de Kyneber, et totam decimam firme mee de Salorch. Et
xx solidos ad lumen ipsius Eccl. de eadem Salorch. Et decimam firme me de Munros
et de Rossin.—*Orig. in Saltoun Charter Chest, copy in Miscell. Aldbar ;* Fraser, *Hist.
Carnegies of Southesk,* i. pp. xi, xii ; ii. pp. 475, 533. Mr. Fraser discusses the
Salork or Salorch question, and prefers to regard the name as a territorial designation
for " probably the peninsular tract to the east of the Basin."

and Montrose—one is led to the belief that the well-known lands and hamlet, now called *Tayock* (the situation of which tallies with that of Salork in the charters), is a corruption of the ancient name Salork.

A charter in the archives of the burgh, which, if not altogether of doubtful character, bears greater evidence of the time of King David II. than that of David I. to whom it is commonly attributed, describes the lands of Salork as "lying and situated nigh to the haven of Stronnay towards the south, measuring in extent four carucates of land and a half," or as much as four and a half teams could plough in one year. But the site of the harbour or haven of Stronnay is now unknown, although so late as the fifteenth century the collectors of customs refer to ships having been freighted there.[1]   Perhaps, since *Stron-i*, signifies "the nose or projecting part of an island," it may refer to some point of the Island of Inchbrayock, which is situated in the middle of the South Esk, immediately south of the Forthill and town of Montrose. That island, separated from Montrose only by an arm of the river, and joined to the town by the suspension bridge, now forms part of the parish of Craig, but in old times was an independent cure, the church, dedicated in honour of St. Braoch, giving name to the district.[2]

It ought to be mentioned, however, that the Island of St. Braoch is rather more than a mile to the south-east of Tayock, the supposed site of the ancient Salork; and that tradition (relying perhaps upon certain points in Slezer's view of the town) says there was a jetty or harbour in the Basin of the South Esk, near the Forthill. Such may have been the case; but the long piled erection shown in that engraving, as stretching across the Basin from the back of the Forthill, is clearly the

[1] *Chamb. Rolls*, iii. p. 222.

[2] *Reg. Vet. Aberbr.* p. 339.   A curiously sculptured stone monument, now preserved at the parish kirk of Craig, is figured in the *Sculp. Stones of Scot.*, ii. p. 2, and plate ii.   There was another sculptured stone found in the churchyard of Inchbrayock in 1832 ; it is now in the Montrose Museum. The same magnificent volume also contains some conjectures regarding St. Braoch.

Drainer's or *Dronner's Dyke,* which was erected shortly before
Captain Slezer visited Montrose. That dike was raised with a
view to the draining and making arable of about two thousand
acres of the Basin. This extent belonged in property to
Erskine of Dun, but he disposed of it to certain persons who
formed themselves into a copartnery, of which the Earl of
Kinghorn was one. Unfortunately, however, the speculation
turned out to be unsuccessful, for "the embankment had
been scarcely accomplished when, by a sudden storm, it was
thrown down," and in consequence several of the projectors
were rendered bankrupt.[1] At low tides the Drainer's Dyke
still continues to be partially visible, though the North British
Railway Company's line along the edge of the Basin has been
built across one end of it. So far as relates to the beauty of
the Basin, the destruction of the dike need cause no regret,
as this tidal lake forms, particularly at full tides, one of the
grandest natural objects of which any town in the kingdom
can boast, being a fine sheet of water, nearly circular, and
about two miles in diameter.

Apart from the Basin, the leading topographical features
of *Munros,* now Montrose, were three hills, called respectively the Fort, the Horologe, and Windmill hills, but these
have all now given way to the improvements of modern times.
The town stands between the North and South Esk rivers, upon
a tongue of land bounded on the south and west by the last
named of these streams, and by the German Ocean on the east;
and as the Gaelic word *ros,* signifies "the point or promontory
between two waters," whether that point be high or low, and
moine, "a bog or moss," the name most likely signifies the
"bog of the promontory or peninsula." The first is the more
frequent rendering, and had on the whole, perhaps, been
appropriate to the site of the town. So also it had been
to the nearly adjacent lands of Ald or Old Montrose, the true

---

[1] (1670) *Extr. from the Pleadings of J. Erskine of Dun in the Stake-net Case,*
in possession of the late Adam Burnes, Esq., writer, Montrose; *Old Stat. Acct.* v.
p. 26; Headrick, *Agriculture of Angus,* pp. 88 sq.

etymology of which is perhaps *Alt-moine-ros*—"the burn of the mossy point "—for a rivulet, known as the burn of Ald Montrose, traverses that estate, and falls into the Basin of the South Esk a little to the south-east of the mansion-house.[1] The transition from the Gaelic *Ald* or *Alt* to the Scottish " Auld," and the English " Old," is easy and natural, and may account for the fable of the town of Montrose having been situated at that place before the rise of the present burgh.

As already mentioned, Montrose is said to have been a town in the tenth century, and it is alleged that the inhabitants were then massacred by the Danes, but we know at least with some certainty that in the time of Malcolm IV. it possessed both mills and salt-pans. In 1244 the town was consumed by accidental fire ;[2] and the learned Camden, who follows Boece in this theory of *Celurca* being the original name of Montrose, perhaps alludes to this conflagration when he says "the town is built out of the ruins of another of the same name."[3]

Although the period of its erection into a burgh of royalty is unknown, it had burgesses in 1261-2 ; and in 1296, a bailie and several burgesses, as previously stated, did homage to King Edward. Like many other royal burghs of doubtful origin, its creation is attributed to the time of King David I.; but that could hardly have been, since the earliest charters to burghs in Scotland were not granted until the time of King William the Lion. And even these were not charters, properly so called, but merely protective writings, confirming to communities certain privileges held under the superiority of the king, and the inhabitants were consequently called *burgenses regis*.[4] It ought also to be borne in mind that such towns as possessed a royal residence were called King's burghs,

---

[1] Fraser, *Lect. on Maryton*, p. 8, suggests for Old Montrose *Alt-mona-rois*, " the burn from the den on the hill." As " Old " is probably the Gaelic " alt," and has no reference to age, it is a curious question as to what was the connection between the two, and which was the original " Mona-rois " or " Moine-ros."

[2] Hailes, *Annals*, i. p. 332.   [3] Camden, *Britannia*, iii. pp. 402-3.

[4] Chalmers, *Caled.* i. pp. 779 sq.

and Montrose was one of these from at least the time of King
William.

In later times, when it was found necessary to grant *bona
fide* charters to burghs, they were generally confirmations of
the privileges set forth in the writs of earlier monarchs, and
frequently contained certain additions, proportionate to the
importance of the place.   Of this sort the doubtful charter
of Montrose, just alluded to, may be taken as an example.
After confirming to the burgesses the prior grant of "the
whole lands of Salork," which were to be held for ever by
them in "free burgh," the charter not only narrates that they
shall have "all the rights of buying and selling lawfully per-
taining to the business and office of burgesses and merchants,"
but it also describes the boundaries of their trading privileges
as extending "from the water of Thawhoke as far as Findoune,
and from Findoune through the north parts as far as the
water of Carudy, and so descending through the south part as
far as the water of Deychty, as it runs in Drumtay." [1]

During the year 1369, King David II. was himself in
Montrose on two different occasions, in the months of October
and December respectively. [2]   But in 1352 (according to the
charter just cited), he had already confirmed the reputed
grants of King David I.   It is further evident that, in the
course of the year 1369, he granted certain privileges to the
burgesses, consisting of cruive and net fishings in the North
and South Esks, common pasturages, and a right to mill mul-
tures, and customs, etc.[3]   And these were confirmed and ratified
by subsequent kings, but no mention is made by them of the
charter of 1352, or of any such grants as those attributed to
King David I.   There had been older undoubted grants to
Montrose than that of 1369, although these are now lost, for
even in 1357 the town was in such a flourishing condition
that John Clark, then alderman of the town, was chosen as
one of the hostages for the ransom of King David, and it had

[1] *Charter in Panmure Miscel. MS.* i. 5.   [2] *Reg. Mag. Sig.* p. 70.   [3] *Ib.* p. 66.

at that time the middle position among the seventeen chief burghs of the kingdom.[1] In a Parliament, held ten years later, it was represented by two burgesses, being the same number as was allowed to Edinburgh, Aberdeen, and other principal towns.[2]

A great part of the early trade of Montrose had consisted in shipments, for which it was rather famous from an early date, although the common notion of its having been the port from which the Good Sir James Douglas set sail for the Holy Land with the heart of The Bruce, is contrary to the averments of some of our best historians.[3] It is pretty clear, however, that Sir William Wallace landed there in 1303, when solicited to return from France to oppose the haughty arms of King Edward ; and, as illustrating rather an important point in the life of the Great Patriot, and as being locally interesting from the allusions made to certain persons and places of the county, the passage, which sets forth that fact, is here given in full in the quaint language of the poet :—

> " Na ma with him he brocht off that cuntré,
> Bot his awn men, and Schyr Thomas the knycht.
> In Flawndrys land thai past with all thar mycht.
> Guthreis barg was at the Slus left styll ;
> To se thai went wyth ane full egyr wyll.
> Bath Forth and Tay thai left and passyt by
> On the north cost, [gud] Guthré was thar gy.
> In *Munross hawyn* thai brocht hym to the land ;
> Till trew Scottis it was a blyth tithand.
> Schyr Jhon Ramsay, that worthi was and wycht,
> Fra Ochtyrhouss the way he chesyt rycht,
> To meite Wallace with men off armes strang ;
> Off his duellyng thai had thocht wondyr lang.

---

[1] *Acta Parl.* i. p. 157.

[2] Tytler, *Hist. of Scot.* ii. p. 470. It appears that in modern times *female* burgesses were recognised at Montrose, for, on 7th Dec. 1751, there were approved of as burgesses, made with others on the 5th Dec., " The Rt. Hon. Alexander, Lord Falconer of Halkertown ; the Hon. Mr. George Falconer, his brother-german ; the Hon. Mrs. Jean Falconer (Lady Mountain), the Hon. Mrs. Mary Falconer, and Mrs. Marjory Falconer, lawful daughters of the deceased David, Lord Falconer of Halkertown ; James Falconer of Mountain, Esquire ;" etc.

[3] Barbour, *Brus*, p. 478.

The trew Ruwan come als with outyn baid ;
In Barnan wod he had his lugying maid.
Barklay be that to Wallace semblyt fast ;
With thre hundreth to Ochtyrhouss he past." [1]

The shore-dues and customs of the harbour of Montrose,
excepting such portions as were granted to Lindsay, Duke of
Montrose, and enjoyed or given away by his successors, were
collected on behalf of the king until the early part of the
reign of James IV., when the magistrates had the power of
levying the same, with anchorage and other payments for the
maintenance of the harbour—exactions which King Charles
II. permitted to be doubled.   King James VI. also allowed
them to tax liquors " brewen and vented" in the burgh, to
assist in building and repairing the harbour ; and, at a prior
date, the same king, in renewing certain privileges, gave the
town an annuity from the lands which had belonged to the
Carmelite Friars at Inverbervie.[2]

As before remarked, the town and port of Montrose had
the honour of giving the title of Duke to David Lindsay, fifth
Earl of Crawford, and along with that dignity he had a confirmation of a grant, which the family had previously enjoyed,
out of the great customs of the burgh, together with another
gift of the smaller customs ; and he also assumed the armorial
bearings of the town as a part of his coat-of-arms.   At that
time the town possessed considerable powers, having the
privilege or jurisdiction of a sheriffdom or county, and, although
the customs were of little intrinsic value to the Duke, they
were essential to his retaining the title, as it was a feudal
custom to create titles by a grant of land or other heritable
rights.[3]

The trading boundaries of Montrose, as set forth in the
reputed charter of King David I., appear to have been afterwards curtailed ; for in 1641 the Earl Marischal had a tack

[1] Blind Harry, *The Wallace*, p. 243.
[2] *Acta Parl.* iii. p. 504 ; vii. *App.* p. 84 ; x. p. 145.
[3] *Reg. Mag. Sig.* p. 223 ; *Report on Montrose Claim*, p. 512, and Suppl. Case,
p. 180.

from the king of "the customs of all portis, harberies, and creikis alonge the coiste syde frae the North Watter of the towne of Montrose to the watter mouth of Spey," and during the same year Erskine of Dun had also a tack of the customs of the "port and burgh of Muntrois and vthir portis, herberies and creiks along the coast syde" from the North to the South Esk.[1] But long prior to this, the Erskines had a tack of the customs from David, eighth Earl of Crawford, who inherited them through his uncle, the Duke of Montrose. The Earl granted a precept of infeftment to Dun and his heirs in 1525,[2] and of this right the charter above mentioned seems to be a confirmation, the Erskines having previously obtained that right, along with the constabulary of the burgh, by purchase about the time that the fortunes of the Lindsays began to decline.[3]

Apart from the old weekly markets of Montrose, for the advancement of which the "Staplehand" Markets at Brechin and Fordoun were inhibited by King David II.,[4] the principal annual fair was held upon the Rood Day (the third of May), from which it had the name of *Ruidfair*;[5] and upon petition of the magistrates another market was granted to be held within the burgh in the month of July, and it was to "continue for the space of ffour dayes yearly." A weekly market was also allowed "upon ilk Thursday" from October to December "for selling and buying of horse, nolt, sheep, and all manner of cattle yearlie," and of that the magistrates had power to uplift the customs, etc.[6] But all these fairs, excepting a weekly market which is held upon Friday, are now abolished,

---

[1] *Acta Parl.* v. pp. 565, 592.

[2] *Miscell. Spalding Club,* iv. p. 22; and again, in 1541, Earl David granted to Erskine of Dun 40 merks out of the great customs of Montrose, and 15 merks out of those of Aberdeen.—*Ib.* iv. p. 37.

[3] Sir Thomas Erskine, Knight, had a charter of the Constabulary of Montrose from James V., dated 6th Nov. 1541 (*Miscell. Sp. Club,* iv. p. 38), calling him "Noster Thomas Erskin de Brechin." He conveyed it by charter, dated 19th Feb. 1541, to his nephew John Erskine, the laird of Dun, in liferent, and to his son and heir-apparent John Erskine in fee.—*Ib.* iv. p. 40, cf. xii.; Jervise, *Land of the Lindsays,* p. 142.

[4] *Reg. Ep. Brechin.* ii. p. 380.

[5] This fair is celebrated in Smart's *Rambling Rhymes,* p. 90. See also George Beattie's humorous poem of *John o' Arnha'.*   [6] *Acta Parl.* vii. p. 443.

and the chief markets of the year are those at Martinmas and Whitsunday, when the hiring of farm servants, male and female, is the principal business of the day.[1]

SECTION IV.

This above all,—to thine own self be true ;
And it must follow, as the night the day,
Thou canst not then be false to any man.

SHAKESPEARE, *Hamlet.*

Montrose in the 17th Century—Arthur Johnston's Epigram—Modern Improvements —Increase of Trade—Town Hall—Charitable Grants—Infirmary—Lunatic Asylum—North Water Bridge—Suspension Bridge, etc.

ABOUT the time that Parliament allowed the fairs, which have just been referred to, to be established, Montrose was, as it still is, rather a pretty town; and, with the exception of Dundee, it was the largest and most important in the county. Mr. Ochterlony, who gives the earliest account of it, describes it as " a very handsome well-built toune, of considerable trade in all places abroad; good houses all of stone, excellent large streets, a good tolbuith and church, good shipping of their own, a good shore at the toune, a myle within the river of South Esk; but the entrie is very dangerous for strangers that know it not, by reason of a great bank of sand that lyeth before the mouth of the entrie, called Long Ennell, but that defect is supplied by getting pilots from the neighbouring fisher-towns of Ulishavene and Ferredene, who know it so well that they cannot mistake. It is a very cheap place of all things necessary except house rent, which is dear, by reason of the great distance they are from stones, and makes their building very dear; yet, notwithstanding, they are constantly building both in the toune, and suburbs, which are at a considerable distance from the toune, in the Links, where are their malthouses, and kills, and granaries for cornes, of thrie storeys high, and some more, and are increased to such a number, that in a short tyme it is

[1] *Forf. Illust.* pp. 120 sq.

thought they will equall, if not exceed, the toune in greatness. They are well appointed of flesches and fishes, which are extraordinare cheap in that place, and have them in great abundance of all sorts. They have a good public revenue, two wind-milnes, ane hospitale, with some mortificationes belonging to it; they are mighty fyne burgesses, and delicate and painful merchants. There have been men of great substance in that toune of a long time, and yet are, who have and are purchasing good estates in the countrey. The generalitie of the burgesses and merchants do very far exceed these in any other toune in the shyre."[1]

The more celebrated Daniel de Foe, who made a tour through Great Britain in the beginning of the eighteenth century, speaks in much the same terms of the town and the inhabitants as Ochterlony. It "is a pretty sea-port town," he says, "and one street very good; the houses well built, and the town well pav'd: The inhabitants here, as at Dundee, are very genteel, and have more the air of gentlemen than merchants."

Prior to the date of either of these notices, however, Montrose had its praises heralded in Latin verse by John and Dr. Arthur Johnston, both of whom follow Boece in reference to the ancient name Celurca, and begin by calling the town " the Mount of Roses," in allusion to the popular notion that the name was assumed from the Latin *Mons Rosarum*. The Links or common, alluded to in Arthur Johnston's Epigram (of which an old quaint translation is given below), is one of the finest in the kingdom, and the ancient exercise of the bow noticed by him, for which new butts were erected at the expense of the town about the beginning of last century,[2] was lately revived, the corporation of the burgh having, in 1850, presented a fine silver arrow, of the value of ten guineas, to

[1] *Spot. Miscell.* i. p. 383. Monipennie (1612) says, "Montrosse; a commodious harborough for shipping; this toune is all builded with stone, and populous, abundant with all kinde of fishes."—*Miscell. Scot.* i. p. 163.

[2] *Burgh Records*, 1704.

the Royal Company of Archers of Scotland. This arrow has
been four times shot for upon the Links, the last occasion being
on 21st July 1882; but the old butts have long since disappeared. The amusements of bowling and golf, particularly the
latter, are carried on with great spirit, as are likewise cricket,
curling, and football; for the practice of all these delightful
recreations the Links are well adapted. In Montrose there are
two Rifle Volunteer Companies and one Battery of Artillery
Volunteers. A splendid practice range for rifle-shooting is
provided on the Links, and at the annual gathering in August
of the Angus and Mearns Rifle Association, the concourse of
competitors from all parts of Scotland is very great.

> "The Noble Town from ROSIE-MOUNT doth claim
> Its Present, as from Heaven its Ancient Name :
> Near it 's a hill by which a river glydes,
> Both which to it Delicious Fare provyds :
> The Hill doth Flocks, Salmon the Flood brings forth,
> Or what in Nero's Ponds was of more worth.
> The Lillies on the Banks refresh the night,
> The Roses on the Hills afford delight.
> Towards the East the Seas themselves do spread,
> Which with a thousand Ships are covered.
> A large Field by the Sea is stretched forth,
> Begirt with waters both at South and North.
> Some Youths train Horses here, some use the Bow,
> And some their Strength in rolling Great Stons shew,
> Some Wrestle, some at Pennie-stones do play,
> The rolling Balls with Clubs some drive away.
> Should Jove or Venus view this Town, sure He
> His Capitoll, Her Ida leave would She."[1]

In equally laudatory, but more lucid terms, although in the
less attractive style of prose, Montrose is called " a beauty
that lies concealed, as it were, in the bosom of Scotland ; most
delicately dressed up, and adorned with excellent buildings,
whose foundations are laid with polished stone, and her ports
all washed with silver streams, that trickle down from the
famous Ask"! So wrote the pedantic Captain Franck in
1657-8.[2] But according to popular story these laudatory

---

[1] APPENDIX No. VII. (B).   [2] *Northern Memoirs*, p. 233.

effusions will be of little avail in preserving the town of Montrose, for, as will be seen by the following verse, which is a reputed prophecy of Sir Thomas the Rhymer, it is doomed to destruction, like the more opulent town of Dundee, while the lesser burghs of Brechin and Forfar are prophesied to survive and flourish, when every vestige of the first two are swept away !—

> " Bonny Munross will be a moss,
>   When Brechin 's a borough town ;
> An' Forfar will be Forfar still,
>   When Dundee 's a' dung down ! "

But to return, the *shore* of Ochterlony's time was of wood, and it so remained until about the middle of last century, when the present " old stone port " was erected. This was a great work for the period, and extended from the bridge along the north side of the river, a distance of about 650 feet.

The harbour accommodation was afterwards much enlarged and improved by the addition of the wet dock, and recently the removal of the lower end of the Scaup, a bank of gravel and stones nearly opposite the dock entrance, has still further increased the convenience and safety of the port for large vessels, which can now be moored afloat there at all states of the tide, the depth of water at the lowest springs being not less than 25 feet. At the present date a new low-water wharf and other works, completing the quay wall from the Suspension Bridge to the protection wall at the wet dock, are in course of construction, and will afford very great facilities for the general trade of the port, but more especially for the fishing traffic, which has increased very rapidly of late years. The Scurdyness Lighthouse, built under the authority of the Board of Trade in 1870, at a cost of £2700, should also be mentioned among recent improvements, as, besides its being the only light between Aberdeen and the Bell Rock, and therefore of the utmost consequence to vessels approaching or passing this dangerous coast, it is of the greatest service to vessels making for Montrose.

Although the burgh of Montrose has less claim now-a-days to the high rank assigned to it among the other burghs of the county, than it had either in Ochterlony or De Foe's time, the population of the town is more than threefold, and the shipping has much more than doubled in tonnage, since 1790.[1]

Of late years however, the shipping belonging to the port has, in common with that of other places, considerably decreased, but the general trade of the harbour, as indicated by the revenue collected, has not fallen off. Since the introduction of iron and steel, instead of wood, for the building of ships, that industry has almost entirely disappeared, though boat-building is still carried on vigorously. On the other hand, flax-spinning, which may be considered the staple trade of the town, and the export of grain, have very much increased, while the harbour has become one of the most important on the east coast of Scotland for the importation of timber, the manufacture of which has also been very much extended. The main line of the North British Railway from Aberdeen to the south, which now passes through the town, has greatly improved the means of communication with other places, of which the Caledonian Railway Company had formerly the monopoly; and the competition of the two companies, tending to reduced rates and greater facilities for traffic of every sort, is a substantial advantage.

If the town was worthy of commendation in old times for its buildings and general appearance, it is more so now, the want of water—one of the greatest drawbacks upon domestic comfort—having been completely overcome;[2] and, as it was in the time of Ochterlony, so is it still the resort of families of independent means. Burns the poet, who there visited his cousin, Mr. Burnes, in 1787, calls it " a finely situated handsome

---

[1] In 1790 the population of the town was reckoned at 5194, and in 1881 at 16,280. In 1790, at Montrose and Ferryden there were 53 ships, of 3543 tonnage; and in 1884, there were 42 vessels, with 9245 tonnage.—*Old Stat. Acct.* v. pp. 31-2, 39; *Edinb. Almanac*, Angus and Mearns Supplement.

[2] Water was first brought from Glenskenno to the town in 1741, at a cost of £1300.—*Burgh Records.* The original works for the present supply, from the

town ;" and the broad High Street, which lately contained a
number of old-fashioned houses, with picturesque wooden gables
projecting towards the street, such as are yet to be seen in
many parts of England, now displays a series of substantial
dwelling-houses and shops, elegant in design beyond those of
most provincial towns.   The erection of these wooden-gabled
houses was prohibited in 1739,[1] and the few remaining
examples are now to be met with in Castle Street ; of late
several of them in that street have been removed, and those
remaining are very few indeed.   One stone house, on the north
side of Castle street, with the legend [D]OMINVS · PROVIDE[BIT]
upon the lintel of one of the upper windows, is perhaps the
oldest house in town.   There is another old house, at the top
of Bridge Street, with monograms over the windows and the
date 1688.   A few years ago there was also an old door-lintel
in Apple Wynd, but the date and letters which it bore are
said to have been effaced, as the proprietor " couldna be
bothered wi' *queer folk* gaun to look at them " !

The " good tolbuith," spoken of by Guynd, which stood in
the middle and south end of the High Street, is now removed,
and the site occupied with good effect by a fine colossal statue
of Sir Robert Peel.   In the High Street there is a statue of
Joseph Hume.   The Town Hall, a large building of three stories,
with arcade below and balustrade round the top, and decorated
in front with the armorial bearings of the burgh,[2] is a handsome fabric, projecting into the street.   The Council Chamber
is adorned by some good portraits, the best of which are that
of the late Joseph Hume, a full length of Sir James Duke,
robed as Lord Mayor of London and presented by him to his
native town, and that of the Rev. Dr. Paterson, who was for so
many years minister of the second charge.

Haughs of Kinnaber, on the North Esk, which is calculated to be sufficient for
all the domestic and commercial wants of the town, cost about £8800.

[1] *Burgh Records.*

[2] On a shield argent, a rose seeded and barbed; supporters, two mermaids proper ;
crest, a sinister hand issuing out of clouds, holding a branch of laurel ; Motto, MARE
DITAT, ROSA DECORAT.

It ought also to be remarked that Montrose contains a museum of natural and antiquarian curiosities—perhaps one of the best in the provinces. It originated in 1836, and the collection was formerly contained in a room of the public schools, on the site of the present building, to which it was transferred in 1843, on the birthday of the Society's president, Lord Panmure. There are also two public libraries, the principal one containing a large and valuable collection of books, which number about 20,000 volumes in all classes of literature. Besides these facilities for intellectual improvement, few towns of a like size have so many charitable institutions, or so large an amount for benefactions to the poor. Mortifications to the number of twenty-two, and amounting to more than £20,000, have been given by natives and others connected with the town since the middle of last century, and the whole is applied for educational purposes and for alleviating the wants of the distressed.

Dorward's Seminary and House of Refuge were founded and liberally endowed by a late wealthy merchant of that name, for the education and protection of orphan children, as well as for an asylum for aged men and women. The Infirmary and Lunatic Asylum were reared by public subscription, and for a number of years the two institutions were wrought in combination; but in 1838 the foundation of a new Infirmary and Dispensary, which are found of very great benefit to the town, was laid. The Lunatic Asylum, which has long been considered one of the best conducted in the kingdom (founded in 1779, and incorporated by royal charter in 1810), was the first of the sort in Scotland, and owed its origin to the gentle feeling and spirited enterprise of the late Mrs. Carnegy of Pitarrow. The building near the Dock, formerly used as the Asylum, has been acquired for the dépôt of the Forfar and Kincardine Militia Artillery, and a new asylum, on the most approved principles, was erected at Sunnyside in 1855, at a cost of about £35,000. Since that time it has been extensively enlarged, so as to be now capable of receiving about 500 patients.

It is finely situated on the rising ground to the north of Dubton Station, and commands an extensive view of "flood and field." Though at a distance of five miles from Montrose, the Rossie Reformatory ought to be mentioned among the institutions of the place. It owes its origin to Colonel Macdonald of St. Martin's, for some time proprietor of Rossie, and has proved of very great benefit to the county.[1]

Of recent years the Mid Links has been laid out in an ornamental manner as public gardens, and this improvement adds very greatly to the amenity of the locality. But of all the improvements connected with Montrose, next to the formation of the railways, the bridges across the North and the South Esk, which were previously crossed by boats, must be reckoned as those of the greatest public utility. The former, a fine stone bridge of eight arches, projected by Thomas Christie, Provost of Montrose, a gentleman of shrewd business habits and of a literary taste, was finished in 1775, after a lapse of five years, and while his son was chief magistrate.[2]

In consequence of the island of Inchbrayock being in the middle of the South Esk, the river is there separated into two channels, the more northerly being about 430 feet wide, while the southern is barely 90. Towards the close of last century a wooden bridge was erected over the northern course of the river, but within thirty years it was deemed unsafe, as the water threatened to sweep away the piers. When a suspension bridge had been resolved upon, the foundation stone was laid in September 1828, and the whole completed in December 1829, at a cost of £20,000, but the accidents afterwards caused an additional outlay of £12,000. It was designed by Captain Samuel Brown, R.N., and is one of the finest structures of the sort anywhere to be seen. Unfortunately, it received severe damage on two different occasions, and both these accidents occurred in the year 1838. The first was caused by a crowd of persons, who had assembled to witness a boat race, making a

---

[1] See APPENDIX No. XII.   [2] Jervise, *Epit.* i. p. 43.

sudden rush to the east side of the bridge, when one of the upper chains gave way. When this fell upon the lower one, several individuals were caught between the chains and killed upon the spot. The bridge was soon repaired, but upon the 11th of October following, a fearful gale of wind tore up and destroyed about two-thirds of the roadway and iron work. The principal chains being fortunately uninjured at that time, the damage was soon repaired, and a roadway was formed on a new and more approved principle.[1]

On the erection of the suspension bridge, the arch of the stone bridge across the southern or narrow channel of the Esk was removed, and supplanted by a drawbridge, that by this means vessels might be allowed to pass up and down the Basin to a small port at Ald Montrose, where at one time goods were frequently shipped and delivered ; but even before the introduction of the railway that harbour was very rarely used, and the drawbridge has not been raised for fully forty years.

SECTION V.

I have seen the robes of Hermes glisten—
Seen him wave afar his serpent wand :
But to me the Herald would not listen—
When the dead swept by at his command.

AYTOUN, *Hermotimus.*

Feuds between the Inhabitants and the Erskines of Dun—a Priest killed in the Bell Tower—reconciliation of John Erskine with the inhabitants—His defence of the Town against the English—General Assembly at Montrose—Andrew Melville— Wars of the Covenant—Town invaded by Irvine of Drum—Dun plundered by the Marquis of Montrose—Chevalier de St. George embarks for France—Rebels of 1745 possess Montrose—Captain Ferrier captures the *Hazard* Sloop-of-war —Admiral Byng sinks a French Ship at the Ennet—Visit of the Duke of Cumberland.

THE close proximity of Dun to the town of Montrose naturally brought the Erskines and the inhabitants into close and frequent contact, and the Constabulary of the burgh ultimately became vested in that family. Calderwood and others say

---

[1] See the local newspapers of that period.

that the Erskines were Provosts of Montrose in old times, and also represented the county of Forfar in Parliament. Upon what authority this statement was made cannot be discovered, no trace of the family in either capacity being found in the public records. The only foundation seems to be that, in 1569, "Dominus Dun pro Montrose" appears in the Parliament held at Edinburgh on the 17th of November of that year.[1]

It is certain that the family were no favourites at Montrose towards the close of the fifteenth century, for the laird of that period and the inhabitants were at open war. The cause was one of no uncommon character. In 1491-2, the younger Erskine, as tutor for his relative, Henry Graham of Morphie, had taken possession of certain cruives and fishings in the North Esk against the will of the magistrates. When they carried the affair to a court of law, and the case went to proof, Erskine was declared to have done "na wrang," and so he kept possession of the property.[2]

It was in the month of June 1493 that young Dun obtained this decision in his favour, and, almost immediately afterwards, he began upon the inhabitants a series of reprisals, which afford a striking picture of the rude character of the time. He had previously rendered himself so obnoxious to the officials of the burgh, that Stirling and Scott—two of the chief citizens— procured letters of lawburrows against him, whereby they " sal be harmles and scatheles of him, vnder the pain of two hundred pounds."[3] But heedless of the law and emboldened by gaining the suit over the people of Montrose, young Erskine, accompanied by his father, his three brothers, and several followers, resumed his work of spoliation and insult, and, as it is quaintly described in the complaint of the citizens of Montrose, he destroyed " ande ete all oure corne that grew apone our comone lande, and this beande done onder cilence of nycht, come bodyn with speris and bovis to youre saide

---

[1] *Acta Parl.* iii. p. 57.   [2] *Acta Dom. Con.* pp. 278-9.

[3] *Acta Aud.* p. 161. George Stirling is the first-named commissioner to the Parliament for the burgh of Montrose, March 11, 1503.—*Acta Parl.* ii. p. 239.

burgh, and bostit [threatened] oure alderman, he beande in his
bed, sayand thai suld pul done his houss abuf his hede."[1]

The alderman and burgesses, however, preferred their beds
to an unequal trial of strength, and the marauders quietly
returned home. Still, "dayley ande nychtly," they invaded
the town, looking "quare thai may get vs at opin to stryk vs
done ;" and on St. Ninian's day [16th September] of the same
year the Erskines attacked "oure fyschars, thier wyffis, and
seruandis gaderynde thair bate to thir lynis, ande spuylzeit
thaim of thair claithis."[2]

A messenger was despatched with a complaint regarding
these oppressive proceedings, to Lindsay, Duke of Montrose ;
but the messenger, while on his way to the Duke, was overtaken and slain by the Erskines, and another party, under
an escort of armed men, was sent to the king at Stirling.
The petition had the desired effect, and the defenders were
summoned to appear at the next Justice-air at Dundee, under
certain pains and penalties, but the result is not recorded.

These outrages upon the inhabitants of Montrose, if they
are to be judged of by the decision given in the first case, may
be excused in some measure by the inconsiderate action of the
magistrates. But a fresh source of irritation soon arose on the
other side, when an act of a most sacrilegious nature was perpe-
trated within the precincts of the parish church by the future
Superintendent himself, who, in early life, appears to have
exhibited much of the proud domineering spirit of his ancestors.
The details, however, of the sad occurrence, which, until lately,
formed an unknown incident in the character of Erskine, are
uncertain. It only appears that, out of revenge or in the heat
of passion, he killed Sir Thomas Froster, a priest of Montrose,
within the *campanile* or bell tower of that place ; and in consequence, according to the fashion of the period, he granted a

---

[1] " Walter Ogilby, alderman of Montrose, and Maister George Sterueling, procurators of the toun of Montrose," etc.—*Acta Dom. Con.* p. 355.

[2] Bowick, *Life of Erskine*, p. 144 ; Wodrow, *Biog. Coll.* pp. 422-25.

bond of assythement or blood-money for the offence, to Froster's father, who was a burgess of the town.[1] Erskine was little beyond twenty years of age at the time when this unfortunate affair occurred, and perhaps it may have had some effect in bringing about the change which took place in his religious views and future life. As to whether or not he had been doomed to undergo a penance for the crime by the Church of Rome, and had thereby taken a distaste to her principles, it is matter of conjecture ; but it is certain that soon after the murder he left Scotland for the Continent, and that upon returning, in the course of three or four years, he began to show favour for Church reform, and, as already mentioned, brought along with him a teacher of the Greek language whom he settled and maintained at Montrose.

From that time, the Erskines and the inhabitants seem to have continued good friends, so that Erskine in 1542 had a royal gift of the Constabulary of Montrose ; and in 1548, when the English attempted to land their fleet in the South Esk, he, at the head of a number of the inhabitants and others, vigorously defended the town, and prevented their landing. The loss to the enemy is variously stated at eight and five hundred, and the reader is referred to Buchanan for a detailed account of the transaction, he, it is supposed, having had the particulars from Erskine himself.[2]

Beyond the incidents already noticed relative to the Reformation, little of moment appears to have taken place in Montrose from the period just mentioned (if we except the capturing of the town by Gordon of Auchindoun in 1570, in behalf of Queen Mary), until the year 1600, when a General Assembly was held there, in presence of King James. This was an Assembly of considerable importance, as it was intended to decide the fate of Presbytery, and the presence

---

[1] *Miscell. Spalding Club*, iv. p. 27. See APPENDIX No. XIII.
[2] Buchanan, *Hist. of Scot.*, by Aikman, ii. 374 ; *Miscell. Spalding Club*, iv. pp. xii, 51.

of royalty was expected to strengthen the king in his wish to establish Prelacy, and place himself at the head of the Church in Scotland, as he already was by law in that of England. But the attempt failed, notwithstanding that some of the more influential of the clergy were appointed to vacant bishoprics.   Mr. James Melville, who was present at the Assembly, quaintly says that Mr. Blackburn, the Moderator, who had the see of Aberdeen, " delyverit verie guid doctrine befor noone, bot he was brought in effect to recant it at the efter noone befor the haill Assemblie, to the grait greiff of guid breithring, a grait stepe from a preceise honest Minister to a Bischope of this new strak, quhilk he becam the yeir efter."[1]

The defeat of the king's party was owing, in a great measure, to the power and influence of Andrew Melville, whom the king sharply rebuked for being present at the Assembly.   And perhaps no better picture of the independence and self-possession of a subject in the presence of a king exists in the annals of any country, than the stories related of Melville's conferences with King James, and more particularly the scene which occurred at Montrose upon this occasion.   The sturdy reformer, for Melville was then in the prime of life, was retiring from the presence of. the king, and in so doing he took himself by the throat, and replied —" Sir, tak yow this head, and gar cut it af, gif ye will ; ye sall sooner get it, or I betray the cause of Chryst !   And sa," continues his nephew, " he remeanit in the town all the whyll, and furnisit arguments to the Breithering, and mightilie strynthned and incuragit tham."[2]

King James, being at this time foiled in his wish, had no sooner ascended the English throne than he tried to gain his purpose in another way in Scotland, by having Melville, and some of the other leaders of the Church, removed to distant countries, under the pretence of having them employed in

---

[1] Melville, *Diary*, pp. 469, 537, 542.
[2] *Ibid.* pp. 485, 542.   Andrew Melville died at Sedan, in 1622, aged 77.

preaching the gospel.   Though these plans were partially successful, they were less so than the king could have wished, and,
notwithstanding his partiality for his fellow-countrymen, he
strained every nerve to have the Church subjected to his will.

It need hardly be said, that a desire to carry out these
arrogant measures was leading on to the sad consequences
which followed during the reign of his unfortunate son and
successor, King Charles I.[1]   The history of that important
period—eventful alike in the annals of Scotland and England
—is well known, and need not be here dwelt upon.   Suffice
it to say, that the vacillating conduct of the king was supposed to render it necessary to take strong measures to oppose
him, and a party, composed of the more influential noblemen,
barons, and burgesses of the kingdom, united themselves into
a body for the government and protection of the realm.   They
were commonly called Covenanters, more properly the Estates
of Parliament, and their army, which was large, was placed
under the chief command of the Marquis of Argyll and
General Leslie, while the royalists were latterly led by the
Marquis of Montrose and the Earl of Crawford.

In those important proceedings the town of Montrose bore
some little part.   A committee of the Covenanters met there
in 1639, when an abortive attempt was made by the royalists
to seize some pieces of ordnance which had been placed for
the defence of the town, and in the following year a ship
landed from Holland, carrying ammunition and arms for the
Covenanters.[2]   But it was not until the month of April 1644
that the town and its lieges were seriously endangered.   This
arose from a desire on the part of the royalists to obtain
possession of "tua brassin cartowis," or small cannon; and,
headed by young Irvine of Drum, about three hundred soldiers,
horse and foot, entered Montrose with sounding trumpets and

---

[1] For the dealings with the Roman Catholics, Covenanters, and Episcopalians
respectively, see Burton, *Crim. Trials*, ii. pass.

[2] Spalding, *Trubles*, i. pp. 148, 285.

drawn swords about two o'clock in the morning. The inhabitants, who had been apprised of the invasion, alarmed the neighbourhood by kindling fires upon the steeple and ringing the bells, whilst they themselves stood in arms. " But all was for nocht," as quaintly remarked by Spalding, and he further says that the royalists "dang the toune's people fra the calsey to thair houssis, and out of the foirstaires thay schot desperatlie, bot thay war forssit to yeild by many feirfull schotes schot aganes thame; quhair vnhappellie Alexander Peirsone, ane of thair balleis, wes slayne."

For a brief period Montrose was occupied by the royalists, but, fortunately for the town, an Aberdonian of the name of Burnet resided there, who, though " an anti-Covenanter," so far betrayed the cause as to allow the provost of the burgh and many others, with the " tua brassin cartowis," to be quietly taken on board the very ship which he promised to place at the service of the royalists. To this piece of treachery Drum and his friends were strangers, but upon nearing the shore, the deception became only too palpable ; for, instead of quietly stepping on board the vessel, as they expected to do, and getting possession of the cannon, the " schip schot fyve or six peice of ordinans disperatlie amongis thame, with about fourtie mvscattis, quhair by the gryte providens of God thair wes bot onlie tuo men killit, and sum hurt."

Drum now wreaked his vengeance upon the wheels of the cannon, by breaking them to pieces and throwing them into the water; and, returning to the town, the infuriated soldiers broke up and plundered the houses and shops of the more important merchants, and slaked their thirst from " a pype of Spanish wyne," which they " drank hartfullie." Having thus sacked the town, they carried off two of the principal citizens, whom, however, they afterwards released ;[1] and, leaving about two o'clock afternoon, they marched that night to Cortachy, in hopes of being received by the Earl of Airlie, but, when the

---

[1] Spalding, *Trubles*, ii. pp. 352, 360.

approach of the Marquis of Argyll was announced, they returned to Aberdeen.[1]

The inhabitants of Montrose, afraid of being again invaded by the enemy, had the more valuable of their goods removed to the house of Dun, as the laird was a friend to the Covenant. But when this fact became known to the Marquis of Montrose, as he marched from Atholl through Angus soon afterwards, he attacked and plundered Dun of its contents ; and among other things taken there were several fire-arms, and "four feild brassin peices" which the Covenanters had captured from the Marquis of Huntly at the affair of the Bridge of Dee in 1639.[2]

With the "Fifteen" Montrose had but a slight connection, which was mostly confined to the fact that the Chevalier de St. George, after a brief sojourn of six weeks in Scotland, stopped a night there, and re-embarked for France on the following evening. The house in which he spent the last night of his ill-fated pilgrimage to Scotland is long since removed, and a new one built on its site ; but the passage, through which the Prince and the Earl of Mar went by the garden of the house to the river where the vessel lay waiting, is still pointed out, and had been, in every respect, most fitting for the occasion.[3] Nor ought the fact to be omitted, that it was in this house, on the 4th of February 1716, while waiting an opportunity to escape to the vessel, that the Chevalier wrote his admirable letter to the Duke of Argyll, intimating that he had consigned a sum of money to certain magistrates, to be expended in repairing, to some extent, the loss which the country had sustained by the burning of several villages in the course of the rebellion.[4]

Although there would seem to us now to have been little hope of the Stuarts succeeding to the throne after this unfor-

---

[1] Spalding, *Trubles*, ii. pp. 347-8.   [2] *Ibid.* ii. p. 419.

[3] This house and garden, situated at the south end of the High Street, are now the property of the representatives of the late Mr. George Smart, corn-merchant. Amid much rebuilding, the passage has been preserved intact, and it is thought that some of the old castle walls are incorporated in the present house.

[4] This letter is printed in Chambers, *Hist. of the Rebellion*, p. 312.

tunate attempt, yet the King of France and their friends in
Britain at the time appear to have thought otherwise; and
accordingly in 1745, when the Chevalier's son, Prince Charles
Edward, had attained his twenty-fifth year, the question of
the Stuart succession was revived, with considerably more
talent and tact than that with which it had been pursued
upon the previous occasion.   But the evil day was at no
great distance, and the hopes derived from the transient success that attended the arms of the young Prince in the victories
of Prestonpans and Falkirk, were blasted for ever by the
defeat at Culloden.

The progress of Prince Charles in Scotland is so well
known that it were idle to trace it here.   Unlike that of his
father, which was a series of disappointments from the time
he landed in Scotland until the hour he left it, Charles's was
a mixture of sunshine and cloud—victorious one day, and defeated the next—holding levees in the Palace of Holyrood,
attended by all the pomp and equipage of royalty, and then
wandering a lonely outcast over trackless paths, clothed in the
meanest apparel, sleeping in desolate caves by the sea-shore,
and subsisting on the humblest fare.   Fortune, however, at last
favoured his escape to France, where the Stuarts ever found a
welcome and hospitable asylum in the many dangers and difficulties with which they had the misfortune to be surrounded.

Montrose at this time was made the headquarters of the
royalists.   From this position they had probably been driven
by the rebels, whose greatest strength and influence lay for
the most part in Angus, and who consequently selected this
town as their chief rendezvous.   The royalists, aware of the
favourable character of the position they had lost, attempted
to regain it, and for that purpose sent thither a sloop of war
called the *Hazard*, which was anchored in the river, opposite
the village of Ferryden.   That vessel mounted sixteen guns
and some swivels, and contained a crew of eighty men commanded by Captain Hill.

Prior to Prince Charles going into England, he had, through the solicitation of Captain Erskine of Dun, appointed David Ferrier (one of Lord Ogilvy's men) to be deputy-governor of the town of Brechin and the neighbourhood, a post for which Ferrier proved himself admirably well qualified, and which he faithfully maintained.[1] Aware that the *Hazard* sloop, which had kept up an occasional fire for three days and three nights, was sent chiefly to prevent his party from entering Montrose, he " formed the design of capturing the vessel by raising a battery at the entrance of the river, and thereby to prevent her getting out to sea. In pursuance of this plan he entered Montrose one night, and possessed himself of the island [Inchbrayock], on the south side of the town, opposite to where the *Hazard* lay. Next day the *Hazard* attempted to dislodge the party from the island by her fire, but without success. In the afternoon of the following day a vessel carrying French colours was observed at sea, standing in towards the river. This turned out to be a transport from France, with a party of Lord John Drummond's regiment, some Irish pickets, and six pieces of artillery. On observing this vessel, the *Hazard* fired a gun to leeward as a decoy ; but, upon a signal from the party on the island, the commander of the French vessel ran her on shore out of reach of the *Hazard's* guns. The crew then landed the six guns, and a fire was opened upon the *Hazard* next morning from both sides of the river, on each of which three of the pieces had been planted. With the exception, however, of having some of her rigging cut, she sustained no damage. Before the arrival of Ferrier's party, Captain Hill, the commander of the *Hazard*, had taken four six-pounders and two four-pounders, belonging to the town, and put them on board a vessel in the harbour ; but by oversight he left his vessel at the quay, and she fell into the hands of the insurgents. This circumstance was fatal to

---

[1] Ferrier, who is supposed to have died in Spain, was farmer of Unthank near Brechin, and a merchant in that town.—Jervise, *Land of the Lindsays*, pp. 68, 316.

the *Hazard ;* for, finding that the guns lately landed were not sufficient to force the *Hazard* to surrender, Captain Ferrier carried the four six-pounders to the *Dial-hill* [Horologe], and from this fired upon the *Hazard.* Her commander, seeing escape hopeless, hoisted a flag of truce, and after making an ineffectual attempt to obtain permission to leave the river, surrendered."[1]

The capture of this fine vessel, afterwards named the *Prince Charles,* was one of the best and most timely successes that could have attended the rebels, as they not only obtained possession of the ship and its valuable contents, but for some days were enabled to land troops with impunity. Admiral Byng, however, determined to cripple as far as possible the resources of the rebels, and to revenge the loss of the *Hazard.* He accordingly gave chase to a French gun-ship, which was descried near the river-mouth, and sunk her long-boat full of men, whose bodies were afterwards washed ashore ; yet, heedless of the loss thus sustained, the Roman Catholics are said to have quietly heard mass in the town on the same day that the disaster occurred.[2]

These transactions took place towards the close of the year 1745. In the month of May following, the Duke of Cumberland revisited the town, and found the spirit of Jacobitism reigning as strongly as before ; for, on the 10th of June (the Prince's birth-day), a contemporary Diarist says that "the Jacobite gentle-women in Montrose got on white gowns and white roses, and made a procession through the streets, where the young boys had put on bonfires." This the officers of the army considered an affront, but they overlooked the matter in consideration that the ladies were engaged in it. Cumberland, however, was less lenient, and had the commanding officer deprived of his post : he also threatened, "because the inhabitants are nourishing up their children to rebellion, to cause them to be whipped at the cross, to frighten them from their bonfires."

[1] Browne, *Hist. of the Highlands,* iii. p. 221. The statement of the Chevalier Johnstone, that the *Hazard* was boarded by the Highlanders, is erroneous.

[2] *Miscell. Spalding Club,* i. pp. 357-8, 360.   [3] *Ibid.* p. 397.

CHAPTER IV.

Castles of Kincardine, Glenbervie, and Durris.

SECTION I.

We love
The king who loves the law, respects his bounds,
And reigns content within them.

COWPER, *The Task.*

KINCARDINE AND FORDOUN.

Castle of Kincardine—Occupied by William I. and Alexander III.—Twice visited by
Edward I.—Scroll of Baliol's resignation prepared there—Murder of Kenneth
III.—Proprietary History of the Lands—Old Hostelry—Kincardine made the
County Town—Its Decline—St. Palladius—His Chapel—Town of Fordoun—
Dr. Beattie—Auchinblae—Glenfarquhar—Friars' Glen.

THE earliest authentic notices of the Castle of Kincardine
occur in the reigns of William I. and Alexander III., as they
both occasionally resided there.[1]   During the time of the
former of these monarchs, it was a place of considerable
importance, and to it were attached all the officers common to
a royal household of the period.   The remote progenitor of
the noble family of Kintore was chief falconer or hawksman,
and in virtue of this he held the lands of Hawkerstown in the
immediate neighbourhood, and adopted the name of *Falconer*.[2]
It is also told, but on no trustworthy authority, that an early
member of the noble house of Southesk was Constable of the
Castle, and for that service held certain lands in the barony
of Kincardine.[3]

[1] *Reg. Vet. Aberbr.* pp. 70, 95 ; *Chamberlain Rolls*, i. p. *19.   These *Rolls*
contain accounts of rents received from the lands of the royal manor of Kincardine
during the time of Alexander III., similar to, although not so considerable as those
of Forfar and Glamis.

[2] *Reg. Vet. Aberbr.* p. 100.   [3] Jervise, *Land of the Lindsays*, p. 238.

The only other traces of the ancient greatness of the
place are the names of adjacent fields, such as the King's and
Chancellor's Parks; the Chancellor's and the Dean's Crofts;
the Deer or Hunting Park; the Countess' Croft, and the
Earl's Inns, as also the Lorimer's, the Archer's, and the Palfrey-
man's Crofts.[1]   These names, it will be seen, differ from the
Duray, Bakehouse, Brewhouse, Gardener's, Hen, and other
Crofts, which, common in the vicinity of baronial establishments, are also to be found at Kincardine.   As, for the most
part, these places are described as marching with lands belonging to some of the more ancient and powerful lords of the
Mearns, the persons, from whom these names were derived,
may have filled, in connection with the Court, the offices
indicated by them.

The castle was picturesquely situated upon a natural hillock
in the gorge or opening of the valley descending from the
Cairn-o'-Mount, and on the east side of the parish of Fordoun.
Three sides of the castle were inhabited, and the chief entrance
was on the south-west, between two round towers.[2]   The sides
of the great fireplace of the hall, and the lower steps of a
staircase leading to an upper flat, were not long ago entire.
No part of the ruin now stands more than five or six feet high,
and the whole structure measures about a hundred and thirty
feet square.   There was also a narrow entrance towards the
north-east, on either side of which were two apartments, the
one about fourteen by fifty feet in size, and the other fourteen
by thirty-five feet.   Two apartments on the east side measure
respectively twenty-two by sixty feet, and twenty-two by
fourteen; the door of the former is quite visible.

Record and tradition are alike silent as to the time when
the castle became ruinous.   It was probably during the Wars

[1] For these significant old names, which occur in the charters of the Fettercairn
estates, the author was indebted to the kindness of the late Sir John Hepburn Stuart
Forbes, Bart.

[2] By the compass the line of the eastern wall is 30° west of south.   For a fuller
account of the castle, see Jervise, *Land of the Lindsays*, p. 394, and *Appendix*
No. xvi. there.

of the Independence, or at least soon after King David's visit in 1383, if on that occasion he lived in the Castle. It was one of the national fortresses of which King Edward I. had seisin prior to the settlement of the disputed monarchy, and it was governed for him by a person of the name of John of Gildeford.[1]

King Edward I. visited "Kyncardyn en Mernes meynor" on Wednesday, the eleventh day of July, 1296. It was his first stage after leaving Montrose, a distance of upwards of thirteen miles, and is described in the Diary of his journey as "a farour," or more distant, "manour."[2] He received no homages upon that occasion, but on returning southward, on the 4th day of August, he received that of Ranulph of Kynnard, chief of the noble family of that surname and title in Perthshire.[3] It was in this castle also that the scroll of King John Baliol's resignation of the crown of Scotland was written out, dated the 2nd day of July of the same year,[4] when Edward was himself at the Castle of Inverqueich, in Perthshire.

Tradition assigns a remote antiquity to the Castle of Kincardine, describing it as the scene of the assassination of King Kenneth III. by the stratagem of Finella, wife of the chief of the Mearns.[5]   Finella, it is said, was daughter of Conquhare, the Celtic Earl or Maormor of Angus, and her son, having been convicted of treason, was put to death by order of Kenneth. Out of revenge she had the king murdered within the walls of Kincardine, her reputed residence, into which she treacherously invited him while he was on a pilgrimage to the shrine of St. Palladius at Fordoun.

---

[1] Rymer, *Fœdera*, ii. p. 590 ; *Rotuli Scot*. i. p. 11.

[2] *Bannatyne Club Miscell*. i. p. 277.

[3] *Ibid*. i. p. 279; *Ragman Rolls*, p. 112; Prynne, *Hist*. p. 651 ; Palgrave, *Writs*, p. 196.

[4] Rymer, *Fœdera*, i. pt. iii. p. 161.

[5] A small British fort on the western slope of Strathfinella Hill, now planted, is also called *Finella's Castle ;* and the vitrified site of Green Cairn, near Balbegno, is similarly named.

Such is the story of Boece, who relates the circumstances attending the murder with all the minuteness of an eye-witness. But less fanciful historians, such as Tytler, are of opinion that the king was waylaid or lured into a hunting match, and thus came unwittingly by his death, yet not within the Castle of Kincardine, or by the poisoned darts of a brazen effigy, as related by Boece, but by the swords of a band of hired assassins. Wyntoun, alluding to Finella's personal inability to put an end to the king, says that

> ". . scho cowth noucht do that be mycht,
> Scho made thame traytowyrs be hyr slycht ;"

while, in the following quaint lines, he points to the members of the king's own court as the perpetrators of the deed, and says that it was done at Fettercairn,[1] though others believe he was killed in the neighbourhood of Stracathro. Wyntoun says :—

> " As throw the Mernys on a day
> The kyng was rydand hys hey way,
> Off hys awyne curt al suddanly
> Agayne hym ras a cumpany
> In to the towne off Fethyrkerne :
> To fecht wyth hym thai ware sa yherne,
> And he agayne thame faucht sa fast ;
> Bot he thare slayne was at the last." [2]

The first mention of any portion of the barony of Kincardine belonging to a subject, occurs in the time of The Bruce, when Sir William Oliphant had charters of confirmation in the lands of Moorhouse in Mid-Lothian, in exchange for the " clausura parci de Kyncardin in le Mernis."[3] The same king, in 1323, granted to his brother-in-law, Sir Alexander Fraser, six acres of arable land in the tenement of Auchincairnie, beside the King's manor of Kincardine, bounded on the east by the old

---

[1] Her Majesty the Queen, the Prince Consort, the Princess Alice, and Prince Louis of Hesse, Lady Churchill, and General Sir George Gray, spent at Fetter-cairn village the night of 20th September 1861.

[2] Wyntoun, *Cronykil*, ii. p. 94. The account of Kenneth's death, when traced through the Scotch and Irish Annals and the later Scotch Chronicles, gives a curious, interesting, and very valuable example of the growth of the historical legend.

[3] *Reg. Mag. Sig.* p. 12.

cart road of the town of Auchincairny, on the west by a new ditch, on the north by the burn of Vethi, and on the south by the moor of Cambou. The land was to be held in one free hostilage, with common pasturage in the King's thanage of Kincardine, for two horses, ten oxen, twelve cows, and a hundred sheep, with their followers till these should be a year old, and with freedom to dig peats and turfs within the same thanage of Kincardine.[1]

During the following reign it appears that the thanedoms of Kincardine and Fettercairn, with that of Aberluthnott or Marykirk and the park and Castle of Kincardine, belonged to William, Earl of Sutherland, who married Margaret, sister of King David,[2] whose issue, it is said, David had a wish to advance to the throne in preference to The Steward, although the latter was the nearest heir in right of his mother, the daughter and only child of King Robert I. by his first marriage.

The Earl of Sutherland survived till about 1388, but long before his death he had exchanged these lands with King David II. for the barony of Urquhard, in Inverness-shire,[3] and in 1367 Kincardine is mentioned as held by Sir Walter of Leslie of Rothes,[4] who married Euphemia, Countess of Ross. In course of time the male succession of Ross failed, and when the grand-daughter of the last-named Leslie took the veil, her aunt, the wife of Donald of the Isles, became her successor.[5] For the purpose of enforcing immediate possession of the vast estates of Ross, and with the view of obtaining a still higher position in the nation, Donald raised a powerful army in the Hebrides, and, marching southward, was checked in his premature and lawless enterprise on the fatal field of Harlaw, but, unfortunately, not until a great part of the flower of Scottish chivalry was slain.

The Nun-Countess resigned the estates into the hands of

[1] Hadington's *Coll. of Chart. MS.*, Adv. Lib. Edin.
[2] *Chamberlain Rolls*, i. p. 343.   [3] Robertson, *Index*, p. 49.   [4] *Ibid.* p. 87.
[5] Douglas, *Peer.* ii. pp. 114-15; Leslie, *Hist. Fam. Leslies*, i. pp. 69, 79; ii. p. 37.

the king about the year 1415, and the destination of the
charter, which was then granted, having failed, the lands
ultimately became a royal fief.[1] This must have been very
pleasing to James I., as the object of his life, and the ultimate
cause of his ruin, lay in a foolish desire to crush the Scottish
aristocracy.

During Leslie's time King David II. visited Kincardine
twice. He presided at a jury court there in December 1375 ;
and there also, in January 1383, he gave, among other grants,
a confirmation charter of the lands of Uras in the parish of
Dunnottar to his shield-bearer, Thomas of Rait.[2]

Little is known with certainty of the proprietary history of
the barony of Kincardine from 1383, until a late date. It
appears to have been broken up into several fragments, and
of these the Earls Marischal and the old family of Strachan
of Thornton had the principal parts. The last named had
the *Castelsted* and park, and the greater part of the adjoining crofts, which bear the significant names already noticed ;
while the Earls Marischal had other crofts, together with the
advowson of the Chapel of St. Catherine and the liberties of
the burgh of Kincardine,[3] in virtue of which, in 1473, Earl
William gave the toft of Auchcairnie to John Spalding, Dean
of Brechin, to be held by him for the keeping of a free
hostelry, or inn ; and, as the charter goes on at length to
state, he had the power and liberty of brewing, baking,
buying and selling loaves, and all and sundry other things,
with fuel and pasture within the commonty of Kincardine.[4]
But most of these lands and privileges were subsequently
held by the Earls of Middleton, and the property of Kincardine, upon which the ruins of the ancient palace stand, was
bought soon after the fall of the Middletons by an ancestor of
the present proprietor.

---

[1] Leslie, *Hist. Fam. Leslies*, i. pp. 80-83.
[2] Douglas, *Peer.* ii. p. 119 ; *Reg. Mag. Sig.* pp. 161-2. James V. was perhaps at
Kincardine in 1526.—*Acta Parl.* ii. p. 315.
[3] *Inq. Speciales*, Kincardinesh., Nos. 18, 70.   [4] *Reg. Ep. Brechin.* ii. p. 384.

It was in 1531-2 that the fourth Earl Marischal obtained a charter for making the town of Kincardine " the principal and capital burgh of the county."[1] How shortly and imperfectly it maintained that position is proved by the Acts of Parliament; for these show that, in less than eighty years after it was made the county town, the Sheriff and his deputes petitioned for the removal of the courts to Stonehaven, in consequence of the extreme poverty of the accommodation at Kincardine, where there was neither a tolbooth, nor any house for " parties to ludge into for thair intertenement;" and in this state, it is said, matters had continued " mony zeiris,"[2]—the free hostelry having been long previously abolished.

The town of Kincardine had probably been in a poor state even when the Earl Marischal obtained the charter, although a late writer supposes that it once was a great place, extending " from the ground at the foot of the castle to near Fettercairn House,"[3] a distance of at least an English mile. That idea had been assumed in consequence of foundations of cottages being often turned up in that line of road, which was the old highway from Kincardine to Fettercairn; but the real extent of the town in that direction had only been from the East to the West Ports, a distance of about two hundred yards.[4]

Although no house remains to show where the town of Kincardine stood, the sites of both ports, and also that of the market cross, are still pointed out, and the old burial-ground of St. Catherine is laudably preserved, surrounded by a rude stone wall and overshadowed by a few trees. It ought to be observed that the Cross, now preserved at the village of Fettercairn, is a memorial of late date, having been erected by the celebrated John, Earl of Middleton, and gifted by him to the town of Kincardine. He was born near that place, and latterly assumed his titles from lands which he held in the

---

[1] Douglas, *Peer.* ii. p. 192.   [2] *Acta Parl.* iv. p. 374.
[3] *New Stat. Acct. Scot.*, Kincardineshire, p. 84.   In 1790 Kincardine contained only seventy or eighty souls.
[4] *Ibid.* p. 84, giving much curious information.

same neighbourhood, and the Cross bears his arms and initials, with the Scottish Lion and the date of 1670.

Apart from its containing within its bounds the stone circle on the hill of Herscha, the Roman Camps at Fordoun and Clattering Brigs,[1] and some other ancient traces, the parish of Fordoun is reputed to have been one of the earliest seats of the Christian faith in Scotland. St. Palladius is said to have settled there in the fifth century, and his church occupied nearly the same romantic site as the parish kirk of the present day. A copious well in front of the Manse still preserves his name, as does also an annual market in the neighbourhood, commonly called *Paddy* fair.

St. Palladius is said to have died and been buried at Fordoun, and tradition relates that many great personages made long and arduous pilgrimages to his shrine. Among these were King Kenneth III., whose tragical death has already been alluded to, and Archbishop Shevez of St. Andrews; of these two, the latter collected together the bones of St. Palladius, which appear to have been then scattered about, and had them put into a new shrine made of silver, or, if we are to believe Butler, he had the old shrine " enriched with gold and precious stones."[2]   St. Palladius' relics, however, seem to have soon lost their value ; for the Reformation followed within fifty years, and Wishart of Pitarrow, the selfish and sacrilegious Comptroller of King James V., is said to have enriched his own coffers by seizing the holy casket, and scattering its still more revered contents to the winds. But from that time, says an old writer, the family " never prospered."

The older part of the edifice in the churchyard, known as St. Palladius' Chapel, is in all probability the church of Fordoun that was consecrated by David de Bernham, bishop of St. Andrews, on Monday the 17th October 1244.[3]   This

---

[1] See an account and engraving of the camp at Clattering Brigs in Chalmers, *Caled.* i. p. 178.   [2] Butler, *Lives of the Saints* (PALLADIUS), July 6.
[3] Robertson, *Stat. Eccl. Scot.* i. Pref. pp. ccxcviii sq. for the list of churches consecrated by De Bernham.

was perhaps raised in the walls and otherwise decorated by
Archbishop Shevez, but its architectural peculiarities are so
few that the age cannot well be ascertained. The east gable
is obviously the oldest portion. It is ornamented by a small
mutilated piscina, terminating in a rude pointed arch, hewn out
of a single stone; and there also, within an arch in the centre
of the wall, behind where the altar had stood, the ashes of
St. Palladius are said to have reposed in their shrine. The old
families of Halkerton and Monboddo used to bury in the vault
beneath this chapel, and to one of the latter there is in the north-
west corner of the chapel a monument, with a quaint Latin
inscription. Here also stands the curiously sculptured stone
which local story associates with the murder of King Kenneth.[1]

The parish church of Fordoun, adjoining St. Palladius'
Chapel, stands also within the churchyard. It was rebuilt
upwards of fifty years ago, and is a handsome structure, with a
square Gothic tower. The churchyard contains some rather
tastefully designed monuments, the most conspicuous of which
is a pillar of Aberdeen granite raised some years ago to the
memory of George Wishart, the reformer and martyr, who is
usually considered a cadet of the old family of Pitarrow. Close
by the church and churchyard are the manse, the school, and
the new and old school houses. In the latter of these, and it
included both school and school-house, the celebrated author of
The Minstrel lived several years, and taught the youth of the
parish, previous to his elevation to the chair of Moral Philo-
sophy at Aberdeen. These, with an old hostelry, constitute
what is now termed the *town* or village of Fordoun.[2] The
stream of the Luther washes the base of the rock upon which the
kirk stands, and the whole forms an enchanting and romantic
spot. It is believed that in the dell between the church and

---

[1] Stuart, *Sculp. Stones of Scot.* i. p. 20 and plate lxvii. ; *New Stat. Acct. Scot.*,
Kincardineshire, p. 79; *Proc. Soc. Ant. Scot.* ii. pp. 464-6.

[2] John de Fordun, the celebrated author of the *Scotichronicon*, is supposed to
have been born at the village of Fordoun about the year 1350, and to have assumed
his name from it.

the rising ground opposite (the solitude of which has since been
broken by the formation of a public road), Dr. Beattie composed the greater part of *The Minstrel,* and he thus beautifully
describes the immediate locality in his Ode to Retirement :—

> "Thy shades, thy silence, now be mine,
>   Thy charms my only theme ;
> My haunt the hollow cliff, whose pine
>   Waves o'er the gloomy stream,
> Whence the scared owl, on pinions grey,
>   Breaks from the rustling boughs,
> And down the lone vale sails away
>   To more profound repose."

Apart from the fact of the quiet of this part of the vale of
the Luther being then unbroken by a common highway, the
village of Auchinblae, on the east side of that stream, was
then also of small importance.   Now-a-days, however, matters
are different: a trade in linen manufactures and general
merchandise is carried on in the village, which contains a neat
Free Church and manse, a Public Hall, a post-office, branch
banks, a gas-work, and several inns, with a population of a
little over 400 persons.[1]

The pretty pastoral district of Glenfarquhar, to the north
of Auchinblae—now studded with comfortable farm-houses
and cottages—long furnished the old monks of Arbroath with
shieling and pasture for their herds of cattle and swine.[2]   In
later times an embattled fortalice of the Burnetts and the
Falconers stood there, sheltered by a cluster of trees, but we
can now scarcely trace even the foundations of what was the
birthplace of Falconer, Lord President of the Court of Session.

A little to the north-west lies Drumtochty, now belonging
to the Rev. J. S. Gammell ; beyond is the romantic gorge of the
Bow Glen, separated from the valley of Strathmore by the Hill
of Strathfinella, which, it is conjectured, is so named from the
reputed murderess of King Kenneth III.   Near the middle of

---

[1] Though much improved in outward appearance the village has lost 159 in its
population since 1861.   The whole parish of Fordoun has decreased by 305 in the
same period.   [2] *Reg. Vet. Aberbr.* p. 60.

the valley, and a short distance off the road, is the Friars' Glen with its reputed Hermitage, surrounded on all sides by mountains, and watered by a transparent brook. The remains of the dwelling-house, barn, and byre of the last occupant stand in a corner of the glen, and these the writer of the *Old Statistical Account* calls " the ruins of a small friary "—a mistake that had originated in the fact that, in 1402, Fraser of Frendraught granted the property to the Carmelite or White Friars of Aberdeen, who continued to draw the revenues of it down to the Reformation.[1]   Then the glen passed to the Earl Marischal, who granted it to the Marischal College of Aberdeen, from which it passed by purchase more than half a century ago to the proprietor of Drumtochty.[2]

SECTION II.

Sun comes, moon comes,
Time slips away ;
Sun sets, moon sets,—
Love, fix a day.

TENNYSON, *Poems.*

CASTLE, AND KIRK OF GLENBERVIE.

Edward I. at Glenbervie Castle—Submission of the Baron, and the Parson of the Kirk—Kirkyard—Drumlithie—Chapel burned—Curious Epitaph on the Hassas, Olifards, Melvilles, Auchinlecks, and Douglases—Account of the Melville Family —The Sheriff boiled at Garvock—The ninth Earl of Angus—His Successors in Glenbervie, and failure of that line of the Douglases—Stuarts of Inchbreck— Ancestry of Burns the Poet—Burneses of Montrose.

WHEN King Edward I. left the Castle of Kincardine, he passed to " the mountagne of Glonberwy,"[3] or Glenbervie, the parish adjoining Fordoun on the east, and there he remained for the night. Both history and tradition corroborate the fact of a castle having been at Glenbervie from a very remote period, and there is no doubt but the king made it his residence upon

[1] *Reg. Ep. Brechin.* ii. p. 386.
[2] *New Stat. Acct. Scot.*, Kincardineshire, p. 86.
[3] *Bannatyne Miscell.* i. p. 277 ; *Ragman Rolls*, p. 179, has Glombrvy.

the occasion referred to, although the silence of the writer of the royal Diary on that particular point might lead those unacquainted with the locality to infer that the party had somewhere encamped among the mountains; the designation "mountagne," however, is merely descriptive of the appearance of the district as the point of departure from the plain into the hills.

The old Castle of Glenbervie is believed to have occupied nearly the same site on the Bervie Water, as the present mansion-house; and at the time of the king's visit it belonged to a branch of the old family of Melville. Many barons of that name did homage to Edward, and among these was "dñs Johannes de Maleuill, miles," who probably was Johan de Malevill, Chevalier, the laird of Glenbervie. His submission took place at Lumphanan, in Aberdeenshire, on the 21st of July; and, from the writs printed by Sir Francis Palgrave, it appears that 𝔍𝔬𝔥𝔫 𝔬𝔣 𝔖𝔱𝔬𝔴𝔢, parson of the kirk of Glenbervie, performed the same service at the same time and place.[1] Subsequently, after the king had returned southward to Berwick-upon-Tweed, the same churchman repaired thither, and again took the oath of allegiance;[2] but nothing further is known of his history.

The old church stood within the present burial-ground, opposite to the mansion-house. A new one was erected in 1826, in the corner of a field by the road-side, some distance from the former site. The name of the patron saint is in all probability still retained in Michael Fair, which is held in October. Nothing but a fragment of the old kirk now remains. It adjoins the burial aisle of the Douglases, which is wholly covered with ivy and shaded by a few good specimens of the yew—a beautiful tree, much too rare in Scottish graveyards.

The church, which belonged to the diocese of Brechin, is

---

[1] Palgrave, *Writs*, i. p. 77; *Ragman Rolls*, p. 94, gives the submission of Jacobus de Maleuill at Aberdeen on July 16, 1296, and (*Ib.* p. 158) Jacobus de Malueille de Aberden, at Berwick-on-Tweed, in the end of August following.

[2] *Ragman Rolls*, p. 142; Prynne, *Hist.* p. 657; Rymer, *Fœdera*, i. pt. iii. p. 163.

rated in the ancient *taxatio* at £20 Scots.[1] The first recorded parson is described as "Henricus, persona de Glen-
beruin," in a grant of the lands of Bractullo, in Kirkden,
by Randulph of Strathechyn to the Cathedral of Brechin
about the year 1222;[2] but, from the time of Stowe until
nearly the middle of the fifteenth century, there are few
notices of much moment regarding either the kirk or its
priests.   Some of them, as we may infer from their names,
were nearly related to the chief heritor or patron; but the one
who attained the most influence in his day was Robert
Erskyn, the rector, belonging to the family of Dun, who was
Provost of the Collegiate Church of Holy Trinity, Edinburgh,
and also apparently Dean of Aberdeen, about 1539.   Towards
the close of the preceding century, while the property belonged to the family of Auchinleck, and during the wardship
or minority of the heir-apparent, an action was raised by the
king against Sir John Auchinleck of that Ilk for ' the wrang-
wis vsing and disponyng apon the samyn kirk," which was " a
sequele and pertinentis of the said landis," first " to vmquhile
Maister William Auchinlek his brother, and thereafter to
Maister Johne of Auchinlek his sone,"[3]—a dispute of which
the issue is not recorded.   A chapel, situated at Drumlithie,
was dependent upon the kirk of Glenbervie, and the patronage
of both livings went along with the estates.[4]

Drumlithie has been *the* village of the parish from a remote
date, although the Douglases had the Kirkton of Glenbervie,
which has long been lost to memory, erected into a barony.
That village, like other small villages in the county, had long
a slight trade in linen and other manufactures; but now
for some years the looms have entirely disappeared.   The
Parochial School, the Episcopal and Free Churches, and the
Public Hall, are situated there.   The Episcopalians have been
settled at Drumlithie since the time that Episcopacy was

---

[1] *Reg. Vet. Aberbr.* p. 241.
[2] *Ibid.* ii. p. 3; *Reg. Vet. Aberbr.* p. 179.
[3] (1493)—*Acta Aud.* ii. p. 180.
[4] *Reg. Ep. Brechin.* ii. p. 348.

disestablished in the country ; and in 1746, when the Duke of
Cumberland and his forces were putting down the Jacobites in
this quarter, he not only burned down the chapel, but had its
parson, Mr. John Petrie, seized as a non-juror and imprisoned
in the county jail, because he persisted in his ministry, and
" did not pray for his Majesty *by name*, his heirs, and successors, and all the royal family."[1]

Although none of the monuments in the kirkyard of
Glenbervie have any pretensions to beauty or design, few rural
graveyards contain so many memorials of the ancestors of those
who have rendered themselves famous in the annals of their
country.   The most interesting to the historian and antiquary
are those within the Douglas aisle—the one a mural tablet, and
the other a chest-shaped tomb. It is, however, the former alone
that calls for any special attention here, as the other is interesting only in so far as it marks the burial-place of the ninth Earl
of Angus, and his lady, Ægidia Graham, of the old family of
Morphie. The mural tablet is a renewed monument of date 1680,
and shows some curious mortuary ornaments, with the armorial
bearings of the ancient families of Hassa, Olifart, Melville,
Auchinleck, and Douglas. The inscription, which is in old
contracted Latin, narrates the valiant deeds, and the matri-
monial alliances, of the lairds and ladies of Glenbervie, from
the remote period of A.D. 730.   About that time (so at least
we find in the inscription), Hew Hassa, a German by birth,
came to this country and married Germunda Dervies, the
heiress of Glenbervie ; and the last of their male descendants
fell at the battle of Barry in 1012, while attempting to expel
the Danes from Scotland.   Helen, the last of the Hassas,
married Duncan Oliphart, a captain or soldier of the Mearns
(*Merniæ Decurio*), and from Margaret, his great-granddaughter,
is sprung the present family of Arbuthnott.[2] Walter Oliphart,
the son of Helen Hassa, had by Matilda, daughter of Sinel,

---

[1] *Black Book of Kincardineshire*, pp. 28 sq.

[2] *Cf.* Jervise, *Land of the Lindsays*, p. 388, for the connection with the Olipharts
or Oliphants.

Thane of Angus, an only son called Osbert, who fell in the
Holy Wars with Godfrey of Boulogne; his only daughter
married James Melville, a Hungarian noble, and their son
Hew married Geruarda, daughter of Macpender, that Thane
of the Mearns who murdered Duncan II. in 1095.

Although little reliance need be placed upon any portion
of this sculptured narrative, it seems to contain a traditional
view of the line of family history, not entirely erroneous,
especially in its later details.   It is unquestionably one of
the most singular of its kind extant, and its perpetuation
of the sobriquet of the fifth Earl of Angus, "Bell-the-Cat,"
as he is designed upon it, is not the least curious of its
features.   The lands of Glenbervie in the twelfth century
were in possession of a baron whose surname probably was
Melville, which was a common name in the district at that
period.[1]

The Melvilles came to Scotland with King David I.,
under whom they had a settlement in the Lothians, and their
progenitor is said to have borne the name of *Male*, and so
called his lands Maleville.[2]   Chalmers holds that they were
of Anglo-Norman lineage, while Crawford asserts, perhaps
following the tablet in the burial vault of Glenbervie, that
they were from Hungary, where, he adds, some families bear
the same name and arms.[3]   The family had settlements both
in Angus and Mearns in King William the Lion's time, for
in 1189, Richard of Melville made over part of the lands of
Kinblethmont, and the patronage of the Chapel of St. Lawrence
on that estate to the Abbey of Arbroath.[4]   Nothing is recorded
of the parentage of Richard; but Philip, the founder of the
Kincardineshire branch, is called the son of Galfrid of Melville,
who was eminent during the reigns of King David I. and the
two succeeding monarchs.[5]   Some time before the year 1200,
Philip of Melville married Eva, daughter of Walter the son

[1] *Reg. Vet. Aberbr.* p. 63.   [2] Chalmers, *Caled.* i. pp. 524-5.
[3] Crawford, *Peerage*, p. 324.   [4] *Reg. Vet. Aberbr.* p. 99.
[5] Douglas, *Peer.* ii. p. 110.

of Sibbald, with whom he received the lands of Monethyn or
Mondynes, in the parish of Fordoun,[1] which were previously
owned by Richard of Freuill.[2]　His son, also called Philip,
was Sheriff of Aberdeen in 1222, and subsequently Sheriff of
the Mearns.　Afterwards, in 1241, he was joint Justiciary of
Scotland proper, along with Richard of Montealt,[3] and from
him was descended the knight who did homage to Edward I.
at Lumphanan.

　　Another of the Melvilles is said to have been John,
Sheriff of Kincardineshire (but more probably a sheriff-depute,
if indeed either) in the time of James I.　Of his horrible death
by being boiled in a caldron on the hill of Garvock, Sir Walter
Scott, in noticing the similar fate of Lord Soulis, says :—
" The tradition regarding the death of Lord Soulis, however
singular, is not without a parallel in the real history of
Scotland.　The same extraordinary mode of cookery was
actually practised (*horresco referens*) upon the body of a
Sheriff of the Mearns.　This person, whose name was
Melville of Glenbervie, bore his faculties so harshly that
he became detested by the barons of the county.　Reiterated
complaints of his conduct having been made to James I. (or,
as others say, to the Duke of Albany), the monarch answered,
in a moment of unguarded impatience, ' Sorrow gin the Sheriff
were sodden and supped in broo!'　The complainers retired
perfectly satisfied.　Shortly afterwards, the lairds of Arbuthnott, Mathers, Lauriston, and Pitarrow decoyed Melville to the
top of the Hill of Garvock, under pretence of a grand hunting
party.　Upon this place, still called the Sheriff's Pot, the
barons had prepared a fire and a boiling caldron, into which
they plunged the unlucky Sheriff.　After he was ' *sodden*,'
as the king termed it, for a sufficient time, the savages, that
they might literally observe the royal mandate, concluded the
scene of abomination, by actually partaking of the hell-broth.

---

[1] *Reg. Vet. Aberbr.* p. 64.　　　　　[2] *Ibid.* p. 62.
[3] Douglas, *Peer.* ii. p. 110 ; Chalmers, *Caled.* i. pp. 524-5.

The three lairds were outlawed for the offence, and Barclay, one of their number, to screen himself from justice, erected the Kaim (*i.e.* the fortress) of Mathers, which stands upon a rocky and almost inaccessible peninsula overhanging the German Ocean. The Laird of Arbuthnott is said to have eluded the royal vengeance, by claiming the benefit of the law of the clan Macduff. A pardon, or perhaps a deed of replegiation founded on that law, is said to be still extant among the records of the Viscount of Arbuthnott." [1]

Of the Angus branch of the Melvilles there were the celebrated Andrew and James Melville of the Reformation, sons of the lairds of Baldovie and Dysart near Montrose; but the original or Kincardineshire branch survived in the male line no later than 1468, when Alexander Melville's only daughter and heiress, Elizabeth, was married to Sir Alexander Auchinleck of that ilk in Ayrshire. A granddaughter of Elizabeth Melville, in 1492, married Sir William Douglas of Braidwood, second son of Archibald, Earl of Angus, and by her he had the barony of Glenbervie. These last were the grandfather and grandmother of Sir William Douglas, afterwards ninth Earl of Angus, from whom were descended the Dukes of Hamilton and Douglas, and many others among the nobility. [2]

The lands of Glenbervie passed to Robert, second son of the ninth Earl of Angus, and a Nova Scotia baronetcy was created in the family in 1625. There were seven baronets in direct succession, and the sixth, Sir Robert, was compiler of the *Peerage and Baronage of Scotland.* He was succeeded by his only son, Alexander, the seventh and last baronet in the male line, who became physician to his Majesty's forces in Scotland, and married Barbara, daughter of Carnegie of Finhaven. Sir Alexander had no surviving issue, his only son, Robert, having predeceased him in 1780. The baronetcy was restored in

[1] *Border Minstrelsy*, i. p. 162; Sibbald, *Fife*, etc., pp. 216-7 *n.*; *New Stat. Acct.* Kincardinesh., p. 94 : *Anal. Scot.* ii. 30: Stuart, *Sculp. Stones of Scot.* ii. pp. lxvi. sq.

[2] Douglas, *Peer.* ii. 110; Nisbet, *Heraldry*, ii. *App.* ii. p. 25, on the alliance of the Auchinlecks and Douglases.

1831 to Kenneth Mackenzie of Kilcoy, in Ross-shire, nephew of Sir Alexander Douglas by his only sister, Janet, whose descendants continue to enjoy it, but the estates have long since passed to other hands.[1]

Here also is the burial-place of the Stuarts of Inchbreck. A brass plate, affixed to a part of the ruins of the old kirk, commemorates the names of the various lairds from the year 1550. Prior to the middle of the sixteenth century, these lands formed part of the Glenbervie estate, and were then granted by Sir Archibald Douglas to David Stuart, in order to reward him for the care he had taken of the baronet while he lay wounded upon the field of Pinkie. Stuart subsequently took part with Queen Mary's forces at the battle of Corrichie, and, according to the ballad, he killed the corpulent Earl of Huntly with his own hand :—

> " The Murray cried tak the auld Gordone,
> An' mony ane ran wi' speid,
> But *Stuart o' Inchbraick* had him stickit,
> And out gushit this fat lurdane's bleid."

Inchbreck, and the properties of Kair, Redmyre, and Castleton, which had been acquired by marriage, passed, in uninterrupted succession from father to son until about the close of last century, when the late Mr. John Stuart, W.S., succeeded his grandfather, and the properties were disposed of. Kair was first sold, and Redmyre and Castleton soon afterwards passed into other families. But Mr. Stuart's uncle, Professor Stuart of Aberdeen, a native of the adjoining parish of Fordoun and an industrious antiquary, purchased the patrimonial estate of Inchbreck. In it he was succeeded by his elder son, George Andrew, who bequeathed it to his surviving brother and sister. In this way, for the first time for many generations, the destination of Inchbreck was altered ; it is now, however, protected, so far as that can be done, through the present proprietor, Alexander Stuart, of Inchbreck and Laithers, who succeeded to the one

---

[1] For the later account of the estate and its proprietors, see Jervise, *Epitaphs,* i. pp. 90 sq.

half *pro indiviso* on the death of his father, having purchased her right to the other half from his aunt, Mrs. Glennie of Maybank, Aberdeen, and strictly entailed the whole property.

The first Stuart of Inchbreck was a younger son of the laird of Johnston near Laurencekirk, and a lineal descendant of the old family of Stuart of Morphie.[1] The succeeding members of the house of Inchbreck continued for many generations to exhibit that martial spirit, at home and abroad, which characterised their founder. Captain James, after serving some time in Holland, returned to Scotland in the memorable " Forty-five," and enlisted in the cause of the Prince under Lord Ogilvy. He was present at the battle of Culloden, and from that time until his escape to France he shared in the privations and calamities of his proscribed associates. Of this interesting period of his life, he kept a Diary, which is printed in the first volume of the *Spalding Club Miscellany*. This soldier was created a knight or chevalier of the Order of St. Louis of France, and died at St. Omer in 1776.

But, although late in being noticed, it may be of some interest and importance to the general reader to know that the parish of Glenbervie was the " fatherland " of the Scottish Poet ROBERT BURNS, and that within its humble graveyard lie the ashes of many of his ancestors. Four of the old tombstones record the death of various members of this family, and a brief notice of them may not be out of place here. William Burnes, father of the Poet, was the third son of Robert Burnes, farmer, first of Kinmonth in his native parish of Glenbervie, and then of Clochnahill in Dunnottar. The Poet's father, it is well known, left his native county when about nineteen years of age ; and upon that occasion, as he used to tell his children, he took a sorrowful farewell of his brother at the last point from which the roof of their lowly dwelling could be seen. He first went to the neighbourhood of Edinburgh, where he was employed as a gardener, but soon afterwards removed to

---

[1] Prof. Stuart, *Essays*, p. xi.

Ayrshire. He married there in 1757, and his illustrious son ROBERT was born near Alloway on the 25th of January 1759.

Although the Poet is now best known by the name of *Burns*, it may be proper to remark that his father always signed his name as *Burnes*, and so also did the Poet himself down to within about ten years of his death. And then, because the name was pronounced in Ayrshire as if written *Burns*, he and his brothers, about 1786,[1] " consulted together and agreed to drop Burnes and assume Burns."[2]   Such is the family account of the change of the name, but this form, as adopted by the Poet and his brothers, has no claim to antiquity. Not so, however, with the name they rejected, which can be traced from remote times, through the records of both kingdoms, in all the varieties of spelling that individual caprice or the peculiarities of ages could suggest. " The name of Burnes," says Sir J. B. Burke, Ulster King of Arms, " is of great antiquity.   Godric de Burnes appears in the Domesday Book as the lord of ample domains in Kent, in the time of Edward the Confessor ; Raoul de Burnes made gifts to the Abbey of St. Acheuil, in France, in 1189 ; and Godeholt and Eustace de Burnes, with others of the same name, are mentioned in the registers of the *curia regis* of Richard I. and John, and in the rolls of knights' fees of Henry III. and Edward I.   In 1290, John de Burnes *miles* was Edward's envoy to Rome, and in a charter of Edward II. Willielmus de Burnes is included amongst the benefactors to St. Thomas's Hospital at Canterbury.   In the 16th and 17th centuries the name is again prominent in Staffordshire, where John Burnes of Aldershaw was of high consideration at Lichfield early in Elizabeth's reign, and his grandson of the same name was an active Parliament-man and magistrate under Cromwell.   The name is supposed to have been carried into Scotland either by some of the followers of Edgar Atheling, after 1066, or during the time of Edward I.   About 1500, the

---

[1] Letter to Mr. Aitken, dated Mossgiel, 3rd April, 1786.
[2] *Scottish Journal of Topography*, etc., Nov. 6, 1847.

ancestors of Sir Alexander Burnes were settled as leaseholders of Bralinmuir of Inchbreck, in Kincardineshire."[1]

It is certain that Edward I. had followers of the name in Scotland, and that the king himself was in the parish of Glenbervie.[2] Bernes appears there as the name of a place, in two charters of Robert I., and the word is variously spelled *Bernis* and *Bernes*, while the lands are described as lying "within the thanedom of Aberbothnoth." The same lands, it is believed, were afterwards known as Burnhous of Kair in the barony of Mondynes,[3] and may be the present Burnside of Monboddo.

It is within a few miles of this place that the present family of Burnes are discovered, in the early part of the sixteenth century, as leaseholders of the lands of Bralinmuir and Bogjorgan, which form the estate of Inchbreck. The late Professor Stuart of Aberdeen, proprietor of Inchbreck, who died in 1827, at the age of 76, averred that his ancestors had found them there in the reign of Queen Mary,[4] and some of them remained there till 1807, thus showing an unbroken connection with the lands for about three centuries. This is confirmed by the tombstones at Glenbervie, and also by a deed of the Earl of Traquair, Lord High Treasurer of Scotland, to Alexander Straitown, dated 5th April 1637; it is signed by John Burnes, residing at Thornetoun, near the same locality.

Of the four tombstones which belong to the Burneses, the most notable are those of James Burnes of Bralinmuir, and his wife, Margaret Falconer, who were the great-grandparents of the poet Robert Burns; and William Burnes of Bogjorgan, and his wife, Christian Fotheringham, the great-grandparents of John Burness,[5] author of the legendary rhymes of *Thrummy*

---

[1] Burke, *Visitation of Seals and Arms.*   [2] *Ragman Rolls*, p. 147.

[3] Robertson, *Index*, pp. 17, 23.   Burnside is still commonly called Burnies.

[4] Ancestry of Burns, *Edinburgh Courant*, April 26, 1851.

[5] This name, like Forbes, has frequently but not generally, been spelt with a double *s*. The Poet received the single *s* from his father, then adopted the double *s*, and finally ended by shortening the name to Burns. But in 1705 we see the family at Bogjorgan spelling the name as Burness, Burnesse, and Burnasse.—*Life and Works of Robert Burns*, Ed. by R. Chambers, 1853, i. p. 333.

Cap, The Ghaist o' Garron Ha', etc. There were two younger brothers of the same family; of these one, named Robert, settled in the parish of Benholm, while the other, Colonel John Burnes, was included in the Act of Parliament of William and Mary, " rescinding the forefaulters and fynes since the year 1665," as having been a partisan of the House of Stuart.[1]

The family of William Burnes continued, in the persons of three successive Williams, to occupy Bogjorgan till 1784, when John, the above-named poet, and son of the last William, quitted that place for Stonehaven, and near that town, after a life of penury and hardship, he perished in a snowstorm in 1826, his remains being interred in the Spital churchyard of Aberdeen.

The descendants of James Burnes and Margaret Falconer can be more clearly traced by the records of the Lyon Court. With two daughters, they had five sons, William, Robert, George, James, and Thomas. William and Thomas died early, and the former, having left no issue, was succeeded at Bralinmuir by his brother James, whose son relinquished it so late as 1807. Robert and George became lease-holders on the domains of the Keiths Marischal, the former at Clochnahill of Dunnottar and the latter at Elfhill of Fetteresso, and it is to them that Robert Burns, the grandson of the former, particularly alludes when he says :—" My ancestors rented lands of the noble Keiths Marischal, and had the honour of sharing their fate. I mention this because it threw my father on the world at large. They followed boldly where their leaders led, and welcomed ruin and shook hands with infamy, for what they believed to be the cause of their God and their king."[2] The Earl Marischal, it is well known, proclaimed the Chevalier King of Great Britain on the 28th September 1715, at the head of his retainers, at the market cross of Aberdeen, and again, after the battle of Sheriffmuir, repeated it at the gate of his own house of Fetteresso, in presence of the unfortunate Prince himself, and his general, the Earl of Mar. Under such circum-

---

[1] *Acta Parl.* ix. p. 166.   [2] Letter to Dr. Moore, 2d August 1787.

stances it is obvious that the parochial tenantry, even if they wished, could not altogether escape the pains attached to the treasonable practices; but although it is said that they lost all their goods in the misfortunes which overtook and scattered them, yet the dignity of their moral worth was not removed.

Robert Burnes married Isobel Keith (a circumstance which has probably led the Ettrick Shepherd to call the family cadets of the Earls Marischal), and, besides six daughters, he was the father of four sons, James, Robert, William, and George. As before noticed, William went to the south country, where he married Agnes Brown, by whom he had his son Robert Burns, the Poet.[1]

Of remoter relations therefore the Poet had no lack, as most of his grandfather's family, including three of the sons, James, Robert, and William above mentioned, arrived at maturity. None of the families, however, with one exception, departed materially from the " noiseless tenor of their way." Those who obtained the most honourable position were some of the descendants of James, uncle of the poet, who, when his brother William left the district, settled in Montrose, and became a burgess of that place and town-councillor, and died there in 1761, leaving by his wife Margaret Grub an only son, James, and a daughter. His son, James *secundus*, who died in 1837, and grandson, James *tertius*, who died at Edinburgh in 1852, were both writers in Montrose, and the latter was long its Chief Magistrate, and a Justice of Peace for Forfarshire. He married Elizabeth, daughter of Provost Glegg of Montrose, and of the marriage were born Sir James Burnes, at one time Physician-General of the Bombay Army; Sir Alexander Burnes, C.B.; and Lieutenant Charles Burnes, whose tragic and melancholy fate at Cabul in 1841 is now matter of history. Sir James Burnes, with his lamented brother Sir Alexander, not only gained the frequent thanks of the Indian Government for professional and diplomatic services, but also wrote various important works upon the geography and

---

[1] *Supra* p. 154.

manners of the East. He died at Manchester 19th September
1862. James Burnes *secundus,* above referred to, is the gentleman that all the Poet's biographers applaud for having responded
so readily to the necessitous appeal of his then neglected,
though now so highly honoured kinsman. It was he also who,
when the Poet and his friend Mr. Ainslie were on a northern
tour, met Burns by appointment at Stonehaven in 1787, and
conducted him into the circle of his paternal kindred.[1]

SECTION III.

Norham is grim and grated close,
Hemm'd in by battlement and fosse,
And many a darksome tower.

SCOTT, *Marmion.*

CASTLE OF DORES, OR DURRIS.

Route and Visit of Edward I. to Durris—Story of Hog of Blairydryne, etc.—Castle
of Durris—Visited by Alexander III.—Thanedom gifted to Sir Alexander Fraser
—Sold to Hay of Errol—Lands harried, and Castle burned—subsequent Proprietary History—Red Beard's Well—The Kirk.

THE Castle of Dores stood on the south bank of the Dee,
upon a rising ground, or rather a conical knoll, which in
Gaelic would be written and pronounced *Torr;* but the name
is usually considered to signify a mouth or entrance, as mark-
ing a pass though the mountains.[2]   The site is about twelve
miles south-west of the city of Aberdeen, the place to which
King Edward next repaired, and little more than the same
distance north of the House of Glenbervie.

In going northwards from Glenbervie, Edward crossed by
the mountains of that parish, and through a swampy pass, dreary
even at this day, called the Cryne Corse: he thus reached
the Castle of Dores or Durris, which his Diarist describes as

---

[1] See Burns's letter to his brother Gilbert, Sept. 17th, 1789, and Lockhart's *Life.*
Chronicle of the Hundredth Birthday of Robert Burns, by J. Ballantine, gives the
pedigree and collateral branches in sheet-form; also Rogers, *Gen. Mem. of the
Family of Robert Burns,* 1877.

[2] *Old Stat. Acct.* iii. p. 258; *New Stat. Acct.,* Kincardineshire, p. 170.

"a manour among the mountains."[1] By this route, which was
the most direct, and probably no worse than many others that
the king had seen in Scotland, Edward passed near the Stone
House of Mergie, crossed the Blackburn and Water of Cowie at
romantic spots, and, if he ascended the hill of Cairnmonearn,
was in view of the sea and the ancient town of Aberdeen. In
the swamp on the east, and almost at his feet, there lay a
trackless wild that is traversed now-a-days by the Slug road,
along which, prior to the formation of the Deeside Railway,
Her Majesty used often to pass in going to and returning from
her Highland retreat of Balmoral.

One of the places on Edward's route through these mountains is called Eshintillie *Regis*,[2] to distinguish it from another
Eshintillie which belonged to a subject. It is said that King
James V. travelled there *incognito*, and from the kindness
shown to him by a person named Hog, then farmer of Blairydryne, the Earl Marischal, who had a proprietary interest in
Durris, gifted that farm to Hog, and one of his descendants
married the heiress of Skene of Raemoir, in a neighbouring
parish.[3] The family of Hog has long since died out, but
the name is preserved in the district by a charity which was
left in 1787 by a native of the parish, and is still used, as
directed in the will, for educational and other purposes;
among the latter, with a kindly remembrance of the pleasures
and scenes of his boyhood, Mr. Hog has provided a payment
to the cattle-herds on the hill of Cairnshee, upon which he
himself had tended sheep and cattle, for the purpose of raising
a midsummer fire there.[4]

The site of the old Castle of Durris, which the agricultural

---

[1] *Bannatyne Miscell.* i. p. 278, has "Downes," but *Ragman Rolls*, p. 179, has
"Dores," which is also the provincial pronunciation of the name.

[2] *Acta Parl.* iii. p. 591; *Inq. Spec.*, Kincardineshire, No. 69.

[3] *Coll. Shires of Aberd. and Banff*, p. 638; *Inq. Spec.*, Kincardineshire, No. 135.

[4] *New Stat. Acct.*, Kincardineshire, p. 177; *Old Stat. Acct.* iii. p. 601. From the
fund, which is managed by the kirk-session, ten boys and girls, natives of the parish,
are educated at the Board School. About £15 are distributed annually to non-
registered poor in the parish, and ten shillings are devoted to beer and a bonfire for
the herds on the 24th of June.

improvements of the present century have greatly reduced in size, appears to have been moated in old times, and the castle itself was burned by the Marquis of Montrose; but no record or tradition of it remains in the district, except the significant name of " the Castle-hill." It was occupied as a residence by King Alexander III., and the earliest mention of it occurs in the *Chamberlain Rolls* of that period, when certain sums of money were paid for repairs to the houses of Collyn [Cowie], and the vessels and bridge at the house of Durris,[1] but whether the bridge was of stone or wood is not recorded : it may have been a drawbridge for the castle.

The visit of King Edward occurred on the 13th of July 1296, but of the subsequent history of the castle little has been learned.   In 1373, King Robert II. granted to John Fraser, son of the deceased Sir William Fraser, knight, the land of Wester Essyntoly (which John of Dalgarnok had resigned), for the blench ferme of a silver penny yearly at the castle hill of Durris—" apud castri montem de Durrys."[2]   On the lands of the Castletown of Durris, which lie but a short distance from Maryculter, the Knights Templars had a residence, and from them the fields are called " the Templarie lands ;"[3] but Durris proper was more anciently a thanedom, and the collectors of the rents of the king's lands take credit for payment of these.[4]

Sir Alexander Fraser, who was Chamberlain and brother-in-law to The Bruce, was the first baron of Durris, and received that thanedom and the old royal hunting forest of Cowie, with many other lands, from the king for his services as a soldier and statesman.   These lands continued in possession of the Frasers till about the end of the fifteenth century, although in 1413 the pecuniary affairs of the knight of the period had become so embarrassed that, reserving only the life-rent interest of his mother-in-law, he agreed to sell the whole

---

[1] *Chamberlain Rolls*, i. p. *34.   [2] *Reg. Mag. Sig.* p. 99.
[3] *Acta Parl.* vii. p. 591, has Templaria.   [4] *Chamb. Rolls*, v.Y. : *sup.* p. 13.

property " for euirmare," to Hay of Errol, Constable of Scotland, for, as the disposition quaintly bears, " a sowme off sylure before hand in my mykyle mistre [great necessity], to me payit."[1] Still, the estates did not pass out of the family, for long afterwards one of the Frasers held an interest in them, and, in 1494, the Bishop of Brechin raised an action before the Lords of Council setting forth that William Fresale withheld from him and the kirk of Brechin, " the secund teynd of his relief of the landis of Durris," which was claimed as belonging to that bishopric.[2]

During Montrose's wars the Castle of Durris was occupied by Forbes of Leslie, whom Spalding describes as " a gryte covenanter;" and, fearing that his house might be plundered by the royalists, he had part of his effects hidden or carried away to a place of greater safety. As anticipated, the castle was soon afterwards assailed by the Gordons, who, in the absence of better fare, regaled themselves upon " beir and aill," and " bruk up girnellis and book [baked] bannokis at good fyres, and drank mirrellie vpone the lairdis best drink, syne careit away with thame alss mekill victuall as thay could beir, whilk thay culd not get eitin and distroyit."[3] This was in 1639, and in 1644 the place was subjected to a similar raid, and the house garrisoned by " ten soldiouris " under command of Robert Irving, for the purpose of preserving the girnells or granaries, which were well stocked with grain ; and during that time " thay leivit upone [Lord Fraser's] nolt and scheip and vther commodeteis."[4] But it was upon Monday the 17th of March, in the following year, that Durris suffered most severely, for the Marquis of Montrose, then on his march southward to Dundee, plundering and burning the lands and houses of such of the Covenanters as lay in his route, set fire to " the place, lauche bigging, and haill cornes [of Durris], and spolzeit the haill ground of horss, nolt, scheip, and vther goodis."[5]

---

[1] *Antiq. of Shires of Aber. and Banff*, iii. p. 364.
[2] *Acta Dom. Con.* p. 355 ; *Antiq. of Shires of Aber. and Banff*, iii. pp. 365-67.
[3] Spalding, *Trubles*, i. p. 188.　　[4] *Ibid.* ii. p. 338.　　[5] *Ibid.* ii. p. 458.

In the year 1669, Sir Alexander Fraser, who was many years royal physician, had a charter of confirmation of Durris from King Charles II., upon the resignation of Lord Fraser.[1] On the second of December of the same year we find John Burnett served heir to his father, Andrew Burnett " of Dooris, merchant burgess of Aberdeen," in these lands,[2] and over these it is probable that he held a mortgage.

Sir Alexander Fraser was twice married, and by his first wife he had two sons and a daughter; the younger of his sons, Charles, translated Plutarch's *Lives*, and is supposed to have been author of *The Turkish Spy*. By his second marriage he had a son and daughter, the former of whom became Sir Peter, and was the last Fraser of Durris. Sir Peter's daughter Carey, a maid of honour to Catherine, Queen of Charles II., married the celebrated General, the Earl of Peterborough and Monmouth, by whom she had an only daughter, Henrietta Mordaunt, who became the wife of Alexander, second Duke of Gordon, and by this means the estate of Durris was eventually carried to that ducal house.[3]

The mansion-house, which was enlarged by John Innes, Esq. of Leuchars, lessee of the Durris estate, is pleasantly situated near the Dee. When the entail was transferred to property in the neighbourhood of Gordon Castle, the lands of Durris were sold, under the provisions of an Act of Parliament in 1837, to the late Anthony Mactier, who was a successful merchant in India, and by his enterprise and heavy outlay the estate was so greatly increased in value that, when his son sold it in 1871, it realised three times the buying price. It now belongs to the representatives of the late Dr.

---

[1] *Acta Parl.* vii. p. 591.   [2] *Inq. Spec.*, Kincardineshire, No. 115.
[3] This lady had four sons and seven daughters. The eldest son, Cosmo George, succeeded as third Duke of Gordon; the second died a Captain; the third was "Lord Lewis Gordon," famous in Jacobite Minstrelsy; and the fourth, Lord Adam, was Commander in-Chief of the Forces in Scotland, and builder of the house of The Burn, near Fettercairn. The third and sixth daughters were married respectively to the Earls of Aberdeen and Wemyss. They were all educated by their mother in the Protestant religion, and for this she had a pension from George II. of £1000 a year.—Douglas, *Peer.* i. p. 654; Jervise, *Land of the Lindsays*, pp. 122 sq.

Young of Kelly, but the mansion-house has a special interest as being the birthplace of the late Mr. Cosmo Innes, Edinburgh.[1]

The parish is meagre both in antiquarian remains and in traditionary lore. The few prehistoric traces that have been found are noticed in the *New Statistical Account*, and consist of several tumuli, of which one, by the side of the Dee, contained stone coffins with human remains. At the 'Spital Croft, a reputed seat of the Knight Templars, which lies to the south-east of the church, an old bronze pot was found some years ago, and the same is now preserved at the house of Durris. It holds about half a gallon, and is similar in form to the old-fashioned broth or *kail-pot* of Scotland, having three feet to rest upon, and two ears for fixing the bow or handle to.

The chief tradition of the parish is one regarding a free-booter called *Red Beard*, who is said to have lived in a cave on the hill of Craigbeg, where a spring-well at the side of the Cryne Corse preserves his name; but, beyond his dexterity in cattle-lifting and the like, there is nothing related of him.

The kirk, which is first mentioned in 1249, is rated in the ancient *taxatio* at ten merks; and the second teinds of the relief of the lands of Durris belonged to the Bishop and church of Brechin.[2] The church of Durris was in the diocese of St. Andrews; but the names of the early pastors are unre-corded, with the exception of Mr. William Crychtoune, who was appointed to the parish church, by the Archbishop, in 1487.[3]

The present church, erected in 1822, is a plain building: it stands by the side of the Dee, near the mouth of the romantic burn of Sheeoch, and two burial aisles are near it in the church-yard—one is called the Innes aisle, the other the Fraser. The first had its name from the forementioned lessee of the estate, and the latter bears a rough carving of the Fraser arms, and the initials, T. F., S. A. F., also the dates of 1537 and 1595, and the words " MEMENTO MORI."

---

[1] See APPENDIX No. XIV.

[2] *Reg. Vet. Aberbr.* pp. 169, 240; *Acta Dom. Con.* p. 355.

[3] *Antiq. of Shires of Aberdeen and Banff*, iii. p. 360.

CHAPTER V.

The Round Tower, Cathedral, Castle, and City of Brechin.

SECTION I.

Fairer wreaths are due, though never paid,
To those who, posted at the shrine of Truth,
Have fallen in her defence.

COWPER, *The Task.*

First Notice of Brechin—The Culdees—The Round Tower—Pagan and Eastern Origin refuted—Christian Symbols, etc., on Doorway—Supposed Date and Purpose of Erection—General Description—Saved from Destruction—Satirical Poem suggesting the joining of the Tower to the Church.

THE name of Brechin is first perhaps to be met with towards the close of the reign of King Kenneth III., and at that time it appears to have been a place of some consequence. It is next mentioned about the year 1012, soon after King Malcolm II. defeated the Danes at Aberlemno, and in honour of this victory he is said to have erected a monastery at Brechin, which he inscribed to the Blessed Virgin;[1] but no trace of it now remains.

There appears to have been at Brechin, in the twelfth century, a body of clerics called Keledei, who came to be better known in Scottish history as the Culdees. From what is known of these, it is likely that they were closely allied to the Continental secular canons, who received their rule from

---

[1] Butler, *Lives of the Saints* (MOLOC), June 25; Black, *Hist. Brechin*, pp. 1 sq., gives authorities, but none of value, for the earlier period. If Christianity in Scotland followed the same order as to propagation that it did in Ireland, it would naturally work from monastic centres.

Chrodegang, bishop of Metz, and had it reformed or modified in 816 at the Council of Aix-la-Chapelle. In Ireland and Scotland they were called Keledei, or servants of God; and from this we have from Boece and Buchanan the corrupted form of Culdee, which has been the object of so much controversy. That they had the same constitutions, and performed the same duties as the secular canons of other countries, is now well established;[1] and under the reforming system of King David they were gradually merged into, or often supplanted by, the regular canons in the cathedral chapters.

The Colidei were also at York, as early as the year 936, and in the history of the foundation of the Hospital of St. Leonard of that city, it is stated that when King Athelstan was on his way northwards to fight the Scots, he came to the Church of St. Peter's at York, where the ministers of that church were still called Colidei, and on his return after a victory he conferred on them valuable rights.[2]

Two of the best-known seats of the Culdees in Scotland were Abernethy, near Perth, and Brechin, and at both of these places the Culdee chapters survived down to the reign of King Alexander II. Their *colleges* at both of these places exist only in name, although ruins of the houses were visible at Brechin in the time of Maitland the historian, who was a native of that place, and those of Abernethy are engraved by Captain Grose.[3]

But whether we are to attribute those erections to Culdeeism or not, we have both at Brechin and at Abernethy the only Scotch specimens of the Round Tower. Few things have excited so much controversy as these, not only regarding the

---

[1] In our Scotch charters they are "Canonici qui Keldei dicuntur"—"Keldei qui se Canonicos gerunt"—"Keldei sive canonici." On the whole question of Culdeeism, see Reeves, *Culdees;* Robertson, *Stat. Eccl. Scot.* i. Pref. pp. ccvii sq. ; Dr. Wm. Smith and Prof. Cheetham, *Dict. Chr. Ant.* i. pp. 282, 402. On the Culdees of Brechin, see *Reg. Ep. Brechin.* i. Pref. pp. iv sq.

[2] Dugdale, *Monasticon,* vi. p. 608.

[3] *Antiquities of Scot.* ii. 251. College Burn (*Reg. Ep. Brechin.* ii. p. 247) is that part of the burn which passes the foot of College Yards, to the west of the Cathedral of Brechin.

history, age, and use of the buildings, but also the fact of their being found only in Ireland and Scotland. They have been ascribed to Eastern worships and Druidical rites, to ante-Christian times and to a late mediæval age, as well as to Danish artists and to monastic requirements. In all probability they were places for security in times of disorder; if the space in the several floors was small for the shelter of persons and valuables, the round smooth outer circumference and the narrow doorway, which was always at a considerable distance above the ground, made resistance the easier, while a bell or a fire at the top would readily spread any alarm.[1]

The architecture of the round towers of Ireland agrees with that of ancient churches erected there from the fifth to the twelfth centuries. In one case a round tower is placed *on* a church, as at Glendalough. In another the tower is built into the walls of the church, as at Roscrea; and one forms part of the west gable of S. Magnus Church, Egilshay, in Orkney. At Donoughmore and Antrim, as at Brechin, the towers, while having well-known Christian symbols, differ in no respect in plan from those more numerous examples which are destitute of such.[2]

Apart from the representation of Christ upon the Cross which surmounts the doorway of the Brechin tower, two ecclesiastical figures are sculptured near the middle on either side of the door. These are mutilated to such an extent that it is hopeless to attempt their identification, though Mr. Gough supposes them to represent the Virgin and St. John, and Dr. Wilson, St. Serf and St. Columba.[3] Both are habited in loose garments, of which the upper may be a cope or cloak. The figure on the left seems to grasp a crozier or pastoral staff with both hands,

---

[1] See article "Round Towers" by the Editor, in Dr. Wm. Smith and Prof. Cheetham's *Dict. Chr. Ant.* ii. p. 1820.

[2] There are no peculiar symbols on the Abernethy tower, but the four upper windows present traces of Norman architecture. For the Round Tower at Brechin, its measurements and ornaments, see Black, *Hist. Brechin*, pp. 230 sq.; *Proc. Soc. Ant. Scot.* iii. pp. 28 sq., iv. pp. 188 sq.

[3] *Archæologia*, ii. 85; Wilson, *Prehist. Ann.* ii. p. 381; also Pennant, *Tour*, p. 162.

while that on the right has a cross-headed staff on which rests an open book held by the left hand. These figures, each of 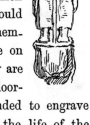 which is about eighteen inches high, are cut out of the same two stones as form the solid jambs of the door, are in bold relief, and rest upon pedestals which project about four inches. Both appear to have had beards, and something like a nimbus or glory seems to have surrounded the head of the figure on the right, which is altogether of a more portly mould than the other. There are two unembellished blocks in the tower, one on each side of the crucifixion, but they are *outside* the sculptured part of the doorway, and upon them it may have been intended to engrave some special incident, perhaps illustrative of the life of the founder of the tower, whoever he may have been.

There is also a diamond or lozenge-shaped figure, cut in low relief on the centre of the front of the door-sill, bearing an illegible centre ornament, from which possibly a *fleur-de-lis* had issued, in four points, as one point of it is faintly visible in the north-east angle of the diamond.[1] The two recumbent animals by the sides of the door-sill, which have also been variously described, are much worn. They are here represented. Woodcut No. 1, which represents that under the left-hand figure, has (despite the laughter that Mr. Gough's averred credulity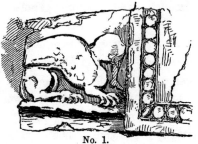

No. 1.

has furnished to succeeding writers), much of the form of

---

[1] The question as to this being an ornament or an armorial coat is discussed by Black, *Hist. Brechin*, p. 248.

the skull and *proboscis* of an elephant, certainly not "a fish in the animal's mouth," as suggested by Dr. Wilson; while

the head and fore-quarters of the object No. 2 have much the appearance of a horse. But it is idle to speculate on the sort of animals which these represent — most probably they are only objects

No. 2.

of the artist's own imagination. No. 1 has feet and claws pretty similar to those of the nondescript animal that was figured upon a stone built into the west and outer gable of Meigle church, but now preserved in the Museum there.[1]

A button-shaped border surrounds the doorway, and resembles that upon some of the ancient sculptured monuments, particularly that on the Farnell Stone, and the fragment which was found in a garden within the old boundary of the kirkyard of Brechin. Upon this fragment there are the Virgin and Child, and St. Peter, and allegorical representations of the Four Evangelists. These, however, are greatly inferior in execution to those upon the doorway of the tower, for in the latter a good knowledge is shown of proportion, and of the joints and extremities in both the human and animal forms, while in the others the figures are the squat and unshapely productions of untutored genius.[2]

As to whether the old sculptured stone monuments and the round towers of Scotland are coeval, it is too early in the study of the subject for us to determine, the age of the former being fully more uncertain than that of the latter. But it may be found that both the towers and the monuments had a common origin. The analogy of the architecture of the towers in Ireland to that of those in Scotland appears to go far in proving this point, and some of the mystical and Christian symbols on the sculptured stones of both nations are

[1] Stuart, *Sculp. Stones of Scotland*, i. pp. 22 sq.   [2] *Ibid.* ii. p. 1, and plates.

alike.[1] As the round towers are peculiar to Scotland and Ireland, so also are the monumental stone crosses.

The clergy, called the Keledei, Colidei, Culdees, were not exactly peculiar to Scotland and Ireland, and yet they first appeared in the latter country and then passed over to the former. This leads us still more firmly to believe, that both the Scottish round towers and the sculptured stone crosses were the work of native artists, who had been educated in convents under the eye of the primitive abbots and canons, who came from Ireland to instruct the youth in the useful and ornamental arts, and that among these accomplishments, doubtless, had been that of building and carving in stone.

These secular canons, as before shown, are first mentioned in the ninth century; but written evidence proves that some of the Irish towers have a much more remote antiquity. Dr. Petrie supposes that the Brechin Tower was built some time[2] between 971 and 994, or during the reign of Kenneth III. In connection with this there are two facts that deserve attention as showing something deeper than a mere coincidence. In an ancient Scottish chronicle[3] it is stated that in the year 990 Kenneth III. gave the large city of Brechin to the Lord; and again Boece relates how the Danes, in 1012, burned down and destroyed the town of Brechin, and all its great church, except a certain round tower that was built in a wonderful manner. It seems therefore to be in every way likely that the still existing Round Tower was a witness of the Danish invasion, and is a remnant or memorial of Kenneth's gift to the Lord.

Within the tower of Abernethy,[4] and in most of the Irish

---

[1] See Petrie, *Christian Inscriptions in the Irish Language*, 2 vols. : Anderson, *Scotland in Early Christian Times*, 3 vols.

[2] Petrie, *Round Towers of Ireland*, pp. 93-5, 377, 410 ; Simpson, *Arch. Essays*, i. pp. 109, 131 sq.

[3] " Hic est qui tribuit *magnam* civitatem Brechne Domino."—Innes, *Crit. Essay*, ii. p. 788.

[4] Small, *Roman Antiquities in Fife*, App. p. 12. Mr. Small supposes that "the Pictish race of kings" was buried within the Abernethy tower. This, however, is not so certain as the fact that there were hereditary lay abbots of the Culdees at Abernethy, who were also lords of the manor of Abernethy.—*Reg. Vet. Aberbr.* p. 256.

towers, sepulchral remains have been discovered ;[1] and in some cases, as in that of Kilkenny, round towers have been erected in churchyards *after* they had been Christian cemeteries, thereby showing that the round towers were perhaps sometimes to be used as places of interment. But although the Tower of Brechin was searched in 1842, and excavated down to the original soil, no such remains were found there. Whether these towers were originally erected as belfries or not, it is certain that many of them, including those of Brechin and Abernethy, have been used as such.[2]

The Round Tower of Brechin is a tapering building, eighty-five feet high, and the stones are neatly dressed and jointed into one another, in some parts slightly resembling the twistings of a screw. It gradually tapers from an *external diameter* of nearly sixteen feet at the base or sill of the door, to twelve feet eight and a half inches at the four top windows. The walls are three feet eight inches thick at the door-sill, and two feet five inches at the upper windows. It is divided into seven unequal apartments (exclusive of the spire or upper portion), by corbels of hewn stone, which project five or six inches, and on these are rested the wooden floors and ladders by which the top is reached. The fourth and fifth stories are each lighted by a small aperture on the east and south respectively, and the seventh by four apertures, or windows, facing the four cardinal points. A comparatively modern octagonal spire of about fifteen feet in height, in which there are four angular-headed windows, covers the top,[3] making a total elevation of about 101 feet nine inches. The entrance door has a circular head, and is six feet two and a half inches high. The sill of the door is six feet eight inches from the ground.[4]

[1] Betham, *Etruria-Celtica*, ii. pp. 211-24.

[2] On the tower at Abernethy, see Black, *Hist. Brechin*, pp. 240 sq. ; Simpson, *Arch. Essays*, i. pp. 131 sq. ; Wilson, *Prehistoric Annals*, ii. pp. 373 sq. For an account of the tower, with plans and measurements, see *Proc. Soc. Ant. Scot.* iii. pp. 303 sq.

[3] "The head of the Litl Steeple, blowen ower," 5th November 1683, was immediately restored.—*Brechin Session Records.*

[4] For minute and detailed measurements see Black, *Hist. Brechin*, p. 238 n.

Local story says that this tower vibrates in high winds, but this idea has probably originated in the fact that the lime or cement, by which it is bound to the corner of the church to the height of about thirty feet, naturally wastes and is shaken off by the storm. It is told, however, that with a view of testing the truth of its movement in stormy days, people have put knives into these fissures, and had them snapt across by the tower suddenly reverting to its old position. These, although stories of mere hearsay, may not be altogether unfounded; but this fact may be mentioned, as an instance of taste perverted by a professional idea, that in 1807, when it was proposed to make the present unshapely alterations upon the cathedral, an Edinburgh architect, who submitted plans for that purpose, gravely suggested that the Round Tower be demolished, and the stones used to assist in building the new walls!

It is difficult to say what the consequence of this monstrous suggestion would have been, had not Lord Panmure and the somewhat eccentric Mr. Skene of Careston promptly interfered, feeling so indignant at the spirit which dictated this outrage, that they not only rejected the plans of the architect, but vowed to hang from the top the first man that dared to remove a stone of the tower!

The following *Pharos loquitur*, written about 1807, satirising the joining of the tower to the church, suggests an improvement which might yet be acted upon with good effect :—

> " In ages dark, when men had light,
>   I reared my head on high,
> And when they view'd me, to the sight
>   I seem'd to reach the sky !
> In lighten'd times, when men were blind,
>   And priest-craft ruled the roast,
> A kirk they tuckled-to behind,
>   And made me like a post !
>
> In modern days, if men be wise,
>   Alone again I'll stand,
> And long be deemed by curious eyes,
>   The wonder of the land !

What tho' I shake in stormy days,
I 'm hale and sound, ye see,
While *terra firma* 's at my base,
There 's little fear of me !" [1]

SECTION II.

Let thy alms go before, and keep heaven's gate
Open for thee : or both may come too late.

HERBERT, *The Church Porch.*

Foundation of the Cathedral—The Culdees—The Chapter of the Cathedral—Seal of
the Chapter—Roman Catholic Bishops—Gifts by Bishop Carnoth—Extent and
Revenues of the Bishopric—Reformed Bishops—The Cathedral—West Door
and Window—Modern Alterations—The Steeple—Bishop's Palace—Canons'
Houses—Foundation of the Hospital or *Maisondieu*—Dispute regarding the
Patronage of it—The Rents granted by the Earl of Panmure to the Master of the
Grammar School—Ruins of the Hospital—Public School—Eminent men, etc.

THE Cathedral Church of Brechin was founded by King
David I., probably about the year 1150, and dedicated to the
Holy Trinity. The Culdees were then in a transition state,
and the Cathedral Chapter was composed, in whole or in part,
of those canons who, by the bishops, were always spoken of
with affection as " Keledei nostri." The names of two of these
still survive—Brice and Mallebryd; the first flourished A.D.
1178-98, and the latter A.D. 1202-22.[2]   After the Culdees
disappeared, the Chapter of the Cathedral was somewhat differ-
ently constituted, eleven of the old benefices being erected
into canonries. Those of Fothnewyen (Finhaven) and Lethnot were subsequently added, the former by Sir Alexander
Lindsay of Glenesk, and the latter by his son Sir David, afterwards Earl of Crawford. This made a Chapter of thirteen,
exclusive of the Bishop who sat as rector of the parish ; and
this state of matters continued, with but little change, till the
time of the Reformation.[3]

[1] In *Old Stat. Acct.* v. p. 461 ; xxi. p. 128 ; the tower is said " to bend like a
willow in high winds, so as almost to touch the steeple" ! The tower is about thirty-
four feet south of the steeple.

[2] *Reg. Ep. Brechin.* ii. pp. 255-69.   [3] *Ibid.* i. pp. xvi, xvii.

It was some time during the thirteenth century, and before the additions made by the Lindsays of Glenesk, that the beautiful brass matrix was executed for the Seal of the Chapter. It is one of the best examples of the art of seal-engraving of the early period to which it belongs, and "represents the Trinity under a Gothic canopy. The Father, seated, supports between his knees the Son extended on the Cross. Over the head of the former is inscribed, on the under edge of the trefoil arch, the word PATER: on the arms of the Cross, the word FIL: and between them, over the head of the Son, is the Sacred Dove, with the designation, S. SPS. The legend is ✠ S. CAPITULI · SANCTE · TRINITATIS · D · BRECHIN." This beautiful seal is represented in the woodcut No. 1: the reverse side, as shown in woodcut No. 2, is richly ornamented with scroll work.[1]

No. 1. No. 2.

According to Keith, the first known Bishop of the diocese flourished about A.D. 1155-6, and is designated by the initial

[1] *Proc. Soc. Ant. Scot.* i. p. 189. This matrix, and also those of the seals of the Official of the Provincial of the Dominicans or Friars Preachers of Perth, and Bishop David Strachan, were found in the office of Messrs. W. & C. Anderson, writers, Brechin, and presented by them to the Society of Antiquaries through the

letter T.[1]   Subsequently, in various charters granted by Bishop
Robert of St. Andrews, who died in 1159, " Samsone Episcopus
de Brechin " appears as a witness ;[2] and although the succession
of the Bishops to this see is not so clearly ascertained as could
be wished, it is evident that Samson had at least twenty-one
successors in office down to the period of the Reformation.[3]
Some of these were of noble birth and eminent in their day,
such as Bishops Leuchars and Shoreswood, both of whom were
Chamberlains of the kingdom, the one in the reign of King
David II., the other in that of King James III.[4]

Shoreswood's immediate predecessor, Bishop Carnoth or
Crannoch, was also deeply engaged in State matters, and
accompanied Princess Margaret to her luckless marriage
with the Dauphin of France. Carnoth is the only one of
the old bishops of whose gifts to the church there is any
notice, and these consisted of two silver candlesticks and seven
silver cups. The cover of one of the cups is described as
having the rays of the sun spread over it (*cum radiis solis
super*), and it is ordered to be kept for the special use of
the Dean and Canons at the ordinary festivals.[5]   Of these
vessels themselves, which are minutely described, even to the
colour of the leather in which they were wrapped, there is now
no trace ; and, valuable as they had been, they do not seem
to have either preserved the donor from the assaults of the

---

late P. Chalmers, Esq. These seals had in all probability been in the possession
of a family surnamed Spence, who held the office of Town-clerk of Brechin for five
generations, down to 1815.

A brass matrix, of the 15th century, beautifully executed, shows the front of the
head of a mitred Bishop, probably St. Ternan. Below is a hunting-horn stringed,
and the background is diapered. The legend is : SIGILLUM · CURIE · OFFICIALIS ·
BRECINENSIS. This was found on the Links of Montrose in 1848.—*Proc. Soc. Ant.
Scot.* i. p. 73.

[1] *Catalogue of Scottish Bishops*, pp. 156 sq.

[2] *Reg. Prior. S. Andree*, p. 128.

[3] A list of the Bishops is given in *Reg. Ep. Brechin.* i. pp. vi-xvi ; and in Black,
Hist. Brechin, pp. 298 sq.

[4] Crawford, *Off. of State*, pp. 20, 36. A stone with Bishop Shoreswood's
armorial bearings upon it—(1 and 4, three lions' faces, 2 and 3, lion rampant ; crest
(perhaps) a wreath of thorns)—is built into the outer wall at the west gate of the
kirkyard of Brechin.   [5] *Reg. Ep. Brechin.* i. p. 61.

members of his Chapter, or inculcated a thorough system of morality amongst them; for soon afterwards Bishop Carnoth found cause to excommunicate the Archdeacon for laying violent hands upon him, and to threaten pains and penalties against the Dean for maintaining a concubine in his house.[1]

The Cathedral of Brechin had twenty-three churches and chapels attached to it, all situated within Angus and the Mearns. They were so curiously scattered over different parts of both counties that the ancient diocese may be likened to a piece of patchwork, for in every corner of the bishopric— even to the very ports of the burgh—parts of other dioceses intervened. This peculiarity in the capricious disposition of ecclesiastical territory in Scotland is paralleled by the older diocese of Dunkeld alone.[2] The annual revenue or income amounted in 1566 to £410 sterling, exclusive of payments in kind, which consisted of about 188 chalders of grain and meal, together with a quantity of salmon, capons, poultry, and geese.[3]

Down to the episcopate of Alexander Campbell, who, through the intrigues of his kinsman, the Earl of Argyll, was raised to the see while yet a youth, the property of the church of Brechin remained of much the same extent as it had been during its best days. But, out of regard to the extraordinary part which Argyll played at the Reformation, he succeeded in obtaining for Bishop Campbell the unlimited power of disposing of all the benefices within the diocese, and this right the Bishop unscrupulously exercised in favour of Argyll and other relatives. Campbell died Bishop in 1608,

---

[1] *Reg. Ep. Brechin.* i. p. 124.

[2] St. Michael's Mount, within the enclosures of Brechin Castle, opposite Bearehill gate, was in the diocese of Dunkeld, and there the Bishop held consistorial courts.—*Inf. from the late P. Chalmers, Esq.* The hollow adjoining St. Michael's Hill or Mount is called *Michael Den.—Reg. de Panmure*, ii. p. 181. The Archdeacon's Barns, a curiously moated place with ditches and walls, on the farm of West Drums, on the estate of Aldbar, is surrounded on all sides, by the diocese of St. Andrews. John, Archdeacon of Brechin, did homage to King Edward of England at Berwick-upon-Tweed, in August 1296.—*Rag. Rolls*, p. 164.

[3] *Reg. Ep. Brechin.* ii. p. 417; Black, *Hist. Brechin*, p. 40.;

after having held the office upwards of forty years.[1]   He was
succeeded by Andrew Lamb, of the Chapel-Royal, who was one
of the three bishops that received Episcopal consecration in
England by order of the king.   Bishop Lamb was translated
to the see of Galloway in 1619, but, four years before, he
gifted the beautiful brass *herse*, or chandelier, which still
ornaments the church.   This and the horologe or clock,
which was given by Bishop Strachan, and continued till near
the close of the last century to warn the inhabitants of the
ceaseless "course of time," are all the recorded gifts which
the bishops of post-Reformation times made to the church.[2]
Inclusive of Alexander Campbell, there were eleven bishops
down to the Revolution, and there have been eleven since,
including the present Bishop of the Scottish Episcopal Church,
who was formerly Bishop of Colombo.

The Cathedral or parish church is a collegiate charge, and
has been so since 1641, when a second minister was appointed
by Charles I., "after some of the nobilitie and utheris" had
made inquiry, and reported upon the state of the church and
the bishopric.[3]   In 1836 a new extension church, now called
the East Church, was built, and a district having been attached
to it, it has been erected into a parish *quoad sacra*.[4]

The Cathedral was, as already mentioned, dedicated to the
Holy Trinity, and, down to the beginning of the present century, presented much the same appearance as it did during the
Middle Ages.   It was a stately fabric, partly in the Early
English, and partly in the Decorated style of Gothic architecture, with nave, side aisles, and chancel,   The nave, as it
now stands, is a hundred and fourteen feet long by fifty-eight

---

[1] *Supra*, p. 79. For the spoliations under Campbell, see Black, *Hist. Brechin*, pp.
40 sq., 314 sq.   In *Orig. Letters of the Reign of James* VI., preface, pp. xxxvi-ix—
and the statement is accepted by Dr. Grub (*Eccl. Hist. Scot.* ii. p. 490)—Campbell was
only titular bishop, and resigned his dignity in April 1607, dying in February 1608.
Bishop Lamb, his successor, was successively minister in Arbroath and Leith, before
being appointed to the Chapel-Royal and made Commendator of Cupar.—Maxwell,
Old Dundee, pp. 364 sq.   [2] APPENDIX No. xv.
   [3] *Register of Privy Council Seal*, cx. p. 56.   [4] Scott, *Fasti*, vi. p. 817.

feet broad, the roof being supported by a row of six pillars on either side. At the late period alluded to, the aisles were demolished, the carved capitals of the pillars plastered over, and on both sides new walls built, from which couples were laid to the tops of the arches between the pillars.[1] The windows and mouldings of the clerestory were thus entirely hid from view, and covered in addition with an unseemly roof, which has not inaptly been designated "a quarry of slates."

The west door of the church, although much decayed, still presents some beauti- ful pieces of carved work, and among these are traces of an almost unique figure in Gothic architecture, called the *reed pattern,* the only other example of which, so far as is known, is on the north doorway of Ely Cathedral. The large west window over the doorway (here represented) with grace- ful mullions and flam- boyant tracery, is still pretty entire; and al- though little exists of the east end or chancel of the church, the por- tion still remaining is a fine specimen of the

Early English style of architecture, being decorated by the bay-leaf and dog's-tooth enrichment.[2]

[1] An engraving of the kirk, prior to these alterations, is given by Grose, *An- tiquities of Scot.* ii. p. 261.

[2] The west door and chancel (with details) are engraved in *Reg. Ep. Brechin.* i. Pref.

Some suppose that the church had originally extended farther towards the east, and in digging graves in that direction foundations of walls have frequently been found, while in these were stone coffins, hewn out of single blocks.[1] Some part of the building is also said to have been destroyed at the Reformation, and this is by no means improbable. Others believe that the structure was never finished, but both of these views are purely conjectural. Better evidence remains to show that in 1617, " the bishop and haill sessione " thought " it good that all the pictours be destroyit off the loftis ;"[2] and also, that the alterations, which took place at the beginning of the present century, did more to rob it of its ancient appearance than anything that had previously been done. The "PICTOURS" alluded to were perhaps the figures of saints and the insignia of the different trades, but if these latter were removed at that time they had again been restored, for down to about 1808 some such decorations were in existence.

Although a great want of taste is displayed in the alterations which were made upon the kirk at that time, it had previously been an ill-cared-for and comfortless place of worship. In the north porch the incorporated trades met for the despatch of business, and the aisles (ironically called the *horse market*, in consequence of children being allowed to amuse themselves in them during divine service) were filled with all sorts of lumber, and used as a woodyard by the carpenters of the town.[3] The cold damp earth formed the floor of the

---

[1] The remains of some of these coffins (one of which is pretty entire) and the curiously ornamented top of a sarcophagus, lie in the kirkyard. The latter is engraved in Mr. Chalmers's *Sculptured Stone Monuments*, plate xiii. It had at one time been used as a gravestone : the remains of an inscription . . . . FEARED ˙ GOD ˙ AND ESCHEVED ˙ ILL ˙ AND ˙ DEPAIRTED . . . . are on the reverse of the stone, cut in characters of the 17th century.   [2] *Brechin Session Records.*

[3] The parish ministers and many of the heritors were buried in the south aisle, and there also lie the ashes of the celebrated Mr. W. Guthrie, of Fenwick, author of *The Christian's Great Interest.* He was born at Pitforthie, near Brechin, in 1620, and died Oct. 10, 1665. Mr. David Blair, first minister of the parish, was also buried in the south aisle, and, according to the inscription on his tombstone, he instituted at Brechin, about 1760, the first Sabbath-school that was opened in Scotland.

nave or area of the church, and loose unseemly joistings of oak supported a shattered and leaky roof. The graveyard was enclosed by a low ruinous dry-stone dike, and the ground on the north side of the church, now overcrowded by graves and tombstones, was a common thoroughfare, and also occupied in part by saw-pits and dunghills.

The square tower or belfry is at the north-west corner of the church, and, with its octagonal spire, is a beautifully proportioned and imposing object of a hundred and twenty-eight feet in height. An octagonal staircase at the north-east angle leads to the bartizan, from which an extensive view of a beautiful and interesting country is to be had. A fine floral moulding runs along the base of the bartizan on the west, and on the battlement, on the east side of the bartizan, is the date 1642, probably the date of some renovation. This tower may be said to be divided into several compartments, and the lowermost, in which the presbytery and kirk-session meetings are held, has a groined roof, with arches springing from sculptured corbels, terminating in a plain circle. The great and two smaller bells are placed in the upper compartment, and from this springs the base of the spire of the tower. The four corbels on which the

base rests bear beautiful carvings in high relief. These sculptures are about seven inches in height, and from ten to twelve inches in breadth. Three of the ornaments are floral, and bear no marked peculiarity, excepting the broad and effective manner in which they are executed; but the fourth, here represented, is more remarkable. It abuts from the north-east corner of the tower, and, as will be seen, represents a whimsically combined design of a dog with its tail strangely turned over its back, picking a bone, and supported by a ram's head and horns.

The date of the erection of this tower is not ascertained, but probably it was built during the episcopate of Bishop Leuchars, 1354-73. This may be inferred from the fact that, upon an inquiry being made at an after period regarding the non-payment of an annual rent from the kirk of Lethnot, which was due to the cathedral, the debt was declared to have been partly discharged in the time of that bishop, by the debtor having given the use of a white horse and cart to lead stones to the building of the belfry of the church.[1] Doubtless, also, at the same time, the spire had been placed upon the Round Tower.

The Bishop's Palace, of which no trace is now left, except a very small portion of the arch of the gateway (on the inner and south side of the Bishop's Close), stood near the site of the old manse.[2] The ruins both of this edifice and of the Canons' houses were to be seen towards the close of the seventeenth century, and also remains of Bishop Carnoth's tower, which formed part of the old city wall. The mere localities of the residences of the treasurer and of some of the other members of the Chapter, which adjoined the cathedral, and occupied the space from the Bishop's Close westward to the Chanonry Wynd, are traceable only through the ancient writs of the church. But in the garden of the old treasurer (now the property of Mr. Prain, late parochial schoolmaster) is a carving in stone of a female dressed in Roman costume, with a drawn sword in her hand. It ought also to be noticed that in 1848, while workmen were digging the foundations for a house on the east side of the High Street, nearly opposite to the Bishop's Close, the fragment of a carving of the crucifixion, executed in rather a superior style, was found several feet below the surface of the ground. It is said that the house in which

[1] *Reg. Ep. Brechin.* i. p. 74.

[2] When the old manse was taken down in 1850, a mutilated door or window lintel (now preserved in the garden wall of the new manse) was found, with the initials M. W. R. (Mr Wm. Rate—*v.* APPENDIX NO. XV.), dated 1644, and these words:

. . . CRVX ' SERRATA ' MIHI ' INSIGNE ' EST ' CRV . . . . . .

. . . SVS ' SIT ' TVTELA ' MIHI ' CRVXQVE ' CORONA ' N . . .

this relic was found belonged at one time to the church, and was possessed by some member of the Chapter, and also that by the accidental discovery, in the wall of the more ancient house, of an image, which is popularly described as " A LITTLE JESUS IN GOLD," the owner, previously poor, became wealthy and independent !

The names of many of the altarages of the cathedral are lost, and little remains relating to the chapels in the neighbourhood,[1] with the exception of the Hospital or *Maisondieu* which was the more important of these institutions, and from which sprung the Grammar School.   The ancient Hospital, founded in 1264, by Sir William of Brechin, son of Henry, and grandson of David, Earl of Huntingdon and Garioch, Lord of Brechin and Inverbervie, brother of King William the Lion, was supported by the revenues of certain lands in the parish, as described in the foundation charter; and for this the " chaplain and poor of the said house were not to pay anything except only due and devout prayers and orisons."   The Lord of Brechin bound himself, his heirs, and successors in the lordship, to protect all the lands, and other rights, which he had given to the Hospital, reserving to them the sole power of presenting the Master to the house, the bishop having " the care of spiritual things only."[2]   A charter by which an " isch and entry was given of a road thirty feet broad, from the chapel towards the town of Brechin," was granted to the Hospital in July 1267, and from that time until about the close of the fifteenth century, when a dispute arose betwixt two parties regarding the Mastership of the house, nothing interesting is recorded of it.   At that time the lordship of Brechin, previously in possession of the Crown,[3] was held by the Duke of Ross, son of James III., and in virtue of this he had the right of presentation to the Hospital.

---

[1] APPENDIX No. XVI.

[2] *Reg. Ep. Brechin.* i. pp. 4-8.   Black, *Hist. Brechin*, pp. 17,255, in his account of the Maisondieu, seems to prefer " about 1256;" *Reg. Ep. Brechin.* i. p. xix stands by 1264.   [3] *Acta Parl.* ii. p. 42.

This he appears to have exercised in favour of an Archibald Pattonsoun, and, in opposition to him, James, son of George Ramsay of Foxtoun, claimed the office of Master "to pertene to him be presentacioun of our souerane lord that last decest;" but the Duke of Ross being found "vndoutable patroune of the semmyn," Pattonsoun was not only declared to have the proper right to the emoluments arising from it, but Ramsay was also ordered to restore those which he had uplifted from the time of Pattonsoun's appointment. Besides, the "king's liegis" were warned "that nain of thaim tak apone hand to mak ony maner of persecucioune, or folowing of the said mater at the court of Rome, sen it pertenis to land patronage, under the panis contenit in the act of parliament, proscripcioun and bannysing." [1]

The further history of this foundation is obscure until about the time that the lordship of Brechin became the property of the family of Panmure, when, during the preceptorship of Alexander Norrie, minister of Dunipace, the chapel underwent considerable repairs at Norrie's private expense. These, in 1636, he agreed to waive on consideration that Sir Patrick Maule, afterwards Earl of Panmure, was to "apply the fruits and rents" of the preceptory "to the maintenance of the schoolmaster of Brechin, and of ane second minister there," to which he added the more selfish clause, "upon expectation of the said laird of Panmure his favour." Immediately after this, Robert Norrie, his son, had a presentation to the office of Preceptor of *Maisondieu,* upon condition that he and "his successors shall serve the cure of an actuall and ordinar minister within the Chapell of the said Preceptory; and also should teach the youth of the city of Brechin in grammar, and exercise the place and charge of an master of the grammar school within the samyne." [2]   The right of

---

[1] *Acta Dom. Con.* pp. 103, 128 ; Black, *Hist. Brechin,* p. 256.

[2] *Reg. de Panmure,* ii. p. 321.   This MS. was placed, before its publication, in the hands of the author by the Earl of Dalhousie, to whose kindness and liberality he was also indebted for the use of many other valuable MSS. and books.

presentation continued with the Earls of Panmure down to the forfeiture of 1716, when their property was annexed to the crown; and the revenues of the Hospital, in terms of the original grant, belong to the rector of the Grammar School.

Part of the front and east walls of the Hospital, presenting several fine though decayed points of Early English architecture, with piscina and ambry, still stands in the vennel, and the original mason-marks are yet visible on many of the stones.[1] It had never been a building of great extent, and probably these are the ruins of the chapel which was erected by Sir William of Brechin. At a late period this was appropriated to the humble use of a stable, during which a fire broke out in it, and the wood-work and one or two horses then in the building were burned to ashes.

As the Hospital or *Maisondieu* was the parent of the Grammar School of Brechin, it may be well to remark, before closing this portion, that an Alexander Hog, who also held a chaplaincy in the cathedral church in 1485, is the first individual recorded as assuming the title of *Rector* of that school.[2] The designation occurs frequently afterwards, and, as shown by the presbytery and session records, the rectorship was often a preliminary to church preferment.

After the passing of the Education (Scotland) Act in 1872, the Grammar School was incorporated with the High School, under the general name of the High School. This again includes and takes the place of the former Parish and Burgh Schools, as these, along with the Grammar School, were, prior prior to 1873, worked as one school. The present Classical Master in the High School, Mr. Andrew Robertson, M.A., holds the office of Rector, to which, on the recommendation of the Town Council, he was appointed by the Crown in 1865, and,

---

[1] Detailed engravings of these ruins are in *Reg. Ep. Brechin.* In *Archæologia* (xxxiv. 36, plate iii.) the mason-marks on the Hospital, Round Tower, and Steeples of Brechin, etc., are engraved in connection with an excellent paper " On the use of Mason-marks in Scotland," by the late P. Chalmers, Esq. of Aldbar.

[2] *Reg. Ep. Brechin.* ii. pp. 119, 121.

as Rector, draws the revenues of the Preceptory of the
Maisondieu. Of the other schools in the town those that call
more particularly for notice are the Tenement Schools which
were built in 1859, by Mr. John Smith of Andover, Massachusetts, to supply a good education to the "children of the
labouring, manufacturing, and other poorer classes." They
were first placed under the management of nine Directors, but
in 1877 were transferred to the School Board, when, as before,
they were arranged as a boys' and a girls' school. In 1883,
however, another change was made : the one became a mixed
school, and the other a school for all the half-times in the
burgh. From the money contributed by Mr. John Smith
and his brother, Mr. Peter Smith, for the endowment of the
Tenement Schools, and for the promotion of education of their
native place, there are bursaries given by competition to boys
and girls who " have been receiving their education within
any school of the burgh and parish of Brechin."

Several persons, who have obtained distinction in science
and literature, have been born in Brechin and educated at
the public schools. Among these may be mentioned the Rev.
William Guthrie of Fenwick, already noticed ; John Glendy,
Dean of Cashel and Prebendary of St. Michael's of Dublin ;[1]
William Maitland, historian of Edinburgh and London ;
William Guthrie, compiler of the *Geographical Grammar* ; Dr.
John Gillies, historian of Greece, and his brother Adam (Lord
Gillies), a Senator of the College of Justice ; Alex. Laing,
author of Scottish Poems and Songs ; Rev. Dr. Thomas Guthrie
of Edinburgh ; Dr. J. P. Nichol, author of *The Architecture
of the Heavens ;* D. D. Black, Town-Clerk for many years,
and the writer of *The History of Brechin ;* John Hendry,
writer in Edinburgh, author of *Styles of Conveyancing ;* Colvin
Smith, R.S.A., artist. And to the list the editor must add our
author, Andrew Jervise, who to the last retained a special
affection for Brechin, its people, and memories.[2]

[1] See APPENDIX No. XV.   [2] APPENDIX No. XVII.

SECTION III.

Sing on, sing on, my bonny bird,
The song ye sung yestreen ;
For weel I ken by your sweet sang,
Ye hae my true love seen.

SCOTT, *Old Ballad.*

Earl David of Huntingdon, Lord of Brechin—Family of Brechin—Sir David of Brechin—His homage to Edward I.—Services to England—Sir David of Brechin executed—Sir David Barclay—The Earl of Athole—Edward I. at Brechin Castle —Surrender of King John Baliol—Sir Thomas Maule's defence of the Castle—Burned by Edward I.—Its Past and Present State—Battle of Brechin—The Castle besieged by Regent Lennox and Gordon of Auchindown.

ALTHOUGH there is no record of a castle at Brechin until the days of Henry of Brechin, son of David, Earl of Huntingdon, it is probable that there was a fort there about the year 1012, when the Danes are said to have burned the town.

The lordship of Brechin was part of the appanage that William the Lion granted to his brother, the Earl of Huntingdon, and the Earl would appear to have transferred it to his natural son Henry, who assumed the surname *Brechin*, which his descendants afterwards bore. As Henry, son of Earl David, he witnessed a grant by his father to the Canons of St. Andrews, of the kane, conveth, and service of the lands of Eglesgirg (Ecclesgreig, or St. Cyrus, in the Mearns) ;[1] and, in Stephen of Kinardley's charter of Pitmengartenach (Pittengardner, in Fordoun), dated 1221, he is similarly designed.[2]

Edward I. is the first king, so far as recorded, who honoured the castle with his presence. It then belonged to David of Brechin, who did homage at two different times to that prince, first at Berwick-upon Tweed in August 1296, and then at Macclesfield, in Cheshire, in May of the following year.[3] David of Brechin, although brother-in-law to The Bruce, entered into the service of England, and for many years

[1] *Reg. Prior. S. Andree*, p. 238.   [2] *Reg. Vet. Aberbr.* p. 179.
[3] *Ragman Rolls*, p. 126 ; Prynne, *Hist.*, p. 654 ; Palgrave, *Writs*, p. 193.

fought against the interests of his native country; in 1360, he took Sir Simon Fraser, one of the Scottish patriots, prisoner at the battle of Methven. He was long a favourite with King Edward, but ultimately made his peace with King Robert, and joined the Scots.

This Sir David was the third in succession from Henry, the first of that race and lord of Brechin, whose son, Sir William, founded the Hospital or *Maisondieu*, and became one of the most influential barons of his time. Sir William married a daughter of Alexander Comyn, Earl of Buchan, and by her had Sir David, the baron who did homage and was so serviceable to Edward I. This last knight again had two sons and a daughter; the eldest son, also Sir David, commonly called the "flower of Scottish chivalry," succeeded to the estate of Brechin. The second son became Thomas of Lumquhat, in Fife, and the daughter was married to Sir David Barclay.[1]

The last-named Sir David of Brechin distinguished himself in the Holy Wars, asserted the Independence of Scotland as a Kingdom in 1320, and was otherwise one of the staunchest of Bruce's friends. But, having been made privy to the plot of William of Soulis and others against the life of the king, and having, unfortunately for himself, maintained the oath of secrecy that he had given to Soulis, he was executed as a traitor, along with his brother of Lumquhat, only four months after he had subscribed the letter to the Pope at Arbroath. Sir David Brechin was " jugit till hang and draw," then a common death for traitors, and it appears, by the following lines, that his death was much regretted—[2]

> " And, as tha drew him for till hing,
> The pepill ferly fast can thring
> Him and his mischef for to se,
> That till behald was gret pite."[3]

---

[1] Given in more detail in Anderson, *Scott. Nat.* i. pp. 378-9 ; Jervise, *Land of the Lindsays*, p. 139 et al.

[2] Tytler, *Hist. Scot.* i. pp. 373-5.   [3] Barbour, *Brus*, p. 440.

Upon this, The Bruce, who had implicit confidence in Sir David Barclay, the husband of Margaret of Brechin, gave him the greater bulk of these estates. Barclay was slain at Aberdeen in 1350, and was succeeded by an only son. That son died about 1364, leaving an only daughter, who became the wife of Walter Stewart, Earl of Athole and Caithness, second son of Robert II.; and Stewart, being the chief actor in the murder of King James I., "was beheaded at Edinburgh in 1437, his hoary head fixed on a spear, encircled with a crown of iron, and his titles and extensive estates forfeited." It was on this occasion, that Sir Thomas Maule of Panmure laid claim to the estates of Brechin, in right of his mother Marion Fleming, daughter of Jean, sister of David, the last Barclay of Brechin. In consequence of these alliances, the family arms of Maule of Panmure are quartered with those of the ancient lords, Brechin and Barclay.[1]

Sir David of Brechin, who did homage to King Edward I., had his castle garrisoned by the English in 1296. King Edward, while marching towards the south, after having been so far north as Elgin, reached "the cytye of Breghan," on Saturday the 4th of August in the same year.[2] There he abode for the night, but did not receive any homages, and it was now nearly a month since King John Baliol, by the deed of resignation to the English Commissioner, the Bishop of Durham, had there surrendered the Crown and Kingdom of Scotland into the hands of the King of England.[3]

> "Bathe Scepter, Swerd, Crowne, and Ryng,
> Fra this Jhon, that he made Kyng,
> Halyly fra hym he tuk thare,
> And made hym of the Kynryk bare."

In the following year, while Sir William Wallace proceeded towards the south, leading a powerful army, he drove the

---

[1] Jervise, *Land of the Lindsays*, pp. 139 sq. ; but specially *Reg. de Panmure*, i. pp. xxiii sq., ii. pp. 201 sq.

[2] *Ragman Rolls*, p. 179.

[3] Prynne, *Hist.* p. 647, is accurate in his brief summary of the proceedings before the English envoy, who was there "cum plenâ potestate regiâ."

enemy from this castle and took temporary possession of it, but history is silent as to the length of time the Scots then held it. It was certainly possessed by them in 1303, for Sir Thomas Maule, younger brother of Sir William of Panmure, then commanded it for the Scottish interest.

Edward I. is supposed to have placed his besieging engines in the field between the river and Butherkill (Burghill), on the south side of the castle. The engine used was called the war wolf (*lupi guerre*), the same kind of instrument as Edward subsequently employed at the siege of Stirling; it was capable of discharging stones of two or three hundred-weight. It is worthy of notice, that stone coffins have been found in the field alluded to, and about a quarter of a century ago, while it was being ploughed, a rounded freestone, of about the weight here noticed, was discovered some inches below the surface. It appears to have been fashioned by a hammer or similar instrument, and is probably one of the stones which the English had intended to use at the siege of the castle.

Although the garrison of Brechin was small, and the force large that Edward brought to bear against it, Maule remained undaunted, and held the enemy at defiance for the long space of twenty days, wiping away the rubbish with his handkerchief, as did Black Agnes of Dunbar a few years afterwards, until a missile, thrown from the enemy's engine, struck him on the breast. He survived the blow until evening, and, notwithstanding the favourable terms upon which the English offered to treat for a surrender, he disdained to capitulate so long as he lived. As if to emulate their fallen general in bravery, the noble little band held out until next day, when, unable longer to maintain their position, they were forced to let down the bridges and throw the gates open to the invaders.[1]

This noble and solitary resistance which the English arms received in Scotland at that time, had perhaps occurred in July

---

[1] Chalmers, *Caled.* i. p. 669.

or August, immediately after which the castle appears to have been destroyed by the English; for during the last-named month a payment of 3s. was made by King Edward's Chamberlain "for sulphur for burning the castle of Breghyn." Before the burning, however, care was taken by the English to insure the safety of the charters and other writings, and for these a "wooden coffer" was made at a cost of 2s. 6d.[1] The castle had been soon restored, perhaps by Sir David of Brechin, for he took refuge in it a few years afterwards, when pursued by Bruce, whose service he then entered.

The bravery of Sir Thomas Maule is extolled by all historians. Even Matthew of Westminster, who is slow to acknowledge anything good or patriotic of the Scots, says that "Maule was a soldier of undaunted boldness and resolution of mind, that the vigour and strength of his body were very great, and that he did not fear to hold out the small fortress committed to his charge against a royal enemy."[2]

The most ancient fortress of Brechin had occupied much the same romantic spot as the present castle, which stands upon a rock about eighty feet in height, overhanging the South Esk. It was surrounded by water in old times, and on the north and east there was a natural fosse, which separated the castle from the town; through this the Skinner's Burn still runs. The Esk formed the southern defence, and, as represented in Captain Slezer's view, there was a ditch on the west, whether natural or artificial cannot now be said.[3] The river has encroached considerably upon the rock on which the castle stands, for at one time there was a cart road along the base of it, and this existed even in the end of last century in the form of a foot-path. Probably the western fosse had been filled up by the forfeited Earl, who, in 1711, made large additions to the house, and gave it a new front, upon which are fine carvings of the Vallognes and

---

[1] *Reg. Ep. Brechin.* p. xxi, giving other curious entries.
[2] Lord Hailes, *Annals,* i. 302-3; Math. West. *Flor. Hist.* p. 446; Black, *Hist. Brechin,* p. 18.   [3] *Theatrum Scotiæ,* plate iii.

Maule arms.   The latter are upon a separate shield, quartered with those of the ducal house of Hamilton, the forfeited
Earl having married Margaret, third daughter of the fourth
Duke of that title.   The castle was still further enlarged by
William, Lord Panmure, near the close of last century; and
after his death his son, Fox Maule, afterwards Earl of Dalhousie, had both the interior and exterior much improved.
Fox Maule was born there on the 22d of April 1801, and it
was his favourite residence; it has also been frequented by
the late and present Earls as their principal seat.

From the time that King Edward I. besieged the castle,
neither it nor the district had been the scene of any warlike
deed of much moment until about the middle of the following
century, when the battle of Brechin was fought between the
Earl of Crawford and the king's forces.   As the incidents of
the event are given more fully elsewhere, it need only be
remarked here that this was a struggle between the Douglas
party, as represented by Earl Beardie, and the king, by
his lieutenant the Earl of Huntly; and the tide of battle was
luckily turned in favour of royalty.   This battle was fought
at the Haercairn, in the parish of Stracathro, between two
and three miles north-east of the town of Brechin, and a farm
in the immediate locality still bears the name of *Huntly*-hill,
in honour of the leader of the royalists.[1]

The next, and indeed the only other affair of note which
took place at Brechin (with the exception of some skirmishing
during the Wars of the Covenant, and certain incidents in the
rebellions of the following century, not very dissimilar to those
of other towns in the county at the same period), relates to
the times of the unfortunate Queen Mary and the Regent
Lennox, when both the town and castle were captured by
the Earl of Huntly "in the Queines name and behalff."

Upon this Huntly gave the castle in keeping to Captains
Couts and Muir, and proceeded northwards himself for the

[1] Jervise, *Land of the Lindsays*, pp. 180 sq.

purpose of raising a larger army, while Lennox, taking advantage of Huntly's absence, besieged and captured the castle, and hanged the two captains, with a number of their soldiers, in front of it.[1] This was in August 1570,[2] and in the following year Earl Huntly's brother, Sir Adam Gordon of Auchindown, also took Brechin, in what is known as the "Bourd of Brechin;" but, in direct opposition to Lennox's brutality, as well as his own when he burned Towie Castle and twenty-seven of its inmates, he displayed one of the finest traits of humanity and chivalry on record. It appears that after his defeat of the Earl of Buchan, he returned thanks to God in the kirk of Brechin for the victory he had obtained, and, calling the prisoners to the number of nearly two hundred before him—and most of them were gentlemen—he dismissed them all upon the one condition of their becoming, in future, faithful subjects to the Queen.

SECTION IV.

For all the vision dies,
As 'twere, away : and yet the sense of sweet,
That sprang from it, still trickles in my heart.

DANTE, *Paradise.*

Brechin in 990, etc.—The Town three times burned—Royal Grants—Weekly, and Trinity Muir Markets—First represented in Parliament—Disputes between the Bishop and the Earl of Panmure—Election of Magistrates—The Bishop Provost —The Earl of Panmure Hereditary Justiciary—the Bishop's power in civil matters annulled—Usurpation of power by the Church—Incorporation of Trades— Hereditary Blacksmiths, etc.

As in the case of many other old towns, a remote and hazy antiquity, with an unauthenticated dignity, is often ascribed to Brechin.[3] Not content with calling it the chief seat of Druidism north of the Forth, and the Pictish capital, tradition

---

[1] Gordon, *Genealogy of the Earldom of Sutherland,* p. 155.

[2] Tytler, *Hist. Scot.* vii. pp. 280, 301 ; *Diurnal of Occurrents,* p. 183 ; Lamont, *Diar.* p. 227 ; Black, *Hist. Brech.* pp. 46-7.

[3] The Gaelic *Braigh-chein,* signifies "a hilly brae," and is quite descriptive of the situation of the town of Brechin.

also affirms that it was anciently the county town.   As already
seen, it is first mentioned in the year A.D. 990, and this is the
earliest authentic notice of any of the towns in Angus, but even
at that time it is described as a *large city*.   It was then a
considerable ecclesiastical seat, and afterwards, being the
cathedral city, appears to have had the Bishop as chief magistrate or ruler of the burgh down to a late date.   Chalmers
classes Brechin among the burghs-royal of King David II.;
and in the charter of King Charles I. it is stated to have been
a " frie burgh royall " when King James III. granted a charter
for levying petty customs in 1488.[1]   The first mention of a
Provost occurs in the same Act, but no person is specially
named as holding that office until the year 1696.[2]

The town was burned at three different times—first, it is
said, by the Danes, in 1012 ; next in 1645, by the Marquis of
Montrose, when about sixty houses were destroyed ; and the
third time in 1672.   The origin of the last fire is unknown,
but, as was then customary, collections were made throughout
the country in behalf of the sufferers, and a considerable sum
was raised for their relief.[3]

It was a market-place in at least the reign of King David I.,
and in an early grant by King William, the Bishop and Culdees
had a renewal of David's charter, which empowered them to hold
a free market on Sundays, in *villa* of Brechin.[4]   This term
seems rather at variance with that of *civitas* in the Pictish
Chronicle already quoted, but the name *city* was and still is
given to cathedral towns or those having the seat of a Bishop.

This charter of right of market, and that regarding the
trading privileges of the town, were confirmed by subsequent
monarchs.   Under the provisions of the latter charter, the
inhabitants continued to trade in various parts of the county,
and to carry merchandise to and from the waters of South Esk

---

[1] Chalmers, *Caled.* i. p. 776; *Acta Parl.* v. p. 631.
[2] Black, *Hist. Brechin*, pp. 111, 339.
[3] Spalding, *Trubles*, ii. p. 461 ; *Brechin Sess. Records.*
[4] *Reg. Ep. Brechin.* i. p. 3.

and Tay, which were the most convenient places for shipments, without interruption, until towards the close of the reign of King David II. At that time the burgesses of Montrose, proceeding on the narrative of their doubtful charter of trading privileges before noticed, questioned the right of the merchants of Brechin to traffic with ships lying at their port, and a like objection was raised against them by the people of Dundee in regard to their harbour on the Tay. These difficulties were soon overcome, however, and in 1372, King Robert II. not only confirmed the ancient privileges of the burgh, but provided that the Bishop and merchants of Brechin should receive the protection of the king's officers, if the people of Montrose or Dundee disturbed them in these matters at any future time.[1]

In 1483, the modified burgh tax of Brechin amounted to £4 Scots, being somewhat less than that of Montrose, and considerably more than that of either Forfar or Arbroath;[2] but now the population and revenue of either of these towns greatly exceed those of Brechin. Still, notwithstanding the apparent wealth of Brechin at the above date, its revenues seem to have been quite inadequate to meet the expenditure; for, in 1488, King James III., in consideration of the *poverty*, and at the same time the loyalty, of the burgh, empowered the citizens to levy a small payment (*unum obolum*) as custom on all sorts of goods brought into the town, and to employ collectors of the same.[3] This is the first and only time that mention is made of a royal grant concerning the customs of the burgh, but, in virtue of that charter, the petty customs are still levied. So far as ascertained, the customs were first let in 1580, at the annual rent of £60 Scots,[4] and since that time they have naturally increased in value, so that now they yield a considerable income.

The weekly markets were held on Sunday until the year

---

[1] *Reg. Mag. Sig.* p. 65-6; *Reg. Ep. Brechin.* ii. pp. 314, 380; Black, *Hist. Brechin*, p. 20. [2] *Miscell. Spald. Club*, v. p. 27. [3] *Reg. Ep. Brechin.* ii. p. 122. The *obolus* is 1s. Scots, or 1d. sterling.— Ruddiman, *Vocab.* p. 114. [4] *Min. of Bailie Court, Brechin.*

1466, when they were altered to Monday. In 1640 the day was changed to Wednesday. Subsequently it was altered to Tuesday, which is now the weekly market-day. This alteration probably took place in 1647 ; we know at least that the kirk-session and magistrates met that year to consult regarding such a change.[1] Besides the ordinary weekly market, there were and still are other fairs held within the parish. Lammas Muir, established by Act of Parliament in 1695, continued in old times for the space of eight days ; it is now limited to one day. But the most ancient and principal fair is that of *Trinity*, so styled in honour of the name in which the cathedral is believed to have been dedicated. This fair was long held in the town,[2] but now stands upon a common about a mile to the north, and continues three days, which are devoted respectively to the sale of sheep, cattle, and horses. From time immemorial and until lately, the magistrates, who are superiors of the market and attend it in a judicial capacity, went there in procession, preceded by a guard of two free members from each of the incorporated trades of the burgh. These were armed with halberts of various devices, and had precedence in the procession according to the dates of their respective incorporations. But the marching of the guard, as well as the custom of " taking in the market," at which there appears to have been a good deal of amusement, may now be said to be obsolete.[3]

Brechin had no lay representative in Parliament until 1585,[4] but he often occurs after that period ; and the town's commissioner to the celebrated Parliament of 1647, when King Charles I. was sold to the English, was one of the four commissioners of Scotch burghs that voted against that transaction.[5] This had perhaps been owing chiefly to the influence of the Earl of Panmure, who was one of King Charles's firmest friends. There was no bishop in Brechin at

---

[1] *Acta Parl.* v. p. 301 ; *Brech. Sess. Rec.*   [2] *Acta Parl.* ix. p. 499.
[3] *Old Stat. Acct.* xxi. p. 124 ; Black, *Hist. Brechin*, pp. 97, 274.
[4] *Acta Parl.* iii. p. 374.   [5] *Sup.* p. 59 *n.* ; Black, *Hist. Brech.* p. 69.

that date, Bishop Whitford having fled to England and died, and no successor being appointed till after the Restoration. So soon as they were reinstated, the magistrates of Brechin, as had been previously the case, were greatly influenced in their doings by the bishop and his court. The bishop not only sat, as of old, in the capacity of provost or chief magistrate, but had at the same time the power of electing one of three bailies, and thus had little difficulty in carrying matters according to his wish. Another of the bailies was elected by the community of the town, and in that too the bishop is believed to have had a considerable hand; while the appointment of the third lay with the proprietor of the lordship of Brechin and Navar.

Soon after Sir Patrick Maule of Panmure had bought these estates in 1634, a misunderstanding took place between him and the bishop, and the elections became a source of great annoyance to the public, being frequently attended by " ryot and bluid." With a view to putting a stop to this unpleasant state of matters, the king appointed a commission to inquire into the subject, and to adjust differences ; by this it was recommended that the bishop and the Earl of Panmure should mutually concur in making choice of bailies, and that the latter should also "give ane deputation" of his hereditary office of Justiciary " to the person qwhome he names to be baillie of the toun."[1]

If this recommendation was at all acted upon, it had been only for a very short time, for soon afterwards it became necessary to pass a special Act of Parliament, whereby the power of the bishop in civil matters was annulled. It was likewise declared that Sir Patrick Maule should continue as before to elect one bailie, and that the community should only have the power of electing the remaining magistracy and Council. From the bishop to the magistrates was also transferred, at the same time, the power of granting charters over Church and other lands in the town and neighbourhood, thus

---

[1] Black, *Hist. Brechin*, p. 64 ; *Reg. de Panmure*, i. p. xl, ii. p. 320. The Earls of Crawford and Mar had previously been Justiciaries of Brechin.

depriving the kirk of all power in the civil jurisdiction and management of the affairs of the burgh.[1] Still, with that tenacity which has characterised the Church in all ages, she clung to her ancient powers, and, despite the prohibition of Parliament, successive bishops continued to sit in the Councils of the burgh, and to elect a bailie, down even to the disestablishment of Episcopacy. It is needless to say that the Panmure family only ceased to exercise their right of hereditary Justiciary and the election of a magistrate, on the occurrence of the attainder of 1716.[2]

Although the trades were not incorporated until the year 1600, or a Guildry formed until 1629, there appears to have been a considerable and varied traffic long previously carried on ; and so early as 1580, a standard price was set upon candles, and a committee was appointed "to prove flesh meat." Both were named by the Bailie Court ;[3] and although there is no record of the special excellence of any of the trades of Brechin in early times, it may be presumed, from the fact that a load of "quhyt breid" was sent from Brechin to Aberdeen in 1603-4, "to try the baxteris witht," and that, at a later date, the community of the same city were charged for "ane calsie maker," who went there from Brechin, "for wndertaking the bigging of the tounes commoun calsies"—that those trades, at least, were in good repute.[4] The first still stands deservedly high, but the latter is now little known in Brechin, the old causeways of the town having, several years ago, given place to the plan of Macadam, when, as if to verify

---

[1] *Acta Parl.* v. p. 631.

[2] Subsequently the Town Council consisted, as at present, of thirteen members, including a provost, two bailies, dean of guild, treasurer, and hospital master. According to the *Report of Grievances of Royal Burghs*, the affairs of Brechin, like those of many other places, appear to have been sadly mismanaged, as it was shown that the Provost and others "possessed themselves of large tracts of the public territory," which at one time extended to "several thousand acres, and that now (1789), it is not possessed of an hundred," for which the town received an annual fee of £15 !

[3] *Minutes of the Bailie Court of Brechin,* bound up with *Minutes of the Hammermen, MS.,* the property of the Hammermen Trade. For supposed history of the entries in this minute-book, see Black, *Hist. Brechin,* p. 44. APPENDIX No. VI.

[4] *Miscell. Spalding Club,* v. pp. 74, 144 ; Black, *Hist. Brechin,* pp. 58 sq.

the reputed prophecy of Thomas the Rhymer—that the streets would one day be turned over by the plough—the boulders were removed by that means.

The Guildry Incorporation still exists in Brechin, and, together with the six trades (hammermen, glovers, bakers, shoemakers, weavers, and tailors), forms a numerous and influential body. The glover trade has long ceased to be practised. That of weaving or the linen manufacture, now the staple trade of the burgh, is rapidly on the increase. The hammermen was the first incorporated of the trades, and the office of common blacksmith to the lordship of Brechin had long existed under the bishops. It was hereditary in the family of Lindsay, who held the appointment for many ages until about 1616; and for the making and mending of ploughs and sheep-shears, they had certain annual payments in meal and wool from various farms in the lordship, and pasture for two cows and a horse at Haughmuir.[1] The minute-book of the hammermen, which begins on 2d February 1579, contains some curious entries, and these, with the records of the kirk-session, throw considerable light upon the ancient manners and customs of the district.[2]

SECTION V.

The rays of night, the tints of time,
Soft-mingling on its dark-grey stone,
O'er its rude strength and mien sublime,
A placid smile have thrown.

HEMANS, *Tale.*

Almshouse established by James VI.—Increase of Beggars—Prohibited from appearing during the King's Visit—Privileged Beggars—Badges made for them, etc.—The Plague—The Presbytery meets on Butherkill (Burghill) Hill—People leave the Town and live in Huts—Murlingden—Weekly Markets held at Kintrockat.

APART from the Hospital or *Maisondieu* already mentioned, there was also a bede-house in the town, which was established by James VI., 1572-87, and supported by the annual rents

[1] Jervise, *Land of the Lindsays*, pp. 335, 336.
[2] Black, *Hist. Brech.* pp. 58 sq., gives a fuller account of the Guildry, and also extracts from the minute-book of the Hammermen.

paid to prebendaries and chaplains of the Church prior to
the Reformation.   These the king decreed should go in
future towards the support of an hospital or asylum for the
accommodation of the destitute and helpless of all ages,
whether men, women, or children.[1]   But this act of royal
beneficence does not appear to have taken effect until the
beginning of the following century, as it was only then that
the magistrates of the burgh, whom the king constituted
patrons of the hospital, found themselves at liberty to purchase
a house for the purpose.   "Wnderstanding," as the deed goes
on to narrate, "that our Souerane Lord hes erectit within thair
citie ane hospitalitie for the ease and sustentatioune off the
edgit and puir placit and to be placit thairine, and for thair
intertinement hes dottit and gewine to thame dyuerss rentis
and benifices, and thai [the bailies and Council] being
cairfull to haiff ane speciall mansioun and residence to the
saidis puir in all tyme cumming," resolved to purchase the
" mansionis" of the chantor and of the chancellor of the church.

These stood near the present manse of the second minister
of the parish, and were bought in 1608;[2] but in less than
eighty years from that date, on account of the house being
" neither wind nor water tight," the inmates had to leave the
building, and were boarded in various parts of the town.
Since that time there has been no Hospital, properly so called,
in Brechin, but the rents belonging to that foundation are annually dispensed among such of the poor as have a claim to
them, the Hospital Master being a member of the Town-Council.

As is still customary in many such foundations, the inmates
of the Hospital of Brechin had to wear a peculiar habit; and
at one period, when a debauched member of the tailor craft
applied for admission to the house, the kirk-session granted
his request upon the wary provision " that he be not fund a
drunkard quhairunto he is suspect to be given; as also that

---

[1] *Reg. Ep. Brechin.* ii. p. 224 ; Black, *Hist. Brechin*, p. 43.
[2] *Reg. Ep. Brechin.* ii. p. 236.

he keip the houss and wear the habit suitable, and behave himselff modestlie and soberlie thairin."[1]

About this time, the number of beggars, both local and general, appears to have been greatly on the increase. They seem to have made the church-doors their chief place of resort, and to have become so obstreperous in their behaviour on Sundays, that it was found "vnpossible for men to open thair pursis to serve the broddis" at the kirk-door, without being "violentlie" attacked by them; the collectors of the alms were at the same time unable to perform their duty "becaus off the manie beggaris that ouer hauled both thame and the people." Still, anxious to make every person and thing appear as pleasant as possible to royalty when the king came to the town in 1617, each officer had a new "sout off blew as his livray," and had strict orders to "suffer neither uncouth nor couth beggers to resort aither to the kirk-yaird or streitt" while the king was in town.[2] The king, it appears, was expected to visit the church, and it may be taken that he did actually attend worship in it, for *the king's loft* is mentioned in the records soon after that date.

It was during the early part of the same year that a list of the really poor was made up, and a pewterer was instructed " to mak ane number off badges to be marks to the puir off the paroch;" it was at the same time declared that no other person shall have "libertie to begg but those that haue these marks." This was the origin of the order of *privileged beggars*, who, down to the change in the Poor-law in 1845, perambulated the streets in a body upon Thursdays, visiting the merchants' shops and the houses of the wealthier inhabitants. This procession was headed in its later days by "Sandy Maukim," a gaunt crippled veteran, that had a shining blazon dangling from his coat, and

"Whose spacious scrip, and boundless conscience bore
A double alms from many a bounteous door."

---

[1] *Brech. Sess. Rec.* 1618.
[2] On the Brechin beggars, see Black, *Hist. Brechin*, pp. 69, 196.

Soon after the year 1617, we find the kirk-session busying themselves as to the propriety of "bigging ane hous to lodge puir young vnes"—perhaps the children of wandering beggars ; and some years later, when an "ordinance" had been passed by the Justices of the Peace, prohibiting the poor from being allowed to wander abroad in the streets, they again met to consider the best means of complying with the order, and ultimately resolved upon settling "the puir within honest menis housses."

In little more than twenty years from the date of the last of these minutes, in 1645-48, Scotland was visited by a dreadful pestilence, which is said to have carried off more than half of the population of the country.   Like other parts of the kingdom, Brechin also suffered from that awful scourge, and, according to an inscribed tablet in the churchyard, it appears that no fewer than six hundred of the inhabitants fell victims to it in the short space of four months.   Labour of all sorts was suspended for a time, the very streets are said to have been overgrown with grass, and no meeting of the people took place at church, or in the kirk-session, from April to November 1647.   Nor did the Presbytery sit from the first of these dates until the 25th of July ; and even then, fearing to meet in the town, they are recorded to have convened upon "Buthergill Hill." On that occasion, however, which was their first meeting as a body "because of the pestilence," they elected a ruling elder to the famous General Assembly of that year.   It was not till the 20th of January 1648, that the Presbytery met in the town, and at that meeting Mr. David Carnegy, minister of Farnell, preached "a sermon of thanksgieving for the merciful delyverance quhilk the Lord did grant to the city of Brechin from the pestilence," choosing for his text the striking words of the Psalmist—"Fools, because of their transgressions, and because of their iniquities, are afflicted." [1]

Every precaution was used, both in the urban and land-

[1] *Brechin Presbytery Records.*

ward parts of the parish, to prevent the pestilence from spreading, and parties, who acted as *cleansers* during its ravages in Edinburgh, were brought thence to Brechin to fumigate or otherwise disinfect the dwelling-houses. In this work of cleansing the poor often lost their household furniture, which in many cases it was advisable to burn; and, after the severity of the pestilence had abated, collections were made throughout the country to replace the lost articles, as we see in the case of a poor woman at Craigend of Aldbar. Among the inhabitants, who perished at that time, were the wife and two daughters of David Donaldson, a bailie of the town and commissioner for the burgh to Parliament in 1644;[1] also, a person of the name of Erskine, to whose memory a stone is said to have been erected bearing this rude verse :—

> " Here lies JOHN ERSKINE,
> Who died of the affliction ;
> No one must disturb his bones
> Until the Resurrection."

It is said that the piece of ground on the north side of the church, known as the *fore* kirkyard, was set apart for the burial of those who died of the pestilence. From a superstitious belief that the *plague* itself was interred in the graves of those who died of it, and that, upon these graves being opened, it would reappear in the form of a bluish mist or vapour, and spread over the country with as much severity as before, the place was not used for general burial until the idea was shown to be groundless by the interment of Mr. Patrick Bowie of Keithock, in 1809.

Although there is no account of the population of Brechin in 1647-8, the great number of persons who are recorded to have died there in so short a space of time, goes far to confirm the striking record of the ravages which the malady is

---

[1] *Acta Parl.* vi. p. 96. A tombstone, still extant, thus records the death of the Donaldsons—" Heir lyes Bessie Watt, spovs to David Donaldsone, bailzie of Brechin, and Elspet Donaldsone, and Iean Donaldsone, their dochters,—1647." According to the kirk-session records, David Donaldson and Betsy or Elizabeth Watt, were married in 1620.

said to have made in Leith, where the number of the dead was believed to be greater than that of the living.[1]   Tradition asserts that the more deeply afflicted of the town's-people were sent to the common muir, where huts were prepared for them, and that there they were allowed to die unheeded, and be buried by their surviving fellow-sufferers.   The latter part of this story, however much it may savour of inhumanity, is by no means improbable, and the first portion is corroborated by the kirk-session records, where entries occur, in the months of January and October 1648, of payments having been made by the kirk-session to several persons who are described as "lying in *the seikness in the huts.*"   These but too clearly show that many of the poor and plague-smitten had been living in the fields during the most inclement season of the year.[2]

Record is silent as to the precise place of the exile of these unfortunate creatures, but tradition affirms that the small estate of Murlingden, about two miles north of the town, which was feued off the common muir, received its name in consequence, and was known of old as *Mourningden.*   A burn runs through that den towards Cruick Water, and the sides of the den seemed at one time as if studded here and there with artificial works about six feet square, surrounded by low walls of mud or turf.   Tradition also says that, instead of the weekly markets being held in the town at that time, they stood upon the estate of Kintrockat, about two miles to the westward, and also that a caldron was used for purifying the money which was exchanged on these occasions.   In commemoration of that event, a late proprietor is said to have had a mound raised upon the site of the reputed market-place.

---

[1] Robertson, *Antiquities of Leith*, p. 84.
[2] On the plague at Brechin, see Black, *Hist. Brechin*, pp. 70 sq.; also APPENDIX No. XVIII.

SECTION VI.

Thine, Freedom, thine the blessings pictured here,
Thine are those charms that dazzle and endear.

GOLDSMITH, *The Traveller.*

Brechin in the 17th Century—Johnston's Panegyric—Ochterlony's Account—The
Bridge—Mismanagement of Burgh Affairs—Mechanics' Institute—Smith's
Schools—Episcopal Church and Library—East Free Church—Cemetery—
Modern Improvements—the Den, etc.

IN the preceding sections, we have attempted to give an
epitome of some of the more important incidents in the history
of the town of Brechin from remote antiquity. Those desirous
of making themselves more particularly acquainted with the
state of the church and the burgh in old times, are referred to
the *Registrum Episcopatus Brechinensis,* so frequently referred
to in these pages ;[1] while details of the more modern history
and progress of the burgh will be found in Mr. Black's interesting *History of Brechin.*[2] Particulars of the modern history of
Brechin are not intended to be given here, and this chapter
will be concluded by brief quotations regarding the state of
the town from trustworthy writers of the seventeenth century,
and a few general remarks on its present condition.

Of *ancient* Brechin, apart from what has been already
noticed, very little remains. A large three-story house on
the north side of the Nether Wynd is perhaps the oldest
dwelling-house in town. Tradition says it was at one time
the town residence of the Earls of Crawford, and a spring-well
in an adjoining garden is called *Beardie's Well.* At a later
date, during the memorable Wars of the Covenant, it was the
"ludging" of the laird of Findowrie, a great friend to the
Covenant, and representative elder for the Presbytery of

[1] This invaluable local work was the second contribution of its talented Editor
to the Bannatyne Club, and his best literary effort. See notice of Mr. CHALMERS,
below, Part IV.

[2] *History of Brechin,* by David D. Black, Town Clerk, fp. 8vo. 1839, and 2nd
Edition 1867.

Brechin to the General Assembly.   In consequence, the
Marquis of Montrose, in 1646, burned and plundered this
house and the adjoining ·stables at the same time that he
set fire to the town.   But it is from Captain Slezer's view,
taken towards the close of the seventeenth century, that we
can form the best idea of the appearance of the town in old
times.   No vestige remains either of the city cross, its walls,
or its ports, or of the *Catis cross,* which stood near the South
Port.[1]   The south side of the Castle, as seen in Slezer's day,
had, as before remarked, much the same appearance as at
present, but neither the bridge nor cruives is shown in his
print.   The ruins of the Bishop's Palace, however, and the
Little and Meikle Mills, with several houses along the line of
road called the Cadger Wynd and Upper Tenements, are indicated, as are also the farm-house of Pitforthy, and the
Grampians in the background, with the opening to the valley
and mountains of Glenesk.

Arthur Johnston is the only poet of olden times who has
celebrated the praises of Brechin, and it will be seen by the
following translation of his poem, that it is characterised by
the same fancy as the rest of his Epigrams, particularly in
regard to the Round Tower.   Among other points, he alludes
to the defeat of the Danes, which is said to have taken place
at Aberlemno, and also mentions the Bishop's Palace, the
Bridge of Brechin, and the Bridge over the North Esk at Logie
Pert.   The latter bridge is believed to have been built by
Superintendent Erskine of Dun.

> "This fertile Town doth 'twixt two Rivers stand,
>   One to the North, one to the Southward hand :
>   The Watters down betwixt the Rocks do glyde,
>   Both Bridges have, and many Foords beside.
>   The Vict'rie of the Northern KING doth much
>   Commend this City, since its men were such
>   As stood, and by their Valour vanquished,
>   When as their Neighbours treacherously fled.

---

[1] *Reg. Ep. Brechin.* ii. p. 113.

> Here is a Bishop's House, and near to it
> A Tower seems built by Phidias' Art and Wit,
> Its bulk so little, and its top so high,
> That it almost doth reach unto the sky :
> Its Structure's round, look to it from afar,
> You would imagine it a Needle were :
> It's built so strong, it fears no Wind or Rain,
> And Jove's three-forkèd-Darts it doth disdain.
> > Compare the Fabricks ; BRECHIN's Tower exceeds
> > (Proud Egypt) all thy stately Pyramids." [1]

Camden mentions little else than the name of Brechin ; but Ochterlony describes the town as lying "very pleasantlie upon the north syde of the water of Southesk, which runneth by the walls. The toune is tollerablie well built, and hath a considerable trade, by reason of their vicinity to Montross, being fyve [eight English] myles distant from it; but that which most enriches the place is their frequent faires and mercats, which occasion a great concourse of people from all places of the countrey, having a great fair of cattle, horse, and sheep, the whole week after Whytsunday, and the Tuesday thereafter a great mercat in the toune; they having a weekly mercat every Tuesday throughout the yeare, where there is a great resort of Highland men with timber, peats, and heather, and abundance of muirfoull, and extraordinarie good wool in its seasone." [2]

Apart from the antiquities of the Round Tower, the Church, and the Castle, Brechin has few attractions for the stranger, excepting the beauty of the surrounding scenery; but in this respect, especially when viewed from the south side of the river, it has, as thus noticed by an anonymous rhymer, few rivals in the county :—

> " The finest view of Brechin may be got
> > From a soft rising ground beyond the bridge,
> Where you may see the country every spot,
> > And the town rising up a sudden ridge ;
> The castle, old cathedral, and what not,
> > And the spire's griffin 'minished to a midge."

The bridge is the same "stately fabric" that is lauded by Ochterlony and Slezer, though it is found to be much too narrow for the increased traffic of modern times; and the southern arch (the northern having been rebuilt towards the end of the last century), is, so far as known, the same that existed during the thirteenth century, when a payment was made for the support of the bridge out of the rents of Drumsleid in the Mearns.[1] Until within these hundred years, the highway, which led from the south to the north of Scotland, passed along the ridge, and sloped down the Burghill Hill to the bridge, which was the only stone bridge on the South Esk until 1796, when another was erected at Finhaven.[2]

In 1789, the Committee of Burghs, in enumerating certain grievances connected with Brechin, declared that, although the "revenue of the burgh is not inconsiderable, it had no public works either of ornament or utility.   'Tis true," they continue, "that water has been brought into town, and the streets paved, but the water was brought in almost wholly at the expense of Lord Panmure, and at present they are assessed for keeping wells and fountains in repair.   They were also assessed in nearly £200 before the streets were repaired."   At same time the cess of the burgh was levied at £80 a year; but, says the Committee quaintly, "let not the enormity of the fact prevent it from being believed that the amount paid into Exchequer does not exceed £40"![3]

Such were some of the evils connected with the *rotten burgh* system, which prevailed in Scotland, to a greater or less degree, down to the passing of the Reform Act in 1832, when, like other Scottish burghs, Brechin had its councillors chosen by the independent voice of the people, and its accounts annually submitted to public scrutiny.   Although several public works existed prior to 1780, they were limited in

---

[1] *Reg. Vet. Aberbr.* p. 184.

[2] Besides the suspension and revolving bridges at Montrose, there are now stone bridges on the South Esk at Gella, Cortachy, Shielhill, Justinhaugh, Finhaven, Stannochy, Brechin, and Dun.   [3] *Report of Grievances, etc.*, pp. 72, 80.

extent, and caused but little stir in the town; for an English traveller of the period (who, however, seems to have been inclined to find fault with everything Scottish) says that Brechin " is a place which requires not the obscurity of night to render it dismal."[1]   But since the end of last century the city is vastly improved by the widening of the old streets and laying out of new ones, by the erection of many handsome public and private buildings, and by the better care of all sanitary matters.   The manufactures of Brechin are mostly white linen, and bleaching of yarns, even from the neighbouring towns, has become an important industry; while the distilleries at the West Port and Glencadam produce large quantities of whisky for home and foreign use.   But the chief gain to Brechin has been the plentiful supply of water from the Mooran, which the Earl of Dalhousie inaugurated in 1874.

Of the more ornamental buildings that grace the burgh, the earliest erected was the East or *quoad sacra* Church.   It is a cruciform building, with a spire 80 feet in height, and, until the erection of some of the modern dissenting churches, was the neatest and most commodious place of worship in town. It was certainly the least costly; for, although fitted up for 860 sittings, the total expense, including the spire, was something less than £1000.

The East Church was followed, within two years, by the Mechanics' Institute and Public Schools.   These were built and endowed by the late Lord Panmure, who also had the lecture-room ornamented by a number of paintings, he and his successors in the peerage being hereditary patrons of the Institution.   Lectures are delivered to the members on various subjects during the winter months, and a reading-room and library of considerable extent belong to it.[2]   This building, as well as the one which falls next to be mentioned, is in the perpendicular Domestic style of architecture, the

[1] George Colman, *Random Recollections*, 1781.

[2] Black, *Hist. Brechin*, pp. 208 sq.

Mechanics' Institute having a square tower in the centre 80 feet in height, which is embellished with a fine carving of the armorial bearings of the noble donor.   Both are after the designs of the late Mr. Henderson of Edinburgh, who was a native of Brechin.

The other educational building just referred to is in the lower or Tenements district of the town.   It owes its rise, as mentioned above,[1] to the generosity of Mr. John Smith of Andover, Massachusetts, who made the handsome gift of £1500 towards the erecting and endowing of a school at Brechin, on condition that other £500 should be raised by the voluntary contribution of his fellow-townsmen within a given period. The sum of £600 being speedily raised, Mr. Smith, his brother, and their partner in trade, Mr. Dove, gave a further and joint donation of £600 for the purpose of giving the edifice an ornamental character, whereby it forms a fine object in the otherwise rather unattractive locality in which it is situated.

A schoolroom, schoolmaster's house, and library were erected about thirty years ago in connection with the Episcopal Church, and the plan embraced the later addition of a chapter-house; but the school has been discontinued, and the buildings devoted to other purposes, under the sanction of the Diocesan Library Committee.   The library, built at the sole expense of Bishop Forbes, is fitted up with oak shelving, and lighted by a Gothic window, with armorial bearings in stained glass; and at the Bishop's death there was a very substantial addition made to the books from his library : his portrait in oil, presented by himself, occupies the only vacant place on the wall.   An oak cabinet contains, among other curiosities, a richly illuminated copy of the Offices of the Virgin, executed on vellum by Nicholas Vivien, at Paris in 1515; also an antique backgammon board, beautifully inlaid with ivory, which is said to have belonged to Mary Queen of Scots.   The library consists of a large collection of early and

---

[1] *Supra*, p. 184.

rare editions of the works of the Fathers of the Church, and many other valuable books, which were gifted chiefly by Dr. Abernethy Drummond of Hawthornden, for the use of the clergy of the dioceses of Brechin and Dunkeld. Of the first of these sees the donor was for a brief period Bishop before his translation to that of Edinburgh. Externally the Episcopal Church itself has nothing to boast of in the way of beauty, although the interior is neat and comfortable.

But of all the new ecclesiastical buildings in town, that of the East Free Church is by far the most imposing. It is in the Gothic style of architecture, with a porch on the east side, and a spire on the south-west 150 feet in height. The principal doorway enters through the tower, the basement of which forms the porch, and some good pieces of carving ornament the doorway and other parts of the building. The roof is constructed of plain heavy beams with open timbers, and finished in dark staining. The north-west window, which is filled with stained glass, is a good example of the Early Decorated style in massive but elegant tracery, and, as a whole, the fabric is highly creditable to the congregation.

The New Cemetery, situated near the East Free Church, is approached by a stone bridge, which spans the Den in a line with Panmure Street, and it has an imposing gateway, the top of the arch of which is embellished by the appropriate figure of a phoenix, with an image of Silence on the key-stone. The situation, convenient for the town yet completely separated from it, is in every respect the best that could have been chosen, and no small credit is due to the chief magistrate for the manner in which he combated the numerous objections which were raised against it.[1]

Less than half a century ago, the ground now occupied by the substantial buildings in Panmure Street was the site of the *Croft* or weekly cattle markets, and the depository of the town's

[1] The first interment was made on 26th October 1857 ; on the 12th November following, a portion of the cemetery was consecrated by Bishop Forbes ; and on the addition of a new portion, that also was consecrated by Bishop Jermyn, in 1882.

débris and rubbish.   Southesk Street and Bank Street had no existence, and the only approach to the town in that direction was by a narrow filthy footpath along the Denside.   The *Witch Den*, lately an impassable mire, is now the principal entrance to the town from the south ; and the very place, upon which the fires are supposed to have been kindled, that consumed the persons of those unfortunate beings from whom the locality had its name, is occupied by dwelling-houses.[1]

The Latch, which was in an equally neglected state, is now a clean and favourite walk, decorated with villas and hedgerows ; and the common Den—to which the freemen from a very early date sent their cattle to graze under the charge of a common herdsman, who warned the respective owners to send out and take in their *kye* by the sonorous blast of a *nowt's horn*[2]—was converted into a nursery about sixty years ago. It teems with all that is choice in trees and flowers, for the superiority of which it has long been locally esteemed, and is a welcome and favourite resort for the well-disposed.

[1] *The Witch branks* is still in the possession of the Town Council.   The Presbytery and Kirk-Session books contain several accounts of witch trials and burnings, which took place at Brechin during the 17th century.

[2] " The bailies and Council elected Walter Erskine to be *common hyrd* to their nolt until All-hallowday next, and requested all concerned to deliver their nolt unto him as use is."—*Minutes of Bailie Court of Brechin, April* 11, 1580.

FORFAR WITCH BRANKS.

CHAPTER VI.

The Abbey, and Town of Aberbrothoc.

SECTION I.

Good, inasmuch as we perceive the good,
Kindles our love, and in degree the more
As it comprises more of goodness in't.

DANTE, *Paradise.*

Edward I. at Arbroath—Abbot Henry and the Convent did homage to Edward I.
at Berwick—Foundation of the Abbey—its Dedication to Thomas à Becket—Its
Situation—Origin of Abbeys—State of Scotland during the Middle Ages—
Grants to, and Revenues of, the Abbey—Visited by Alexanders II. and III.,
James V., etc.—Parliament held there in 1320—Letter of the Barons to Pope
John XXII.—Abbot Bernard.

WHEN King Edward I. and his court left Brechin, on the 5th
of August 1296, they went to the Abbey of Aberbrothoc.[1]
This was King Edward's first visit to the place; for, though
submissions had been given in at Arbroath on the sixth
of the preceding month, when Edward was proceeding northward, the king, according to his custom, received them
through his officials while the royal cortege was passing on
to Farnell and Montrose. Upon that occasion four knights,
together with Abbot Henry and the whole Convent, performed
homage to him; but Prynne is altogether silent in regard
to the knights, although their names are given in the Ragman Roll.[2] Both authorities, however, agree that on King
Edward's visit a baron named Mark of Clapham took the
oaths of allegiance, though they differ in regard to the day

---

[1] *Bannatyne Miscell.* i. p. 280; *Ragman Rolls,* p. 179. This is miswritten
"Berbrodoch" in the Diary of the King's journey.

[2] *Ragman Rolls,* p. 80; Prynne, *Hist.* p. 650.

upon which these were taken.   The former authority gives it as on the 5th, and the latter as on the 6th of August or on the day when the king passed from Arbroath to Dundee.[1]

It was Abbot Henry who placed King John Baliol's final renunciation of the kingdom in the hands of King Edward I., and the abbot's being thus a person of mark and influence had perhaps been the cause of his previously acknowledging[2] the power of Longshanks, which he did at Berwick-upon-Tweed so early as 1292.[3]   Henry does not appear in the charters of his abbey, but his name is preserved in consequence of the part he acted during the Wars of the Independence.[4]   If the writer of the royal progress is to be credited, the king may have had cause to suspect Abbot Henry's loyalty; for he appears to have held up the English nation to ridicule by insinuations of cowardice and effeminacy, making " the people believe," as the diarist writes, " thatt ther were butt women and noo men in England "—an absurdity, it need hardly be said, which was but too plainly disproved by the daring and martial spirit displayed by the English during the period under review.

The Abbey of Arbroath, at which King Edward I. rested while on his subjugating tour through Scotland, was founded by King William the Lion in 1178.   It was dedicated to St. Thomas à Becket, Archbishop of Canterbury, who was slain at the altar of his own cathedral on the 29th of December 1170 by four knights, who committed this murder in order to deliver the king from a formidable and obnoxious enemy. This incident, it ought to be remarked, forms the device of the ancient seal of the Convent of Arbroath.[5]

So far as has been ascertained, the name of Arbroath does

---

[1] Prynne, *Hist.* p. 113 ; *Ibid.* p. 651.   [2] Hay, *Hist. Arb.* pp. 195 sq.

[3] *Ragman Rolls*, p. 20 ; Rymer, *Fœdera*, i. pt. iii. p. 105.

[4] His exact place in the line of abbots it is hopeless to attempt to fix accurately : he was about eleventh.   *Reg. Vet. Aberbr.* p. xiv ; Miller, *Arbroath*, p. 105 ; Hay, *Hist. Arb.* p. 70.

[5] See engravings of the seal in *Reg. Vet. de Aberbrothoc;* an account of St. Thomas of Canterbury is given by Hay, *Hist. Arb.* pt. ii. ch. i.

not occur in any form until the foundation of the Abbey.   It
is true that Buchanan says its old name was *Abrinca;* but
this seems doubtful, and is perhaps merely a pun or witticism,
since it was at the church of the ancient city of Avranches, in
Normandy, that Henry II. first did penance for the death of
À Becket.[1]

Various surmises have been made as to the cause which
induced King William to inscribe the Abbey to that Saint,
but no satisfactory conclusion has been arrived at.   Some
suppose that he and À Becket were personally acquainted
" when there was little probability of the latter ever becoming
a confessor, martyr, or saint;" and it is well known that the
king invoked À Becket's help when led captive to Richmond.[2]
But, whatever was the cause of the king's favour for St.
Thomas, or however various the opinions may be upon that
subject, only one idea can be entertained of the imposing
situation of the Abbey, the ancient splendour of its architecture, and the greatness of its revenues.

A fine view of Fifeshire and the Lothians, and of the
country more immediately surrounding Arbroath, is obtained
from the site of the Convent.   The Romans, among the
earliest of their visits to Scotland, had a small encampment
in the vicinity, and the Northern marauders were conquered
within a short distance of the same place in the days of King
Malcolm II.; while, at the time the Convent was founded, the
neighbouring lands were possessed by some of the more important of the Anglo-Norman families who had acquired
settlements under the two previous kings.   According to
tradition, King William himself had an occasional residence
in the same locality, and, according to history, he was interred
in the Abbey.[3]   Apart from the old historical importance of
the district, it had many natural and acquired advantages,

---

[1] The story of a mint having been here, and of coins being struck with the word
Abrinca, is unfounded.   [2] *Reg. Vet. Aberbr.* p. xi ; Hay, *Hist. Arb.* pp. 25-6.
[3] On the finding of his remains before the High Altar in 1816, see Hay, *Hist.
Arb.* p. 98.

such as its proximity to the sea, and the long period the surrounding lands had been under cultivation.

Prior to the foundation of this Abbey, there was no similar establishment on any part of the long and rugged coast of Forfarshire, or within many miles of it; and the crazy huts, which were here and there scattered along the beach, were ill adapted for the reception of those whom natural and adventitious circumstances had sent to raise and improve the condition of Scotland. It was therefore important that a proper asylum should be planted in such a part of the country, so that travellers, whether for devotional commercial or warlike purposes, should have a place wherein to rest in peace and safety, and where they could enjoy all the luxuries and necessaries of life, which the intelligence and skill of the age could afford.

It was for these as well as for other more spiritual purposes that monasteries were established, and the condition into which by degrees they fell, is no criterion of their exceeding necessity and value in the rough times when weary men and helpless women began to seek refuge in them. They met a need and served their day, and we do not always consider how much we owe to them. But those who will study the chartularies of the ancient abbeys, and the old history of the nation, will readily admit, that when the Abbey of Arbroath was founded, and even long afterwards, the monastic system was perhaps the best calculated of all systems to meet the wants and intelligence of the people. Besides the knowledge suitable for the different grades of offices in the Church, and for the government of the State, the youth of the country were often trained by the monks in the useful and mechanical arts; and to those cloister-bred tradesmen, as we may call them, we owe most of the gorgeous, though now ruined, piles of religious buildings which were erected in the country from the twelfth to the fifteenth centuries.

Although the state of general intelligence and the commercial interests of the country were at a very low ebb when the new or monastic scheme of religion became universal in Scotland—that is, during the period from King David I.'s accession to the death of King Alexander III.—the kingdom was making steady and healthy progress in the arts of agriculture, commerce, and architecture, also in letters and the fine arts, as we find amply testified by the few remaining writings and illuminated missals of the monks.   Indeed it has been remarked by all historians that at that early epoch Scotland was in a singularly forward state ; roads and stone bridges, which are the precursors of all civilisation, were then common throughout the country, and everything seemed to be going forward as the best friends of Scotland could wish.   But, by the fatal divisions which followed, improvements of all sorts were suspended, and the peaceful arts were forgotten in a long reign of war and bloodshed.   An acute literary antiquary has well remarked, that at no period of the nation's existence, down to the Union in 1707, was it in a more prosperous and civilised state than it was at the death of the last Alexander.[1]

The Convent of Arbroath was composed of Tyronensian monks, who were so named from the first abbey of the order at Tyron near Chartres.   They were brought to Scotland in 1113 by David, Prince of Cumbria (afterwards King David I.), who built for them the Abbey of Kelso.   Reginald, a monk of that house, was the first Abbot of Arbroath, but he died during the first year of his incumbency.[2]   By the original constitution of the Abbey, its independence was secured apart from that of Kelso ; and the lands and revenues attached to it, by the foundation charter of King William, were so great

[1] *Reg. Vet. Aberbr.* p. xxix Pref. ; also see Chalmers, *Caled.* i. p. 643 ; Fordoun, *Scot. Chron.* b. x. c. 40.

[2] There were six convents of Tyronensians in Scotland.   Besides those of Kelso and Arbroath, there were Lesmahagow, in Clydesdale, founded by David I., 1140 ; Kilwinning, in Ayr, founded by Moreville, Constable of Scotland, also in 1140 ; Lindores, in Fife, founded by the Earl of Huntingdon, 1178 ; and Fyvie, in Aberdeenshire, which was a cell of Arbroath, founded by, it is supposed, the Earl of Buchan, 1179.   Walcott, *Anc. Ch. Scot.* pp. 236 sq. ; Keith, *Cat. Scot. Bps.* pp. 404 sq. ; Gordon, *Monast.* iii. pp. 439 sq.

that, with the grants that were made to it by the barons throughout the counties of Forfar, Kincardine, and Aberdeen, as well as elsewhere, it acquired a revenue and influence exceeding that of any other monastic establishment in the kingdom, St. Andrews alone excepted.

King William himself gave the monks of Arbroath the territory of Ethie and Achinglas, the shires or parishes of Dunechtyn and Kingoldrum, fishings on the Tay and on the North Esk, the ferry-boat of Montrose with its land, a salt work in the Carse of Stirling, lands also in Mondynes, and a toft in each of the King's boroughs, with licence to cut timber in his forests, and the patronage of no fewer than twenty-four churches. To these were added the custody of the Brecbennach, the consecrated banner of St. Columba, and a toft of land in Forglen, which went with the office. This was one of the most interesting of the Abbey's privileges, and underneath that banner the vassals of the Abbey went forth to war.[1]   The custody of this was held under the Abbot by the knights of Monymusk of that Ilk, from whom it passed by descent to the Urrys and Frasers, till it became vested, about the year 1420, in the Irvines of Drum.[1]

Next in importance to King William's donations, were those of the old Earls of Angus, who gave it the patronage of four churches and various lands in the neighbourhood of Broughty-Ferry and Monifieth. The Countess of Buchan gave the church of Turriff; Ralf le Naym, that of Inverugy; the Bishop of St. Andrews, Arbirlot; and the De Berkeleys, Inverkeilor, together with the lands of Balfeich in the Mearns.

Thomas of Lundyn, the Durward, gave the church of Kinerny, and the wood or forest of Trustach on the Dee; and Robert of Lundres, the king's bastard son, the kirk of Ruthven. To these gifts most of the minor barons in Angus and adjoining counties added lands, fishings, money, and other privileges. The church of Abernethy was also granted by Laurence,

---

[1] *Reg. Vet. Aberbr.* pp. xv, xxiii; *Miscell. Spalding Club*, iii. p. xxiv.

son of Orm of Abernethy, with half the tithes of the property belonging to himself and his heirs, as hereditary Abbot of the Culdees and lord of the lordship and manor of Abernethy. Among the more recent gifts to the Abbey were the church and revenues of Kirkmahoe in Nithsdale, which were given to it by King Robert the Bruce.[1]

In 1561-2, the money revenue of the Abbey was about £3064, with upwards of 422 chalders of victual, 37 barrels of salmon, besides services, kain, capons, and other perquisites. Still, notwithstanding the largeness of these revenues, it appears that in 1530, two years after King James's visit, when there is no word of princes or other great personages visiting the Convent, these payments in kind were not only insufficient for the maintenance of the Abbey and its visitors, but an extra purchase was made of 800 wedders, 180 marts, 11 barrels of salmon, and 1500 dried cod fish, with 52 chalders of victual.[2] The reasons for this enormous excess of expenditure are not very clearly accounted for by any document now extant.

Though the revenues of the Abbey were great, the demands upon its hospitality were equally so. Even in the time of the founder, while the buildings were in progress, he and his court met there to grant charters, and for the disposal of other matters which concerned the nation. His successors, Alexander II. and III., met there for like purposes, and the former had pecuniary aid from the monks while in difficulties, and this, he pledged himself, should not be to the disadvantage of them or their Convent.[3]

During the period of the Interregnum, King Edward I. and his suite, as already mentioned, passed a night here when on their return southward. King James V., familiarly designated "the king of the poor," was, with his vast retinue, on two occasions in the year 1528 entertained in the Abbey; and

---

[1] *Reg. Vet. Aberbr.*, Pref., for a summary of the abbatial endowments.
[2] *Reg. Nig. de Aberbr.*, Appendix. Miller, *Arbroath*, pp. 168; Hay, *Hist. Arb.* pp. 41 sq.   [3] (1229) *Reg. Vet. Aberbr.* p. 79.

Archbishop Beaton of St. Andrews, whose train was nearly as great as that of the king, also visited his nephew, who was then Abbot and afterwards more celebrated as Cardinal, no less than three times in one season.

But by far the most important assemblage that ever graced its walls was that which was held on the 6th of April 1320, presided over by King Robert the Bruce. It need scarcely be said that that assembly had its origin in a secret negotiation between King Edward II. and the Papal Court, when that king prevailed upon Pope John XXII. to despatch a nuncio to Scotland and threaten both King Robert and the whole nation with excommunication if they refused longer to own the superiority of the English king.

The Pope, however, miscalculated the character of the people with whom he had to deal, and the message was met with all the characteristic boldness of the surviving heroes of Bannockburn. The assembly consisted of thirty-eight of the most powerful magnates and barons of the age, and of these nearly a third part were connected with the counties of Angus and Mearns. In name of the whole community of Scotland they framed and despatched a singularly spirited letter to the Pope, setting forth the wrongs which the country had sustained at the hands of King Edward I. They maintained the independence of Scotland as a nation, and declared that they had been freed from their calamities by the valour of Robert the Bruce, and that with unanimous consent they had chosen him to be their " chief and king. To him," continues this remarkable letter, " in defence of our liberty we are bound to adhere, as well of right, as by reason of his deserts, and to him we will, in all things, adhere; for through him salvation has been wrought unto our people. Should he abandon our cause, or aim at reducing us and our kingdom under the dominion of the English, we will instantly strive to expel him as a public enemy, and the subverter of our rights and his own, and we will choose another king to rule and protect us; for, while there exist a hundred of us, we will never submit to England."[1]

This noble appeal, at the reading of which Pope John is said to have trembled, set the unfortunate question of our national independence at rest; and, as no representative of the English Court appeared to debate the matter, Scotland was left free to assert its ancient privileges, and that in a way suggested afterwards by the Pope himself.

Bernard of Linton, then Chancellor of Scotland and Abbot of Arbroath, was the writer of that manifesto. He was perhaps descended of a family who assumed their surname from the parish of Linton in Roxburghshire, and several of this name and county did homage to King Edward I. in 1296, as did also Bernard himself. [2] He was at that time parson of the kirk of Mordington in Berwickshire, was appointed Abbot of Arbroath in 1311, and Chancellor of the kingdom during the same year; both of these offices he held until the 30th of April 1328, when he was promoted to the see of Sodor or the Isles, where he continued down to the time of his death, which occurred in 1331-2.[3]

Combined with the highest qualifications as a diplomatist and Churchman, he also possessed, to no mean extent, those of a poet, and celebrated the battle of Bannockburn in a heroic Latin poem, of which a fragment has come down to our own times.[4] Although Bernard ceased to have connection with the Abbey of Arbroath, it is pleasing to find that, by permission of the Bishop of St. Andrews, he had an annuity or pension from certain lands belonging to the monastery over which he had so long presided[5]—a fact which shows that, even in those days of reputed darkness and bigotry, the services of the worthy were not always allowed to go unrewarded.

[1] Original is printed and engraved in facsimile in *Acta Parl. Scot.* i. p. 114; also in Anderson, *Dipl. Scot.* plate li.; translated in Lord Hailes' *Annals of Scotland,* ii. pp. 105-6. The original writing is preserved in the Register House, Edinburgh.

[2] *Ragman Rolls,* pp. 134-67.

[3] Keith, *Cat. Scot. Bps.* p. 302; Grub, *Eccl. Hist. Scot.* i. pp. 349, 354.

[4] Fordoun, *Scot. Chron.* ii. p. 248.   [5] *Reg..Vet. Aberbr.* p. 316.

SECTION II.

Sermons in stones.

SHAKESPEARE, *As you Like it.*

The Abbey Church—Chapter or Charter-house—Armorial Bearings of Abbot Panter
—Supposed Effigy of King William the Lion, and other Sepulchral Monuments
—Regality Tower—The Abbot's House—The Abbey burned by Lightning—Its
Repair, and Contract with the Plumber—Notices of its History after the Reform-
ation—Altars—Chaplainries—Hospitalfield, etc.

ALTHOUGH the ancient grants to the Abbey, and some other
interesting circumstances relating to its history, can be traced
with much certainty, the names of many of its early abbots
are lost, and little remains to show by whom the different
portions of it were built. It appears, however, that the Abbey
Church, begun in 1178, was not finished until 1233, a period
of fifty-five years, when, on the 8th of March, it was dedicated
by Ralph de Lamley, who held the office of Abbot from 1226
to 1239.[1]   Abbot Panter or Paniter is believed to have erected
what is now variously called the Chapter-house and the
Charter-house. We often read of fires occurring in the Abbey,
and the charters bear frequent testimony to the care taken by
the monks to keep the buildings in repair. A new dormitory
was being erected about 1470, during the time of Abbots
Brydy and Guthrie, and in the construction of this it was
stipulated that Norwegian timber should be used.[2]

The Abbey was built chiefly in the Early English or First-
Pointed style of Gothic architecture. The church was two
hundred and seventy-six feet long within the walls, the nave
and side aisles sixty-eight feet broad, and about sixty-seven
feet high. Only portions of the nave and choir (the east and
west ends) and the south transept, now remain.[3]   Small as

---

[1] *Chron. de Mailros*, p. 143 ; Grub, *Eccl. Hist. Scot.* i. p. 317.

[2] *Reg. Nig. de Aberbr.* pp. 163-7.

[3] Theiner, *Monumenta*, pp. 524-26, enables us to picture the Abbey as it was in
the beginning of the sixteenth century. The narrator was a priest of the diocese of
Brechin.—Hay, *Hist. Arb.* p. 39.

these are, they present some beautiful mouldings and details. The Abbey gateway, upwards of sixty feet long, which was only unroofed about the beginning of the present century, seems, with the exception of the Chapter-house, to be the most recently erected portion of the building, and shows a dawning of the Decorated or Second-Pointed style, which followed that of the Early English and prevailed down to the reign of King Robert II.[1]

The so-called Chapter-house, supposed by some to be a Vestry or Sacristy (for it is difficult to say for what purpose the chamber was really used), is now made the depository of such relics as are found among the ruins, and is by far the most entire portion of the fabric, being two stories high, and having a short spire at the south-west angle. The lower apartment measures about eighteen by twenty feet, and is surrounded on all sides, except the north, by an *arcade* or ornamental dressing of arches, which appear to have run round the whole edifice. The room is about thirty-two feet high, and the groins of the roof spring from four columns, two of the capitals of which are formed of shields. Those on the south-east capital are wholly unembellished; but the centre shield, or that on the north-west (as represented in woodcut No. 1)

 is charged with the armorial bearings of the old family of Panter of Newmanswalls, near Montrose, of which family the Abbot was a cadet.[2] The other two shields, as represented in woodcut No. 2,

No. 1.   No. 2.

appear to be both charged with a crozier or pastoral staff, and two old-fashioned keys formed into a St. Andrew's cross, tied together in the middle, and united at the bottom by a chain. A shield bearing the Panter arms is in another part of this room; and thus the not improbable idea has

---

[1] Rickman, *Essay on Gothic Architecture*, p. 381.

[2] On a fess with three roundels, in chief, a crozier between two mullets, with a rose in base, the latter figure perhaps for Montrose.

been advanced, that this Abbot, who held office from 1411 to 1443 and resigned it in consequence of old age, was builder of the house.[1]   The capitals of the two remaining columns represent floral ornaments and birds sitting upon trees, picking at the branches.

The relics preserved here consist entirely of the remains of ancient tombs.   The most interesting is, perhaps, the fragment of a recumbent effigy in the dark spotted kind of marble called *madrepore*.   Although the head is gone, and the figure otherwise mutilated, there are a grace and elegance in the disposition and folds of the drapery, and a truthfulness in the remaining details of the lion at the feet, that indicate the chisel of no mean sculptor.   All history agrees that William the Lion, the founder of the Abbey, was buried before its high altar (*ante majus altare*, says Fordun), on the 10th of December 1214 ; and, from the fact of this effigy having been found in the chancel of the church, immediately in front of the supposed site of the High Altar, and covering a stone coffin in which were the bones of a person of goodly stature, the grave and statue were presumed to be those of King William. Apart from the figure of the animal at the feet, which is a common accompaniment to such effigies, a pouch or purse is suspended from a belt on the left side which begirts the waist ; and on various parts of the figure are fragments of four armed Liliputian knights, with spurs on their boots, as if in the act of arranging or adjusting the dress.[2]

There is another mutilated statue in bluish sandstone, con-

---

[1] On these remains at Arbroath, see Laing's account in *Proc. Soc. Ant. Scot.* i. p. 13.

[2] This statue and the one next noticed, are engraved in *Reg. Vet. de Aberbrothoc*, and the supposed grave of King William is now covered by an old gravestone, which bears a monogram, embodying the four initial letters—A. F. Y. P.— and a shield charged with *a crane* (the armorial bearings of the old Forfarshire family surnamed Fithie) ; the stone had perhaps belonged to a descendant of the Fithies. Near the same place were found three stone coffins, cut out of solid blocks, in one of which was the skeleton of a female, sewed up in a leather shroud, similar to, but not so entire as, that found in a stone coffin at the Abbey of Dunfermline, in 1849. The latter discovery is described in *Proceedings of the Society of Antiquaries of Scotland*, ii. p. 75.

jectured, on no very plausible grounds, to be that of St.
Thomas à Becket. The person represented is in a devotional
attitude, and habited in richly carved sacerdotal robes. The
folds of the drapery flow even more gracefully than those of
the first-mentioned fragment, while the ornamental parts of
the dress are carved with a delicacy and finish unsurpassed,
perhaps, by any contemporary piece in Scotland. The effigy
of an old priest, very similar to this, and nearly entire, the
stole of the robes being decorated by carvings of the sacred
dove, lies in the garden of Dun House, whither it was taken,
as one story says, from the Abbey of Arbroath, or according
to another, and the more probable, from the old kirk of
Montrose.

Another sepulchral monument, with an inscription round
the sides, now nearly effaced, is embellished with a full-length
effigy, in low relief. From the remains of the legend, the
person represented appears to have been one of the *monks* of
the Abbey. The name and date are illegible, but there is a
shield over the head, charged with two, or, it may be, three
bendlets—doubtless the armorial bearings of the Churchman
commemorated—and from this, it may be inferred that the
surname had been Alexanderson, or Sanderson, although there
is no trace in the chartulary of any monk bearing such a
name.[1]

The front of a mural tombstone, of a class commonly found
in old ecclesiastical buildings, somewhat resembling a chimney-
piece, is preserved in the same apartment. This fragment,
which was found near the site of the high altar, is divided
into four compartments, each of which contains a figure carved
in bold relief. The first division is occupied by an angel,
with outstretched wings, holding a shield, which is placed
upon a crozier and charged with the Panter arms. The figure

---

[1] In 1486, a William Alexanderson held the fourth part of the lands of the town
of Dunnychthin (Dunnichen), under the Abbots of Arbroath.—*Reg. Nig. de Aberbr.*
p. 249.

in the second compartment holds a pitcher, and the aspergillum or brush for sprinkling the holy water.   That in the third bears what seems to be a paten, and the figure in the fourth holds an open book with both hands.   Panter's bearings being upon this stone, it may be taken that it had formed a portion of the tomb of that Abbot ; and as the style in which this fragment is carved is not very dissimilar to that of the so-called statue of St. Thomas à Becket, that effigy may in reality have represented Abbot Panter, and at one time adorned his tomb.

The remains of another draped statue and the elbow of a mailed effigy are the only other remaining relics of the ancient sepulchral monuments of Arbroath, with the exception of three stone slabs, which lie in the graveyard, and are adorned with variously designed crosses and swords, of a type similar to those found in England and Wales.[1]   These few traces of old monuments show that the destruction which had taken place at Arbroath about the time of the Reformation had been great ; for doubtless the statues and other works of ancient art, which had adorned that magnificent place in its palmy days, were much more numerous than we have now the means of knowing.

But it ought to be added that the Regality Tower and adjacent buildings, with the stone arched roofs of the lower story, present works of considerable extent, and strength of workmanship.   The Abbot's house, now called the Abbey House and held in private hands, is of various periods.   The ground floor, which is evidently the oldest portion, is peculiarly constructed, the part called the kitchen having in the centre a strong pillar from which the arches of a low groined roof spring.   The upper portion of this house is of much more recent date.   Of the many pieces of carved oak panellings

---

[1] Boutel, *Christian Monuments of England and Wales.*   Numerous examples are there engraved.   Having found several similarly carved slabs in Angus and Mearns, etc., our author proposed, had time and circumstances allowed, to publish accounts of them at some later date.

which are said to have adorned it, even down to a late period, only two remain. One of these represents the Annunciation, with the common attributes of the dove descending on the sunbeam, and the cross-crosslet on the head and breast of the angel. The figure holds a cross in the hand, without the scroll or ordinary legend, and kneels on a geometrical pavement supported by an ornamented pedestal, enclosed in a Gothic arch.[1] The other panel contains a carving of the Scotch Thistle.

That the buildings of the Abbey suffered injuries from a variety of causes long anterior to the Reformation is matter of record, and in the frequent forays many of its earlier monuments had doubtless perished. Although its position was favourable in many respects, it was not so in others, for its proximity to the sea made it easy of attack by foreign fleets, and from these it frequently suffered, particularly from the English about the middle of the fourteenth century.[2] At the same time its elevated situation and towering spires rendered it liable to be struck by lightning, from which it suffered on two occasions within the space of about a hundred years. The first accident occurred in the winter of 1272, a year which seems to have been peculiarly disastrous to Scotland; for Fordun, in whose chronicle alone this burning is mentioned, says, "the land was barren, the sea unproductive, the air stormy, and sickness reigned among men, and mortality among cattle." The storm on that occasion came on upon a Saturday about midnight, with a violent wind blowing from the north, and accompanied by showers of hail. Many houses were blown down smothering those that slept within, and by the lightning the Abbey Church of Arbroath and many others throughout the country were destroyed.[3]

On the next occasion, which was in 1380, the damage done to the building was perhaps less serious and chiefly confined to the roof. The monks, however, had to be sent to live in

---

[1] This panel is engraved in *The Architect and Build. Oper.* i. p. 289, Lond. 1849.
[2] *Reg. Nig. de Aberbr.* p. 22.   [3] Fordun, *Scot. Chron.* c. x. p. 30.

other establishments for a time; and that the injury might be speedily repaired and the expenses discharged, the Abbot and his monks were enjoined by the Bishop of St. Andrews to relinquish much of their ordinary comfort and practise economy in all things, until the repairs were finished.[1] Touching this part of the Abbey's history, a singularly interesting document is preserved in the form of the contract with the plumber for "thekyn the mekil quer wyth lede." This indenture shows that in those days, as now, there were inspectors of works, and that penalties were inflicted where the stipulations of a contract were not complied with, and that rewards were given when its terms were duly fulfilled. The contractor, "Wilyam Plumer of Tweddale, burges of the city of Andristoun" (St. Andrews), was "to theke and gutter the mekil quer wyth lede;" and for this he was to receive thirty-five merks "at syndry termys as he is wyrkand," five merks of the sum being kept in the Abbot's hands until the works were finished, when these were to be given him, as well as "a gown with a hude til his reuarde." It was also provided that "the quer be thekyt and alurryt (or parapeted) al abowyt with stane, and qwhen it is alurryt he sal dycht it about wytht lede suffyciandly as his craft askys." The plumber was to provide one man, and the Convent another, together with "al maner of gratht that perteyns to that werk quhil it is wyrkande," and the plumber was to have threepence, and "a stane of ilk hyndyr that he fynys til his travel, and that day he wyrkis he sal haf a penny til his noynsankys."[2]

It is probable that the Abbey suffered also at the hands of the Lindsays and the Ogilvys in 1446, when the battle of Arbroath took place in consequence of the chiefs of these clans contesting the office of Bailie of the Abbey, a struggle which will be briefly noticed in another page. Of the destruction of the building at this time, however, there is no record, neither is it known whether the plan which was laid for a similar object,

[1] *Reg. Nig. de. Aberbr.* p. 35.   [2] *Ibid.* p. 42.

by Wishart and others, in the subsequent century, was ever put in execution. Wishart's attack, which was to be made upon "the Abbey and Town of Arbroath, in common with all the other Bishops and Abbots houses on that side the water thereabouts," was the work of several of the neighbouring barons, with the connivance of King Henry VIII. of England, out of revenge, it is said, for the wrongs which Cardinal Beaton had inflicted on the Protestant Reformers; and to that circumstance, perhaps, we must attribute the local tradition of Auchterlony of Kelly's attempting to destroy the Abbey about the same time.[1] But whether the demolition of the Abbey and its relics is to be attributed to the attacks of the barons, or to its having been made a quarry, out of which many of the houses in the town were built (for which last purpose, it is feared, there is but too good authority that it was used), it certainly maintained its high position among the other monasteries of the country down to the Reformation.[2]

In 1541 it was given *in commendam* to the second son of the Regent Arran, afterwards the first Marquis of Hamilton ; but on the attainder of that family in 1579, the king bestowed it upon his cousin, the Duke of Lennox.[3] Lennox died in 1583. In 1600 the abbacy was restored to the Hamiltons, and a few years afterwards, upon the King and Parliament resolving to disjoin the lands, patronage, and teinds of the Abbey from the Crown, they were erected into a temporal lordship in favour of the second Marquis of Hamilton, with the title and dignity of a lord of Parliament. Subsequently the abbacy is said to have "belonged to the Earl of Dysert, from whom Patrick Maule of Panmure, gentleman of the bedchamber to King James VI., did purchase it, with the right of patronage

---

[1] The story of Auchterlony's attack will be found in Bremner's guide-book—*The Abbey of Aberbrothoc : its Ruins and Historical Associations ;* Hay, *Hist. Arb.* p. 90.

[2] On the "Abbey in ruins," and the attempts to trace its downfall, see Hay, *Hist. Arb.* pt. ii. ch. viii.

[3] Hay, *Hist. Arb.* p. 91, gives a recently discovered precept from Lennox in 1580, allowing the stones, etc., of the Abbey dormitory to be used in building the parish church.

of thirty-four parish churches belonging thereto,"[1] and these the Panmure family continued to hold until the forfeiture of 1716, when the whole reverted to the Crown.   The above grant, however, did not include either the monastery itself, or "the houses, biggings, yeards, orchards, and others within its precincts," for these, together with a yearly revenue of "fyve thousand merks Scots money," were decreed by King Charles I., in 1636, to be given, out of the first and readiest of the revenues of his Majesty's Exchequer of Scotland, to the Bishop of Brechin and his successors in office.   This grant was ratified soon after the Restoration,[2] but reverted to the Crown at the Revolution.[3]

Ever since the attainder of the Earl of Panmure in 1716, the ruins of the Abbey have been owned by the Commissioners of Woods and Forests; but it was not until a century after the forfeiture that Government paid any attention to their condition.   In 1815 the sum of £250 was granted towards their repair, and at that time the tower of St. Thomas, a hundred and two feet high, was partly rebuilt.   The rubbish also or *débris,* which had accumulated to such an extent that it was nearly on a level with the base of the windows of the south aisle, was removed.   All the ruins were in that half-buried state, and bodies were interred among the rubbish, when the Abbey was visited by Dr. Samuel Johnson, in 1773.   Yet he expressed himself as so highly gratified with its appearance, even in that condition, as to say that "he should scarcely have regretted his journey [to Scotland], had it afforded nothing more than the sight of Aberbrothock."[4]   The ruins have still a very imposing appearance, and seem to be of much the same extent as when sketched by Pennant, Grose, and Cardonnell.   Of these antiquarians, the first says that in the year before his visit, "a part adjoining to the west end fell suddenly down, and destroyed much of the beauty of the place."[5]

[1] Spottiswood, *Religious Houses*, p. 446.   [2] *Acta Parl.* vi. p. 432.

[3] Hay, *Hist. Arb.* pp. 82 sq., has a painstaking account of the temporal lordship.

[4] Johnson, *West. Islands*, p. 12.

[5] Pennant, *Tour in Scot.* in 1772, p. 134.

Several grants since that of 1815 have been made by
Government for the further repair of the ruins ; and it is
hoped, now that they have survived so many changes and
chances, that the utmost care will be had for their preservation.   The ground adjoining on the north-east, together with
the aisles and other parts within the walls of the ancient
church, is used as a cemetery, and was the only place of
public burial in the town until 1867, when the new Cemetery
was provided at East Muirlands, and afterwards extended so
as to embrace an area of twenty acres carefully laid out.   In
this new Cemetery Mr. Allan-Fraser of Hospitalfield has, at a
great cost, erected a Memorial Chapel, which will also be the
family mausoleum.   The Abbey churchyard is neatly kept,
ornamented by trees and shrubs, and contains some interesting
monuments with curious inscriptions.   Bishop Henry Edgar, of
the family of Keithock, near Brechin, long Episcopal clergyman
of Arbroath, and Bishop of the diocese of Fife, was buried in
the south aisle ;[1] and near to the High Altar was an old burial-
place of the family of Ochterlony of that ilk, now marked by
a marble tablet.   Adjoining is a stone, commemorating the
death of an old burgess of the name of Pierson.   It is dated
1589, and has a carving of the arms of that family, which has
been connected with the town and neighbourhood of Arbroath
for probably four hundred years.[2]   J. A. Pierson, the proprietor
of Balmadies and the Guynd, is now its representative.

It is somewhat remarkable that there is no account of the
appearance of the Abbey prior to the days of Mr. Ochterlony,
who wrote about 1685.   The oldest known engraving is that
by Captain Slezer, taken much about the same time ; and from
this it appears that the ruins were in a half-buried state even
then.[3]   Mr. Ochterlony's notice is valuable, notwithstanding
that he has confounded the Chapter-house with the tomb of

[1] Jervise, *Land of Lindsays*, pp. 338, 436.   [2] *Reg. Nig. de Aberb.* p. 361, etc.
[3] Slezer, *Theatrum Scotiæ*, plate xii.   Engravings of the ruins of the Abbey of
Arbroath will also be found in Pennant's *Tour*, Grose's *Antiquities of Scotland*,
Cardonnell's *Antiquities*, Billings' *Baronial and Ecclesiastical Antiquities*, etc.

the royal founder, a mistake which had no doubt arisen from
its being then popularly believed to be the real place of his
interment.   He describes the royal tomb as " a very stately
piece of work of thrie storie high. The whole fabrick of the
buriall-place," he continues, " is still entire as at first, and if it
be not thrown downe, may continue so for many generations ;
the laigh storey is the buriall-place, and the second and third
storeys were employed for keeping the chartours of the
Monastrie.   There is one lodging remaining yet entire.   It
had a most stately church, with two great steeples on the west
end thereof; most part of the church is ruined, but was the
largest both for breadth and length, it is thought, in Scotland.
There is much of the walls thereof as yet standing in many
places ; the tower thrie storie high is standing yet entire, and
the roof on it.   There was ane excellent roume, called the
fish-hall, standing, with ane excellent oak roof ; but that with
much more of the building, by the avarice of the town's people
about there, were all broken down and taken away." [1]

Besides the chief altar there were at least five others within
the Abbey Church : in all there is said to have been twelve.
The six that are known were dedicated to St. Katherine, St.
Peter, St. Laurence, St. James, St. Nicholas, and the Virgin
Mary.[2]   The Chapel of St. Ringan or Ninian, bishop and confessor, stood at Seaton Den, to the eastward of the town, but is
long since lost sight of ;[3] while that of Our Lady, in which
were altars to St. Nicholas and St. Duthac,[4] occupied the site of
the old harbour, and was swept away, more than a century and a
half ago, to make room for the better accommodation of the shipping. The Almory Chapel, or place where the poor were relieved,
was at Almerieclose.   It was founded in honour of St. Michael,
and supported partly by the rents of the lands of Hospitalfield.[5]   It was possessed in the days of Mr. Ochterlony of Guynd

---

[1] *Spot. Miscel.* i. p. 343.   [2] *Reg. Nig. de Aberbr.* p. 227, etc.
[3] *Ibid.* pp. 271, 436.   The locality of St. Ninian's Chapel is celebrated by Alex.
Balfour, in his poetical tale of *Mary Scott of Edin-Know.*
[4] *Ibid.* pp. 356, 483.   [5] *Ibid.* pp. 448-56.

by James Philip, a gentleman of learning and poetical talent, who wrote a Latin poem in praise of Viscount Dundee entitled " Grameis," and also two elegies, one on the laird of Pitcur, and the other on Gilbert Ramsay, who volunteered his services in favour of royalty and fell with his leader at Killiecrankie. Mr. Ochterlony says that the house of Almerieclose was built of the stones of the chapel, and had " all the apartments belonging thereto. The fabrick was great and excellent, having many fyne gardens and orchards, now converted to arable ground, about which is a high stone wall." In addition to those chapels, there were other two situated at Kinblethmont and Back Boath, both dedicated to St. Laurence,[1] and another at Whitefield of Boysack, dedicated to the Blessed Virgin; all were dependent upon, and attached to, the Abbey.[2]

In connection with the Abbey there was also a Hospital or Infirmary, of much the same nature as those of the present day. There was attached to it a chapel, which appears towards the close of the fifteenth century to have fallen into a state of great dilapidation, and for the repair of this the rents of the lands of Abernethy and the chapel lands of Dron were mostly appropriated.[3] The Hospital, dedicated to St. John the Baptist, stood nearly two miles south-west of the Abbey; and, in 1325, when the lands are first recorded as being let by the Abbot, the tenants, Reginald of Dunbranun, and Hugh Macpeesis, were bound to build, during the first year of a five years' lease which they had of the lands, a barn and byre, each forty feet in length, and these they were to leave in good order at the expiry of their term.[4] Upon the site of this old byre and barn the fine hall of the mansion-house of Hospitalfield is erected; and it is believed that the agreement regarding the erection of the byre and barn referred to, furnished Sir Walter Scott (who, it ought to be remarked, visited Hospitalfield)

---

[1] *Reg. Vet. Aberbr.* pp. 99, 189; *Reg. Nig. de Aberbr.* p. 165.

[2] The fullest account of the altars and chapels belonging to the Abbey is given in Miller, *Arbroath*, chs. vii. and viii.

[3] *Reg. Nig. de Aberbr.* p. 268.   [4] *Reg. Vet. de Aberbr.* p. 368.

with the locality of "Monkbarns" in his novel of *The Antiquary*.

As a part of the Abbacy of Arbroath, the lands of Hospital-field belonged to the Earls of Panmure down to the time of their forfeiture, and were long held under them by Ochterlony of Guynd. About the year 1664 they were acquired by James Fraser, a cadet of the Philorth family, who had previously purchased the adjoining lands of Kirkton, and from these he and his descendants long took their title.

Down to within the last few years, the mansion-house of Hospitalfield had little pretension to architectural beauty, but under the present proprietor it has assumed a fine castellated appearance. Its principal internal feature is the great hall, which is in the Scoto-Franco style of architecture; and Mr. Allan-Fraser, himself an artist, has introduced, in the spandrels of the roof, carved medallion portraits of some of the more celebrated of the ancient painters. The terminations of the hammer-beams are ornamented by a variety of figures carved in wood, each bearing a shield charged with the armorial bearings of the Frasers of Kirkton, the Parrotts of Hawkesbury Hall, in Warwickshire, and the several houses to which they were allied. It ought to be remarked that the late Mrs. Allan-Fraser was the last descendant of the old families of Fraser and Parrott.

There is a fine oriel window in the west end of the hall. The arch of it is decorated by carvings of the signs of the zodiac, and the room contains a number of original paintings by personal friends of the proprietor, as well as several by himself. There are also some pieces of good sculpture in marble, carvings in wood of game, flowers, etc., and a collection of original drawings by Francis Place, who was an ancestor of Mrs. Allan-Fraser, and by Hollar, the celebrated engraver and painter. As a whole, this is perhaps the most interesting modern hall in the county of Forfar, and should it be properly cared for by posterity, Hospitalfield cannot fail to become a favourite resort for the curious and intelligent traveller.

SECTION III.

Let the world revere us
For our people's rights and laws,
And the breasts of civic heroes
Bared in Freedom's holy cause.

CAMPBELL, *Men of England.*

Origin of Name, and rise of Arbroath as a Town and Burgh—Early Burgesses—
—Customs—Grant by King John of England—Origin, and subsequent History
of the Harbour—Magistracy and Incorporations—Weavers' Toast—Progress of
Manufactures and Shipping—Modern Improvements—Church of St. Vigeans,
and Ancient Sculptured Stones—Ecclesiastical Notices of Arbroath.

THE town of Aberbrothoc, known better by the modern
name of *Arbroath*,[1] is situated upon the margin of the German
Ocean, at the point where the river Brothoc falls into the sea,
and hence the name of the town.   This stream rises in different parts of the parishes of Inverkeilor and St. Vigeans,
and the confluents become united near the mansion-house of
Letham Grange, in the latter parish ; from this it flows along
a muddy channel, skirting the old kirkyard of St. Vigeans on
the east, and running through the town of Arbroath towards
the sea.

The town of Arbroath had doubtless risen under the protection of the Abbey, and it appears to have soon become a
place of importance, for it was a recognised burgh even in the
time of its royal benefactor, King William the Lion, as several
of his charters are witnessed by parties who design themselves
burgess of Arbroath.   Some of their surnames, such as that
of Roger of Balcathin,[2] or Balcathie, seem to have been assumed
from lands in the neighbourhood of the town.   But the burgh
at first was probably under the regality of the Abbey, and to
this the lost charter of King William may refer.   It is now a
royal burgh, and joins with Montrose, Forfar, Brechin, and
Inverbervie in sending a representative to Parliament.

[1] Hay, *Hist. Arb.* p. 2 *n.*, gives a list of thirty spellings of the name.
[2] *Reg. Vet. Aberbr.* pp. 40, etc.

Like other burghs, Arbroath paid dues into the Exchequer of the kingdom, and these in 1328 amounted only to 17s. 6d. Scots, which was the smallest amount paid by any of the burghs in the county. From 1392 to 1405, the customs of the port or harbour, which were little more than £32 Scots, were uplifted by persons surnamed Conon and Seton; the latter appears as sole "customer" in 1425.[1] Probably the names of both of those persons had been assumed from the lands of Conon and Seton, and the parties themselves may have held these as vassals of the Abbey.

In 1483, Arbroath contributed the sum of 40s. to the modified burgh tax, and, again, 55s. to the new levy of 1669.[2] These sums were the smallest paid by any of the Angus burghs, except Forfar. From this it may be inferred that, notwithstanding the advantages which Arbroath enjoyed from being the seat of a rich abbey, and from the early grant that King John of England made to the abbots and monks in allowing them to buy and sell goods free of tax and custom in all parts of England, with the one exception of the City of London,[3] the trade of Arbroath had always been inconsiderable.

It does not appear that there was any harbour, except a natural one, until 1394. In that year, Abbot John Gedy, alive to the advantages which the town and district would derive from having a good harbour, entered into an agreement with the burgesses to erect one, binding his successors to make and maintain it "in the best situation, according to the judgment of men of skill, to which, and in which, ships may come and lie and have quiet and safe mooring, notwithstanding the ebb and flow of tides." The burgesses were also to contribute to this work of common good, by clearing the place fixed upon of stones and sand, and to find certain of the working tools, such as spades and iron pinches. Over and above they imposed a voluntary tax upon themselves of three

[1] *Miscell. Spalding Club*, v. p. 27; *Acta Parl.* vii. p. 542.
[2] *Chamb. Rolls*, i. pp. 12; ii. p. 224; iii. p. 151.   [3] *Reg. Vet. Aberbr.* p. 330.

pennies sterling for each rood of land within the burgh, in addition to the three pennies which they already paid, the extra rent to begin so soon as one ship took the harbour.[1]

This haven, which was constructed of wood, was known as "The Abbot's Harbour," and stood at the mouth of the river Brothoc, where, by being occasionally repaired, it long remained. About 1654, it was either wholly renewed or received extensive repairs, as it appears that collections were then made throughout the county "for helping to build the pier of Aberbrothoc;"[2] but, according to the Rev. Mr. Edward of Murroes, who wrote in 1678, this harbour was then "not much liked by mariners." In 1725 the magistrates and merchants erected one of stone a little to the westward; and the difficulty, complained of by Mr. Edward, was still further obviated by the erection of a long pier in 1788, which was put up as a breakwater between the ocean and the harbour. The bar, a ledge of rock which runs along the front of the harbour, has been much reduced by dredging in the sea-way, and the access and safety of the port much improved by additions and alterations made by Parliamentary Commissioners, so that it is now found suitable to the growing importance of the burgh, and its shipping interests.[3] The registered shipping is about two-thirds of that at Montrose.

From the year 1579 the burgh of Arbroath was as a rule represented by laymen in the Parliaments and Conventions of Estates, and the Commissioner of the town during the time of King Charles I. was a member of the Committee of Estates for the north.[4] There is no mention of a Provost until about the beginning of the seventeenth century, and then he is usually found also as the town's Commissioner. Perhaps the Abbot, as the Bishop did in those of Brechin, sat in the Councils of

---

[1] *Reg. Nig. de Aberbr.* pp. xviii *n.*, 40.   [2] *Brechin Kirk Session Records.*
[3] Hay, *Hist. Arb.* pt. v. chs. v. and vi, gives a minute account of the harbours and their history. Fresh-water springs beneath the piers have recently caused great damage, entailing much expense in restoring the works.
[4] *Acta Parl.* iii. p. 124; vi. p. 91, etc.

the burgh as chief magistrate.   It is certain that, by charter of
James VI., the free burgesses and inhabitants elected their
councillors and magistrates until about the year 1700, when
the system was changed and the Earl of Panmure, as Lord of
the Abbacy, had the power of choosing the First Bailie.   That
privilege was annulled by the forfeiture of 1716, and between
that time and the passing of the Reform Bill various changes
were made in the mode of appointing the civil rulers of the
burgh.[1]

Besides the Guildry, which was incorporated in 1725, there
are seven incorporated trades—the hammermen, glovers, shoemakers, weavers, tailors, wrights, and bakers.[2]   Of these the
first named is the most ancient, being incorporated in 1592,
and the rest are given here in the order of their precedence,
but the second has long existed only in name.   Although
the weavers were a corporate body in 1594, it was not
until 1736 that there was introduced into the town the manufacture of osnaburgh, or brown linen cloth.   This was long
the staple trade, but it has now given way to sailcloth, canvas,
and similar fabrics.   At convivial meetings of the " wabster
craft," the following comprehensive sentiment in rhyme,
known as the *Arbroath Weavers' Toast,* is given by the Deacon ;
and it is needless to say that in the prosperity of the different
points which it embraces, all countries and classes of men are
more or less interested :—

> " The life o' man, the death o' fish ;
> The shuttle, soil, and plough ;
> Corn, horn, linen, yarn ;
> Lint, an' tarry woo' ! "

Between 1736 and 1772, when the town was visited by
Mr. Pennant, the antiquary, it had advanced so much that he
described it as a " flourishing place, well built, and still increasing." [3]   The Abbot's house, before referred to, was the first

---

[1] *Sets of Royal Burghs of Scot.* 1787, p. 51 ; on the constitution of the early
burgh, see Miller, *Arbroath,* ch. ii.   [2] See APPENDIX No. VI.

[3] Pennant, *Tour in Scot.* in 1772, ii. p. 131.

depository of flax in Arbroath; and although the town at that comparatively late period had only a single street, and some lanes, with houses thatched with turf or heather, it has progressed so rapidly since then, as to take rank in Forfarshire next to Dundee in the important points of manufactures and population.[1]

Unlike the rest of the Forfarshire burghs, Arbroath has not had its praises celebrated by Dr. Arthur Johnston, or, so far as known, by any other old poet, and the only key that we have, to either its ancient appearance or state, is Slezer's view and Ochterlony's account of the town.[2] "It is a pleasant and sweet place," writes the latter, "and excellent good land about it, built upon the east syd of the water of Brothock; they have a shore, some shipping, and a little small trade: it hath one long large street, and some bye streets; it is tollerably well built, and hath some very good houses in it."

The more recently erected manufactories are large and substantial. The streets are generally narrow; and, as in most places of trade and bustle, they are not remarkable for cleanliness. Many of the shops, however, are spacious and elegant, and some of the private houses and villas in the town and neighbourhood are neat and tastefully designed; while the public buildings, such as the Town Hall, the Infirmary, and the new Market,[3] would do credit to towns of greater pretensions. The Infirmary and Dispensary are specially worthy of notice, the two being combined in one institution and under one management. The building was opened for patients in January 1845, and has proved a most precious boon to the town. It is under the very efficient management of directors

---

[1] In 1755, the population of Arbroath was 2098; in 1851, 17,008; in 1881, 21,995.

[2] *Theatrum Scotiæ*, plate xl.; *Spot. Miscell.* i. p. 343.

[3] In the hall of this market-place, on the 30th December 1856, the gentlemen of the county of Forfar entertained their Lord-Lieutenant, Lord Panmure, afterwards the Earl of Dalhousie, to a splendid banquet, in testimony of their personal respect for him, and of his efficient services as Minister of War, during the Russian campaign. The hall was appropriately decorated for the occasion, and about 1000 persons were present, presided over by Sir John Ogilvy, Bart., M.P.

belonging to the town and neighbourhood, and is supported by private subscription and the proceeds of invested funds.[1]   The scientific requirements of the people are to a certain extent met by the Public Museum, which was started by Lieutenant Medley, R.N., in 1840.   It is placed in the Public Buildings, and forms a most valuable centre for the illustration of the world's progress in all departments of life, past and present.

The spire of the parish church, which is 160 feet high, took the place of an old square tower in 1831.   It is a well-proportioned object, adding considerably to the appearance of the town, and the kirk itself, though plain, is a commodious building.   Within the last twenty years, several of the churches in the town have been rebuilt, and the new style of ecclesiastical architecture has added much to the appearance of the whole place.

The Roman Catholic Chapel has rather a good Gothic front, and a commanding position on the west or Dishlandton district of the town, while the Episcopal Church of St. Mary's, which was consecrated in August 1854, is among the finest structures of the kind in the county, and may be ranked next to St. Paul's, Dundee, to which it is second only in point of size.   St. Mary's is in the Decorated style of Gothic architecture, consisting of nave and chancel, with north aisle, and a handsome spire at the north-west end 130 feet in height.   The principal doorway enters through the tower, and, besides its rich mouldings, it presents some unique and curious carvings on the corbels. The chancel has a fine arched ceiling, and the east window, which is a beautiful example of the Decorated style, is filled with stained glass representing the Ascension in large figures, with five smaller panels containing the five principal scenes between the Resurrection and the Ascension of our Saviour.[2]

Prior to the erection of this fine building (which was designed by Mr. Henderson of Edinburgh, as was also the

---

[1] Hay, *Hist. Arb.* p. 397.

[2] See a detailed account of this church, and its consecration, in the *Arbroath Guide* newspaper, 2nd Sept. 1854.   For the memorial windows see APPENDIX No. XIX.

spire of the parish church), the Scottish Episcopalians worshipped in a plain unpretending house, which they left in the year 1806, when they and the English Episcopalians united. After this union the old place of worship was used for some time as a theatre, next converted into a dwelling-house, and eventually purchased by the heritors as a manse for the parish minister.

Episcopacy appears to have met with less opposition at Arbroath than in some of the other towns in the county, and this probably arose from the fact that a great majority both of the proprietors in the neighbourhood and of the principal inhabitants were adherents of that Church. Still it appears that Mr. Edgar, who was pastor in 1745, and afterwards Bishop of Fife, was charged by the local authorities for having infringed the statute, by either praying for the Prince or omitting all mention of King George. But Mr. Edgar was a very likely person to be suspected for non-compliance in such matters, as the whole of his family were uncompromising Jacobites, his elder brother James having long been private secretary to Prince Charles.[1]

Arbroath is the seat of a Presbytery, but down to about the time of the Reformation, it merely formed a portion of what is now the parish of St. Vigeans, from which it was then disjoined. Within St. Vigeans parish, a great part of the population still live, and the extended royalty of the burgh also stretches into it.[2] The first mention of Arbroath after the Reformation, so far as relates to its church, occurs in 1562, when Superintendent

[1] Jervise, *Land of the Lindsays*, pp. 337 sq.

[2] St. Vigeans, one of the largest Lowland parishes in Forfarshire, has its name from St. Vigean, who is said by Hector Boece to have flourished towards the end of the tenth century. The teinds of St. Vigeans were first gifted to the Abbey of Arbroath by Hugh, bishop of St. Andrews, who was sometime chaplain to William the Lion. The church, which had a chapel belonging to it dedicated to Sebastian (*Reg. Nig. de Aberbr.* p. 367), is built upon a natural hillock by the side of the river Brothoc. It is in the Romanesque style of architecture, with nave, arches, and side aisles, and in the vaults below lie the remains of Sir Peter Young of Seaton, joint tutor and almoner with George Buchanan to King James VI. In the churchyard are several ancient stone crosses, engraved in the *Stone Monuments of Scotland*. One of these has an inscription upon it, similar to those on the Irish crosses, and the late Sir

Erskine of Dun intimated to the Assembly that Robert Cumming, schoolmaster of Arbroath, was " infecting the youth committed to his charge with idolatrie ;"[1] and the first of its clergymen, whose name occurs in the records, was Mr. Ninian Clement, who had a stipend of 100 merks, while the reader, Mr. Thomas Lindsay, had 40.[2]   Mr. Clement was probably followed in the office of the ministry by Mr. James Melville, brother of the celebrated Andrew Melville.   Melville held the cure in 1574 and there resided for a considerable period, enjoying " the vicaris gleibe and manse " as well as " the twa bolls ait maill " which Thomas Ramsay of Kirkton bound himself to give for Mr. Melville's " awin eating," and to make as " guid and fyne as ony gentill man sall eat in the countrie adjacent about him."[3]

Little has been learned of James Melville's successors.   He that immediately followed was Andrew Lamb, who became Bishop of Brechin.   Mr. Ferguson, the first Presbyterian minister of the parish, is chiefly remembered for the eccentricity of his preaching.[4]   He had much of the sarcasm and indifference of character that marked many of his contemporaries, and delighted to indulge in witticisms and personalities even from the pulpit.   He acquired in consequence so considerable a local celebrity among a certain class, that his church often contained persons from neighbouring towns, who went to listen to his orations ; but, from what is now related of them, they appear to have been silly in themselves and altogether unfitted for the pulpit.

Since the days of Mr. Ferguson, however, a great change

James Y. Simpson, of Edinburgh, read it as relating to " Drosten, the son of Voret, of the race of Fergus," one of the last of the Pictish kings ; but Dr. Skene as " Prayers for Vered and Ferquhard."—*Proc. Soc. Ant. Scot.* i. p. 83, ii. p. 458.   Cairn Conan, in the west of the parish, was the place of the Abbot's law courts.   The still older remains found about the ridge are described in *Proc. Soc. Ant. Scot.* iii. pp. 465 sq., iv. 492 sq.   See APPENDIX No. XX. for a more detailed account of the Church of St. Vigeans by the parish minister, the Rev. Wm. Duke, M.A.

[1] *Booke of the Kirk*, p. 25.

[2] (1567)—*Woodrow Miscell.* i. p. 354 ; Scott, *Fasti*, vi. pp. 785, 807.

[3] M'Crie, *Life of A. Melville*, i. p. 4.   [4] Douglas, *E. Coast of Scotland*, p. 50.

has taken place in the parochial superintendence of Arbroath. In addition to a permanent assistant in the parish church, whose salary, with the exception of a small annuity and the emoluments arising from other offices, is dependent upon the will of the people, there are four churches in connection with the Establishment, called Abbey, Ladyloan, Inverbrothoc, and St. Margaret's. There are also five Free, and three United Presbyterian Churches, and eight others of different denominations, making in all twenty-one, or a church to about every thousand of the inhabitants.[1]   Since 1793, when there were the parish school and two or three private schools, the facilities for education have been vastly extended. There are the High School and six other Public Schools under the charge of the School Board, as well as the Dale Cottage Industrial School, and many evening and art classes, while for education and other charitable purposes a considerable amount of funds has been mortified during the last century and a half.

SECTION IV.

The pious Abbot of Aberbrothock
Had placed that bell on the Inchcape Rock.
SOUTHEY, *The Inchcape Bell.*

Battle of Arbroath—Captain Fall's unsuccessful Attempt to Storm the Town—History and Traditions of the Bell Rock and Lighthouse.

OF battles or forays the neighbourhood of Arbroath has had its own share. The most important was that between the Lindsays and the Ogilvys in January 1445-6. It arose from a quarrel between the Master of Crawford, better known afterwards as Earl Beardie, and Alexander Ogilvy of Inverquharity, regarding the post of Justiciar in the Abbey regality. On Sunday, January the 23rd, they met, with their adherents, " at the yettis

---

[1] The eight remaining denominations are Episcopalians, Roman Catholics, Original Seceders, Catholic Apostolic, Congregationalists, Evangelical Union, Wesleyans, and Baptists.

of Arbroath on ane Sonday laite and faucht." The Crawford party was entirely defeated, and the Earl of Crawford mortally wounded.[1]

From the time of this fatal engagement, and the unsuccessful attempt that Cromwell made to disembark troops at Arbroath in July 1651,[2] when the inhabitants of the upper districts of the county went thither to prevent his army from landing, no warlike transaction of much moment is known to have occurred at Arbroath beyond the occasional attacks made upon the Abbey, as previously alluded to. One circumstance, however, which occurred in the summer of the year 1781, is deserving of notice. At that time the lives and property of the lieges were threatened by the well-known Captain Fall, who, struck, perhaps, by the smallness of the town and its exposure to the sea, hoped to carry by threats and a few shots the feelings of the people in favour of France. He accordingly cast anchor opposite to the town, and sent a peremptory message to the magistrates, informing them, that if they did not "bring to the French colour in less than a quarter of an hour," he would "set the town on fire directly." To this an evasive answer was sent, requesting at same time to know what terms he desired. In the interim a messenger had been despatched to Montrose for a company of soldiers, and such of the inhabitants as could bear arms prepared to resist any attempt that Fall might make to land. In the evening he intimated his demand, which he stipulated at "£30,000 sterling at least, and six of the chief men of the town as hostages;" adding, "be speedy, or I shoot your town away directly, and I set fire to it!"

With a courage worthy the best of causes, the authorities sent a verbal message to Fall, to the effect that he might shoot as much as he pleased on the town, and the best would be done to prevent him from setting it in flames. On this he

---

[1] For an account of this battle, see Tytler, *Hist. Scot.* iv. pp. 49 sq. ; Jervise, *Land of the Lindsays,* pp. 176 sq. [2] *Brechin Kirk Session Records.*

opened a heavy fire which continued several hours, without, however, "doing further damage than beating down a few chimney-tops, and going through the roofs of some houses." Remaining at anchor all night, he renewed the attack at day-break; but, in course of the same morning he gave the inhabitants another chance of coming " to terms," which they answered by hoisting a flag of defiance. That was again followed by another brisk fire from Fall's cutter; and, although admitted to be better aimed than that which preceded, no great harm was done.[1] Finding the inhabitants thus determined to resist, and descrying a ship in the offing, he weighed anchor and set sail.

Owing to the remarkable character of the Bell Rock Light-house, and its proximity to Arbroath, from which it is distant about twelve miles south by east, some notice of it may be expected here. That, however, will be brief. The dangerous reef of rocks upon which the lighthouse is built is 2000 feet long, by 300 feet broad. At high-water the whole is covered to a depth of about 12 feet, and at ebb-water of spring-tides a space of about 427 feet by 230 is uncovered, and the rock visible about 4 feet above the sea. It is then found to be covered with fuci, and is frequented by seals, gulls, shags, and cormorants.

On the appointment of a Lighthouse Board for Scotland, the Commissioners resolved upon the building of a lighthouse on this rock, and an Act of Parliament having been obtained, operations were begun in the year 1807, under the superin-tendence of Mr. Robert Stevenson, engineer to the Board. Commenced on the 17th of August of that year, the work was finished in October 1810, and the lights were first exhibited on the first of February 1811. The lights are two in number —one is intensely bright, and the other tinged by a red shade, both revolving and showing alternately every two minutes. In foggy weather two large bells are tolled night and day, and the sound of these is heard at a great distance. Sir Walter

[1] APPENDIX No. XXI.

Scott, who visited the lighthouse on the 30th of July 1814, alludes to the colour and revolving nature of the lights in the following *Pharos loquitur*, which he wrote in the lighthouse album :—

> " Far in the bosom of the deep,
>   O'er these wild shelves, my watch I keep ;
> A ruddy gem of changeful light,
> Bound on the dusky brow of night :
> The seaman bids my lustre hail,
> And scorns to strike his tim'rous sail."

The tower is circular, and solid to the height of 30 feet, the outer casing being of Aberdeen granite, and the inner work of Mylnefield stone, from near Dundee. From this height it is divided into apartments for the keepers, and the top or lantern room, which is made chiefly of cast-iron with a copper roof, is 15 feet high, glazed with strong plates of polished glass, and protected by a cast-iron rail of curiously wrought network. The tower gradually diminishes from a diameter of 42 feet at the base to 13 feet at the point where the lantern rests. The mean height of the lighthouse from the base to the top is 115 feet ; the spray frequently rises 70 feet upon it, and in great storms it has been known to rise upwards of 100 feet.[1]

One horse, the property of James Craw, a labourer in Arbroath, is believed to have drawn the entire materials of the building. This animal latterly became a *pensioner* of the Lighthouse Commissioners, and was sent by them to graze on the island of Inchkeith, where it died of old age in 1813. Dr. John Barclay, the celebrated anatomist, had its bones collected and arranged in his museum, which he bequeathed at his death to the Royal College of Surgeons, and in their museum at Edinburgh the skeleton of the *Bell Rock horse* may yet be seen.

According to tradition, this dangerous reef was well known

---

[1] See Mr. Stevenson's account of the Bell Rock Lighthouse. The total cost of the building was £61,331 9s. 2d. See also, Hay, *Hist. Arb.* pp. 366-8.

in old times, and one of the Abbots of Arbroath had a bell fixed upon it, which was tolled by the action of the waves, so as to warn the mariner of his impending danger. That bell, it is added, was wantonly cut down by a Dutch pirate, who has received the poetical name of Sir Ralph the Rover; and as a retribution for his deed, it is said that he and his lawless band afterwards perished upon the rock. This tradition has formed the subject of a popular drama, and also gave rise to Dr. Southey's beautiful ballad, so well known to every one, of the Inch-Cape Bell :—

> " So thick a haze o'erspread the sky,
>   They could not see the sun on high ;
>   The wind had blown a gale all day ;
>   At evening it hath died away.
>   On deck the Rover takes his stand,
>   So dark it is, they see no land :
>   Quoth he, ' It will be brighter soon,
>   For there 's the dawn of the rising moon.'
>   ' Canst hear,' said one, ' the breakers roar ?
>   For yonder, methinks, should be the shore.
>   Now, where we are, I cannot tell,—
>   I wish we heard the Inch-Cape Bell ! '
>   They hear no sound—the swell is strong,
>   Though the wind hath fallen they drift along,
>   Till the vessel strikes with a shivering shock,
>   ' Oh, heavens ! it is the Inch-Cape Rock ! ' " [1]

[1] Balfour, *Characters Omitted in Crabbe's Parish Register, with other Tales*, gives "The Legend of the Bell Rock" and some other poems of local interest (*ut sup.*, p. 230 *n* [3].) Among these is the story of "The Piper of Dickmont-law," a tale illustrative of a tradition regarding a bagpiper who lost his way, and entered the "Forbidden Cave," to the eastward of Arbroath, and who was heard playing his pipes for some days below the hearthstone of the kitchen of Dickmont-law ! The caves on this part of the coast are numerous, and interesting alike for their geological and botanical peculiarities, and for their picturesque and singular perforations. They are noticed by Edward, *Description of Angus*, A.D. 1678; by Lyell, *Elements of Geology;* and in the *Old* and *New Statistical Accounts of the Parish of St. Vigeans;* also by Bremner, *Guide to the Cliffs and Caves near Arbroath*, and Hay, *History of Arbroath*, pt. vii. ch. v.

CHAPTER VII.

The Church, Convents, Castle, and Town of Dundee.

SECTION I.

Lord William was buried in St. Mary's Kirk,
Lady Margaret in Mary's quire :
Out o' the lady's grave grew a bonny red rose,
And out o' the knight's a brier.

BALLAD.

The Stories of the preservation of David, Earl of Huntingdon, his landing at Dundee, and founding a Church there—Notice of an Antique Gold Ring—Probable age of the Steeple—Church gifted to the Abbey of Lindores—Gift of Vessels and Ornaments of the Altar—The First recorded Priest of Dundee—Presentation to the Vicarage by Pope Calixtus III.—The First Minister after the Reformation—Mr. David Lindsay—Mr. John Willison—Altars of St. George and All Saints, founded by Sir David Lindsay of Glenesk—Altar of St. Salvator—Altar of St. Margaret, and Presentation to the Chaplaincy—The Churches—Curious Inscriptions—Churches Burned—Rebuilt.

ALTHOUGH it is probable that Dundee was a place of importance, both civil and ecclesiastical, long prior to existing record, there is no authentic notice, even of the name, until past the middle of the twelfth century. As will be subsequently shown, it was then a place of some note, and in the year 1200, David, Earl of Huntingdon and Garioch, brother of King William the Lion, founded and endowed a church there, which he dedicated to the Virgin Mary.

Earl David, like many contemporary princes and barons, joined King Richard I. of England in the third and luckless crusade to the Holy Land. This, as is well known, turned out an unsuccessful enterprise, and but few of those that were engaged in it had the good fortune to return home. Earl David, however, was among those that survived, and his preservation seems to have been almost miraculous. According to the quaint, if not always trustworthy historian of the Holy War, he "was by a tempest cast into Egypt, taken captive by the Turks, bought by a Venetian, brought to Constantinople, there known and redeemed by an English merchant, and at last safely arrived at Alectum in Scotland ; which Alectum he, in memorie and gratitude of his return, called Dundee, or *Dei donum*, God's gift."[1]

Fuller gives the name of Alectum, as indeed he does the whole narrative of Earl David's romantic adventure, and the reason of his building a church at Dundee, on the authority of Hector Boece, who was himself a native of the place, and during whose youth the story had doubtless been generally told and believed in the more minute manner in which it is related by that historian. We are also told by him that the Earl landed in Dundee at a rock called St. Nicholas' Craig, upon which there was then a chapel, and that he built his church in a place near the town termed "the wheat field ;"[2] while Mr. Pennant again informs us that Earl David, unable of himself to erect the church in question, obtained a mandate from the Pope, who recommended a collection to be made throughout Christendom to assist in the building.[3] There is, however, nothing to show that this mandate was issued, or indeed ever had existence.

In addition to these stories, tradition not only gives the very year in which the kirk and tower were finished, but also condescends upon the name of the architect, and asserts that the work, completed in 1198, so pleased King William the Lion, that he presented Allan Dorward (for such is the reputed name of the builder) with a gold ring, and Dorward, being

---

[1] Fuller, *Holy Warre*, (1640) p. 268. On the name and early history of Dundee, see Thomson, *Hist. Dundee*, pt. i. ; *Mun. Hist. of Dundee*, sec. i.

[2] Holinshed, *Scot. Chron.* p. 384.

[3] Pennant, *Tour in Scot.* in 1772, iii. p. 125.

afterwards at a boar hunt in the Sparrow Muir, now the Hawkhill of Dundee, there lost the ring, and offered a reward for its recovery, the advertisement of which is said to be extant.

That an antique gold ring was found about the year 1790, while people were digging the foundations for Heathfield House on the Hawkhill, is matter of certainty. It is of pure gold, weighs eight pennyweights seven grains, and is now in the possession of the family of the late Mr. Neish of Laws and Omachie. It is ornamented by a beautifully engraved head, representing that of an old man, with a crown; and on the breast is a mullet or star of five points. It is impossible to say at what time or by whom the ring was worn and dropt; but in addition to the story of its having belonged to an architect of King William the Lion's reign, another version says it was that of the master-mason of King David II., and that he received it from that prince, and lost it in the manner before related.[1]

But for these, and such like ancient stories, tradition, unfortunately, is the only authority; and, so far as yet known, there is no record to show that Earl David ever, in the literal sense of the word, *founded* a church at Dundee, and the very name of St. Mary's itself is not met with in any chartulary or other writing until about the year 1406.[2] In short, it is only certain that the church of Dundee was granted by Earl David, about the year 1200, to the monastery which he founded at Lindores in Fife, on the opposite bank of the Tay.[3]

If the Earl built a church at Dundee, no vestige of it remains; one story, indeed, says it was destroyed by King Edward I. in 1303. It is worthy of notice, that the old steeple is not in the Early English or First Pointed style of

---

[1] The late Mr. Constable of Wallace Craigie told a former possessor of the ring (Mr. Webster of Heathfield House), that he found the advertisement alluded to in one of the museums at Edinburgh.—*Note from the late Mr. Neish.*

[2] *Reg. Ep. Brechin.* i. p. 24. On the ecclesiastical history of Dundee, see Thomson, *Hist. Dundee*, pt. ii. ; Maxwell, *Old Dundee*, pp. 22 sq., 74 sq., 123 sq. .

[3] *Liber S. Marie de Lundoris*, p. 38.

architecture which prevailed in Earl David's time, but in that of the Decorated or Second Pointed, which was introduced in the reign of King David II.   Several good examples of this style are yet extant, such as the church of St. Monans in Fife, of which Sir William Disschington was architect or master-mason.[1]   It is also to this period, as before remarked, that the *campanile* or bell-tower of the Cathedral of Brechin is supposed to belong; and it is worthy of notice that, whether for architectural or other services in Forfarshire or not, Sir William Disschington had in 1366 a grant from King David II. of the mill of Aberlemno, and the adjoining lands of Tilly-whandland and Balglassie, as also an annuity from those of Flemington.[2]   But whether the steeples of Dundee and Brechin were the work of Disschington or not, the fact remains that the style of both buildings corresponds to that of the architecture which was in use in his day.

Probably belonging to the first half of the fifteenth century, the Steeple of Dundee is now used, as it has been time out of mind, as the bell-tower.   It is a square massive building, a hundred and forty-six feet in height, and the walls are from six to eight feet thick.   The restoration of the Tower was commenced in 1870, under the superintendence of Sir George Gilbert Scott, architect, and completed in 1872, when a peal of six bells was also duly inaugurated and handed over to the municipal authorities.   The bells were presented by gentle-men in the town and neighbourhood, while the cost of repair-ing the tower was met by private subscriptions, and by a grant from the funds of the common good of the burgh.   A spiral staircase, with octagonal top, is on the north-east side of the tower, and a small slated house, which had possibly been a *pharos* or lighthouse to guide mariners in making for the Tay, forms the termination to the tower.   Although it gives a somewhat odd appearance to the building, there is no doubt that it is a part of the original structure—a fact which various

[1] *Chamb. Rolls*, i. pp. 496, 524.   [2] *Reg. Mag. Sig.* pp. 44, 121.

points in the masonry go to corroborate.   Its removal, as has
been sometimes suggested, would be a dangerous and gothic
experiment.   In old times the principal entrance to the church
was from the west, by the door of the Steeple ; but many
years ago, when the prison accommodation of Dundee became
inadequate, the door between the church and steeple was built
up, and this portion of the tower was sanctioned by the County
Justiciary to be used as a prison-house.[1]

In virtue of the grant of Earl David, before referred to, the
Abbey of Lindores was entitled to the tithes of the whole of
the church lands of Dundee, and bound to maintain a perpetual vicar there ; as also to uphold the fabric of the choir of
the parish kirk.   By diocesan and Papal authority, it was
afterwards arranged that the vicar should receive the altarages,
that is, the baptismal, burial, and certain other dues, instead
of the vicarage teinds ; and subsequently, by consent of the
bishop, the burgesses bound themselves to maintain the choir
and the church in general, on receiving an annuity of five
merks from the monastery of Lindores.[2]

The town being thus responsible for the maintenance of the
church, the magistrates and Council naturally became also the
custodiers of its donations, its plate, its vestments, and its
books ; and when gifts were made at any period subsequent to
the last-mentioned agreement, which took place in 1442, they
were always made to the magistrates.   Several donations are
upon record, but the most considerable " adornement and
honor " which the church of St. Mary is known to have
received was in 1495, from George Spalding, a wealthy burgess of the town.   This gift appears to have consisted of some
of the more important vessels and ornaments of the altar, such
as " ane Ewcaryst of siluer owr gylt, ane gryt bell, ane syluer
chalyss owr gylt, ane new mess buyk," as also " ane new war
stall to keip the vestiamentis of the hye altar in till, ane gryt

[1] For its ancient history, see Maxwell, *Old Dundee*, pp. 209-14.
[2] *Dundee Charters*, p. 19.

kyst, and twenty schillingis of annuell rent," the custody of all of which was vested as above, and it was expressly provided that the " buyk and chalyss " were only for the service of " ye Lady preyst."

The intrinsic value of the gift must have been considerable, and that it was viewed in this light at the period is apparent from the honours which the magistrates and Council agreed to confer upon the donor and his memory. The Lady Priest was bound to exhort all the people to pray for Spalding, " hys sawll, hys wyf, and for yar antecessowris and successowris " after his own and his wife's death, and to say psalms and " kast haly watter on yar grawys." An annual mass was also to be said in the choir of the kirk, with " diregeis and torchys at the sawll mess," and they were to " gar ring yar bellis of ye kirk and ye hand bell throu ye tovne as efferis." Spalding and his successors were also to have " larys " or graves " in the quer of ye kirk, under the farrast gree befor ye hye altar."[1]

Although belonging in property to the Abbey of Lindores, the church of Dundee was ecclesiastically subject to the Bishop of Brechin; and it is rated in the ancient *taxatio* at forty pounds Scots. The first recorded pastor was William of Kerneil, and as " person de Dunde " he witnessed a charter by Ranulph, bishop of Brechin, to the Abbey of Arbroath, about 1214.[2] Beyond his appearance at this time, nothing is known of either him or his family; nor, from that early date, until towards the middle of the fifteenth century, is there any trace of the old clergy. The vicar of the last-named date was Richard Craig,[3] who appears to have died soon after, since, at St. Peter's at Rome, on the 20th of April 1455,

---

[1] *Reg. Ep. Brechin.* ii. p. 316.

[2] *Ibid.* ii. p. 261; *Reg. Vet. Aberbr.* p. 132.

[3] *Reg. Ep. Brechin.* i. pp. 94, 153; ii. pp. 67. Mr. Maxwell, in the Appendix to his *Old Dundee*, has given, from a volume in the burgh archives, an " Inventory of all the goods and ornaments of the Church of the Blessed Virgin Mary of Dundee, made and ordered by an honourable man, Henry of Fothringhame, then Provost of Dundee, in the year of the Lord 1454." There are also some very curious entries from the same book and belonging to older documents. The list of "Layris in the Kyrk," paid for in money and kind, is exceedingly valuable and interesting.

Pope Calixtus III. issued a bull in favour of Gilbert Forster, archdeacon of Brechin, in virtue of which he was to receive (notwithstanding that he held the said archdeaconry, and also a canonry and prebend in the church of Moray, of the joint value of £60 sterling) the vicarage of the parish church of Dundee, vacant by the decease of Craig, who is described as *extra Romanam curiam;* and this grant had been ordered to be conferred upon Forster, by the previous Pope, Nicholas V., in the event of the death of Craig.[1]

The only other notice of the clergy prior to the Reformation occurs about A.D. 1490-5, when a person named John Barry was vicar of Dundee.[2] The first minister after the Reformation was Mr. William Christeson,[3] whom Melville describes as " that fathfull pastor of Dondie," and a particular friend of his elder brother Roger Melville, who was a burgess of Dundee. Mr. Christeson had a stipend of £160 Scots, which was payable out of the thirds of the Abbey of Lindores, in Fife, and of " Scone, in the baronye of Angus vndir the Brae," which probably refers to the lands of Kinochtry, an isolated part of the parish of Scone, situated within the parish of Kettins, in Forfarshire. William Kyd, the contemporary " reidare at Dundie "—an official who read prayers or the Scriptures in the church, but did not preach—had the small sum of £40 Scots.

Mr. Christeson probably died in or before the year 1603, but he had previously resigned the charge, and the next incumbent was Robert Howie, who held the benefice but a short time. His successor was Mr. David Lindsay, master of the Grammar School, who held the offices of both schoolmaster and minister in 1606, and during that year he resigned the former on the ground " that he wes not habile to dischairge with ane guid conscience bayth the said offices." As master of the Grammar School he had a salary of 250 merks a year.

---

[1] *Reg. Ep. Brechin.* ii. p. 406.　　[2] *Ibid.* ii. p. 134.
[3] Melville, *Diary*, p. 38. On Christeson and his position in Dundee, see Maxwell, *Old Dundee*, p. 128.

He had for some time the same salary as minister; but it was afterwards raised, for various specified reasons, to the sum of 350 merks, 100 of which were paid out of the Hospital Fund. Again in 1613, in consideration of his great service "als weill in the educatioun and informatione of the youth in letters and gude maneris as in the dischairge of his office and calling of the ministrie," and the difficulty which he had in recovering the portion of his stipend payable out of the lordship of Lindores; also, for the burden "he bears in the sustentatione of his wyiff, bairnis, and familie," the Council resolved to pay him or his heirs, betwixt and Whitsunday 1617, the sum of 500 merks over and above his stipend.[1] Mr. Lindsay, who was a cadet of the Edzell family, remained at Dundee until 1619, when he became Bishop of Brechin.

So far as known, the most eminent of Mr. Lindsay's successors in the ministry at Dundee, though not in St. Mary's, was Mr. John Willison, author of *The Afflicted Man's Companion, Balm of Gilead*, and many other works of a like admirable character and household fame. He was originally ordained minister at Brechin in 1703, but left that charge in the course of a few years. Ever attentive to the first great duties of a minister of the Gospel—by visiting the sick at all hours of day or night, by relieving the poor and distressed, by the free administration of spiritual and bodily comforts, and by following a uniform course in his walk and conversation towards the rich and the poor—he has left behind him a name and fame for consistency of principle and purity of motives which fall to the lot of few. He was one of the most active and zealous of the Evangelical party of the period, and one of three of a deputation which the General Assembly appointed in 1735 to go to Parliament with a view of having the Act of 1712, whereby lay patronage was restored, abolished.[2]

[1] *Appendix of Documents—Mr. Innes's Report.*

[2] Dr. Robert Small, author of the first *Statistical Account of Dundee*, and of an *Explanation of the Astronomical Theories of Kepler*, was long minister of Dundee, and a native of the neighbouring parish of Carmyllie.

The old churches themselves were partly in the Early English and partly in the Decorated style, cruciform in shape, and contained several altars, one of the more important of which seems to have been that of St. George the Martyr. It was founded by Sir David Lindsay of Glenesk, afterwards Earl of Crawford, in gratitude for the victory which he obtained over Lord Wells, in the celebrated " tourney" at London Bridge. That tournament took place upon St. George's Day, 1390, in presence of King Richard II. and of a vast assemblage of English lords and ladies, whither Lindsay went by safe-conduct,

> " With knights, squires, and other men
> Of his awin retinue then ;
> Where he and all his companie
> Was well arrayed and daintilie."[1]

The chantry of St. George consisted of five priests; and the Earl added another altar dedicated to All Saints, with two officiating priests. These were amply endowed by the founder and several of his successors out of their property within the burgh of Dundee and in other quarters, and the whole of these grants were confirmed by the Duke of Albany.[2]

Apart from several foundations of regular religious bodies which were within the burgh, and which will be noticed in another page, there were a great many altarages, chaplainries, and chantries within the Church of St. Mary, besides those of St. George and All Saints;[3] and a number of chapels in different parts of the town were endowed for secular clergy, either by fixed annual rents, or by lands leased or feued. A chapel of St. Mary Magdalene had probably stood upon the high ground above the Magdalen Green, but the name is the only record.[4] Little, however, is known of the history of these, with the exception of the altars of St. Salvator, and of St. Margaret, Queen of Malcolm Canmore. The chaplain of St. Salvator's altar had

---

[1] Jervise, *Land of the Lindsays*, p. 174 ; Thomson, *Hist. Dundee*, pp. 196 sq. for all the altars.

[2] *Reg. Mag. Sig.* pp. 219-22.   [3] APPENDIX No. XXII.

[4] The Magdalen Green or Yard was originally Magdalen Gair. Maxwell, *Old Dundee*, pp. 242-4.

an annuity of £5 for praying for the soul of the young Duke of Rothesay, who was starved to death at Falkland by his uncle, the Duke of Albany, and also the third part of the lands of Milton of Craigie and of Westfield.[1] The first of these grants was paid by the Exchequer, out of the burgh of Dundee, and the lands were granted by Patrick of Inverpeffer, a burgess of the town. These grants were confirmed by King Robert III. in 1390, and he at the same time granted the patronage of the altar to the alderman of Dundee and twelve councillors.[2]

The advowson of the altar of St. Margaret belonged to Scrimgeour of Dudhope, and during the Superintendentship of Erskine of Dun (1562-1589), Scrimgeour made a presentation to him, as "bishop and superintendent" of the district, of Robert Gray, son of Patrick Gray of Baledgarno, on "the decess of vmquhle David Lude, chaiplane, last possessour of the samyn." The deed which confers this gift, dated in January 1580-1, describes Gray, in the quaint language of the period, as a "scolar of gud ingine, hable to encress in literature and sciences, civile and diuine;" and it also narrates the extent and locality of the different pieces of property, as well as their value. These, which included houses and gardens, were all situated within the town of Dundee, and Gray was to enjoy the annuity derivable from them during his lifetime, "to support his burding and expenss at grammar scolis, and scolis of vniversities in his minority, and to by his buiks to help his stude, to the fine, that he may cum to perfectioun of knawledge, and be plantit in the kirk of God, to maintenn the religioun, and set forth the gospel of Jesus Christ."[3] Such was one of the many laudable purposes—the education of poor and meritorious youths—to which the revenues of the old Roman Catholic altarages were intended to be applied from the time of the Reformation down to nearly that of the Revolution, and after that they were chiefly to go to the sustenance of the ministers.[4]

[1] *Dundee Charters*, p. 13. [2] *Acta Parl.* i. p. 577; *Reg. Mag. Sig.* pp. 199, 239.
[3] Crawford, *Officers of State*, pp. 450-2; *Miscell. Spald. Club*, iv. pp. xiii, 66.
[4] *Reg. Privy Counc.* i. pp. 202, 498.

The ancient church, as before remarked, was in the Early English and Decorated styles, with nave, choir, and transepts, and the chancel roof was supported by twelve pillars. At no distant date it was divided into five portions, and each was occupied by a separate congregation : afterwards it was arranged so as to accommodate four, but since the churches were rebuilt (1842-7) there have been but three.

That portion of the old edifice called the *north* transept, afterwards the Cross Church, is said to have been destroyed by King Edward I. in 1303, and to have lain in ruins down to 1588-90, when the magistrates resolved to have it " buildit and repairit," and for that purpose a tax of 500 merks was imposed upon the inhabitants, with private contributions made in the town and neighbourhood.[1] Of these last a roll was ordered to be kept, and such as gave largely to the repair of the kirk, and towards procuring " ane knok," were allowed to have monuments erected to themselves within the church, intimating the extent of their liberality. Some of these monuments were in existence down to 1841, the most curious inscription being perhaps that upon the tombstone of Captain Henry Lyell of Blackness, by which it appears the merit of the whole matter was attributed to him :—

> " To Sol'mon's temple, king Hiram sent from Tyre,
> Fine cedar-wood, but upon great desire ;
> This church, thou HENRY LYELL to repair,
> Didst freely give all that was necessar ;
> Tho' th' Tyrian king gave Sol'mon towns twice ten,
> Thou greater than these all, and best of men." [2]

It is said that this church was twice used as cavalry stables, first by General Monck, during the Wars of the Commonwealth, and next by the royalists, during the rebellion of " The Forty-five." It was here that the chaplain and catechist of the

---

[1] On the reconstruction, see Maxwell, *Old Dundee*, pp. 248 sq. The Cross Church is now represented congregationally by St. John's in South Tay Street.

[2] Many of these inscriptions are preserved, with curious translations of those in Latin, in Monteith's *Theater of Mortality*, first printed in Edinburgh, the 1st Part in 1704, the 2d Part in 1713 ; republished at Glasgow, in 1 vol., with additions, 1834.

Hospital preached ; but it was not until after the year 1788, that either this or the Steeple Church was erected into a separate charge of the Established Church with the ordinary revenues.

The *south* transept is said to have been roofed anew when the north one was repaired, and tradition affirms that the roof of the Abbey of Balmerino, in Fife, was taken off and used for that purpose.[1] Of this there is no good evidence. It is certain, however, that a great part of the structure was corporation and private property ; and the shoemakers were among the trades that attended worship there, and had their pews marked out by the significant words—" HIR SITIS YE CORDNARS." The magistrates had pews in this division, as they had in the chancel. The fleshers and bakers also sat here, and it is said that the former had painted upon the front of their loft the rather appropriate quotation from Scripture, " MAN SHALL NOT LIVE BY BREAD ALONE," an intimation which had stood in humorous contrast to that of an equally applicable character adopted by their neighbours, the bakers, " BREAD IS THE STAFF OF LIFE."

The fabric of the *Old*, East, or Parish Kirk, seems to have been in a bad state of repair about the year 1564, and probably there were no funds to improve it, for the magistrates not only ordered certain fines to be paid towards " the kirk wark," but had also special collections made on Sundays " for gaddering of support to the reparation of the kirk decayit." They also gave a " glaisin wricht " a " maill-free " house or lodging, for having repaired the " glass woundokis," and for agreeing to " uphold the same haill during his lifetyme,"—but the fulfilment of the latter point appears to have been no easy matter, in consequence, as quaintly remarked, of " bairnies recceslie breking the glass." At this time and down to 1589, the "auld kirk" was in much the same state as in the days of Romanism; but at the last-named date it was agreed, for the better accommodation of the people, to have it " repairit, and all impedi-

---

[1] Thomson, *Hist. Dundee*, pp. 208, 216 sq.

mentis within the samin removit, and loftis maid therein." It
was then, in all probability, that many of the mottoes and
ornaments were introduced, and these existed as already mentioned down to the burning in 1841.

This was the principal place of worship, and contained
some fine carvings in oak, the work of a native artist. Several
of the incorporated trades also sat in this portion of the building, and their pews were decorated with armorial bearings, and
mottoes such as those referred to : the most curious was,
perhaps, that inscribed upon the wall adjoining the pew of the
bonnet-makers, which ran thus :—" THIS IS THE BONET-MAKERS
SET QVHA LIST TO SPEYR."

It was in this part of the church that King Charles II.
heard sermon shortly before the disastrous affair of Worcester,
and in memory of him, and the way by which he entered the
kirk, a broad clumsy outside stair ever after bore his name.[1]
But, unfortunately for Dundee, the ravages of accident, more
than those of time, have been ever destroying its memorials
of the past, and the sad conflagration of the churches on
Sunday, 3d January 1841, brought the work of destruction
to a crisis. It was then that, with the exception of the venerable Steeple which still forms the most prominent feature of
the town, every vestige of the old ecclesiastical remains of
Dundee was for ever lost.

The Steeple Church, which escaped the fire of 1841, was
built so late as 1789, to afford additional accommodation for
the inhabitants of the town and parish. The site was that of
the nave of the original structure, which had long lain in
ruins, and the burned churches were replaced in due time
by two fine Gothic buildings which have an imposing external appearance, and are commodious and comfortable in the
interior. They were built after plans by Mr Burn, late of
Edinburgh. The large window of the East Church is in
the Decorated style, divided into three parts, and filled with

---

[1] Balfour, *Annals*, iv. p. 240.

stained glass. In the centre division are the armorial bearings and other emblems of the town of Dundee. The arms
of the masons, wrights, and slaters, with the motto, " TRIA
JVNCTA IN VNO," and those of the maltmen, occupy the
southern part. On the northern division is inscribed—
" FRATERNITY OF MASTER SEAMEN," with their arms (a ship full
rigged), and the " GVILDE TAODVNENSIS SIGILLVM." The shield
also bears a merchant's mark, differing only from that represented in woodcut No. 8 (page 271), in so far as it wants the
initial on the perpendicular line, and the St. Andrew's Cross
at the right of the horizontal line.

SECTION II.

Hark ! the convent bells are ringing,
And the nuns are sweetly singing.

BAYLEY.

Convent of St. Clare, or Franciscan Nuns—Trinity Friars—Hospital, or *Maisondieu*
—Black Friars—Grey Friars—National Assembly of 1309—Destitution of the
Grey Friars—Gift to the Friars by the Countess of Errol—Value of Provisions
in the *Deir Yeir*, 1481—The Burial-place of the Earls of Crawford—Destruction
of the Convent.

As previously remarked, there were a number of other religious
houses in the town of Dundee, apart from the Church of St.
Mary. The names and sites of most of these, however, are
little else than matter of conjecture, but lanes and streets in
the town bearing such names as St. Clement's, St. Paul's, and
St. Roque's, are supposed, with every probability, to indicate
the situation of churches or chapels dedicated to these saints.

The Convent of St. Clare, Franciscan Nuns, or the Grey
Sisters, as they were variously termed, is believed to have been
situated in the Overgate, and a large pile of building, at the
top of the Methodists' Close, is said to have been the abode of
the nuns. The rooms of the house, which is now occupied by a
number of poor families, are large and lofty; the ancient hinges,
yet on some of the doors, are of elegant floral patterns ; but one

of the skew-put stones bears the date of 1621, a period long subsequent to the abolition of monasteries in Scotland, and to this date the style of the building corresponds.   It is, therefore, more probable that this house had been built as the private residence either of a country gentleman or of a wealthy merchant.   Perhaps the latest remains of the monastery were the four vaulted apartments, on the east side of the same entry, supported by rude but not inelegant pillars.   At the period of the Reformation, the rents of this Convent amounted to twenty-eight shillings; and a patch of ground, on the west side of the town, was called the Grey-Sisters' Acre.[1]

The Red or Trinity Friars, an order which is known chiefly in connection with their Hospital, had also a convent in Dundee.   About the year 1391, Sir James Lindsay of Crawford granted to the brethren of the Holy Trinity, his house or tenement in the town to be an Hospital, or *Maisondieu*, in which the old and infirm might reside.   In confirming this charter of Lindsay's foundation of the Hospital, King Robert III. enriched it with a gift of the church of Kettins and its revenues.[2]   Subsequently, several other donations were made to it by different parties; and, among others, it is stated that William Duncan, proprietor of Templeton of Auchterhouse, granted the Master of the Hospital a donation from these lands, by a deed which is said to be thus attested—"Villiame Duncane, with my hand twitching ye pen, led be ye notar, becaus I can nocht vryte myself."[3]

It need hardly be said, that long anterior to the date of this reputed grant (A.D. 1582), the regular religious orders in Scotland were scattered, and their convents mostly destroyed. Among other plans which Government adopted to preserve the hospitals and to relieve the poor, there was that of appropriating the revenues of the monastic establishments for these and

---

[1] *Mr. Innes's Report;* Warden, *Angus,* ii. pp. 130 sq.

[2] *Reg. Mag. Sig.* p. 202 ; *Dundee Charters,* p. 16.

[3] Thomson, *Hist. Dundee,* p. 240 ; Warden, *Angus,* ii. p. 128.

similar purposes. In this wise enactment the poor of Dundee, in common with those in other parts of the kingdom, participated; and, the better to carry out these objects, the Council of the burgh, in 1563, appointed "masters of the Alms-house." But it was not until 15th April 1567, that Queen Mary made a special grant of the old kirk-lands of Dundee and their revenues to the magistrates. This grant, according to the charter, was given for two specific objects—first, to provide for the ministers of God's Word at Dundee; and next, for the preservation of hospitals within the burgh for the accommodation of poor, mutilated, and miserable persons and orphans.[1]

This grant was confirmed by subsequent sovereigns, and the terms of the ratification charter of King Charles II., dated 12th July 1661, are not less distinct than those of Queen Mary as to the appropriation of the funds, for it declares that the rents are to be uplifted and applied for the twofold purpose of "intertaining of the poore within the Hospitall," and "for sustenance of the ministers serveing the cure at the kirk of Dundie," excepting "the person" (that is, the minister of the parish), who, it is expressly declared, "shall have no parte of the forsaids viccarage, since he is otherwayes provided."[2] The annual revenue of this institution, known as the Hospital Fund, has, as a matter of course, become very considerable, in consequence of a great part of the lands situated within the burgh being feued for building and other purposes; but the provision, requiring that a fair share of the funds be divided among the town ministers, was long overlooked, and the money withheld by the magistrates. For many years they were inadequately paid, but the matter having become the subject of a law-suit in the Court of Session, the ministers had a decision in their favour, and their stipends received considerable augmentation from the rents of the properties which, as the Act says, "belonged of befor to the Friers Predicants,

<hr/>

[1] *Report* (*July* 20, 1855), *by Mr. C. Innes*, in causa *The Presbytery of Dundee against The Magistrates of Dundee; Mun. Hist. Dundee*, pp. 39 sq.

[2] *Acta Parl.* vii. p. 351.

Dominicans, Minorits, and Franciscans, and other monkish friars, chaplanes, and prebends."

The Hospital stood at the foot of South Tay Street, and was burned in 1645, most probably by the Marquis of Montrose. In 1678 Mr. Edward of Murroes describes it as a large and splendid hospital for old men; and the cluster of houses, with the tower in the centre, given in Slezer's views of the town, is supposed to represent the building. In one of these prints it appears on the left, and in the other on the right of the Steeple.[1] In 1726, it is described as a " handsome Hospital, with the Garden running down to the River," and at that time the hall contained lists of its benefactors.[2] In 1746 the house was vacated by the pensioners, but in 1757-9 a party of French prisoners occupied it, and for this the town received a handsome rent.

It would seem that in old times, as now, it had required considerable interest to get admission into these establishments, for in 1581, in consequence perhaps of the interest which the Lindsays had taken in the prosperity of the institution, a citizen of Dundee applied to Sir David of Edzell, requesting him to recommend to the magistrates and Town Council the admission of a decayed burgess into the house. He describes him as " ane agit father of lxxiiii years, named Andro Michelsoun, wha is your kinsman, his mother being ane dochter of the House of Morphie—my Lord," continues the writer to Sir David, " your father (the ninth Earl of Crawford), of guid memory, lovit him weill; he has been ane honest merchant in this town; but now both agit and failzeit in substance."[3] It may be added that, at the time of the burning of the Hospital in 1645, there were nine men in the house, and that from the earliest period on record down to 1746, when it ceased to be used as a residence for the pensioners of the fund, the number of inmates never appears to

---

[1] Slezer, *Theatrum Scotiæ*, pl. xxxviii. xxxix.
[2] De Foe, *Journey through Scot.* i. p. 97.   [3] *Lives of the Lindsays*, i. p. 337.

have exceeded twelve. Since the latter date there has been no Hospital for decayed burgesses, but the allowance has been paid to out-door pensioners.

The Monastery of the Black or Dominican Friars was perhaps one of the latest foundations of the kind in Dundee. It was erected by a burgess named Andrew Abercromby,[1] probably the same person as that to whose widow Abbot David Beaton of Arbroath, in 1525, leased the teinds of the kirk of Monifieth and the fishings of the Craig, for a period of eleven years.[2] Nothing further is known of its history beyond the fact that the lands belonging to it were included in Queen Mary's grant, and that its rent, after the period of the Reformation, amounted to £6, 3s. 4d. The convent stood on the west side of Barrack Street, of old called Friars' Wynd, nearly opposite to the west gate of the *Howff*.

If the Convent of the Black Friars was the latest religious foundation of Roman Catholic times, it may be safely presumed that that of the Grey or Franciscan Friars was one of the earliest, for it is said to have been founded by Devorgilla, grand-daughter of David, Earl of Huntingdon, mother to King John Baliol. It was also the most important in the town, and occupied the site of the *Howff*, near which was St. Francis' Well. This house was remarkable as the place where the great National Assembly met in February 1309-10, when the members declared that, seeing the kingdom betrayed and enslaved, they had assumed The Bruce for their king, and had willingly done homage to him as such.[3]

Although this Convent had a larger revenue than any of the others, it appears that, towards the close of the fourteenth century, the Friars were so impoverished that they were compelled to part with their sacred vessels and their books to procure the necessaries of life, and, their house having fallen into ruin, they were unable to repair it. It was at this

---

[1] Spottiswood, *Religious Houses*, p. 492.
[2] *Reg. Nig. de. Aberbr.* p. 450.　　　　[3] Hailes, *Annals,* iii. p. 221.

unhappy juncture that Beatrice Douglas, Dowager Countess of Errol, made the welcome donation to the house of a hundred pounds Scots, for which the Friars bound themselves and successors " till saye or synge a dayly mass perpetually and for evir," for the welfare of the soul of the Countess and of those of her son and deceased husband.   The mass was to be performed at the high altar of the Convent " ay and on to the tym it pleis the said Lady to big and reparal ane altar in the said Kirk of the Three Kings of Colan, aftir the whilk biggin the said mass to be done at the said altar of the Three Kings, and to be callit the Countis mass perpetually."

It may be remarked that the " Three Kings of Colan," here alluded to, were the Three Kings of Cologne—the name by which were designated the Wise Men, who came to visit the infant Saviour in his cradle at Bethlehem.   The legends of the Middle Ages regarded the Magi in art and literature as Kings, and gave them the names of Melchior, Gaspar, and Balthasar.   They were in great repute throughout Christendom, and, being the patrons of Cologne Cathedral, where their relics are still exhibited in a costly shrine, they were popularly spoken of in Western Europe as the Three Kings of Cologne. There were altars to them in almost every large church, their names were used as spells and inscribed on charms, and from their fine scenic effect in the representations of the Epiphany they took a strong hold of the popular imagination.   It is uncertain whether this altar was ever raised by the Countess of Errol, but from the grateful record of the poor friars the more generally interesting facts are disclosed, that the Countess made this gift in 1481, which is significantly characterised as a " deir yeir," and that the Convent then consisted of at least fourteen friars and a warden, whose names are all given.   To the dearth and famine is perhaps to be attributed the cause of the destitution which prevailed in the Convent ; for it appears that provisions were then very high in price, as shown by its being stated in the deed already quoted that "meill gives 24s. ;

mawt, 30s.; beir, 11 merks; qwhyete, 32s.; a lytill haddok, 7d.; a kellin (large codfish), 30d.; a gallon of hayll, 32d. etc."[1]

By charter, dated at Panmure 22d April 1509, Sir Thomas Maule, and his wife Elizabeth Rollock, mortified the sum of 20s. annual rent to the Minoret or Franciscan Friars of Dundee, out of the lands of Skeichan. The grant was made to Father Andrew Russell, professor of Theology and guardian of the Convent, and for this mass was to be celebrated for the souls of the donors and their relatives. To this charter the seal of Father John Zare, " Ministri Provincialis Fratrum Minorum intra Regnum Scotie," was appended, and it was witnessed by Alexander Guthrie de eodem, knight; Alexander Strachachin, Domino juniore de Kermylie; John Guthrie de Balnabriech; Geo. Guthrie and Dom. David Bell, chaplain and notary-public.[2] By Sir Thomas's last will, the same Convent received £3, 12s.

A portion of the south wall of the *Howff* is said to be part of this monastery; but all trace of the " gret artir windows " is now lost, the " mendyne " of which is specially noticed as a portion of the Countess's donation. Even the tombs of the noble family of Lindsay-Crawford (for it ought not to be forgotten that this Convent was long their place of sepulture, and that they were among its chief benefactors) including those of the celebrated " Earl Beardie," and his still more illustrious son, the original Duke of Montrose, were for ever swept away by the infuriated zealots of the Reformation. At the Reformation the rents of this Convent were stated at £25, besides a chalder of bear.

---

[1] *Panmure Miscell. MS.* iv. pp. 133-5.   [2] *Reg. de Panmure,* i. pp. 351-4.

SECTION III.

Each in his narrow cell for ever laid,
The rude forefathers of the hamlet sleep.
GRAY, *Elegy.*

The *Howff*—Its Origin—Old Tombstones—Curious Epitaphs—Monograms, and Merchants' Marks—New Cemeteries.

IN the year 1564, Queen Mary granted the burgh a licence to bury its dead in the yard or garden of the Convent of the Franciscan or Grey Friars, now called the *Howff*,[1] but previous to that time it had been used for interments by both the friars and their benefactors. Perhaps it was scarcely, if at all, enclosed until 1601, but during that year collections were made at the kirk-doors for the purpose of fencing it with stone dikes; of these the western portion is still partially entire. This part of the wall was a piece of fine ashlar work, upon which the monuments of the more opulent merchants seem to have been raised. Some of the earliest of these are yet to be seen, such as that of the family of Mudie, which bears the initials of the erector and his wife, and the words—IN . MONVMENTVM . SEPVLTVRÆ . FAMILIÆ . MVDEORVM . EREXIT . IACOBVS . MVDEVS . ANNO . 1602. The names . . . ZEMANE . . . THOMAS . IACOBVS . WEDDERBURN . . . MALCOM . . . IONET . FRASER . . . ALEXANDER COPPING . . . GVTHRIE . . . with the legends—DOMINO . CONFIDO—SO . SAL . THE . LORD . BLIS . THE . IN . AL . THY . PROCEIDINGIS . . . are sculptured upon different parts of the wall, and some of them had been gilded.

Upon another part of the same wall :—

Mon . . . . . . m . M . . ab . . . . . . Flet
cher of Innerpeffer . . . their . . p . . . ritie
S
A.F : I.F : R.F. Sonnes . . vsed bvild . . no Doñi 1627
FOR JAM
ES FLETC
HER . F
ECI

---

[1] *Mun. Hist. Dundee*, pp. 39 sq. ; *Dundee Charters*, p. 40 ; Maxwell, *Old Dundee*, pp. 206-9. *Howff, houff,* or *hoif*, a haunt—a place of frequent resort. "*Kirch-hof,* area ante templum, a churchyard."—Jamieson, *Scottish Dict.* HOIF.

Some of these were ornamented with armorial and mercantile emblems and monograms, the remains of which, as represented in the following woodcuts, are still to be seen. The first two are upon the Mudie monument, and the third upon that of Copping, who was a burgess and seaman :—

With the exception of the Old Greyfriars' Churchyard, Edinburgh, perhaps no other burial-place in Scotland possesses a greater number of generally interesting tombstones, whether we regard their antiquity, their quaint inscriptions, or their strange and elaborate carvings. Collections of epitaphs from these stones have been frequently, but not always correctly printed. Such is that from the rather famous stone of *Epity Pye*, which is commonly rendered thus :—

" HERE LIE I, EPITY PIE, MY TWENTY BAIRNS, MY GUDEMAN AND I."

The inscription of which this purports to be a copy, although said to have been effaced in 1819,[1] is still in existence, the monument being No. 613 in the register of gravestones. Like too many others, it lies across one of the middle walks of the cemetery, is pretty entire, and surely deserves a better place and fate than have been assigned to it. The true reading of the inscription is as follows:—

HEIR LYIS ANE GODLIE AND HONEST MAN IOHNE ROCHE
BRABENER AND BVRGES OF DVNDIE QVHA DEPARTIT THIS LYFE
THE 10 OF FEBRVAR 1616 ZEIRS BEING OF AGE 43 ZEIRIS
VITH HIS SPOVS EVFIANE PYE
QVA HES CAVSIT THIS TO BE MADE IN REMEMBERANCE OF HIM
AND THAIR 14 BEARNES.

---

[1] In *Dundee Delineated* (1822), p. 163, this stone is not only said to have been effaced, but the name of the husband is given as " Walter Gourlay." There is another stone (registered No. 214), to such a person, with this inscription :—" Heir lyis ane honest man WALTER GOVRLAY, maltman and bvrgess of Dvndee, qvha decessit in 28 day of Apryil 1628, of the age of 46 zeires, with hys twentie bairnis."

The inscription is in raised Roman capitals carved along the margin and head of the stone, and some of the letters are in the interlaced style common to the period. In the centre of the stone are the armorial bearings of the family of Roche (Rough) and Pyot. Above these are two rows of skulls and cross bones : the first row contains two large skulls, and a small one between them, to the latter of which wings are attached ; the second row is closely set with seven small skulls. Another row, near the foot of the stone, had originally contained six skulls, but the centre two have been effaced, and a pair of compasses and a barrel *incised* in their place.

Our limits will not permit many examples of these inscriptions to be given, but we may notice such of the more curious emblems as have not before been pointed out. It is needless to say that here, as in other places, and from the earliest date, the tombstones of many of the burgesses bear carvings of objects which are intended to illustrate their *crafts* or trades. The scissors or goose is found on the tomb of the tailor ; the glove, on that of the skinner ; the broad Scotch bonnet, on that of the bonnet-maker ; the hammer and crown, or anvil, on that of the blacksmith ; the loom, or shuttle, on that of the weaver ; the circular knife, on that of the cordiner or shoemaker ; the compasses and square, on that of the mason ; the expanded compasses or saw, on that of the wright ; the axe and knife, on that of the flesher ; the crossed peels, on that of the baker ; the ship in full sail, on that of the seaman ; the plough, coulter, harrows, or yoke, on that of the farmer ; the millstone, pick, and rynd, on that of the corn miller ; the lancet or other surgical instruments, on that of the surgeon. To these professional emblems it not unfrequently happens that accompanying mottoes bear some quaint allusion, such as the following at Dundee, of date 1628 :—

"Kynd Comarades heir COVPARS corps is layd,
    WALTEIR by name, a tailzoyr of his trade ;

Bothe kynd and trew, and stvt and honest hartit,
Condol vith me that he so sone depairtit,
For I avow, he never *veyld a sheir*,
Haid beter pairts nor he thats bvrid heir."

Apart from the mortuary emblems of the " passing bell"
and the hour glass, the scythe and dart, the mattock, spade
and shovel, the coffin, the skull and crossed bones, and sometimes the terrific effigy of the grim messenger himself, which
are incorporated with the representation of articles of everyday
life, some of the older monuments present the more interesting
figures known as monograms and merchants' marks.

Both are objects of high antiquity, particularly the monogram or cipher which is formed of interlaced letters.   These
were known among the ancient Greeks, and from the seventh
and eighth centuries the Roman Pontiffs and Continental
Sovereigns used them as signatures.   As signatures they were
of comparatively recent introduction into Britain, one of the
earliest being that of King Henry v.[1]   Marks and monograms
had, however, been long before used as the seals of private
individuals ; for in Scotland, so early as 1337, we find,
as represented in the accompanying woodcut, that the
seal of Robert of Glen, a burgess of St. Andrews, was
composed of a mark resembling a cross, under which were
curiously entwined the initials R. G.[2]

Soon after the introduction of printing into England, both
monograms and merchants' marks were pretty generally
adopted, and were placed by artists in the corners of paintings
and engravings, and by letterpress printers and publishers on
the first and last pages of the books which they issued.
Tradesmen in general also used them, not only as signs or
distinguishing marks over the doors of their shops—a practice
which has been superseded by the naming of streets and the
numbering of houses—but as stamps or labels on the cloth or

---

[1] Fosbroke, *Encyclopædia of Antiquities* (Lond. 1843), p. 4820.
[2] Willis, *Current Notes*, Lond. Jan. 1857.

other goods in which they dealt.[1] This custom had been long
followed in the principal mercantile towns on the Continent,
before it was introduced into Britain; and in fashioning these
marks after the initial letters or names of parties, there is
often great ingenuity displayed in the arrangement, as well as
delicacy in the execution.

These monograms and marks are now occasionally found
upon town houses of the sixteenth and seventeenth centuries,
but more commonly on contemporary gravestones; and from
the similarity in the design of the merchants' marks to the
marks of the Freemasons, both may possibly have had a
common origin.[2] Although these marks are to be seen in
different parts of the country, perhaps no single place contains
so many, and such oddly designed specimens, as the *Howff* of
Dundee. Of these—a species of the minor antiquities of our
country, which has not hitherto been much noticed—a few
examples are subjoined. No. 1 is from the tombstone of a
burgess, named Thomas Simson, dated 1579; in the quaint
design his mark and initials may be traced. The armorial
bearings (on a fess, three crescents, a mascle in base), are also
carved upon the stone, with these graphic and admonitory
lines :—

> " Man, tak hed to me, hov thov sal be,
>   Qvhan thov art dead :—
> Drye as a trie, vermes sal eat ye—
>   Thy great bovti sal be lik lead.
> Ye time hath bene, in my zovt grene,
>   That I ves clene of bodie as ye ar ;
> Bvt for my eyen, nov tvo holes bene,
>   Of me is sene, bvt benes bare."

Woodcuts Nos. 2 and 3 are the marks of two burgesses,

---

[1] Paper-makers also used such figures in their *water-marks*. On the waste paper
of a copy of Bisschop's *Signorvm Vetervm Icones* [foolscap folio (158 plates) Hague,
1671], which belonged to the author, a mark similar to No. 20 (p. 273), with three
circles ⚬ instead of the letter M, hangs from the mark of the *cap* of the king's *fool*,
a quaint figure which gave name to this particular size of paper. The binding of the
book is English, and apparently of about the end of the 17th century.

[2] See engravings of masons' marks in *Archæologia*, xxiv. plates iii., iv. ; and in
Wilson, *Prehistoric Annals*, ii. p. 446.

named respectively John Garden and Robert Peblis, dated
1581 and 1582. The name is illegible on the stone from
which mark No. 4 is taken—the initials P. A. E. S. and date
1598 being alone traceable ; and No. 5 gives the mark and

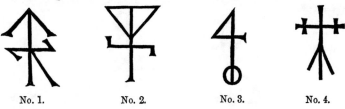

| No. 1. | No. 2. | No. 3. | No. 4. |

initials of Thomas Bover, skinner and burgess, 1603. The
mark and initials of " Robert Fairvedder," litster or wool-dyer,
who died in 1609, are represented in No. 6 ; and in No. 7, the
oddly conjoined initials, D. Z., stand for the curious monogram
of David Zemane, or Yeaman, 1610, whose descendants long
exercised much influence in the affairs of the burgh. One
of them represented Dundee in the last Scottish Parliament,
and the district of burghs in the first and second British
Parliaments. The *Yeaman shore* was named in honour of the
former, and, till lately, the family were landowners in the
county. Upon Zemane's stone is the following couplet, not
uncommon in Dundee :—

> " To honor ye sepvltor ve may be bald :
> Ve lerne of Abraham ovr father avld."

Woodcut No. 8 shows the mark and monogram of William

| No. 5. | No. 6. | No. 7. | No. 8. |

Davidson, merchant and burgess, who died in 1617 ; and Nos.
9 and 10 are the marks of John and James Goldman, father
and son, dated respectively 1607 and 1632. The Goldman
family were, in their day, the " merchant princes " of Dundee,

and owners of considerable landed estate. One of them, named Patrick, was a poet of merit, and some of his Latin eulogiums are printed in Johnston's *Poetarum Scotorum*. But the Goldmans have long since passed away, and even their

No. 9.   No. 10.   No. 11.   No. 12.

name has become extinct in the district, the last of them, a female, having died many years ago, so reduced in circumstances as to be dependent on the charity of a neighbouring kirk-session. In 1609, John Goldman, above-mentioned, mortified the large sum of 800 merks " to the puir resident within the Hospitall ;" and subsequently another of them, named William, gave 100 merks to the same charity—facts which form a strange contrast with the fate of the last recorded of the family.

No. 11 is the monogram of Robert Kandow, also a burgess ; and No. 12 is upon a stone raised by William Chaplane in memory of his wife, Agnes Dorward, who died in 1603. The arms of the Chaplane and Dorward families are upon this stone, and at the foot there is the quaint intimation, " VILIAME CHEPLANE VOS YE DOEIR OF YIS."

No. 13.   No. 14.   No. 15.   No. 16.

The dates of Nos. 13, 14, and 15 are doubtful, but they appear to be of the early part of the seventeenth century. The first is on a stone to the memory of a David Blair, and the second is from that of one John Zoung or Young, who possibly was related to Sir Peter Young of Seaton, co-tutor with Buchanan to King James VI.[1] Sir Peter's father was a burgess of Dundee, and died there in 1583. The name and date on the stone, bearing mark No. 15, are wholly illegible.

The stone from which No. 16 is taken bears date 1617. No. 17 gives the mark and monogram of Robert Mureson, 1637 ; and a slab, built into the wall, at the head of the stone, bears these words—" TO YE FAMILIE OF YE MVRESONS." The initials and mark No. 18 are those of John Pierson, a burgess and seaman, who died in 1660 ; but nothing remains to show to whom the mark, initials, and monogram No. 19 refer. No. 20 is the mark from a comparatively modern gravestone at the Cathedral of Dunblane, in Perthshire, dated 1758, and is here

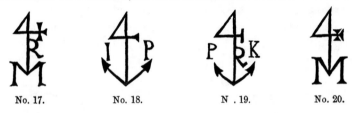

No. 17.   No. 18.   N . 19.   No. 20.

given merely to show the more common form in which these curious marks are found throughout the country—those previously noticed being of much more rare occurrence.

It was during the year 1834 that the present walks were made out in the *Howff*, the handsome cast-iron gates and railings erected, and the ornamental trees, shrubs, and flowers planted. These improvements contribute much to its beauty, and render it an interesting and pleasant resort for the inhabitants of the town, as well as for visitors from a distance. The ground was at the same time levelled, and the tombstones shifted, numbered, and placed in lines. Many of the stones have unfortunately been renewed, and, as may be supposed, none of those remaining are of very old date ; indeed, so far as can be seen, the monument of Thomas Simson, noted in a previous page, is one of the most ancient, if we except

---

[1] On the Youngs, see Maxwell, *Old Dundee*, pp. 253-4.

the fine coffin slabs, sculptured with various beautifully designed crosses, which were discovered in the foundations of the Church of St. Mary. These, which are preserved at the old church, are of the sort previously referred to as common in England and Wales, and are unquestionably the most ancient sepulchral remains in Dundee—some of them older possibly than the tower of the church.

Although the *Howff* is now the oldest place of burial in the town, tradition says that the most ancient were those of St. Paul's, between the Murraygate and Seagate ; St. Roque's, at the east end of the Cowgate ; and St. Clement's, which occupied the site of the present Town House. The Church of St. Clement, to which the last-named place of burial was attached, seems to have been in existence in the time of King James VI. It had a chaplainry within it, dedicated to St. Mary, and to this was attached the third part of the lands of Craigie.[1]

But of these burial-places there is no trace save the names. The later places of burial were at Constitution Road, St. Andrew's and St. Peter's Churches, Rood Yards, and Logie. The *Howff* was closed by an order of Her Majesty in Council in 1860, and now all intramural interments are forbidden unless in very exceptional cases. Previous to the formation of the new cemeteries, the revenue derived from burials in the *Howff* was an important item of the Hospital fund, yielding from £300 to £400 a year. Those now in use are the Western and the Balgay Cemeteries, and the Eastern Necropolis. They are very tastefully laid out and ornamented. Among the monuments in the Western Cemetery, that of the unfortunate William Thom, best known as "the Inverurie Poet," who died in Dundee in 1848, is perhaps the most generally interesting.

Holy-Rood.—This burial-place, situated on the Broughty

---

[1] *Dundee Charters*, p. 27. The late Mr. Cosmo Innes (*Proc. Soc. Ant. Scot.* ii. p. 348) said in 1857 : "I have not yet unravelled the puzzle of the patron saint of the burgh and his church. Dundee is generally said to have been under the guardianship of St. Clement, and I have no doubt correctly ; yet the parish church was dedicated to the Virgin, and its tithes were a very valuable possession of the Convent of Lindores."

Ferry Road, is practically closed as the others are. But some sixty years ago or more, the property, upon which this burial-place is situated, is said to have been in the possession of a writer in Dundee, of the name of Smart, who determined to have it swept away, and, as a preliminary, he had the old gravestones broken to pieces and carried into the Tay. He next engaged a neighbouring farmer to send a plough and horses, to complete the work of sacrilege; and the plough and horses were actually at the spot and ready for work, when the farmer, conscience-stricken, refused to begin operations, and returned to his more legitimate work at home. Long after this some of the people in the neighbourhood had a wall erected around it, and by-and-by it came to be used again as a place of sepulture. There is in it a mausoleum of the Guthries of Craigie, and also a vault to cadets of the same race.

SECTION IV.

'Tis pleasant, through the loopholes of retreat,
To peep at such a world.

COWPER, *Retirement.*

Castle of Dundee—Governed by Umphraville, Earl of Angus—Obtained by King Edward I.—King Edward there in 1296 and in 1303—At Baledgarno in 1296—Castle of Dundee captured and destroyed by Wallace—Scrimgeour, Constable of Dundee—Dudhope Castle—Dundee taken by Kings Edward I. and II.—Retaken by Bruce—Ransom for King David II.—Preaching of Wishart—Vicar Wedderburn—Paul Methven—Provost Haliburton supports the Reformation—Slain near Edinburgh—His Son denounced Rebel—Appointed a Lord of the Articles, King's Commissioner to the Assembly, etc.

THE Castle of Dundee is said to have had a prominent position upon a rock at the head of Castle Street. The rock has been almost completely removed, and the site is now occupied by St. Paul's Episcopal Church. The legend of Sir William Wallace having killed the son of the English Governor of the Castle, when both were school-fellows at Dundee,[1] is the first notice that occurs of a stronghold at that place; but it is not until

[1] *Blind Harry*, by Jamieson, p. 7.

the Wars of the Independence that anything is known of the real history of the Castle. At that time it became the scene of some interesting historical incidents, and as many charters are dated at Dundee, our early kings must often have lived there.[1]

In the year 1291, when King Edward I. received the kingdom from the four Regents, the Castles of both Dundee and Forfar were in the keeping of Umphraville, Earl of Angus, who held them from the Regents of Scotland; and, as has been already mentioned, while the governors of other national strongholds unconditionally resigned their charge, Umphraville refused to give up his, until he received a letter of indemnity from the claimants to the Crown and the guardians of the Kingdom. There being little difficulty in obtaining such a guarantee, King Edward was soon in possession of the keys of these fortresses, and the care of them both he intrusted to an Englishman, Brian Fitz-Alan, who, about the same time, was also made one of the Governors of Scotland, the number of these being thus increased to five.[2]

On Monday the 6th of August 1296, King Edward is recorded to have visited Dundee, after leaving the Abbey of Arbroath;[3] and in the year 1303, when he invaded and desolated Scotland, he again rested there on the 20th of October.[4] He had perhaps also been there two or three months earlier, when on his way from Perth to the siege of the Castle of Brechin, which, as before noticed, took place either in July or in August of that year.[5]

It does not appear that the king received any homages on the occasion of his visit to Dundee in 1296, and his stay extended only until the following day, when it is stated that he was " at Baligarnach," from which he went the day after to Perth. This is clearly a place now called *Baligarny*,

---

[1] *Reg. Mag. Sig.* pass.

[2] Rymer, *Fœdera*, ii. p. 531 ; Hailes, *Annals*, i. p. 251; *Dundee Charters*, p. 1. This Gilbert de Umphraville became eighth Earl of Angus in right of his mother, Maud or Matilda, only daughter of Malcolm, fifth Earl of Angus. Malcolm died before 1242. Laing, *Scot. Seals*, i. p. 22, for their seals.

[3] *Ragman Rolls*, p. 179.   [4] Prynne, *Hist.* p. 1015.   [5] *Ut sup.* p. 188.

although, from a want of local information, the editors of the *Diary of Edward's Progress* were unable to identify it. It is situated in the parish of Inchture, in the Carse of Gowrie, and lies about ten miles west of Dundee. There appears to have been a castle at it, which was most probably built of the deep red-coloured sandstone peculiar to the district, for it is described in the Diary of the King's progress as "le roge Chastel."[1] The Castle Law or hill is still pointed out.

In little more than a year after the first visit of King Edward, Sir William Wallace, taking advantage of the absence of the King of England in Flanders, attempted to rescue the kingdom from his grasp, and succeeded in expelling the English from the Castles of Forfar and Brechin, and at same time laid siege to that of Dundee. Hearing, while there, that the enemy, under the command of the Earl of Surrey, were on his track, he left the citizens to continue the siege themselves, while he and his army marched toward Stirling; and, in a few days after, having succeeded in gaining the celebrated victory at that place, the garrison of Dundee unconditionally surrendered to him.[2] The inhabitants also rewarded him with a handsome gift of money and arms; and, that the fortress might not afford shelter to the invading army, Blind Harry says that Wallace had it immediately destroyed :—

> "Masons, minouris, with Scrymgeour furth send,
> Kest doun Dunde, and tharoff maid ane end."

Scrimgeour, the knight who is so worthily mentioned by the blind poet, in connection with both the capture and destruction of the Castle, is said to have been descended from a baron who rendered signal service to King Alexander I., by pursuing and routing a band of rebels who had attempted to take the king's life.[3] But it is in the person of the cele-

---

[1] *Ragman Rolls*, p. 179; "Balygernatthe, the redde Castell."—*Archæologia*, xii. p. 467. For a further notice of Baledgarno or Baligarny, see below, ii. p. 68.

[2] The siege of Dundee caused great anxiety to King Edward. *Mun. Hist. Dundee*, pp. 11 sq. ; *Dundee Charters*, pp. 3 sq.

[3] Wyntoun, *Cronykil*, ii. pp. 174-5 ; Campbell, *Balmerino*, p. 318.

brated follower of Wallace that we have the first authentic record of the family.   According to tradition, King Alexander conferred upon it the office of Hereditary Standard-bearer of Scotland, at the time alluded to ; and it is matter of record that, in consequence of the knight of the period having carried the national banner before the armies of Wallace, that great warrior, while Governor of Scotland, conferred upon Scrimgeour and his successors the office of. Constable of Dundee, along with certain lands and houses on the north and west sides of the town.[1]   This curious grant is dated at Torphichen, on the 29th of March 1298, and the property of Dudhope is believed to be a portion of the lands that were conveyed by it.

The Scrimgeours erected a castle at Dudhope ; and, from Slezer's view of the town [2] (c. 1680), it appears to have then had a large square keep resembling those of the castles of the fifteenth century.   The greater part of the house now remaining, however, is a much more recent work, and has been long used as military barracks, for which it is well adapted, whether we consider its commanding position, or its healthy situation, being built on the south side of the Law, and overlooking the town.   Here the Scrimgeours had long their chief residence. The family were latterly ennobled, first as Viscounts of Dudhope in 1641, and next as Earls of Dundee in 1661 ; but the Earl dying without issue, in 1668, the title became extinct, and Charles Maitland of Hatton, brother to the Earl of Lauderdale, acquired the hereditary estates and honours, upon, it would seem, rather questionable grounds.[3]   The date of 1600, upon a stone built into the back wall of the old house, refers to the time of Scrimgeour ; and the two stones upon the front of it, bearing respectively the initials D.M.L. and S.M.L., possibly relate to the Lauderdales.

---

[1] *Acta Parl.* i. p. 97 ; iv. p. 90 ;   Maxwell, *Old Dundee*, p. 19.

[2] Slezer, *Theatrum Scotiæ*, plate 38.

[3] Douglas, *Peer.* i. pp. 462-8 ; Anderson, *Scot. Nat.* ii. p. 99 ; iii. p. 424 ; Campbell, *Balmerino*, pp. 318 sq. ; *Forf. Illust.* pp. 48 sq. ; Maxwell, *Old Dundee*, pp. 347 sq.

As before stated, King Edward recaptured Dundee in 1303, and, according to tradition, committed great havoc in the town, by destroying and sacking the churches and other public buildings ; in the churches the inhabitants are said to have deposited the more valuable of their goods. The Castle appears to have been rebuilt after its destruction by Wallace, and was perhaps spared by Edward at the last-mentioned invasion ; if not, it had been rebuilt a third time. It was in existence, and in the hands of the English in 1312, for the force which Bruce brought against it was so great, that Sir William of Monfitchet, the Governor, found it advisable after a stout defence to enter into a treaty of surrender with the Scots. This so annoyed King Edward that he ordered the treaty to be violated, and at the same time commanded David of Brechin (who had again left the ranks of his uncle King Robert) to assist Monfitchet in his emergency, and to act with him as a joint-warden. Thus refortified, as it were, it was not until the subsequent year, while Bruce himself was engaged in an expedition against the Isle of Man, and Ulster in Ireland, that his brother, Sir Edward, succeeded in capturing the town and Castle from the English.[1] Bruce at that time appointed a commission to inquire into the liberties of the burgesses of Dundee, as the English had carried off or destroyed the old charters, and in 1327 he confirmed the ancient privileges and rights.[2]

From that time little is known of it, but it must not be supposed that, in consequence, the town and neighbourhood were long allowed to slumber in quietness. Dundee, as one of the four chief burghs in the kingdom, became bound for the payment of £90,000 as a ransom for King David II., when he had been taken prisoner by the English at the battle of Durham; and it was doubtless, also, owing to the importance of the place that it was attacked, and, as some accounts say, burned, by the army of the unfortunate King Richard II. of England, in

[1] Tytler, *Hist. of Scot.*, i. pp. 256, 290, 296.   *Mun. Hist. Dundee*, pp. 10 sq. ; *Dundee Charters*, pp. 4 sq.   [2] *Dundee Charters*, pp. 8 sq.

1385.[1] More lately, the deeply-rooted animosity and jealousy
which subsisted between it and the neighbouring town of Perth,
regarding the real or supposed infringement of certain liberties
and the precedence of Dundee over Perth in the royal pro-
cessions, together with the tumults which took place between
the Constable and the burgh, formed, from time to time, good
cause for retarding the progress of business, and not unfrequently afforded scenes of riot and bloodshed.[2]

Apart from these forays and the fact that it was off this
port that Admiral Wood, with only two ships, *The Flower* and
The Yellow Carvel, encountered in 1489 a fleet of three English
vessels, under the command of Stephen Bull, and capturing
them carried them into the harbour of Dundee[3] (exploits which
form the groundwork of Mr. Grant's popular novel, *The Yellow
Frigate*),—apart also from some of the skirmishes which took
place during the reign of Queen Mary, the only other hostile
affrays connected with Dundee may be said to relate to the
times of the Reformation and the Covenant, two of the most
important epochs in the more modern history of our country.

It is well known that the Reformation was warmly espoused
at Dundee, and that the inhabitants were greatly incited in
the cause by the ministrations of Wishart and others.   Influenced by their preachings, they destroyed the houses of the
Black and Grey Friars of Dundee; they also went to Perth,
and destroyed the fine sculptures in the Church of St. John;
but the magistrates of Dundee, fearing the occurrence of still
greater evils, happily succeeded in prevailing upon Wishart to
leave the town.   His absence was short, however, for as soon
as he heard that Dundee was afflicted by the plague, he
hastened back, and there preached and visited the sick with
all the devotion and energy of a friend and enthusiast.

It is said that he preached from the top of the East Port

---

[1] *Acta Parl.* i. p. 155 ; Froissart, *Chron.* ix. p. 147.
[2] For these disputes, see Maxwell, *Old Dundee*, pp. 114 sq.
[3] Pitscottie, *Hist.* i. pp. 240-5 ; *Mun. Hist. Dundee*, p. 27.

or Cowgate,[1] an ancient fabric which is laudably preserved though it seriously interferes with the traffic along the street; and there, as tradition represents it, the lame and sick stood without the gate, and the hale and healthy within. It is added that, on these occasions, Wishart was often in danger of being murdered, and that he was always accompanied by a strong guard of personal friends; one of these was armed with a two-handed sword, and this, it is said, was once borne by John Knox. Perhaps these precautions had not been altogether needless, for the Popish party were probably as anxious to obtain the life of Wishart as the Reformers were to obtain that of Beaton. It is told that one day, while preaching, Wishart observed a priest in the crowd with a dagger secreted under his cloak, ready, when an opportunity should occur, to strike him to the heart. Wishart himself is said to have wrested the instrument from the priest, and then to have kindly shielded him from the hands of the infuriated mob.

But this severity of conduct and determination on the part of the Papists to stifle liberty of conscience, only emboldened what it was meant to frighten, and produced, in the town of Dundee, as it did elsewhere, many new advocates of the Reformed doctrines. Among these were the Vicar Wedderburn and his two brothers, whose writings of "godlie playis and ballatis,"—acted as they were, and sung in many parts of Scotland,—contributed greatly towards the advancement of the cause.[2] So deeply did these incur the displeasure of Cardinal Beaton and his party, that the Vicar had to flee from Scotland, and only returned after the Cardinal's death. But a much more conspicuous propagator of the cause was one Paul Methven, who was originally a baker by trade. Not only was he destitute of almost the rudiments of an ordinary education, but even after he had assumed the garb of a priest, his conduct was far from circumspect;[3] still, possessed of great

---

[1] But this is doubted. *Forf. Illust.* p. 26; Maxwell, *Old Dundee,* pp. 221-2.
[2] Anderson, *Scot. Nat.* iii. p. 627.   [3] *Booke of the Kirk,* i. p. 31, etc.

natural eloquence and an intimate acquaintance with Scripture, he rendered so good service to the Protestant cause that he became obnoxious both to the prelates and to the Secret Council, so that the latter not only issued an order for his apprehension, but also forbade the people to listen to his orations, or to harbour him in their houses.[1]   Methven escaped apprehension only through the intrepidity of Provost Haliburton, who was one of the firmest, most politic, and courageous of the promoters of the Reformation; but, to show their disappointment at the escape of Methven, the Secret Council fined the town of Dundee in the sum of £2000.

Haliburton was among the first to join the Protestant Assembly at St. Andrews in June 1559 ; in October following he was appointed one of the Council of the Congregation for civil affairs, but, on the 5th of November thereafter, while attempting, in company with the Earl of Arran and Lord James Stewart, afterwards the Regent Moray, to rout a party of the French, near Leith, he was defeated, while his brother Captain Alexander Haliburton, with many of their followers, was slain in a marsh between Restalrig and Holyrood Park.[2] In the vicissitudes of political life in Scotland, the Assembly, within five years from this time, appointed Provost Haliburton Commissioner for the district of Angus, but during the following year he was denounced an enemy and rebel to the Queen ; then, two years later, we find him one of the Committee of the Lords of the Articles, sanctioning the Queen's demission of the crown, the King's coronation, and the appointment of a Regent.[3]   He does not appear to have taken any part in the General Assembly which was held at Dundee

---

[1] *Ut sup.* p. 99; Pitcairn, *Crim. Trials*, i. p. *406. He removed to Jedburgh, where he became the minister, but was excommunicated for adultery, and finally left Scotland without finishing the penance.—*Booke of the Kirk*, ii. pp. 205 sq. ; Knox, *Hist.* ii. pp. 363 sq. ; Calderwood, *Hist.* ii. pp. 205 sq. A curious use of the *fama* is made by Burton, *Hist. Scot.* vi. p. 245.

[2] Tytler, *Hist. of Scot.* iii. pp. 113-4, 393 : " . . was slain Alexander Halliburton, brother to the tutor of the laird of Pitcur, one of the best captains of Scotland."

[3] *Booke of the Kirk*, i. p. 47 ; Pitcairn, *Crim. Trials*, i. p. 467 ; Tytler, *Hist. of Scot.* vii. p. 164 ; *Reg. Priv. Coun.* i. pp. 348 sq., 501 sq., 537 sq.

in 1580, when the office of Bishop was disavowed, but in the next and subsequent years he was appointed to the high office of King's Commissioner to the Assembly ; and, down almost to the very day of his death, he took an active part in the proceedings of that court, in which he appeared for the last time on the 6th of August 1588, as " the Tutor of Pitcur,"[1] to the head of which family he was uncle.   He died in the year 1588, having " for the space of thirty-three years, happily administered the Provostship within the city of Dundee," and, with all public honour, was interred in the choir of St. Mary's Church.[2]

Unfortunately the monument, which commemorated his name, was one of those that perished at the burning of the churches in 1841, and we hope it is worthy of consideration as to whether Dundee should not restore it in the form of tablet or brass in the East Church, where he was buried nearly three centuries ago.

SECTION V.

There is more of virtue in one single year
Of Roman story, than your Volscian annals
Can boast through all their creeping dark duration.

SHAKESPEARE, *Coriolanus.*

Wars of the Covenant—A Royal Messenger imprisoned—Dundee Soldiers at Bridge of Dee—The Town fined, and two of its Merchants robbed—Captured and burned by the Marquis of Montrose—Stormed by General Monck—Inhabitants and Soldiers slaughtered—Hilltown burned by Viscount Dundee—Chevalier de St. George—Prince Charles.

FROM the decided part which the inhabitants of Dundee took in the Reformation, it may naturally be supposed that they also became deeply engaged in the affair of the Covenant, and, notwithstanding that the hereditary Constable of the burgh favoured the opposite side, the people contributed largely towards the cause, by supplying both men and money.   The

---

[1] Melville, *Diary*, p. 276 ; *Booke of the Kirk*, ii. pp. 585-729.   From 1580 to 1598, there were four General Assemblies of the Church held at Dundee.

[2] *Mun. Hist. Dundee*, p. 37 ; *Forf. Illust.* p. 148 ; Maxwell, *Old Dundee*, pp. 189, 199, etc.

first decisive step which they appear to have taken was on the 5th of January 1639, when a messenger came to intimate, at the cross of the burgh, the proclamation of the king against the Acts of the General Assembly of the previous year. Two of the Bailies not only protested against the proclamation being made, but violently seized the messenger, and had him put in prison, "quhair," says Spalding, "he remainit a long tyme."

The Earl of Montrose was, at this period, a supporter of the Presbyterians, and, in the month of March of the same year, he led an army against the town of Aberdeen, and forced the inhabitants, very much against their will, to take the Covenant. Upon this occasion Dundee mustered in such strength that its soldiers carried two of the five banners which were then borne by the army. Soon afterwards the same force was employed against Lord Aboyne at the Bridge of Dee, and routed him with great loss. It may be added that, apart from other considerations, Aboyne had incurred the vengeance of the Dundee portion of the army by carrying off some pieces of ordnance which Montrose had sent for the protection of the town.[1] But Aberdeen soon suffered for the part it took in this matter, for the inhabitants were not only forced by the king's party to pay the large sum of 10,000 merks, but some of its merchants, with some also from Dundee, were waylaid while travelling to St. James's market at Elgin, and "reft and spoilzeit" of nearly as much again in money and goods.[2]

Before the time of the last of these transactions, the Earl of Montrose (notwithstanding the Presbytery of Brechin had elected him one of their commissioners to the General Assembly of 1639)[3] had deserted the cause of the Covenant, and become one of its most resolute enemies. Accordingly, as a general in the king's army, he appeared before the town of Dundee on the 6th day of September 1644, and demanded

---

[1] Spalding, *Trubles*, i. pp. 128-200.
[2] *Ibid.* i. p. 339 ; ii. p. 392. [3] *Brechin Presbytery Records*, July 18, 1639.

its surrender. As it was then strongly garrisoned both by
soldiers and others, who had fled to it for protection, he was set
at defiance. But, unfortunately, upon the occasion of his next
visit, which happened on Friday, the 4th of April following,
it was altogether defenceless ; and, being chagrined, as is said,
by the rebuff he received on the previous occasion, Montrose
forced an entrance at four different points, and, overpowering
the inhabitants, left his soldiers to their own will. Infuriated
by rage and intoxication, they committed all sorts of depreda-
tion and brutality. The Bonnet-Hill, then a populous suburb,
is said to have been nearly reduced to ashes, and several houses
were set fire to in other parts of the town.

While thus employed, Montrose was apprised of the approach of the Covenanting army under the command of General
Baillie ; and so close, it is said, were they upon him, that
before he could muster his followers to march out at the east
end of the town, his pursuers had entered at the west. But,
by making that dexterous movement, which is characterised
by historians and soldiers of all shades of politics as one of
the noblest specimens of generalship upon record, he made a
successful retreat, and gained the fastnesses of the Grampians
before the Covenanters well knew the route he had taken.[1]

The walls of the town, which were demolished at that
time, were rebuilt soon after,[2] but, in the course of three or
four years, they were again assailed by the soldiers of General
Monck, who were even more merciless in their conduct than
were those of the Marquis of Montrose. The burgh had, at
this time, incurred the vengeance of Cromwell, in consequence
of having given shelter to King Charles II. after his coronation
at Scone. This ceremony took place on the 1st of January 1651,
and on the 7th of September following, the town, after a brief
siege, was entered by the army of the Commonwealth, which

---

[1] Spalding, *Trubles*, ii. pp. 404, 462 ; Jervise, *Land of the Lindsays*, pp. 294 sq.

[2] "Rebuilding walls demolished at siege of the town, etc., £162, 10s."—*Accounts*,
1645-47 ; *Dundee Charters*, p. 173. On the old walls generally, and the ports, see
Maxwell, *Old Dundee*, pp. 215 sq. ; its suffering in wars, *ib.* pp. 479 sq.

followed up the capture with the utmost cruelty; for it is said that the slaughter of innocent women and children was regarded by Monck and his army more as a work of delight than of horror. Tradition says that it was not until the third day of the carnage, when there met the eye of the General himself, the moving spectacle of a living child lying on the street, and sucking the cold breast of its murdered mother, that his heart relented.

The local version of this assault, excepting several exaggerations as to the length of the siege, and the number of those massacred, differs little from fact. Altogether, the transaction seems to have been a disgrace both to the inhabitants themselves and to Monck; for, by the undisguised narratives of contemporary historians, it is evident that the former had been so intoxicated by drink as to be utterly unable to offer resistance to the latter, whose conduct at the same time was inhuman and severe. "The tounesmen," says Sir James Balfour, " did no dewtey in ther auen deffence, but wer most of them all drunken, lyke so many beasts;" and Dr. Gumble remarks, that both the strangers and soldiers within the walls took " such large Morning draughts, that before the Twelfth (hour) they were most of them well drenched in their Cups." The latter authority gives but few particulars regarding the conduct of the English soldiers after the capture; but the former informs us that " Mouncke commandit all, of quhatsumeuer sex, to be putt to the edge of the suord," by which about two hundred women and children perished, and about eight hundred of the inhabitants and soldiers. Robert Lumsden of Montquhaney, Governor of the town, was at first granted quarter, but afterwards he also fell a victim to their cruelty; and Sir John Lesley of Newton and his servant, who were in Dundee at the time, were both killed. Two of the clergymen, who, it appears, had opposed "hollding out the toune, knowing that such a drunken, debosht people could doe no good against so wigilant and actiue ane enimey," were sent by sea, along with some others, as prisoners to England; and it is graphically told that on one of them attempting to speak in his own defence, Monck told him, in a rage, that if he presumed to say a word, " he wold scobe his mouthe."[1]

The plunder on this occasion was great. Balfour says it exceeded two and a half millions Scots ; while Gumble affirms that, in consequence of many people, among whom were not a few of the nobility and gentry of Scotland, leaving Edinburgh and other unfortified places for those of greater security, Dundee afforded " the best Plunder that was gotten in the Wars throughout all the Three Nations." The same writer remarks that most of the spoil was shipped for Leith and England " upon several Ships that were taken in the Harbour, and that the ships were cast away within sight of the Town, and the great Wealth perished without any extraordinary storm"—a circumstance upon which Gumble briefly comments, closing with the appropriate adage : " Ill got, soon lost."

Monck appears to have remained some time at Dundee after capturing the town. It is certain that he was there on the 19th of October following, as on that day he received a letter from the Marquis of Argyll (whom the news of the massacre had reached at his Castle of Inveraray), imploring that a meeting of the responsible parties of both kingdoms might be held at some convenient place, " as a meins to stope the sheding of more Christian blood."[2] To this Monck refused to accede without an order from Parliament ; but soon after, his army was withdrawn, and the garrison occupied by other soldiers from England, who appear to have been generally well-behaved and certainly more humane in their conduct.

From this time until the unhappy reign of King James VII., Dundee was comparatively tranquil. Any disaffection which arose at that time appears to have been owing chiefly to quarrels

---

[1] Balfour, *Annals of Scot.* iv. p. 315 ; Gumble, *Life of Gen. Monk* (1671), pp. 42-4 ; Maxwell, *Old Dundee,* pp. 542 sq. ; Dr. Small, *Old Stat. Acct.* viii. pp. 209 sq., gives an interesting account of the posthumous children born at Dundee after this siege ; *Mun. Hist. Dundee,* pp. 75 sq.

[2] Balfour, *Annals of Scot.* iv. p. 316.

with Graham of Claverhouse, who had been made Constable of Dundee.   In revenge for insults cast upon him in the Town Hall, he is said to have burned the houses of that part of the town called the Hilltown, and committed several other out-rages upon the burgh.   On the whole we must infer that the authorities favoured the establishment of Episcopacy, for, in 1678, they received the thanks of the Privy Council for having dispersed a conventicle and imprisoned the preacher.   It is said by Wodrow, that at that period no person was allowed to live in the town but such as attended upon the ministrations of the Episcopalians, and family worship, conducted in any other form, was strictly prohibited, and the performers and abettors imprisoned.[1]

Soon after this, *the bluidy Clavers*, as Viscount Dundee is derisively termed by his enemies, had a gift from King James of the Castle of Dudhope and Constabulary of Dundee.   But, in the course of four or five years afterwards, he and the cause of his master ended with the famous battle of Killiecrankie, fought on the 27th of July 1689, at which, as is well known, Dundee was mortally wounded.   His body was buried in the Athole family vault at the church of Blair-Athole.[2]

The events which followed this battle settled the crown firmly on the heads of William and Mary of Orange, during whose reign, as well as during that of their successor Queen Anne, the nation had peace.   But soon after the death of the latter, it was broken by the Chevalier de St. George, eldest son of King James VII., who set up a claim to the throne of his ancestors.   He landed at Peterhead, from France, on the 22d of December 1715; and, although guided by a more sincere, gene-rous, and humane spirit than his father, his success was equally hopeless.   Travelling by easy stages from the north, he reached

---

[1] *Sufferings of the Church* (Burns's edit.), ii. p. 481; iii. p. 191; iv. p. 455. There was a long-standing feud between the Constables of Dundee and the Magis-tracy regarding the extent of jurisdiction.   For this see *Dundee Charters*, pp. 103 sq., 219.

[2] A brass to his memory was erected in St. Drostan's Church, Old Deer, in 1864.

Glamis Castle on the 5th of January. Next day, accompanied by the Earls of Mar, Panmure, Marischal, and Southesk, and a great many others of his adherents, he made a grand entry into Dundee, where he was heartily welcomed by the Jacobite magistrates. He remained at the cross for about an hour, showing himself to the people; and afterwards held his Court in a house adjoining the old Hospital.[1] He then retired to the town mansion of Stewart of Grandtully, where he slept, travelling next morning to the camp at Perth.

The magistrates and their friends were enthusiastic in their reception of the Chevalier, but the great mass of the inhabitants are said to have looked on in silence, and, contrary to the will and proclamation of their rulers, they repaired beyond the boundaries of the burgh on the 28th day of May thereafter, and celebrated the birthday of King George I. Upon the following day, the magistrates celebrated the anniversary of the Restoration of King Charles II., and, on the 10th of June, being the Chevalier's birthday, the more zealous of the corporation went to the cross and publicly drank to him as King James VIII.[2]

The connection which Dundee had with Prince Charles and his cause was comparatively slight. He does not appear to have been there personally; but so soon as he made his public entry into Perth on the evening of the 4th of September 1745, he sent a party of the Macdonalds, commanded by the lairds of Keppoch and Clanranald, to Dundee, where they captured two of the king's vessels containing ammunition and arms, and sent these supplies to the army at Perth. Some of the clergy were also ejected from their pulpits at this time, because they did not consent " to pray for King George;" and the town being in the possession of the rebels, many of their " gentlemen prisoners" were sent there.[3] It is also stated that when the

---

[1] De Foe, *Journey through Scot.* i. p. 97. This book is commonly attributed to De Foe, but Lowndes says the author of it was John Mackay.—Lowndes, *Bibl. Man.* i. 614.   [2] Aikman, *Hist. of Scot.* vi. p. 188; *Dundee Charters*, pp. 136 sq.   [3] Chambers, *Hist. of the Rebellion*, p. 58; *Miscell. Spalding Club*, i. p. 367.

Prince received his first supplies from France, the houses in Dundee were illuminated, and such of the windows as did not display the loyal taper were broken by the Jacobites.

SECTION VI.

Glory of Virtue, to fight, to struggle, to right the wrong.
TENNYSON, *Poem.*

Supposed site of *Ad Tavum*—Law or Hill of Dundee, a vitrified site—Traditionary Notices regarding the Town—Etymology of the Name—Destruction and Renewal of the Town's Records—Shipping—The Harbour—Linen Manufactures—Population — Trades — Parliamentary Commissioners — The Town's Mason, A.D. 1536-7—His Wages—Hours of Labour—His Apprentice, etc.

THE stories of Dundee being a town when the Romans invaded Scotland under Agricola, and of its having once borne the name of *Alectum*, seem to be supported by no better evidence than the fancy of Hector Boece, or, at least, no writer prior to the publication of his *History of Scotland* (1526) makes allusion to either incident.   The mythical Roman station, *Ad Tavum*, is placed by some writers at Broughty-Ferry, about three miles to the east of Dundee;[1] while others suppose it to have been at Invergowrie, about as far to the west.   At the latter place the remains of a Roman camp, with high ramparts and spacious ditches, were visible in Maitland's time.[2]

As a proof, however, of the early importance of the surrounding district it may be added, that there is still evidence that the *Law* or Hill of Dundee had been vitrified, possibly from being a beacon hill.   Although it may be a fact that both the Marquis of Montrose and General Monck occupied and altered the surface of the ground to suit their own purposes, we have no good reason for imagining that the vitrification, formerly seen, belonged to any definite system of fortification.

Boece also states that Donald I. and his court visited

---

[1] Roy, *Military Antiquities*, p. 130.
[2] Maitland, *Hist. of Scot.* (1757), i. p. 215; Richard of Cirencester, *Descrip. of Britain*, p. 490 (Bohn); Chalmers, *Caled.* i. p. 123; see generally Thomson, *Hist. Dundee*, pt. i., for the early history of Dundee.

Dundee, A.D. 860; that King Malcolm II. lodged his army there the night before he is said to have attacked the Danes at Barry, in 1012; and that it was the scene of the death of King Edgar, in 1106. Some say that Edgar died at Edinburgh; but Wyntoun thus favours the claim of Dundee :[1]—

> " Edgare, oure nobil Kyng,
> The dayis wyth honowre tuk endyng:
> Be-north Tay intil Dunde
> Tyl God the Spyryte than yhald he.
> And in the Kyrk of Dwnfermlyne
> Solemply he wes enteryd syne."

It need scarcely be said that these incidents are traditional; and it is a matter of certainty that the name of *Dundee,* or any other by which it can be identified, does not occur at all until between 1153 and 1165. The name was then spelled " Dunde"—nearly the same form, it will be seen, which it still retains—the other names and spellings, which tradition assigns to it, being altogether fanciful and the invention of later times. Like the ancient names of most places in Scotland, that of *Dundee* had doubtless been given to the district by the Celtic or early inhabitants, as descriptive of its leading topographical features, and had probably been conferred upon it either as characteristic of the Law which may have had a fortification, or of the more modern castle, which, as before noticed, stood upon what is said to have been a high dark-coloured rock, at the head of Castle Street.[2]

The Law, however, had been in old, as it is in modern times, the most striking natural object in the district. It is an isolated conical hill, rising immediately behind the town, 572 feet above the level of the sea. A magnificent and varied prospect is obtained from it, not only of the north-eastern portion of Forfarshire, but of large tracts of the counties of Perth and Fife, with the windings of the Tay; and no place, for many miles round, had been so well adapted, either for the site of a fortification, or for the lighting of sacrificial and beacon fires,

---

[1] Wyntoun, *Chron.* i. p. 282; Balfour, *Annals,* i. p. 6. [2] *Ut supra,* p. 275.

which are believed to have formed part of the early religious
and warlike customs of the ancient inhabitants of Scotland.
Although the Law has now a verdant hue, yet in former days
it may have had a dark bleak aspect, when surmounted by some
place of strength, and clad with stunted heath, through which
peered large masses of the conglomerate rock, of which the hill
is composed, and from which—(as the Gaelic words *Dun-dubh*
mean either the " black fort " or the " black hill " or " law," for
dun is applicable to either a fort or a hill)—the name had
most probably originated, and been transferred to the town or
district.   This rendering is so far corroborated by the spelling
of the name of " Logyn *Dundho*" in a charter of Richard, bishop
of St. Andrews, 1163-78.[1]

In consequence of the ravages to which the town was subjected during the Wars of the Independence, the Covenant,
and the Commonwealth, the greater part of its ancient muni-
ments and charters was destroyed.   The oldest of these
papers appear to have been lost during the first of these
periods and to have belonged to the reigns of King William
the Lion and King Alexander III.   These writs were subsequently renewed by King Robert the Bruce, and added to
by several of his successors; but during the siege of 1651
they also were taken out of " the charter kist of the burgh
which wes broken vp by the English souldiers," and most
of them were " burnt and destroyed, and verie few of them
gotten bak."   Fortunately, the Charter of Ratification by King
Charles II., granted in the year 1661, contains a recital of

---

[1] *Liber Eccl. de Scon.* p. 26. *Dun-deo* (the hill or fort at the mouth of the
river) is another, and not improbable origin which might be suggested, *deo* being
a term applicable to the embouchure or place where a river enters a lake or sea.
The name *Alec*, or *Alec-tum*, which is perhaps a corruption of the Gaelic *aill-
each* (beautiful or handsome), and the Saxon *tun* (a town)—for the word *Alectum*
has been translated " a beautiful place "—is said to have been the name of Dundee
in Agricola's time, but no such name occurs in Tacitus, or even in Richard of Cirencester's *Iter*. *Dei-donum* (God's gift) is its reputed name in the Earl of Huntingdon's day, but for this there is no authority; and *Tao-dunum*, which has been rendered
"The hill of Tay," was given to it by Buchanan. *Dun-tigh*, in Gaelic, signifies
" the house fort, or hill," which, it will be seen, is not very dissimilar to the rendering adopted in the text. But all the etymologies of Dundee are very doubtful.

the honours and privileges which the burgh had from the different monarchs, but to its terms it is needless to refer here.[1] Suffice it to say that Dundee appears to have been made a burgh, though not a royal one, about the time that Earl David gifted the church to the Abbey of Lindores.

Apart from the notices in the charter referred to, the oldest records which relate to the burgh are those in the Chamberlain Rolls, from which it appears, as perhaps indicating the importance of Dundee as a place of trade in early times, that, during the residence of King Alexander III. at Forfar, in 1264, a charge was made for the transmission of sixteen pipes of wine from Dundee to the county town. At that period there had doubtless been a port or harbour at Dundee, although there is no reference made to it in any public document until about a century afterwards, when certain persons were appointed to collect shore-dues and also the customs which arose from bread and animal food, of which the revenues, even then, were considerable.[2]

Notices of the shipping of Dundee frequently occur after the date of these entries, and we have curious glimpses of the times in the disputes regarding the rights of Dundee and Perth in the navigation of the Tay.[3] It was a vessel of this port, called *St. Mary*—so named, probably, in honour of the patron of one of the churches—which conveyed the Earl of Crawford and his suite to London to the celebrated tournament in 1390; and in 1491, another ship bearing the name of "Marié of Dunde" appears to have been owned by more than one individual.[4] It is also affirmed that in 1567, when a fleet was despatched in search of the Earl of Bothwell, who had adopted the desperate life of a pirate on the northern coast, the best three vessels employed in the expedition belonged to this port.[5]

---

[1] The charter is printed in *Acta Parl.* vii. pp. 350-3; see also iii. p. 44; v. p. 546. See *Municipal History of Dundee*, pp. 19 sq., 295 sq. The oldest charter extant is from Robert I., 1327, and the next is from David II., in 1359. See *Dundee Charters*, passim.   [2] *Chamb. Rolls*, i. p. 13; ii., iii., passim.

[3] *Mun. Hist. Dundee*, pp. 23-24; Maxwell, *Old Dundee*, pp. 103 sq., has an interesting account of the old harbour and shipping.

[4] *Lives of the Lindsays*, i. p. 88; *Acta Aud.* p. 154.

[5] Dr. Small, *Stat. Acct. of Dundee*, p. 71; *Forf. Illust.* p. 33.

But there are no means of knowing the real state of the
shipping until 1652, when the record of the Seamen Fraternity
begins.   It is said, but evidently erroneously, that about a
hundred ships belonged to Dundee prior to the capture of the
town by General Monck in 1651; and, although Dr. Gumble says
that there were sixty vessels "of all sorts" in the harbour at that
time, the greater part of them had doubtless belonged to other
places, and been brought there by those who then took refuge at
Dundee.   It is certain that, in 1654, there were only ten vessels
belonging to the port; fifty-two years afterwards there were
twenty-two.   In the course of twenty-five years that number was
more than doubled, and a similar result followed towards the
close of the last century.   The number pretty steadily increased
until about 1848, when larger vessels were required for the
foreign trade, and the general tonnage has gone on increasing,
but the number of ships diminishing.   In the end of 1884
there were, belonging to the port of Dundee and entered upon
the register, 191 vessels, having an aggregate tonnage of 115,829
tons : of these 60 were screw-steamers, with the gross tonnage of
63,832 tons and 7590 horse-power.   But large as this fleet of
steam and sailing vessels is, it gives only a very partial idea of
the trade of the port, foreign outward and inward, and coasting.[1]

Of the state of the harbour in early times there is little
record.   Monipennie briefly describes it, in 1612, as " a commodious haven."   In October, 1668, as was the case with many
other places, the harbour and shipping suffered severely from
a violent storm, and Parliament recommended a collection to
be made throughout the kingdom to aid in the repair of the
former.   Ten years after this disaster, Mr. Edward of Murroes
says that " the harbour, by great labour and expense, has been
rendered a very safe and agreeable station for vessels ; " while
a few years later, Mr. Ochterlony describes it as " a good shore,

---

[1] *Dundee Year Books* for 1883-84.   See APPENDIX No. XXIII.   The figures at the
end of 1883 were slightly different :—199 vessels, having an aggregate tonnage of
115,649 tons ; the screw-steamers were 62, with the gross tonnage of 64,649 tons
and 7835 horse-power.

well built with hewn stone, with a key on both sydes, whereof they load and unload their ships, with a great house on the shore called the Pack House, where they lay up their merchant goods." Another author, who visited the place about 1728, says that "it is rather a mole than a harbour, having no backwater to clean it ; and that there are three entrances into it which may contain a hundred sail of ships, but not of any great burthen."[1] But since those days, the harbour has been entirely changed, and the "soft clay or slike," for the removal of which "by flat-bottomed boats, as in Holland," that author says, there was then no revenue, is now carried off by the most approved apparatus—the harbour being, as a whole, one of the best in the kingdom, whether in respect of size or of safety. It consists of four docks, which give a water surface of thirty and a half acres, and to the King William Fourth and Victoria Docks there are attached two graving-docks for the overhauling of ships requiring repairs.

As the chief seaport of the county Dundee has been, from earliest record, the principal seat of its commerce. For upwards of two centuries, the staple trade has consisted in the manufacture of linen cloth, of which it is now the greatest and most approved mart in Britain. Many of the manufactories and warehouses are handsome buildings and of great extent. The population of the town and neighbourhood has naturally increased with the growth of trade ; and, with the exception of Glasgow, no other Scottish town has grown at such a rate. In 1801, the population was 27,396 : since then it has gone on increasing with great rapidity, numbering in 1881 140,239, exclusive of Lochee[2] with its population of 12,370. Within the last thirty years the advance in trade and all material wealth has been very great. Although the jute fibre had reached Dundee so early as 1840, it was not until about 1860 that it took a strong place in the list of manufactures. Entirely dis-

[1] De Foe, *Journey through Scot.* i. p. 96.

[2] Lochee is about a mile and a half north-west of the town, but within the Parliamentary and municipal boundaries.

placing cotton, and largely pressing upon flax and hemp, it has become one of the staple manufactures of Dundee, which is the chief centre for its employment in manufactures. During 1883 no fewer than 1,144,327 bales of jute were discharged at Dundee Harbour from 114 ships, of an average burthen of 1427 tons.[1]

Our space will not allow us to give detailed accounts either of the different trades that have been, or that still are, carried on in Dundee, or of the rise and progress of the population. This is the less to be regretted, however, as detailed information on this subject will be found in other publications. But it may be remarked that, although there was a Lodge of Free-masons, at least during the early part of the sixteenth century, it is probable that here, as in most other places, the weavers were the earliest incorporated body. The various dates of the incorporation of the several trades are not known with certainty, but are supposed to vary from 1555 to about 1610.[2]

The privilege of trafficking in "wooll, skins, and hides," which was granted to the town by King David II., must have added greatly to the prosperity of the burgh ; while the more modern and peculiar departments of manufacture, such as those of men's worsted bonnets, of buckles, and more lately of thread—particularly the first mentioned—gave the town a name which will not soon be forgotten. None of these trades are practised now-a-days ; but the Bucklemaker Wynd (now Victoria Road) and the Bonnet Hill are supposed to have been the places where the manufacture of these two articles was chiefly carried on.[3]

---

[1] *Mun. Hist. Dundee ; Dundee Year Books. The Dundee Year Book*, 1884, says of the Local Trade :—" The history of the trade of the district for 1884 is a record of low prices, glutted markets, and slow demand." The jute imported direct from India fell to 605,518 bales in 52 ships of an average burthen of 1576 tons. See APPENDIX No. XXIV.

[2] Thomson, *Hist. of Dundee*, p. 247 ; *Mun. Hist. Dundee*, pp. 175-6 ; *Dundee Charters*, pp. 129 sq., 169. See APPENDIX No. VI.

[3] The following popular rhyme, which has reference to the Bonnet-makers, may be taken as significant of their dirty, and at the same time, of their industrious habits :—

> " Ulie byke—ulie bee ;—
> The Bonnetmakers o' Dundee."

It is not until 1467 that we meet with a commissioner of the town sitting in Parliament,[1] but from that time, down to the Union, the burgh was almost continuously represented. The first commissioner was David Abirkerdor ; and in the Parliament held at Edinburgh in 1560, when the proposition was made by the Estates to the haughty Queen Elizabeth of England, "to june in mariage with the Erll of Arrane," the representative of the burgh (Mr. Haliburton) subscribes himself " Prowest of Dundij."[2]

We have already seen that there were recognised provosts in the time of Queen Mary, and seemingly even before that date, for the designation occurs both in the confirmation charter of the Guildry of 1527, and in the indenture or agreement between the town of Dundee and its master-mason in 1536-7 ; at an earlier date the chief magistrate bore, as in most other burghs, the title of *alderman*. The first of these documents shows that there was also a Dean of Guild, by whose sanction and advice alone ships could be freighted, and by whom freights were collected.[3] The indenture contains many interesting points, not elsewhere to be found, in regard to " the mason craft " of the period, such as the mode of payment, the hours of labour during the two seasons of summer and winter, provisions for the workman in case of distress, the duration of masons' apprenticeships, their wages, and the like.

At the date of this deed, it appears that the box-master of " the paroche kirk of Our Lady " was the " maister of warkis " for the town, and under his superintendence " the mason " obliged himself to " exerceiss the best and maist ingeniouss poyntis and practikis of his craft," whether "at the kirk werk or commone werkis of the said burgh, or at ony other werkis that the said toun plesis best to command hym thairto oney tyme quhen neid beis." His hours of labour were regulated accord-

---

[1] Warden, *Angus*, ii. pp. 196 sq.

[2] *Acta Parl.* ii. pp. 89, 606. In 1467 there appears to have been two commissioners, George and David Abirkerdour. See Warden, *Angus*, ii. pp. 196 sq. for the representation of Dundee.   [3] Thomson, *Hist. Dundee*, pp. 277-80.

ing to the "ald vss and consuetud of *Owr Lady luge* of Dunde."
He began work at five o'clock in the morning, and continued
until eight, when he had "ane haf hour to his disiune" or
breakfast; from nine he wrought till half-past eleven, when
he probably had dinner; then from one to four when he again
had "ane half hour to his none-schankis;" and finally, resum-
ing work at half-past four, he closed for the day at seven.[1]

In winter, which was calculated to begin and close at
Hallow-Day and Lady-Day respectively, he was bound to enter
upon his work "ilk day als sone as he ma se, and wirk as long
as he may se at eweyn," and during that time he was to labour
constantly, having "na tyme of licence of dennar nor none-
shankis, causs of the shortnes of the dais." He had few
holidays. On Eves that were "Fastryns dayis" he worked
till four o'clock, except on those of Christmas, Pasch, Whitsunday, and Assumption days, when he laid work aside at
twelve. His wages were settled at £20 Scots yearly, payable
by instalments every six weeks. If employed at any time by
private parties his wages were paid by the burgh, under de-
duction of that time; and, in the event of his being unable,
from sickness, to attend to his work for a period of not more
than forty consecutive days, he was to receive his full wage;
but, if his illness exceeded that time, his pay was stopped. The
town allowed him an apprentice, who was to be sufficiently
big and strong for the business, and "nocht ane small child;"
the term of apprenticeship was fixed for seven years. During
the first year the apprentice had no wages, but the town
agreed to pay him £10 Scots, or 16s. 8d. sterling a year during
the rest of his engagement; and he was also provided for, in
case of sickness, in much the same way as his master was.[2]

---

[1] *None-schankis*, or *nonysanks*, has also been said to signify "luncheon"—(*Reg.
Vet. Aberbr.* xx.)—but here it must have been a rest or light refreshment in the
afternoon. *Ut sup.* p. 226.　　　　[2] *Reg. Ep. Brechin.* ii. pp. 317-19.

SECTION VII.

If life an empty bubble be,
How sad for those who cannot see
The rainbow in the bubble!

NORTHERN ADVERTISER *Scrap.*

Lodging, or Hostelry of the Abbots of Arbroath—Its Furnishings—Lodging of the
Earls of Crawford—Argyllgate and Port—Whitehall Close—Reputed Palace—
James VI. at Dundee—The Mint—Ancient Houses—The Cross—Johnston's
Panegyric—Old Notices of the Town—Town Hall—Public Seminaries—New
Improvements—University College, etc.

ALTHOUGH little remains to be noticed regarding the history of
Dundee in old times, there are still a few additional facts
which may be interesting.

The lodging or hostelry of the Abbot and Convent of
Arbroath was the abode of the Abbot and his followers, when
on the business of the Convent at Dundee, and perhaps stood
upon the toft or piece of ground which Earl David granted to
the monastery at the time of its foundation. Prior to the
year 1327, it was held of the Abbey by Stephen Fairburn, a
burgess of Berwick-upon-Tweed, who made it over to William
of Irwyn and Mariot his spouse by a charter which was confirmed by the celebrated Abbot Bernard.[1] This document
throws a very interesting light upon the domestic manners and
customs of the period, and shows that, apart from a small
money rent, which the tenant paid to the superior, and after
the house had been provided by the Convent with kitchen
utensils, which the occupiers were bound to uphold, they were
obliged to furnish the Abbot and monks, according to their respective ranks, when they visited Dundee, with a hall plenished
with tables and trestles or stools, as well as with white tallow
or Paris candles to burn in the evenings, and white salt to use
at table. Besides this, they were to have a spense, with a
buttery ; sleeping chambers, and a kitchen, a stable, and also

[1] *Reg. Vet. Aberbr.* p. 315.

litter, which probably included both straw and rushes. The former was probably used for their horses, and the latter for strewing upon the floors of the hall and bed-chambers. This, it may be added, was long previously the fashion, not only in Britain and on the Continent but also in the East, and continued in use among princes and nobles in our own country, down to the introduction of carpets. Shakespeare oftener than once mentions the fact; and when Thomas à Becket, Archbishop of Canterbury, had his apartments strewn daily with fresh hay or straw, it was accounted one of the luxuries enjoyed by that prelate.

On the south side of the Fleukargait, now the Nethergate, there is said to have stood the royal palace, frequented by the Kings James IV. and James V. and also by Queen Mary. The name and site are fixed by the modern Whitehall Street.[1] It appears to have been surrounded by the houses of the nobility; of these, the one of most note in point of antiquity and importance was the Lodging of the Earls of Crawford. It is probable that this house belonged, at one time, to the good Sir James Lindsay, uncle of the first Earl of Crawford, and the great benefactor of the Hospital. It is variously described in ancient records as the 'Palatium Comitis,' the 'Earl's Palace,' the 'Great Lodging,' or the 'Earl's Lodging,' and formed a vast and antique edifice, part of which was still standing about eighty years ago, with the letters 𝔏𝔦𝔫𝔡𝔢𝔰𝔞𝔶 embossed on the battlements. Standing as already mentioned in the 'Fluckargait,' to the west of the present High Street or Market Place, it occupied, with its offices and 'viridarium,' or garden, the whole space between that street and the river. A chapel, or oratory, dedicated to St. Michael the Archangel, was attached to the palace, and served for the daily devotions of the family.[2] Many of the Earls of

---

[1] *Mun. Hist. Dundee*, pp. 194 sq. But it must be noticed that some doubt the existence of a royal palace, and prefer to think that the above royal personages were guests of the Grey Friars or other religious bodies.

[2] *Lives of the Lindsays*, i. pp. 110, 329, 337.

Crawford were born in this town residence, and among them, it is believed, were *Earl Beardie* and also his son, the original Duke of Montrose. Here also, it is said, Archibald, fifth Earl of Douglas and Duke of Touraine, was married to Lady Margaret, eldest daughter of the first Earl of Crawford, " with sic pomp and triumph," Pitscottie quaintly remarks, " that never the like was seen at no man's marriage."

The old Earls of Argyll also, it is supposed, had a residence in Dundee, but all trace of it has long since disappeared. It possibly stood in the Overgate, and is believed to have given the name of " Argilisgait," or " Ergaylisgat," to that street—a name which it bore from at least the middle of the fifteenth century. The site of the house is perhaps marked by the name of Argyll Close, but, unlike that of the Earls of Crawford, no description of it has been handed down. At the west end of the street, there was a Port or gate.[1]

In a house in Whitehall Close the Convention of Royal Burghs on one occasion met, and King Charles II. is also said to have lived there during his short stay in Dundee. On a house fronting the street, which, however, was of a date long posterior to King Charles's time, there was a good carving of the royal arms, encircled by the legend—" HONI SOIT QVI MAL Y PENSE," with the words " GOD SAVE THE KING," and the royal initials "C.R.G.," and date 1660. In all probability this shield had been put up by the loyal owner of the house at the period of the " glorious Restoration." [2] The close may have been named at the same time.

In the same entry was a grotesque carving, in stone, of the Fall of our First Parents; it was represented in the ordinary way, with a serpent twisted round a tree, and over that there hovered a not ungraceful figure of an angel. On the opposite side of the close, also built into a wall, there was part of an old carved door or chimney lintel, dated 1589. It was ornamented

---

[1] *Reg. Ep. Brechin.* i. pp. 93, 185; ii. p. 353.
[2] *Forf. Illust.* p. 29.

with the crown and royal lion of Scotland, and bore the following remains of a legend inscribed upon a ribbon :—

OBAY . ZE . KING .... KING . IAMIS . 6 ..... IN . DE[FENCE]. .

Near the north-west corner of the High Street, there stood a timber-framed house, called " Our Ladie Warkstayris," which is supposed to have been a religious house for females.[1]

It is certain that King Robert the Bruce and his two immediate successors on the throne were frequently in the town, and that King David II. held at least two State Councils and one Parliament here ;[2] it is probable that these monarchs not only transacted business in the Monastery of the Grey-Friars, but also may have lived in it.

It is said that when King James VI. landed in Dundee, on the 21st of May 1617, he passed the night at Dudhope Castle, the residence of Sir John Scrimgeour, Hereditary Constable of the town.   At that time the king remained only a night in the neighbourhood, having left early next morning for Kinnaird Castle, near Brechin, the seat of his favourite, Lord Carnegie.[3] The king returned from Kinnaird to Dundee after an absence of ten days, and gave audience to the magistrates and chief men of the town and its vicinity ; these, the better to evince their loyalty and attachment to him, are said to have presented him with two Latin poems, in celebration of his visit.

But although there is no convincing evidence of a royal palace having ever been there, it is certain that Robert III.

---

[1] Maxwell, *Old Dundee*, p. 149 ; Thomson, *Hist. Dundee*, p. 177.

[2] *Acta Parl.* i. pp. 60, 100 ; *Reg. Mag. Sig.*, passim.

[3] This has been mistaken by some for Kinnaird, in the Carse of Gowrie ; but the Kirk Session Records of Brechin, etc., set the matter at rest.   The king seems to have spent much of his time in hunting with Lord Carnegie in Montreathmont Muir (*Land of the Lindsays*, p. 242), and he was oftener than once in the town of Brechin, where preparations were kept up for his reception (*ut sup.* p. 199).   He also held a court both there and at Kinnaird, which was attended by the Presbytery of Brechin. His last visit to that town appears to have been made on the 27th May, and on the day following, being unable to visit the city of Aberdeen himself, no fewer than twenty of the royal suite went there, and all of them, from Sir Thomas Gerard, Bart., down to Archie Armestrang, the King's *pleasant* or fool, " wer creatt, maid, and admittit burgesses of gild."—*Burgh Rec. of Aberdeen*, ii. pp. 352-3.

established a mint at which groats were coined.[1] The mint, however, ceased with that king, and was not again resumed until May 1585, when, in consequence of the severity of the pestilence in Edinburgh, the " cunzie house" was removed to Dundee. But it was there only until the month of October following, when, the infection having broken out, the mint was removed to Perth.[2] During the short period referred to, gold, silver, and alloyed pennies were coined, and the words " OPPIDUM DUNDEE " were substituted on the coin for "OPPIDUM EDINBURGI."[3] The mint is said to have been in St. Margaret's Close,[4] and a portion of it was visible in the end of last century. But, apart from the regular coinage, it ought to be noticed that Dundee, like many towns of less importance in Britain, had, towards the middle and close of last century, an issue of local coins and medals, among the former of which was the rather uncommon piece of *a silver shilling*. These, as will be seen from the Appendix, contained views of remarkable buildings in the town and neighbourhood, such as Broughty Castle, the Cross of the burgh, the Churches, the Tower, the Town House, and many other public edifices ; to the dates of the building, the improvement, or destruction of some of these, they form valuable keys.[5]

The Mauchlin or Mechlin Tower, which is supposed to have been a part of the old wall that surrounded the town, stood a little to the east of the *narrow* of the Murraygate, where an adjoining court still bears the name. Common report says that the tower was named from some unrecorded proceeding of one of the Lords Mauchlin ; but it is more probable that the name

[1] Cardonnell, *Numismata Scotiæ*, p. 57. The front of the coin had the royal head, with the sceptre before the face, surrounded by the words—ROBERTVS DEI GRA. REX SCOTORV., and the reverse bore a St. Andrew's cross, with a spur rowel of five points in the angle of the cross, and the legend—DNS PTECTOR MS ET LIBATOR MS VILLA DVNDE. [2] *Reg. Priv. Counc. Scot.* iii. pp. 26, 37, 38.

[3] Chambers, *Dom. Annals of Scot.* i. p. 158.

[4] Maxwell, *Old Dundee*, pp. 261 sq., in giving an account of the Mint in Dundee, says St. Margaret's Close or Mint Close was a passage on the north side of the Market Gait or High Street, and not St. Margaret's Close on the south side of the Nethergate.

[5] *Mun. Hist. Dundee*, pp. 230-2. APPENDIX No. XXV.

had originated in consequence of the seamen and merchants of the town of Mechlin in Belgium, who visited the port, making that locality a rendezvous.

The place in the Seagate where Grizell Jaffray was executed for witchcraft, on the 11th of November 1669, is still pointed out.[1] Near it was the house in which the Chevalier lodged in 1716, and where the celebrated Admiral Duncan was born, fifteen years afterwards; it was previously the town residence of the Stewarts of Grandtully. The Wishart Port stands near the east end of the Cowgate. The house in which, after capturing the town in 1651, General Monck had his residence, occupies the foot of the Overgate, and nearly opposite to this there stood the so-called remains of the Nunnery of the Grey Sisters. These, and the picturesque building in the Green Market once used as the custom-house, together with those in the adjoining street, and in the Vault, behind the Town House, in which stands the stately tenement of "Strathmartin's Lodging," at one time a residence of the lairds of that place, are perhaps the only remaining traces of the ancient houses of Dundee.[2] The old-fashioned buildings, with curiously plastered and wooden gables, resembling those on the Continent—buildings that used to be seen in different parts of the streets and closes of the Overgate, Seagate, and other portions of the town, are now almost entirely things of the past. The Cross of the burgh was taken down in 1777, and is now preserved within the enclosure between the Steeple and the Nethergate. It originally stood in the Seagate, and thence was removed to the High Street, in front of the Town Hall. It was afterwards taken from the High Street, and has only in 1876 been set up on the present site with the old base and shaft, but with new top in imitation of the old.[3] Its shaft bears a rude representation of the arms of the town, " the pot and the lily "

---

[1] *Mun. Hist. Dundee*, p. 227.   [2] Marshall, *Forfarshire*, pp. 38 sq.
[3] For the history of the Market Cross, see Maxwell, *Old Dundee*, pp. 244-8. It was made by John Mylne, the king's master-mason, whose initials it bears, and whose name was famous in bridge-building.

(which is the badge of the Virgin Mary), with the motto, "DEI DONUM," and date 1586. [1]

Like some of the towns previously noticed, Dundee had a Latin panegyric written in its praise by Dr. Arthur Johnston of Aberdeen, and another by John Johnston of St. Andrews. Both poems are only curiosities in their way—for they throw no light either on the antiquity or history of the place—and the following quaint translation of the lines by the Aberdeen poet may suffice :—

> " An Ancient Town to which Tay's entrie do
> Willing obedience, and subjection shew.
> The bones of conquer'd and slain Danes are found
> Here scattered, ill buried in the ground.
> When Genoa thee views, it doth despise
> Its marbles, nor doth barbarous Egypt pryse
> Her Pyramids, and Gargara doth deem
> Its Harvests to deserve but small esteem.
> The Lyburne Land thinks not her veshells fair
> When as she them doth with thy ships compare.
> Venice her self in poverty thinks lost,
> And Cnidus of her Fishes dare not boast.
> The Spartan Youth to equall thine doth fail ;
> Rome's Senators unto thy Consuls veil.
> *He* as an Artless fool should branded be,
> Who from Tay's-Gulph did beg a name to Thee ;
> Since Thou by more than Human-Art are framed
> DON-DEI the *gift* of GOD thou should be named." [2]

The notice of the town by Captain Franck, who, in his usual pedantic and mysterious style, speaks of having been transported from "the beautiful port of Dundee to the fragrant levels of Fife," in a boat "steer'd by a compass of straw," is comparatively valueless, while the description of the town by Mr. Edward, though quaint and curious, is rather lengthy to be quoted in this place. [3]   Mr. Ochterlony, the most trust-

---

[1] Edmondson, *Heraldry*, i. pt. i.

[2] APPENDIX No. VII. (D). The Panegyric by John Johnston is printed in Slezer's *Theatrum Scotiæ*, and a translation, with additions, will be found in *Dundee Delineated*.

[3] Franck, *Northern Memoirs* (c. 1669-70), pp. 238-9 ; Edward, *Descrip. of Angus*, p. 21 ; Warden, *Angus*, ii. p. 244 ; In *Acta Parl.* ii. 486, the "ferryaris" charges between Dundee and New Port are thus stated—"Gif ane man desyris ane boit

worthy and correct of the local writers of the period, says Dundee " is a large and great towne, very populous, and of a great trade, and hath many good ships. The buildings are large and great, of thrie or four stories high ; a large merkat place, with a very fyne tolbuith and cross ; two great churches, with a very high steeple well furnished of bells, as is also the tolbuith. They have thrie ministers, whereof the towne presents two, and the Constable of Dundie one ; their Magistrates are a Provost, four Bailies, Dean of Gild, and others are shirreffs within their own bounds : they are joyned in nothing to the shyre except the militia, whereunto they furnish 150 foot. It lyeth upon the water of Tay very pleasantlie, and hath good yards and meadows about it. They have four great fairs yearly, two mercat days everie week, and a great fish mercat dayly. There is a great consumption there of all kynd of victualls ; the excyse of malt there being little short of the whole excyse of the shyre and burghs, besyd a great victuall mercat twice a week for service of the towne, besydes great quantities of all kinds of grain, coft by the merchants, and transported, by which returns they import all kynd of commoditie from Holland, Norway, Denmark, and the east countrey. They export lykwayes all other our native commodities, and import other things necessary for the service of the countrey, which serves above 20 myles round about their towne."[1]

Mr. Morer, who visited the town, as chaplain to a Scottish regiment, in 1689, observes that " the buildings are such as bespeak the substance and riches of the place ;" and adds that he and his companions were entertained by the corporation, and made burgesses.[2] " The town is the best built of any I have yet seen, except Edinburgh," says an English traveller

---

be himself to pay for his portage, 4s. ; and euerilk man and horss, 8d. ; and ilk man or woman be thame self, 4d."—Maxwell, *Old Dundee*, pp. 111-12. There has long been hourly communication on this ferry by steamers.

[1] *Spot. Miscell.* i. pp. 326-7. In the *Mun. Hist. Dundee*, there are most interesting accounts of Dundee in 1746, 1789, 1799, 1820, and 1873.

[2] *Short Account of Scot.* p. 105.

in 1728, " and hath a great face of trade : it is good two miles in circumference : its market-place is almost as spacious as that of Nottingham, and the town house, a stately venerable pile of free stone, is a great ornament to the market. The City runs in four large Streets, each from this Market Place." He also alludes to the Church and the Tower, the latter of which, he says, is like that of Wrexham in Wales ; also to the Hospital, the monuments in the *Howff*, and to Dudhope Castle. But one of the chief beauties of Dundee at that time appears to have been " a pleasant walk " from the harbour to the town, " paved with Flagstones, and with Rows of Trees on each side," which, he continues, " serves for an Exchange to the merchants and masters of Ships." The restoration of such a walk in the neighbourhood of the harbour, and the introduction of trees about such places as the Exchange, Meadowside, and other parts where they could be planted without interfering with public thoroughfares, would perhaps be one of the most pleasing improvements that could be effected in the burgh, and a commencement has already been made upon the Esplanade and in Albert Square.

It is only natural to infer, from the growing wealth of the town, that the style of the dwelling-houses and shops in the new streets, and other buildings, public and private, corresponds with the advancement of the times, and with the increase of the trade and population of the burgh. The Town Hall, erected in 1734, is a fine specimen of the architectural genius of the elder Adam ; and the High School or Public Seminaries, at the top of Reform Street, is a good example of the Grecian style of architecture. These were built in 1833, and some years since received additions in keeping with the original plan. This was chiefly for the accommodation of the recently established Government School of Design, and at the present date a building in Euclid Street is being reconstructed for use as the Harris High School for Girls, in connection with the High School itself.

In speaking of this institution, it may be mentioned that the schools of Dundee are of old date, and have long and justly enjoyed celebrity as places of elementary education.[1] Blind Harry says that Sir William Wallace was taught there. The Grammar School had long for its rector the learned David Lindsay, afterwards Bishop, first of Brechin and then of Edinburgh, who was so closely connected with the attempt to introduce the Liturgy into the Church in 1637.[2]

But it was not merely the departments of reading and writing which were attended to at that early date, for music also formed an element in the education of youth, and, contemporary with Mr. Lindsay, in 1603, was one John Williamson, who is designed "master of the sang schole," and for this "within the burgh," he received a salary from the magistrates of 16 marks yearly.[3]   It is said that the Grammar School was held at one time in the nave of the old church.   Of this there is no record; but it is certain that, so early as 1435, which is the first authentic notice of the public schools, a new school and school-house were built by Laurence Lownan, then master, and that, in consequence of his having erected the buildings without consulting the Bishop of the diocese, he incurred his displeasure, and received the censure of the Church.[4]   Prior to the erection of the present fine buildings, the school was held near the town's churches.   Many of the masters have been men of first-rate abilities, and the school has produced a number of eminent scholars.[5]

It is difficult to select where so much of beauty and interest is to be met with, and so many munificent gifts have been presented to the town.   Passing over such public build-

---

[1] Maxwell, *Old Dundee*, pp. 86 sq., gives an account of the schools in Dundee down to 1597.

[2] *Lives of the Lindsays*, ii. p. 16 ; Jervise, *Land of the Lindsays*, p. 356 ; *ut sup.* pp. 107, 252.   [3] Maxwell, *Old Dundee*, pp. 336 sq.

[4] *Reg. Ep. Brechin.* i. p. 62.

[5] On the High School and other Educational foundations, see Thomson's *History of Dundee*, pp. 287 sq. ; at *Ib.* pp. 357 sq. Mr. Thomson gives an interesting list of eminent men born in or identified with Dundee.

ings and institutions as the Morgan Hospital, the Royal
Infirmary, the Royal Lunatic Asylum, the Royal Orphan
Institution, and the Royal Exchange, the Court House, the
Kinnaird Hall, the Victoria Triumphal Arch, and the many
handsome Churches, Banks, and Public Offices, we would
briefly advert to two that are specially marked, the one by
private liberality and the other by public recognition of greatness, while both have a splendid mission to fulfil. First is
the Albert Institute, erected as a Memorial to the late Prince
Consort, and built after plans provided by Sir Gilbert Scott.
It contains a Free Lending and Reference Library of 42,778
volumes (October 1884), Museum, and Fine Art Gallery.
Soon after the passing of the Free Library Act it was adopted
in Dundee, and the library has proved a great boon to the
town.   Within the Institute enclosure there are placed three
statues, erected by public subscription—to George Kinloch of
Kinloch, the popular advocate of Reform ; to James Carmichael,
inventor of the fan-blast in the manufacture of iron ; and to
Robert Burns, our national poet.

University College, Dundee, is almost entirely due to the
munificence of the Baxter family, who have long been connected with the town.   After the late Sir David Baxter had
given in 1863 the fine recreation grounds of the Baxter Park
—in which there is erected a handsome marble life-size statue
of Sir David, as an acknowledgment of his kindness—his sister,
the late Miss Baxter of Balgavies and Ellangowan,[1] and his
kinsman, the late Dr. John Boyd Baxter, who was for many
years Procurator-Fiscal and Preses of the Society of Procurators
in Dundee, devoted the sum of £100,000 as a permanent
endowment fund to University College, which was not then
founded, and £50,000 to be spent in the purchase and equip-
ment of suitable buildings.   No time was lost in carrying out
the trust, and in buildings purchased in the Nethergate and
fitted up with every appliance for all scholastic and technical

---

[1] Miss Baxter died Dec. 19, 1884, aged 83.

forms of study, the University College was formally opened by the Right Honourable the Earl of Dalhousie, K.T., on Friday, October 5th, 1883.[1]

In conclusion, we would but briefly advert to the water supply of the town.[2]   For many generations the supply was limited and the quality not always wholesome, but at last a Joint Stock Company obtained an Act of Parliament, empowering them to introduce water from Monikie, and in February 1848 the water was laid on and proved of unspeakable benefit to the inhabitants.   But in 1869 the water-works were transferred to the Corporation, which obtained another Act of Parliament for procuring an increased supply from the Loch of Lintrathen.   This was purchased from the Earl of Airlie at a reasonable price, and now yields to Dundee a constant supply of 12,000,000 gallons a day for all the purposes of the town. On the other hand, the drainage of the town is most satisfactory, and the sewers alone, in all their windings underground, extend to about forty-six miles.

[1] APPENDIX No. XXVI.
[2] For a short account of the different water schemes from 1743 to the present time, see *Dundee Charters*, p. 225.

END OF VOL. I.

EDINBURGH UNIVERSITY PRESS:
T. and A. CONSTABLE, Printers to Her Majesty.